Stalin's Reluctant Soldiers

Stalin's Reluctant Soldiers

A SOCIAL HISTORY OF THE RED ARMY
1925–1941

Roger R. Reese

 University Press of Kansas

Photographs on pages 18, 19, 20, 45, 81, 85, 94, 112, 167, and 186 are reprinted courtesy of the Slavic and Baltic Division, The New York Public Library; Astor, Lenox and Tilden Foundations.

Published by the University Press of Kansas (Lawrence, Kansas 66049), which was organized by the Kansas Board of Regents and is operated and funded by Emporia State University, Fort Hays State University, Kansas State University, Pittsburg State University, the University of Kansas, and Wichita State University

Library of Congress Cataloging-in-Publication Data

Reese, Roger R.
    Stalin's reluctant soldiers: a social history of the Red Army, 1925–1941 / Roger R. Reese
    p.   cm. — (Modern war studies)
    Includes bibliographical references and index.
    ISBN 0-7006-0772-2 (alk. paper)
    1. Soviet Union. Raboche–Krest ĭanskaĭa Krasnaĭa Armiĭa—History. 2. Sociol-ogy, Military—Soviet Union—History—20th century. 3. Soviet Union—Politics and government—1917–1936. 4. Soviet Union—Politics and government—1936–1953.   I. Title.   II. Series.
    UA772.R44 1996
    355'.00947'0904—dc20   96–4252

British Library Cataloguing in Publication Data is available.

Printed in the United States of America

10 9 8 7 6 5 4 3 2 1

The paper used in this publication meets the minimum requirements of the American National Standard for Permanence of Paper for Printed Library Materials Z39.48-1984.

To Frederick and Samantha

Contents

This book is not a comprehensive history of the Red Army before the war. It is an essay that explores several important but neglected social-historical themes of the Soviet military that are essential to understanding why the Soviet Union, a rising industrial power with the world's largest and most mechanized army, came close to being eliminated as a geopolitical entity in only a matter of six months. I contend that the Soviet military found itself swamped by an enormous influx of conscripted enlisted men in the years 1936 to 1941 but without enough officers to lead them because of inadequate officer procurement. The Great Purge of 1937–1938 exacerbated the situation, reducing the Red Army to a hollow, ineffective fighting force.

There are several possible reasons why this hypothesis has not arisen before. The first is the plausiblity of the Soviet explanation, which attributes the great success of the German invasion in the first year of the war to what the Soviet military terms "strategic surprise" and to the technical superiority and combat experience of the German army versus Soviet armed forces handicapped by Stalin's cult of personality and by the purges that decimated the officer corps and industrial management. The German army did, in many cases, achieve tactical surprise on 22 June 1941; many of its soldiers and leaders did have combat experience from conquering Europe; and it did have the reputation for technical excellence. The Red Army, by contrast, had the reputation of being technologically backward, and the purges surely did eliminate some experienced men in the Red Army.

A second explanation is that the purges were such an extraordinary and unprecedented event that they easily capture the imagination and direct attention away from the more mundane aspects of administering and training an army, which is where things began to go awry very early in the Soviet military. Historians have universally neglected three major negative factors in Soviet military development in the 1920s and 1930s: the negative social impact of rapid industrialization and urbanization, the negative impact of collectivization on the peasantry, and the rapid expansion of the armed forces.

Industrialization was generally beneficial to the Soviet armed forces, but in the initial phase (1929–1941) it added to the many problems facing the military. The short-term negative impact of industrialization has been entirely missed in the rush to acknowledge the great accomplishments of the first and second five-year plans. What could possibly have been negative about industrialization for the military? Inherently, nothing, but in the attitudes it fostered, much indeed. Industrialization provided complex weaponry, sophisticated equipment, and motorization and mechanization. These innovations enabled the Soviet armed forces to undertake, or at least envision, more complex military operations. Industrialization meant that the nation could support a larger armed force, yet it required an educated population to man it. In effect it created possibilities before it created capabilities. The material was produced, the men conscripted, and the tactics written up, but the appropriate knowledge and social orientation were a bit slower in coming.

Moshe Lewin's concept of the "peasant nexus," elaborated on in *The Gorbachev Phenomenon* (1988), provides the best context in which to understand this. The Soviet Union of the Stalin era was a peasant society in transition. The transition itself proved to be an unpredictable series of actions and reactions between the state and the peasantry, which resulted in each side adapting itself to the other, both knowingly and unknowingly. The armed forces, as a juncture between state and society, was inescapably caught up in the "peasant nexus." The army assigned peasant soldiers and officers complex tasks associated with a modernizing army for which their social background, education, and general life experiences had not prepared them. Consequently they often performed poorly.

Collectivization, as well, created challenges for the army. The greatest was to absorb recalcitrant and angry peasants and change them into "new Soviet men." In the eyes of the peasantry, collectivization was a great evil perpetrated by the regime. The army, as an agent of the regime, participated in collectivization and thereby lost a great deal of the goodwill it had built in the twenties. Military service was discredited among many peasants and workers as an honorable and worthy endeavor.

The rapid expansion of the armed forces, made possible by industrialization, created challenges that could not be met by a social, political, and cultural system that was hard-pressed to produce men prepared to lead a modern mass army. There proved to be too much work and not enough officers to supervise it. The purge compounded this situation.

These mundane social "nuts and bolts" aspects of creating and maintaining an army have been overlooked or ignored by both Western and Soviet historians. Focusing greater attention on these factors is only a partial step in uncovering what truly occurred in the Red Army before the war to affect its performance. To date there has not been very extensive scholarly treatment of the Soviet armed forces in the decade before the Russo-German conflict of 1941–1945. Soviet historians dedicated a section in one volume of each of their official histories of World War II, *Istoriia Velikoi Otechestvennoi Voiny Sovetskogo Soiuza 1941–1945* (1960) and *Istoriia Vtoroi Mirovoi Voiny*

1939–1945 (1973), to the military in the prewar years, and all subsequent writings have followed the line they set.

Soviet military memoirs generally do not address the issue of preparedness until the latter phase of the Spanish civil war or the Winter War with Finland. Memoirs of people involved in the defense industry seem to be direct responses to Khrushchev's de-Stalinization speech, in which he accused the defense industry of not providing enough weapons for the armed forces. These sources fail to deal with the organization, structure, and social problems of the military before the war. There are only three significant works on the Soviet military between the wars by Western historians: D. Fedotoff-White's *The Growth of the Red Army* (1944); John Erickson's *The Soviet High Command* (1962); and, most recently, Mark von Hagen's *Soldiers in the Proletarian Dictatorship* (1990). Erickson and Fedotoff-White support the argument that the Great Purge of 1937–1938 was the key factor in the eventual dysfunction of the military in 1941; von Hagen does not deal with the 1930s. My research both challenges and complements their work, shedding light on the daily workings of the divisions and lower-level units in the areas of training, organization, morale, personnel turnover, and socialization.

I have chosen to organize this book thematically, but as chronologically as possible. The major themes are organization from 1925 to 1941, the daily life of the soldier, the nonmilitary side of service, the officer corps to 1937, the purge, the drive to prepare for war during 1939–1941, and, finally, the German invasion from 22 June to December 1941.

Many people and experiences helped to shape my ideas on the interwar Soviet military. I owe a tremendous debt to Sheila Fitzpatrick, who guided me through graduate studies and work on my dissertation, from which this book is derived. Sidney Monas, co-supervisor of my dissertation, also played a powerful role in my scholarly and intellectual development. Yuri Slezkine and Konstantin Gurevich taught me Russian and about Russians. Tamara Chapman went far beyond the call of friendship to help improve my writing style. My colleagues at Texas A&M University, Roger Beaumont, Jonathan Coopersmith, Chip Dawson, and Chester Dunning, who patiently read my work and offered helpful commentary, also deserve thanks. I thank Mark von Hagen for offering insightful aid at the very early stages of this work and the final version as well. I thank David Glantz for his input. I owe an intellectual debt to Moshe Lewin, whose insights into Stalinist society inspired much of my outlook.

My own experiences as an infantry officer in the U.S. army—as a mere lieutenant, to be sure—actually caused me to raise the questions that I did. My time in training in the Texas A&M Corps of Cadets, the Infantry Officers Basic Course, and other specialized and advanced courses, and the people I came to know or just observe, provided me with a "real life" context for the study of military life and military training institutions. I learned how people from different backgrounds—not just Americans—are trained to follow orders, and I rather quickly became aware of how education, culture, social origin, and race shape attitudes toward authority. My several years of service in a light infantry battalion provided me with first-hand experience in military organization and unit training, as well as knowledge of the various types and ramifications of disciplinary problems that have a personal basis—problems based on a soldier's home life, love life, or financial solvency, to name a few—that classroom instruction alone cannot convey.

One incident in particular had a profound effect on my outlook on military organizations. When I had been in the U.S. Army only a few weeks I saw a large World War I poster outside the office of my tactical officer. Beneath the illustration of a dead soldier caught on barbed wire, the caption read: "Let it not be said, 'If only he had been properly trained.'" From that point on I internalized the idea that all army personnel have a responsibility to those who serve beneath them to do their utmost to give soldiers a fighting chance of surviving combat. In studying the Red Army, the foremost question in my mind was, did the peacetime leadership do all it could to give its men a fighting chance in wartime? Sadly, the answer is no.

Funding for my research came from a variety of sources. In graduate school the history department of the University of Texas provided me several Dora Bonham grants to participate in the Summer Research Program on Russia and Eastern Europe at the University of Illinois at Urbana-Champaign and the Sheffield Dissertation Research Fellowship in European History. The Kennan Institute for Advanced Russian Studies of the Woodrow Wilson Center awarded me a short-term grant for research. My travel to Russia for research was jointly financed by a National Endowment for the Humanities grant for archival research, an International Research Travel Grant from Texas A&M University, and a summer research grant by the Military Studies Institute of Texas A&M University. I also owe thanks to Brett Cooke for helping to arrange my stay with the Moscow Technical University of Signals and Communications and the faculty and the staff of MTUSI for their kind cooperation. Finally, I would like to express my gratitude to the staff of the *Rossiiskii gosudarstvennyi voennyi arkhiv* (formerly *Tsentral'nyi gosudarstvennyi arkhiv Sovetskoi Armii*), particularly Masha and Larissa for their energy, patience, and humor.

Introduction

This book is a social and organizational history of the Red Army from 1925 to 1941. The purpose of this study is to illustrate the basic internal causes for the Soviet military's defeats at the hands of German forces in 1941–1942 through an exposition of how the Workers' and Peasants' Red Army (*Raboche Krest'ianskaia Krasnaia Armiia*, RKKA) organized and utilized its human resources. According to conventional wisdom, the early defeats of the Red Army were caused by the internal problems of the purge of officers in 1937–1938 and the reinstitution of dual command with military commissars, which undermined the military's preparedness and disastrously weakened the army. Such external factors as the size, experience, and technological advantage of the German army; the surprise achieved by the German attack; Stalin's interference in operational matters; and the lack of up-to-date weapons in the Red Army's inventory are also blamed for the debacle.[1] There is ample evidence, however, to suggest that the Red Army had significant internal problems that were not at all related to the purges, which in and of themselves contributed far more than all other factors to its defeats in 1941 and 1942 and compounded all other disadvantages. Difficulties with social cohesion, officer manning, discipline, and training mostly brought on by rapid expansion degraded the Red Army's ability to fight effectively.

The book examines the Red Army from the bottom up, that is, at the regiment and division level and, in some aspects, from the top down as well, to achieve a more complete understanding of the reasons for the great changes in the Soviet military as it evolved from a revolutionary to a traditional army that was incapable of preventing a devastating enemy invasion deep into the USSR. In order to appreciate the causes of the Red Army's failure in 1941, the army must be understood as a society in and of itself, but one cut from the whole cloth of the larger civilian society that produced it. I examine the social composition of the enlisted ranks and officer corps, as well as elements of social mobility, education, morale and discipline, party membership patterns, and the social and political factors external to the military that affected the dynamics of military life. In the course of tracing the growth and transformation of the Red Army, I describe the daily life of the soldier, both his military duties and his nonmilitary experiences, in order to show the profound influence of preservice societal influences on the soldiery and the effect of regime social policy on the outlook of the average conscript. The soldiers' behavior in peace and wartime was perhaps influenced more by civilian experiences than military service.

A traditional army is generally assigned only one task by its government: to defend the interests of the state by force of arms or by the threat of their use through offensive or defensive military action. The Red Army was an exception in early twentieth-century Europe in that it had an additional mission: to act as an instrument of social and cultural modernization. To defend the state, the army had to do three things: establish a doctrine for defense, train the forces to carry out the doctrine, and procure the necessary material means to enable trained men to fulfill the doctrine. It is implicit in all modern armies that military service acts as a modernizing force for naive and uneducated youths, but the Red Army went further by making an explicit commitment to educate and socialize its soldiers, most of whom came from the backward peasant masses. To perform its mission of modernization, the army adopted as part of its organization a basically nonmilitary agency, the Political Administration of the RKKA (*Politicheskoe Upravlenie RKKA*, PURKKA, normally rendered PUR), which competed for leadership personnel, training time, and even a share of the military budget. PUR had two tasks: political indoctrination and social modernization through instruction in Marxist-Leninist doctrine, literacy, atheism, personal hygiene, and culture.

This book is not about doctrine but about the way the Red Army organized and prepared itself to carry out its two assigned tasks and how domestic social, budgetary, and foreign policies of the state affected its preparation. The methodology used for this study is primarily sociological and organizational. The organizational development of the Red Army is charted through two key aspects: manpower policies and training. The role of matériel procurement, allocation processes, and budgetary considerations are included where appropriate. All these factors are intertwined, and a change in one affected the others.

The influences on manpower and manpower policies were by far the most diverse. At the same time, the influence of manpower policies on the rest of the army's activities was the most important. The army depended on state authorization for decreases and increases in personnel. Its leader-to-led ratio depended on officer recruiting, which in turn was affected by social and political constraints on whom it could recruit. When authorized or ordered to expand, the army had to contend with its ability to house and provide training facilities for its soldiers. It also had to compete with industry, the Communist party, government, and PUR for leadership personnel.

Training was affected by manpower policies, matériel considerations, budgetary priorities, and social modernization—tasks which often diverted the army from training. The army's matériel status, that is, its ability to equip and support its personnel in everyday living, training, and combat, was determined by the state's national budgetary priorities, competition with civilian agencies for everything from building materials to fuel, and the army's ability to interact with the defense industry to their mutual satisfaction. Military budget policies in turn were shaped by the government's assessment of foreign military threats, Stalin's expansionist desires, and the capacity of the economy to bear diversions of funds and resources to the military.

In the twenties and thirties, the Red Army evolved from a small revolutionary army with outdated technology and informal relations between officers and enlisted men to a more traditionally organized modern mass army, supplied with modern mechanical and electronic equipment and with formal social distinctions between officers and enlisted men. Such transformations were a response to various changes in the internal order and international stature of the Soviet Union. The Red Army did not change solely as a result of clearly defined and accepted military doctrines, long-term goals, and national defense priorities. Like other armies, it also changed in response to societal trends. This work sheds light on how and why this transformation came about and the subsequent ramifications for the army's combat performance in the opening years of the Second World War.

The Red Army was one of the focal points of the Bolsheviks' attempt to inculcate socialist ideas among the populace, but, as Mark von Hagen has pointed out, the peasant soldier could be the regime's agent of change in the village or the defender of traditional village life against the regime.[2] Attitudes toward socialism were, to a large extent, influenced by how Soviet social policies had affected a soldier before he entered the military and how they affected him and his family while he served. Collectivization of agriculture, de-kulakization, industrialization, and the rapid urbanization of society were the most important policies affecting the common soldier. Other policies, such as forced grain requisitioning and the antireligious campaigns, also influenced soldiers' attitudes. Although the state had many programs in the army designed to foster goodwill on the part of its graduates from the "school of socialism," the effect of life-shattering social reorganization hardened the attitudes of many peasant soldiers against the military and the regime, thus negating the positive influences of military service and undermining the regime's attempts to convince conscripts that service in the Red Army was a privilege, not the burden it had been in the Imperial Army.

The single most important factor in the defeat of the Red Army in 1941 was the rapid expansion of the RKKA in the thirties, for it increased in magnitude the internal social and organizational problems while simultaneously reducing the leadership's ability to deal with them. The armed forces expanded in three stages. The first stage of significant growth was from 1931 to 1934. In these years, the Red Army selectively mobilized a handful of territo-

rial divisions, which were then brought up to normal active-duty strength—
anywhere from six thousand to eight thousand men. Then, if a division was
sent to another military district, as many were, the losing military district
would organize another territorial division to replace the one it lost. Many of
the mobilized rifle divisions were sent to the Far East in the early thirties because of the hostilities with Japan on the Chinese border. Indeed, it seems
that, along with Deputy Commissar of Defense Mikhail Tukhachevskii's urg-
ings for a larger standing army, tension with Japan was a factor in causing this
first phase of expansion. By this process, the Red Army grew by about a
dozen regular divisions and scores of supporting units. The regular force
added 300,000 men, raising its strength to 885,000 officers and men. Additionally, the army created a similar number of territorial divisions.

The second stage of growth was from 1935 through 1937. In these years,
the army bolstered its regular forces by converting two-thirds of the territorial
units to regular units. As the transitory soldiers finished their service obligations, they were replaced by conscripts serving two years on active service. By
this method, it took until 1939 before the former territorial units were truly
regular units. By shutting off the flow of men into the transitory personnel of
the territorial units and conscripting them instead for full-time duty, the active
forces of the Red Army grew to a force of 1.3 million. The impetus for this
stage of growth can be directly traced to efforts of the army to convince the
party and government that a larger regular army was necessary to confront the
growth of Nazi Germany's armed forces. In 1935, Tukhachevskii wrote a report for the Politburo that gave a detailed overview of Germany's increased
military capacity, which he predicted would soon be unleashed against the
USSR. Partly as a result of this report, Stalin authorized the elimination of the
territorial system and increased the strength of the regular forces.

The army's third and final stage of prewar growth was from 1938 to 1941.
In this period, under the terms of a new law on military service passed in
1939, the duration of conscripted service was increased by one year, from two
to three years for army and air force conscripts. Additional regular units were
created, and the few remaining territorial units were converted to regular
units. The number of regular infantry divisions increased tremendously in the
sixteen months following the phasing out of the territorial system, when the
army created one hundred infantry divisions. In this final stage of expansion
before the war, the manpower of the RKKA increased by nearly 200 percent.
This equaled an influx of around three million men over a two-and-a-half-
year period, bringing the strength of the Red Army and Navy to around 5
million men and women on 22 June 1941.

Even in its very first stage, expansion created a serious problem in recruiting and retaining officers to lead the army. Throughout the thirties, the
army was hamstrung by a constant shortage of officers. In the last of the

post–Civil War demobilizations in 1926, the army demobilized nearly 16,000 officers and political personnel, ostensibly as an economic measure. From that time until the first years of the Second World War, the armed forces were short of leaders. Intensive recruitment and forced service of party members and reservists over a ten-year period were not sufficient to bring the officer corps up to the necessary strength, which increased annually.

Changes in the Soviet economy affected the organization of the armed forces, which in turn affected manpower policies. The industrialization of the Soviet Union through the five-year plans created the necessary conditions for the Red Army to expand. Once industry was on firm footing, increased resources could be allocated for supplying the material needs of the army. The Soviet state could afford to have a larger army after industrializing, but expanding the army in the early thirties brought mixed blessings. It contributed to both discipline problems and the shortage of officers. Because the army continually grew, it constantly needed more officers, but because it could not get as many as it needed, the ratio of officers to men decreased. Thus, fewer leaders attempted—unsuccessfully—to exercise control over more men. The army was forced to adopt traditional authoritarian practices to lead the soldiers because the leaders it got were by and large socially and educationally unprepared for their positions of responsibility. To make matters worse, many conscript soldiers served very reluctantly due to a variety of social factors. In short, the expansion made the military susceptible to the same social chaos evident in a civilian society characterized by labor indiscipline, worker turnover, and shortages of competent and trained managers and engineers.

External stimuli also contributed to the transformation to a traditional army. Throughout the late twenties and thirties, hostilities with Japan along the Sino-Soviet border occasionally flared up, causing moderate expansion of the army. Toward the end of the thirties, the rise of Nazi Germany provided the impetus for a greater expansion of the Red Army and its conversion from a mixed system of territorial and regular forces to an all-regular army, which meant the elimination of the army's organized reserve. Finally, the 1939 invasion of Poland by both Germany and the Soviet Union, the Soviets' war with Finland in the winter of 1939–1940, and the successful German invasion of France in 1940, all resulted in further Soviet military expansion, a major loosening of the national purse strings for defense, and changes in military organization. Such considerable expansion had enormous consequences for the officer corps from the late thirties until the start of the war. The creation of scores of new divisions every year after 1936 caused the army to revamp the officer procurement system and adjust its selection criteria to accommodate its changing needs. This, in turn, greatly affected cohesion, training, and the professionalization of the officer corps.

The purge of officers in 1937 and 1938 also greatly affected the army. At a critical time, it deprived the army of thousands of leaders, at all levels of command. The purge and simultaneous reintroduction of dual command with military commissars affected manning, morale, and efficiency within the units. The army now had an additional obstacle to overcome in fulfilling its missions, but it was not the sole or determining cause of the decline of morale and proficiency in the officer corps.

In general, the organization of the Red Army reflected social and economic changes in state and society and, along with training, it had a marked effect on the combat readiness of the RKKA. Changes in unit organization reflected the success of the five-year plans in supplying the army with more equipment and more sophisticated weaponry. The introduction of motorized, armored, and mechanized forces led to the creation of entirely new types of units that had to be integrated into the army. This created a need for new tactical doctrine and an expanded logistical base of support; yet despite technological and doctrinal change, the Red Army remained in its mentality and matériel predominantly an infantry army. The most important aspect of the army's organization was its manning policies. Rifle divisions were overwhelmingly manned by men of peasant origin, while the more technical units were primarily manned by members of the working class. Another important policy was that of partial manning as a facet of mobilization. This policy was to have important consequences at the start of the Second World War because it hindered both operational readiness and mobilization.

Political reports of regiment, division, and military district commissars found in the *Rossiiskii gosudarstvennyi voennyi arkhiv* (formerly *Tsentral'nyi gosudarstvennyi arkhiv Sovetskoi Armii*), documents from the records of the Smolensk Oblast, documents published in Soviet journals, Soviet military newspapers, and journals of the era, and Soviet memoirs form the body of primary sources for this work. It also relies on Soviet secondary sources, contemporary Soviet military and political journals, biographies, and modern secondary sources in English. These sources have obvious strengths and weaknesses. Almost all of the Soviet military memoirs used were written by colonels and higher-ranking officers who benefited from service to the army and the regime. Not surprisingly, they seldom criticize the system or each other and, because it was taboo in pre-*glasnost'* USSR, most avoid mention of the purge. On the positive side, they do tell about army life in the regiments. Emigré memoirs and reminiscences proved to be useful for their treatment of topics normally shunned by Soviet memoirists, such as the purge and the personality defects of their associates. Nonetheless, these sources have to be treated carefully because anti-Soviet bias sometimes distorts their interpretation of events. The archival sources proved to be the most unique and revealing, disclosing many taboo subjects never mentioned by Soviet historians.

Their usefulness, too, was limited, however: first, many items are still classified and unavailable to Western scholars, and second, many topics of great interest lacked continuity throughout the period.

Soviet secondary sources published in the twenties and thirties are quite useful for their portrayal of the desired ideal. This ideal can be checked against reality, as revealed in commissars' political reports. Letters to the editor of *Krasnaia zvezda*, the RKKA's daily newspaper, also provide a perception of reality. These letters frequently complain about conditions and practices in the army and were often used in press campaigns to call attention to specific armywide shortcomings that the military and PUR hierarchy wanted the units to address. These campaigns would not have been conducted if the problems did not exist, so they are useful for understanding the desires and goals of the military leadership and for identifying problems in the military. These letters and PUR reports were checked against information contained in the records of the Smolensk Oblast. U.S. Military Intelligence Division Reports and British Foreign Office files of the era help to distinguish between the real and the ideal, although the military attaché reports are often flawed by misinterpretations caused by unfamiliarity with the Red Army and the Soviet system and from being too close to the events.

Modern Soviet journal articles, especially those published since 1985, are exceptionally valuable for their wealth of raw data and information gained from party and military archives. Until mid-1991, despite *glasnost'*, the authors still adhered to a "party line." These articles, many written by army officers, offer little serious criticism and tend to be self-serving. Moreover, they often still rely on Stalin and his cult of personality as a scapegoat for the military's past failures. Nonetheless, these sources assist in achieving synthesis. After the coup attempt in 1991, some very valuable archival material has been published in a variety of new journals.

Chapter 1 details the organization of the Red Army and describes conscription, preconscription training, and unit training and their attendant problems. The territorial system and its manning, training, and eventual elimination in favor of an exclusively regular standing army are also analyzed. Chapter 2 covers the daily life of the Red Army soldier and the conditions of service: food, housing and barracks life, discipline, insubordination, crime, and punishment in both the regular and territorial forces. PUR and its work of transforming soldiers into "new Soviet men" is the subject of Chapter 3. Chapter 4 addresses the shaping and growth of the officer corps, conditions of service, officers' civilian and military education, the relations between communist and noncommunist officers, and the shortage of officers and its ramifications. Chapter 5 describes the purge and its impact on military organization, personnel, and morale, and the effect of the reintroduction of dual command in 1937. Chapter 6 covers the reorganization of the Red Army between 1939 and 1941, the last and largest phase of expansion, and the failed efforts to overcome the shortage of officers. It chronicles the efforts of the army to prepare for war in the last years before the German invasion. The concluding chapter analyzes the excuses the Soviet military has given for its failure and, finally, the effect of the state's and army's organizational and manning policies on Red Army combat performance during the opening phases of the German invasion.

CHAPTER 1

Organization and Training of the Regular Army and Territorial Forces

Two reasons the Red Army did poorly at the outset of the Second World War were that it suffered from flawed organization and poor training. These problems were systemic. They did not date from the years just before the war but were inherent in the methods of manning and the insufficient emphasis on training the army adopted from its first major reorganization in 1925.

One of the first questions the Soviet government had to address at the end of the Civil War was what kind of army to have: a standing army or a citizens' militia. As a compromise, the Tenth Party Congress decided in 1921 to create a mixed military system comprising a small, standing regular army and a large territorial army of conscripted citizen-soldiers serving part time, led by cadres of regular army personnel.[1] In the Stalin era, Soviet historiography put forth the assertion, which still stands, that the compromise of a mixed system was purely an economic decision. Economics were undoubtedly an important aspect of the decision, but once the system was established, the mixed system seemed to offer the best of both worlds. Besides its lower cost, the territorial force was defensive and incorporated a great many citizens, thus creating a large trained reserve. Although it put more men into uniform than did the regular army, the territorial force did not take them away from their work for long periods.[2] The mixed system lasted until 1935, at which time the army began to convert to an all-regular force. It took four years to complete the transition.

Once the regime decided on the mixed system, the Red Army sought to establish routines and methods for preparing an armed force to defend the USSR—no easy task. Despite—and in some instances because of—its Civil War experience, the Red Army virtually had to start from scratch in setting up the conscription system, the preconscription training system, and peacetime training routines. Simultaneously, the army had to reorganize unit structures as it reduced its size to adjust to the postwar economic, social, and political situation. The economic situation was marked by a disastrous decrease in industrial output, which meant that industry had to concentrate first on recovery before it could make a serious effort to rearm the Red Army. The low educational level of the population, characterized by continued mass illiteracy, hindered the army's development of technical units. The political situation was complicated by the fact that the organs of soviet power had still not extended completely throughout the USSR. In practical terms, this prevented the army from tapping all the human resources potentially available. In establishing its routines and methods, then, the Red Army had to adapt itself to very real but less than ideal conditions.

THE REGULAR ARMY

Organization after the Frunze Reforms

Mikhail Frunze, Leon Trotsky's successor as chief of the Revolutionary Military Council (RVS, in 1934 renamed People's Commissariat of Defense), made an invaluable contribution to the Red Army in 1924–1925 by establishing the framework that gave the military what little order and regularity it achieved before its transition from the mixed system to an all-regular army in 1935. Under Frunze, the framework of the army was established and the organization of regiments and divisions was standardized, on paper at least. The Red Army's most important tasks in the immediate post–Civil War years included establishing a conscription system and organizing—insofar as the economy would permit—an efficient and modern mixed system of regular and territorial forces.[3]

Frunze adapted the army's organization to fit the nation's economic and social reality. From 1925 until the end of the second five-year plan, divisions were supplied mostly with the Imperial Army's leftover equipment, which in some instances dated from before the turn of the century and had seen hard use during the First World War and the Civil War. In this respect, the army's circumstances mirrored those of society, which was itself hampered by meager industrial output and backward technology. Following the traditional Russian pattern, infantry and cavalry predominated and technical branches lagged far behind. The Red Army's reliance on infantry and cavalry was natural in that it fit the social and educational qualities of the Soviet population, which was overwhelmingly peasant in 1925. After the demobilizations and reforms of 1924, infantry and cavalry formations made up 55 percent of the active army and 80 percent of the territorial forces.[4]

Frunze was not content to merely adapt the army to the conditions reigning in the country; he also sought to modernize the armed forces. His efforts, however, were constrained by the national budget. The regime's priority in the mid-twenties was to get the Soviet Union back on its feet economically. Once the military was deemed able to present a credible defense, its budget became relatively static. At the onset of the first five-year plan in 1928, the army high command pushed for a larger share of the budget and to increase the production plan for the military and defense industries. This had a minimal effect. At the Sixteenth Party Congress in 1930, the military made another effort to get even more resources diverted from the civilian sector to the military, but Stalin remained unconvinced. Through the end of the first five-year plan, civilian industry took precedence over defense industry.[5]

Conscription

Because the Red Army was designed as a conscript army, the organization and efficiency of the conscription organs were vital to the life of the army. The draft officially began on the first of September and lasted until mid-November. It did not, however, take place simultaneously all over the USSR. Moscow, Leningrad, and the major cities of each military district were the first to undergo the draft. From there, conscription commissions filtered out to the smaller cities and towns of their districts.

Responsibility for organizing conscription lay with military district administrations. Some of the numerous tasks associated with conscription and mobilization included (1) registering men, horses, carts, trucks, and automobiles liable for military service; (2) organizing and conducting preconscription training and training men performing their service outside the ranks; (3) organizing annual call-ups, conducting practice call-ups, and organizing supplies, horses, and carts for mobilization; (4) drawing up mobilization plans for the district; (5) organizing local guards; and (6) leading and observing the activities of *raion* (district) military commissariats. The military district chief coordinated the activities of the subordinate *raion* military commissariats with the help of his own mobilization section.[6]

The *raion* military commissariat, under the guidance of the *raion* executive committee *(raiispolkom),* conducted registration and preconscription training. The commissariat consisted of (1) a political section, (2) a mobilization registration section, (3) a section for training men outside the ranks, (4) a billeting section, (5) a section for economic administration, and (6) two commissions, one for *oblast* (provincial) conscription and one to handle deferments. The *raion* administration was in many ways a miniature copy of the district administration. Besides its conscription duties, the *raion* commissariat was supposed to maintain a relationship with the local social insurance and land sections to represent the interests of residents serving in the regular forces.[7]

Regional party organs kept track of men aged twenty-one through thirty who had military obligations and reported this to the army. The military district mobilization section then used this information to formulate orders to the subordinate conscription organs every year. The orders specified the number of young men needed and where they were to be sent once conscripted. The military districts passed down this information to the *raion* military commissariats, which then established quotas for towns and villages.[8]

Raion conscription commissions, consisting of a representative of the *raion* military commissariat, a representative of the *raiispolkom,* a member of the *raion* trade union bureau, two or three doctors, and a military officer, went to predesignated villages during the conscription "season." In the major urban centers, especially Moscow and Leningrad, large factories served as temporary conscription points.[9] In contrast to European armies, in which the military handled conscription and recruiting, conscription in the USSR was a joint effort by the army, the Communist party, trade unions, and the Komsomol. The most important of these was the party.

In areas where no military units were stationed, the *oblast* (province) was supposed to maintain a military commission to oversee conscription and recruiting. In many cases, however, *oblasti* often did not create subordinate military commissions to support conscription at the local level. Throughout the twenties and thirties when the army created or transferred units to areas with no military commissions, *oblast* and *raion* military commissions subsequently had to be created.[10] Thus the population of some of the more remote areas of the Soviet Union escaped military conscription well into the thirties.

Men could secure deferments and exemptions from conscription. The army granted deferments on religious grounds and for university attendance and higher technical schooling, but most often for medical deficiencies. The army also exempted heads of households who were the sole providers of their families. Soldiers with bona fide reasons, however, did not always receive the exemptions they deserved. If a conscription commission had to meet its quota by denying an exemption, it would.[11]

The actual social composition of the regular army in the twenties did not mirror the social composition of the draft cohorts, nor was it intended to. Conscription commissions seem to have been under orders to put as many workers into the regular forces as possible. Workers and those categorized as "other" (among them white-collar workers and government employees) were overrepresented. Peasants were more likely to be assigned to the territorial forces.[12] There is every indication that the trend of putting as many workers and nonpeasants into the regular forces as possible continued until 1939. Wealthy peasants, former noblemen, and middle-class men were neither conscripted nor allowed to volunteer for the military. To keep the army free of these "class enemies," conscription commissions checked (though often poorly) the social background of conscripts to weed out undesirables.

The Red Army sought to achieve two goals by its recruiting policy. The first was to get educated men into the regular army, which meant recruiting as many workers as possible, because they were the most literate segment of society. The second was to enlist as many poor and landless peasants (*bedniaki* and *batraki*) as possible, because the regime wanted not only to ally itself with the rural poor against the rural "rich" but also to prepare those men for leadership in the countryside. The actual social composition of a regular or territorial unit depended on its area of manning. Units garrisoned in urbanized areas had large numbers of workers, while those in the rural areas had vast numbers of peasants. The army, despite its desire for a minimum percentage of proletarians in each unit, made no attempt to distribute workers and peasants between units to obtain uniformity.[13]

The criteria that determined who would serve in the regular forces and who in the territorial forces have yet to be revealed. Since the regular army was just over half infantry and cavalry and the remainder was specialized units that had first pick of the more literate recruits, it is reasonable to speculate that the rest of the regular army must have had a higher claim on the remainder of the best educated conscripts. The territorial force contained mostly infantry and cavalry, so its need for educated and technically trained men was correspondingly less pressing than that of the regular force.

Although the press always reported that 100 percent of the men picked for military duty reported for service, this was not the case. The RKKA never got all the men to show up, whether they were designated for preconscription training, training outside the ranks, training between assemblies or summer camps of territorials, or for active duty. For example, in 1930 the Siberian Military District had 90 percent of soldiers called up report for duty. This percentage was down from previous years. One regiment even reported only 84 percent compliance from its recruiting district.[14]

When conscripts appeared at assembly points for service in the regular forces, they were given another physical examination before being shipped off to their regiments. The men were inspected for vermin and fleas, and tested for contagious diseases. In the words of one conscript, "Our military training began with a steam bath, the disinfection of all our clothes, a haircut that left our scalps as smooth as our faces, and a political lecture."[15] After that, they were supposed to be fed a good meal and issued new uniforms, thus undergoing a full transformation, in appearance at least, from civilian to soldier. In reality, things did not proceed as neatly as all that. Sometimes disturbances broke out among the draftees at assembly areas. Downright mayhem in the form of drunken brawls was not unusual. Many discipline problems at the assembly points were the result of alcohol abuse. In 1930, for example, the rates of drunkenness among new recruits in the 16th Artillery Regiment at its four *raion* assembly points was 50 percent, 20 percent, 15 percent, and 10 percent, respectively. In contrast, the 47th Rifle Regiment of the same division reported only three drunks in all its six assembly points. In the early thirties, conscripts' negative reactions to collectivization also caused problems.[16]

The army required men not chosen to serve on active duty or in the territorial units to train outside the units. These men were surplus to the *raion* quota, or those medically disqualified for regular or territorial service. They were known as "outside the rankers" (*vnevoiskoviki*). They were obligated to perform three years of training, consisting of a one-month assembly each year. According to the military press, the better-off peasants (kulaks) made a special effort to sneak into the army and become *vnevoiskoviki*.[17]

Just because a man was initially assigned to a specific type of service—regular, territorial, or in industry—was no guarantee that he would actually serve there. Procedures existed that permitted the transfer of individuals between the different types of service. Sometimes these procedures were manipulated for personal gain. In 1929, a military tribunal convicted a platoon commander of the 250th Territorial Rifle Regiment and a clerk on the regimental staff of taking bribes from some fathers of men in the regiment. The fathers wanted their sons transferred from the territorial forces to service outside the forces so they could work in local factories. Their standard bribe was forty-five rubles, although the platoon commander would accept twenty rubles in a pinch. Those who could not wrangle their way completely out of the ranks could still get out of the annual assemblies if they had money and knew the right personnel clerks.[18]

Beginning in 1936, conscription commissions found their duties complicated by new policies expanding the recruitment base. Not all conscription organs rose to the challenge, prompting major changes. In place of the former regional corps and divisional mobilization areas, which had been under the charge of the rather ineffective district military commissariats, independent military commissariats were established in the autonomous republics, territories, regions, autonomous regions, and cities. In addition, the number of district military commissariats multiplied by three and a half.[19]

As the army grew throughout the thirties, the People's Commissariat of Defense (NKO) sought ways to expand the manpower pool. Initially, conscription commissions granted fewer exemptions. Then, in 1936, the government lowered the draft age from twenty-one to nineteen. The 1936 "Stalin Constitution" did away with class and nationality restrictions for all purposes, including military service. Those previously identified as kulaks or children of kulaks became subject to military service. The army ended exemptions for religious believers and conscientious objectors in August 1939.[20] Although the draft age was lowered, the RKKA did not immediately draft all the men in the nineteen to twenty-one age group. The armed forces could not have coped with the number of men that would have brought in. Rather, the army worked its way down to the nineteen-year-olds over a three-year period.[21]

Allowing nationalities previously banned from service (Uzbeks, Turkmen, Buriats, Tadzhiks, Kirgiz, and some peoples of the North Caucasus) to serve expanded the draft pool. In addition, on 15 May 1936, the regime published a resolution to organize Cossack units from the Don, Terek, Kuban, and

Stavropol regions. The divisions were not pure Cossack units as they had been in tsarist days; they included peasants, workers, Armenians, and Jews of the territories in question. Nevertheless, they were provided with distinctive Cossack uniforms and were called Cossacks (*kazaki*) rather than Red Army men (*krasnoarmeitsy*). Cossack units were short-lived, however. In March 1938, the Commissariat of Defense decided to phase out all national units and man formations without regard to nationality or ethnic origin.[22]

In 1939 and thereafter, as the army rapidly expanded, creating hundreds more divisions, it parceled out nationalities to units throughout the whole USSR. This practice created numerous problems, language being the most pressing. Most of the Caucasian and Central Asian conscripts did not speak Russian, impeding training and the achievement of unit cohesion.[23]

Responding to the increased importance of efficient conscription, the Commissariat of Defense began a campaign in 1936 to galvanize the local conscription organs. The immediate response was not positive, and the army quickly resorted to public recrimination by making examples of selected deficient organizations. In this vein, the NKO accused the Kiev Military District of being unprepared for the draft in August 1936. Three of its *raiony* apparently had not done their preparatory work for the start of the draft in September. Of their draftees, 5 percent had been identified as illiterate and 41.5 percent as semi-literate, indicating that the *raiony* had not provided the requisite preconscription educational instruction. The army held the *raikom* (*raiou* committee) and other *raion* organs responsible. In other areas, many draftees did not get notices telling them when and where to assemble, and city soviets, trade unions, and local Komsomol detachments did not send representatives to help military commissions. Despite admonitions, many local organs prepared no better for the draft in 1937 than the year before, although the party sent special commissions to several areas ahead of time to prevent mistakes.[24]

Broadening the conscription base served to bring in mostly Russians, but the share of Russians dropped as a percentage of total soldiers. Even so, Russians, Ukrainians, and Belorussians continued to be overrepresented in relation to their numbers in society. Bolshevik rule saw the military become more dominated by these three groups than it had been under the tsars. Before the First World War, in the old army, 75 percent of the army had been Russian, Ukrainian, and Belorussian. In 1941, 84.7 percent were Russian, Ukrainian, and Belorussian.[25]

Preconscription Training

Because the length of service for soldiers was comparatively short, the army wanted conscripts to acquire basic military knowledge and skills before they entered the service. Over the course of two years prior to induction, all young men were supposed to undergo more than 200 hours of military instruction. The training consisted of the rudiments of weapons handling, marksmanship, and individual and squad tactics. Soldiers were familiarized with the various branches of service and the organization of the military, what barracks life would be like, and the daily routine they could expect in active service.[26]

Initially, preconscription training was the joint responsibility of the regular army, the territorial forces, and the Communist party. The military provided instructors, and the party organized the conscripts. Although the army placed much emphasis on this training, it was sometimes conducted in haphazard fashion or not at all. Occasionally, factories would refuse to release men for training. For many years, almost right up to the German invasion, the party and army simply did not have the material and human resources to supervise or conduct training everywhere in the USSR. The preconscription training system was further weakened in 1935 when its supervision was taken out of the army's hands and left up to myriad party and civilian organizations not closely monitored or controlled.

When preconscripts arrived at their instruction points, they often found confusion and chaos. Often there were no billets, so the men had to be quartered among the population. Weapon and equipment shortages plagued the preconscription organs. Such conditions made thorough training rather difficult and probably undermined the army's prestige.[27] At other times, the preconscripts themselves caused chaos. Some men did not come to training, some came late, and others left early, all breaches of the regulations. The experience of the 62d Rifle Regiment in May 1929 is an example of just how much trouble preconscripts could be. In less than a month, the men committed 788 infractions, 346 of which were considered serious. Of the above infringements, 190 resulted in arrests and referral to military tribunes.[28]

Other problems arose because party organs did their jobs poorly. In 1933, the Smolensk *obkom* (*oblast* committee) issued a directive noting that the responsible *raikom* personnel had not paid sufficient attention to training preconscripts at the local level. Support for classes had been very weak. The *raikom* did not fill all the classes, did not provide required materials, and sent irresponsible people for training. The task of training at the local level, the directive said, had been obstructed and undermined.[29] To remedy the situation, the *raikomy* and *raiispolkomy* were ordered to screen draftable men more carefully and assign them to the *raion* military commission in a timely fashion, paying special attention to their health and physical condition. They were also instructed to furnish materials needed for training, conduct political work among trainees, and bring classes up to full strength with responsible men. Finally, the *obkom* ordered the local organs to send inspectors to ensure the directives were followed. Such problems were not limited to Smolensk *oblast* but occurred throughout the USSR up to 22 June 1941.[30]

As the army grew, the ratio of experienced leaders to novice conscripts widened, making preconscription training ever more important. With leadership resources spread thinly, the army needed conscripts to arrive for service armed with basic soldiering knowledge, such as how to march and shoot. Receiving conscripts already trained in the basics would allow leaders to concentrate their efforts on raising their units' military proficiency rather than creating it from scratch. The party and Osoaviakhim worked inconsistently and in general let the army down. Units remained at a low level of proficiency because many men arrived untrained. The army did not have basic training units, so each battalion set aside several months to conduct such training.

Overall, the Red Army was successful in garnering a sufficient number of conscripts every year. Despite widespread reluctance to serve, and despite a high number of medical deferrals, the Red Army, until 1939, still had to train outside the ranks almost a third of the eligible conscripts because the armed forces were not large enough to absorb them all. The army successfully relied on the party's administrative network to reach the men. Even when chaos reigned in the lower party organs, which was not unusual during the first several decades of communist rule, the party managed to enforce conscription, though not necessarily preconscription training.[31]

ARMY LIFE

Initial Training

When soldiers first arrived at their units, their initial reception was geared to reassuring them that life in the Red Army would be good. With this in mind, the army touted service in the RKKA as a better deal than service in the Imperial Army, particularly because the Red soldier had to serve less time. In the Imperial Army, service in the combat arms lasted three years; in specialty branches, four years. The Soviet soldier had a five-year military obligation, but until 1939 active service for all branches was only two years. The remaining years of the obligation were spent on long-term furlough. Once the furlough ended, they were automatically enrolled in the reserve and put on a secondary recall roster for mobilization.[32]

Red Army propaganda described barracks life in glowing terms that emphasized the improvements made since the Revolution. Soldiers were told that they would have time every day for tea and reading the newspaper. In practice this became a political-education event rather than a leisure activity. The army promised soldiers access to movies, plays, sports, and cultural ex-

Typical tent city at a summer training encampment.

cursions. Soldiers were continually reminded that their tsarist predecessors had had none of these benefits and that barracks life in the old army could be so dreary as to trigger suicide. Unlike service in the tsarist army—likened to a prison term—Soviet soldiers enjoyed all the rights of civil society and should consider it a privilege to wear the uniform of a *krasnoarmeets.*[33]

Recruits were told that the Red Army's social composition was crucial to making it superior to the old tsarist army. In particular, the Soviets lambasted the old army for its class nature. The old officer corps was composed of *dvorianstvo*, bourgeois, kulaks, *pomeshchiki*, merchants, and so on. They learned the slogan, "In the Red Army there is no gulf between commanders and Red Army men because they are from one toiling family."[34]

Their superiors taught the new recruits the necessity of discipline for the efficient functioning of the army, but they insisted that revolutionary discipline was different from the discipline of bourgeois armies where discipline was based on class exploitation. The Red Army had socialist discipline, characterized by two facets: a conscious understanding that the mission of all working people was the mission of the Soviet Union; and mastering the particularities of military discipline. To have socialist discipline, a soldier needed to be literate, functionally and politically, and had to work for the goals of Soviet power. According to a soldiers' manual, "These three requirements . . . are no less important than the study . . . of the rifle." Socialist discipline, however, did not go so far as to rule out unquestioning obedience. Soldiers were instructed to obey orders, even if they did not understand them—just as in the old army.[35]

Nonetheless, the Red Army soldier was repeatedly assured that he would not be exploited. On the contrary, there was a strong comradeship, a brotherly relationship, between commanders and Red Army soldiers. Enlisted men and officers addressed each other with the formal "*vy*," helping to eliminate the class distinction that existed in the old army. Ideally, officers associated with their men in an easy and informal manner that would have been unthinkable in the Imperial Army. Soldiers could walk into their commander's office at will to bring matters to his attention. The oath of the Red Army soldier was to the workers' and peasants' class; before the Revolution, soldiers swore allegiance to the tsar.[36]

In addition to teaching military subjects and Soviet patriotism, the army tackled some of the more basic goals of the Soviet state, such as personal hygiene. Cleanliness was supposed to be a high priority in the barracks. Unit doctors periodically checked the cleanliness of barracks and camps to ensure that soldiers followed the rules of proper sanitation. Doctors encouraged the men to brush their teeth and bathe frequently—both new habits to many

Cavalry and light tanks on maneuvers in Central Asia.

Horse-drawn artillery in the field.

peasant conscripts. In its endeavor to get soldiers to understand the importance of general sanitation, the Red Army again made every effort to compare the Red Army's care for soldiers with the tsarist army's lack of concern.[37]
In addition to promoting health and cleanliness, the Red Army also tackled
the long-standing vice of alcoholism. Regulations forbade alcohol in the barracks, and soldiers were discouraged from drinking in local villages during
off-duty hours.[38]

Unit Training

After the Frunze reforms, the Red Army settled down to peacetime training.
Because it was a new army, however, it could not fall back on well established
patterns and routines but had to work out many things from scratch. Understanding the army's inadequate proficiency, Leon Trotsky in 1922 described
how it would have to concentrate on matters mundane to an established
army:

> All our attention must now be directed not toward a fantastic reconstruc-
> tion, but toward improvement and greater precision. To supply sections
> properly with food; not to permit products to rot; to cook good cabbage
> soup; to teach how to destroy body vermin and to keep clean; to cor-
> rectly conduct training exercises, . . . to prepare political discussions in-
> telligently and concretely; to furnish each Red soldier with a service
> book and keep good records; to teach how to oil rifles and grease boots;
> to teach how to shoot; to help the commanding personnel thoroughly as-

similate the statute regulations concerning maintaining communications, gathering intelligence, making reports, maintaining guards; to learn and to teach how to adapt oneself to various localities; to wrap one's feet correctly in pieces of cloth to keep them from getting rubbed raw; once again to grease boots.[39]

Trotsky detailed things most former tsarist officers (*voenspetsy*, literally military specialists) and higher officers with prerevolutionary military experience took for granted. Many regiment and lower unit commanders had joined the army after the Revolution and thus were unfamiliar with such details.

The training year was divided into two parts: winter (15 November to 30 April) and summer (1 May to 15 September). From 15 September to 15 November the army discharged the second-year men and conscripted the new draft cohort. During the winter training cycle, individuals learned skills such as skiing and snowshoeing, as well as some small unit tactical training. As much training as possible was done in the barracks.

As had been the case with the Imperial Army, the annual spring/summer camp was the most important training period of the year for both the regular and the territorial forces. During the summer, the army trained mostly outdoors and focused on unit tactical skills and large-scale maneuvers. Units packed up and moved out of their garrisons and went to training areas where they were free to maneuver across the countryside. Advance parties from each regiment went to their respective camps to get organized before the main body of troops arrived. Despite this preparation, most effort during the first week of camp was usually spent on administrative tasks and very little on military training. The habit of taking a week to settle in did not sit well with those at higher levels. Units were supposed to have their plans made well in advance of the assembly; in fact, territorial units had a special ten-day assembly of officers in late winter or early spring just to do such planning. Nevertheless, all too often units arrived at camp unprepared to begin training.[40]

The training at camp was supposed to be more advanced than what was done in garrisons in the fall and winter. Still, many soldiers arrived at their first summer camp lacking the basic skills necessary to begin advanced training. Consequently, the first weeks of camp had to be dedicated to teaching skills that should already have been mastered. In 1937, for example, in a battery of the 60th Artillery Regiment, only 42 of 134 instruction hours had been utilized in March in preparation for summer camp. A great number of commanders held the attitude that time in garrison was for administrative tasks. What training they did not get done could be made up in the summer.[41]

The training given soldiers and the methods used were not unique to the Red Army. Infantrymen learned fundamental skills, such as the use of cover and concealment; they were taught how to dig foxholes and use a variety of weapons in defense and offense. They learned basic squad fire and maneuver tactics and how to move at night. Leaders stressed teamwork in the squads and took the men on long, conditioning marches carrying up to seventy pounds of equipment. Artillerymen practiced standard firing techniques, emplacement, and displacement of the guns. The cavalry performed mounted drills and tactics normal to all armies of the day.[42] In addition to tactical field training conducted by unit officers, the men were given instruction on the more esoteric subjects necessary to becoming "new Soviet men." Teams organized by the Military Lecture Bureau of the Central House of the Red Army (TsDKA) spoke on such themes as economics, science and technology, art, and literature.[43]

Commanders trained their units according to their own whims and standards, with corps or division commanders providing broad training guidance. Little uniformity existed in large unit tactics and training methods from division to division. In an effort to reduce the inconsistencies throughout the army, the RKKA's Administration for Military Training published a training manual for the infantry in 1933 (MTPP-33). The manual covered training of the individual soldier, squads, platoons, companies, and battalions. It spelled out duties and responsibilities for the individual soldier, squad leader, and others on up through the battalion commander and his staff. The second part covered tasks for specialized units, such as chemical, sapper, and mounted reconnaissance detachments found in infantry regiments.[44]

Through MTPP-33 the army attempted to create a uniform training system for rifle battalions. It provided thorough and exact instructions, yet it left room for initiative on how those tasks could be accomplished. It also served as a resource document with reference to other manuals and regulations. It is evident that sincere men with clear minds struggled to improve the army's training. Constant problems in organizing and conducting training, often because of officer ineptitude, vitiated the efforts of higher military authorities to achieve consistency and quality.

Distractions from Training

One of the most serious obstacles the Red Army failed to overcome in its quest to thoroughly train its men was the assignment of nonmilitary tasks that distracted from military training. Soldiers were taken away from scheduled military training to do fatigue details and administrative tasks, and, most important, entire units were detached from military training to perform tasks in support of state objectives, particularly industrial and agricultural work. Regiments and divisions spent considerable time building quarters. Political instruction should not be understood as a distraction from military training because the army itself scheduled political classes during the training day.

Sometimes soldiers were permanently reassigned to nonmilitary duties. PUR established a program to train men for agriculture, and the military taught skills that coincidentally proved useful to industry, such as mechanics, engineering, and electrical technology. In 1930, the Red Army demobilized thirty thousand technical specialists specifically to work in industry.[45] This represented a substantial sacrifice for the army because it desperately needed technically qualified personnel and had invested considerable time training them.

Besides sending masses of men out of the ranks and into industry, the regime used army units as a labor reserve for constructing industrial sites. The Red Army used regiments and divisions, both territorial and regular, to help build Dneproges, the Kharkov tractor works, the Magnitogorsk metallurgical complex, the Gomel' agricultural machinery factory, and many other industrial plants. This work lasted for months at a time and was important enough that several units were recognized with awards, such as the Order of the Red Banner of Labor and the Order of Lenin.[46] Assigning territorial units to industrial work was particularly detrimental to training because most cohorts only assembled for a month. Consequently, if they spent their month on a construction project, they received no military training that year.

Units participating in industrial projects probably never did a bit of training, yet they were encouraged and rewarded because their work was sponsored by the state. In contrast, the army punished a division commander who, out of sheer necessity, built barracks to the detriment of training, even though he was placed in a position of his superior's choosing. In another instance, an engineer officer complained that the corps commander acted indifferently to the affairs of the battalion except when those affairs involved labor for his dacha and those of other top officers. These and other examples illustrate how unpredictable and variable conditions could be for enlisted men and their commanders due to the unsystematic political and economic state of the USSR during the late twenties and early thirties. Specialized units had their training interrupted as well. For example, a student pilot reported that the garrison commander constantly interrupted instruction at his flying school to have the students hoe potatoes, build fences, and dig ditches.[47]

The state also stole Red Army training time to support agriculture. Originally, the army's participation in agriculture was voluntary, performed on an individual basis and only on weekends, but in time of need the party sent regiments or even whole divisions to the fields for days on end. In 1933, thousands of soldiers spent five weeks of training time helping collectivized peasants with the spring sowing and the harvest in the Urals, the Don basin, and the North Caucasus.[48]

The decision to detach thirty thousand technically skilled men from the ranks to support industry, taking thousands of officers and men away from training for months for construction work (while low budgets forced soldiers to live in substandard housing), suggests that during the first two five-year plans, Stalin considered industrial growth more important than strengthening the Soviet Union's military might. In the end, the military greatly benefited from industrialization, but from the late twenties to mid-thirties, the military appears to have been the servant of domestic policy. As such, it was treated more as a labor army than as a fighting force.

TRAINING ON THE EVE

With war clouds looming in the late thirties, the army put much more emphasis on training; yet, because of the army's rapid growth and the poor preparation of its leaders, the military every year became less able to provide high-quality training to the new recruits. The harder the General Staff tried to think of new and better training methods, the more glaring was the failure of the line units to fulfill training requirements.

The army gave small unit (battalion and below) training more formal emphasis. New field regulations published in 1936 (PU-36) were intended to affect training down to the lowest level. The high command intended that new techniques be taught at the first summer camp after the new regulations were introduced. It turned out to be somewhat difficult to break old habits. For several years thereafter, many units continued to employ the old training methods every summer, with little or no reference to PU-36.[49] Beginning in 1935, the high command gave large unit training more attention than in the past, with military districts holding major maneuvers of corps- and army-size operations at the end of each summer camp.

The Red Army's large-scale maneuvers were on a par with those conducted by the German army and surpassed those of the British and French armies, which had conducted no large-scale maneuvers since the First World War, not even during the phony war period from September 1939 to May 1940. The U.S. army did not conduct its first multidivisional maneuver until 1940 (the famed Louisiana maneuvers) and had conducted only a single division-size training operation before then.[50] The actual quality of the training, however, was probably not the equal of the Wehrmacht. There was little combined-arms work and not much leeway for initiative on the part of lower- and middle-ranking officers.[51] Despite MTPP-33 and PU-36, the army as a whole had not succeeded in standardizing small and large unit tactics and methods of instruction by November 1939, when the USSR attacked Finland.[52] Officers reporting to their units fresh from military schools had been taught different tactics. This variety made a unit commander's job more difficult because he had to teach his subordinates a common set of basic tactics, which they should have possessed when they first arrived.

Once the units got to camp and began training, things were far from ideal. Taking soldiers out of training was widespread, though constantly denounced. In one unit, the commissar ordered thirty new recruits to work in the kitchen. A couple of days later, seventy-eight men were detailed for farm work, cleaning a storeroom, and laboring on a construction project. Sometimes soldiers at their first summer camp spent their initial days working on the unit farm, a rather inauspicious beginning to the year's most important training.[53]

Training Junior Commanders

Training junior commanders was always a controversial subject in the Red Army because units seldom lived up to the ideals of the high command. Such training remained a sore spot in the waning years of the decade. In the regimental school of the 282d Rifle Regiment, for example, as many as thirty-five to forty students were detached for work in the storehouse or for special projects, such as building an ice-skating rink for the regiment. Another regiment usually sent eight to twenty-five men daily to work on fatigue details in the different companies. In the first two weeks of December 1936, one regiment had full participation in training in its regimental school on only two days. These problems were not unique to the infantry.[54] By not training them thoroughly, regiments handicapped junior commanders in their ability to lead, train, and supervise their subordinates and consequently reduced their usefulness to their officers. This failure, in turn, handicapped the officers' ability to make their units function well.

Company, battalion, and regiment commanders and commissars themselves often disrupted training in their regiments. They gave low priority to training prospective junior commanders and future junior lieutenants (*mladshii leitenanty*) in the regimental schools. The standard excuse of these leaders for not devoting themselves to training and leadership development was lack of time. Often the men were quite aware that they were getting short shrift in their training and complained—to no avail.[55]

To be sure, the Red Army was not the only army that took soldiers from training for details. All armies of that day had more potatoes to peel than the cooks could handle, and like the Red Army, they assigned rank-and-file soldiers to the task. What was unique about the Red Army was its willingness to detach junior commanders from regimental schools to do such details. In the German and American armies of the thirties, prospective noncommissioned officers were sent to special training not only to get their specialized instruction but to isolate them from menial details that would detract from their training. Despite rhetoric to the contrary, the Red Army—at least in a large number of line units—did not take their junior commanders seriously as part of the chain of command. The use of junior commanders to perform fatigue duties undermined their status as leaders in the eyes of superiors and subordinates alike.

Officers were absolutely truthful in claiming they did not have time to train their subordinates between 1937 and 1941. In cases where the regiment commander was a major, and company and battery commanders were lieutenants or *mladshii leitenanty*, they justifiably would have been spending most of their time trying to master their own duties. How could they teach junior commanders if they did not know their own jobs? Not all units had serious problems, but enough did to continuously elicit official concern.

THE TERRITORIAL FORCES

For all practical purposes, the Soviet territorial forces, always the stepchild of the regular army, was a reserve army, much like the U.S. National Guard and the German reserve army, based on local recruitment and administration. The army intended the territorial forces to train men on the cheap and add to the reserve of trained soldiers. For most of its existence, the territorial force was larger than the regular army in the number of units and men yet received less than its share of equipment and funding. The territorial force suffered numerous problems throughout its existence because it was unprecedented in Russian military annals and everyone responsible for making it work was unfamiliar with the system. It depended very much on the voluntary cooperation of the average village peasant and factory worker, which was not always forthcoming.[56] The degree of support from the army leadership for the territorial system is hard to gauge, but after Frunze's death it was never very enthusiastic. Many in the high command never fully accepted the mixed system as desirable or necessary.

Transitory personnel—called *terrarmeitsy* as distinct from *krasno-armeitsy*—served a five-year stint. During their tenure, soldiers had to serve in periodic call-ups of a few days every month or so and one or two months in the summer. At the conclusion of their service, territorials' names went on registration lists for recall in wartime. If recalled, they would be used to reinforce either territorial or regular army units. Men drafted into the territorial forces kept their civilian jobs and returned to them after their annual training.[57]

Locational Principle of Manning

The NKO usually formed territorial units as divisions or separate brigades. For most of the year, they existed as skeleton units of regular army personnel who served as leaders, instructors, and custodians of the equipment for the part-time troops. Units trained by conscription-year cohort, so the full complement of men was seldom, if ever, together at once. Soldiers received eight months of training over the course of five years: three months the first year of service; two months in the second; and one month in each of the last three years. Like regular soldiers, territorial soldiers were expected to have received preconscription training before joining their regiments. Each year-group and branch of service trained separately.[58]

The army formed and stationed territorial and regular units in accordance with party and government administrative boundaries. The army allocated each division one *oblast* for recruiting and conscription purposes. Within the *raiony* of an *oblast,* the division's subunits were assigned administrative boundaries as well. A regiment or battalion was assigned to a *raion* and a company to a particular town or village depending on population density. The men in each area liable for service filled the local territorial unit upon conscription, unless designated for the regular forces.[59]

The locational principle of manning made necessary the creation of national formations in the non-Russian areas of the Soviet Union. Normally, national territorial units were formed as divisions. The army created regiments and units as small as separate companies for the less populous minorities. In addition to national units, the RKKA followed the tsarist pattern and established separate military schools for the nationalities. Units and schools conducted daily training and administrative work in the native language of the men but required all leaders to speak Russian.[60]

Organization of the Territorial Forces

The territorial units were categorized into four types of formations, depending on the number of permanent personnel (cadre) in the unit. The cadre consisted of unit commanders, their staffs, and medical, veterinary, administrative, and political personnel. The cadre was responsible for military and political training and the administration of the units. A contingent of regular enlisted men supported the regimental school, provided guard details, and did the menial labor necessary to maintain the units between assemblies.

The four types of formations comprised first-, second-, and third-line divisions and mixed divisions. The first-line divisions initially (1923) were authorized 1,607 full-time Red Army personnel and 10,959 territorial soldiers and officers, but these allocations changed to 2,400 cadre personnel and 10,681 territorials a couple of years later. There were two kinds of second-line divisions: formations associated with a regular division, which had 604 of their own cadre and 11,734 territorial personnel; and formations associated with first-line territorial divisions, which had 622 cadre and 11,734 transitory personnel. Third-line divisions were actually only nuclei of divisions and had 190 cadre. Mixed divisions had one regular regiment and two territorial regiments.[61]

Just over half the leadership in territorial units consisted of regular army men. Territorial personnel comprised most of the enlisted men, as one would expect. Company commanders and above were nearly always regular officers, but all platoon commanders were, in fact, territorial personnel. Like their men, they had a five-year service obligation.[62]

The Red Army never ceased to grow from the moment it ended the post–Civil War demobilizations. In the twenties, the territorial forces experienced the bulk of this growth. In the spring of 1923, only a year after its inception, the territorial forces consisted of ten divisions. By the end of 1925, the RKKA had forty-six territorial rifle divisions. Six months later the army's strength stood at ninety-seven rifle, sixty territorial, and thirty-seven regular divisions. This growth shows how significant a role the territorial forces played in training men for the national defense. They became progressively more numerous and larger over the next three years. At the height of its growth in 1935, the territorial force comprised 74 percent of the army's divisions.[63] The sheer size of the territorial forces suggests its importance as a mechanism for the government to make its presence felt among the population as well as to bolster the national defense.

TRAINING THE TERRITORIALS

Territorial units arranged the training year along the same lines as active units, with winter and summer training cycles. The territorials emphasized summer training camp even more than the regular units and also attempted to conduct training year-round. Cadre of territorial units who conscientiously sought to fulfill their duties were extremely hard pressed to do so successfully. Because their units were spread throughout the towns and villages of the *raion*, training was a much more complex undertaking than it was for their regular counterparts. For example, the following tasks were laid on the cadre of the territorial divisions in just one year's time: train groups of sixteen- to eighteen-year-old preconscript youths in a 210-hour program of preconscription military training in each *raion*; conduct a three-month assembly for newly conscripted young men; conduct month-long assemblies for the other four year groups of territorial soldier conscripts; train territorial officers and political staff for one month; work with *terrarmeitsy* in the periods between assemblies.[64]

Just as with regular units, numerous hitches hampered training. In some cases, units lacked the material necessities for training. One regiment reported that it had to ration water all summer. Some units received supplies late, and soldiers did not get their uniforms and equipment until well into the assembly. Still other units did not receive enough helmets and overcoats. Other units reported that uniforms wore out long before the next issue was scheduled.[65] Overall, the territorial forces had numerous problems—some minor, some major—that hindered training, and, like the regular forces, they experienced distractions from training. During the first five-year plan, many units spent most or all of their summer assembly assigned as labor to industrial sites. The priority placed on industrial development over military development could not have been more clear.

The party records of the Smolensk *oblast* give a glimpse of the organization of territorial training. Tables 1.1 and 1.2 show the upcoming assemblies of XI Territorial Rifle Corps for 1926. The lists of those who assembled indicate that, although the draft age was twenty-one, the new recruits were twenty-three years old, suggesting that in the early years the Red Army worked its way down to the twenty-one-year-olds and drafted older men with military obligations first. Moreover, in the Smolensk *oblast*, more men were drafted in 1926 than in the preceding years. In the previous three years, the combined drafts yielded 13,487 men, while the 1926 draft cohort alone produced 8,096 men: either there were more draft-age men in the *oblast*, the conscription mechanism was getting better, or perhaps the conscription quotas may have been raised because the number of units had significantly increased. The data also show that two territorial divisions, the 29th and 62d, were training close to twenty-four thousand men. Two regular divisions would only train about eleven thousand men, so the ideal of training more men for less was being realized, although the quality of training was questionable.

The most intriguing bit of information to be gleaned from Table 1.2 is the very small number of party members and Komsomols among the *terrarmeitsy* of XI Corps. Of the 8,096 new recruits of the Smolensk *oblast*, only 415 had a party affiliation. In this corps, 0.67 percent of the new soldiers were party members, whereas in the regular army, Communists comprised 14 percent of all soldiers. The logical explanation for the low party membership rate in XI Corps is that Smolensk *oblast* was mostly rural and conscription commissions had a habit of sending party members to the regular forces. Throughout the USSR, peasants had a lower rate of party membership than urban workers. It also suggests that PUR worked less effectively in the territorial units, in part because of the short time *politruki* had to work with the men.[66]

Nine years later, the system of assembling remained virtually unchanged. The 1935 schedule for XI Territorial Rifle Corps started with special assem-

Table 1.1. Assembly of XI Territorial Rifle Corps, 1926

Order of Assembly	Duration of Assembly	No. of Men
1. New recruits of the 1903 contingent	10 May–25 July	8,096
2. Preliminary assembly of transitory commanders and political personnel of special units of divisions (signal and sapper companies)	19 July–1 Oct.	19
3. General assembly of special units of the 1900, 1901, and 1902 contingents	1 Aug.–1 Oct.	852
4. Preliminary meeting of commissars and *politruki* of all units	11 Aug.–1 Oct.	174
5. General assembly of the birth cohorts of 1900, 1901, and 1902	1 Sept.–1 Oct.	12,635
6. Assembly of the rear troops	four days	2,129
Total manpower assembled		23,905

Source: *Smolensk Archive:* WKP 129, 141–142.

Table 1.2. Assembly of New Recruits of XI Territorial Rifle Corps, Summer 1926 (estimate)

Uezd	No. to Receive Instruction	Unit and Place of Instruction	Comments
Smolensk	2,825	Smolensk: 190th, 191st Rifle Rgts., Art. Rgt. rear units of 62d Div., 1st and 2d A. A. bns	192d Rifle Rgt., Cav. Sqd., Sappers, 5th A. A. Bn. are in Orshaik district (1,474 men)
Iartsevso	771		
Subtotal	3,596		
Viazma	1,002	29th Division	
Gzhatsk	676		
Dorogobuzh	914		
Sychevko	941		
Yelnia	321		
Belyi	603		
Subtotal	4,500		

Total number of men to be instructed in Smolensk *guberniia:* 8,096 men.

Preliminary count of Communists and Komsomel members who will attend:

	VKP(b)	VLKSM
From Smolensk *uezd*	17 members	110 members
From Iartsevso *uezd*	8	50
From other *uezdy*	30	200

Total: 55 members of the VKP(b) and 360 members of the VLKSM

Percent Communists and candidates of the total personnel: 0.67
Percent Komsomol of the total personnel: 4.45

Source: *Smolensk Archive:* WKP 129, 143–144.

blies in February and March exclusively for the leadership. At these assemblies, territorial officers met with the cadre to plan the summer assembly and organize training between assemblies to prepare for summer camp. A seven-day assembly was held in March followed by a thirty-day assembly in the spring (March–April). Reservists attended a fifteen-day assembly in June. New recruits trained from 1 June to 1 September. Finally, the entire corps assembled in September. [67]

Training Between Assemblies

In order to train the territorial forces year-round, the cadre conducted training between assemblies. In the ten- to twelve-month interval between assemblies, regulations required that permanent cadre give at least seven one-day refresher courses. At the company level, the only two cadre members—the company commander and the *politruk*—bore the entire burden of training. The training consisted mainly of basic military skills, shooting, and political instruction. Due to limited resources, the cadre generally delivered only sketchy training. For example, a detachment commander of the 2d Ul'ianov Cavalry Regiment had fifteen pairs of skis, two small bore rifles, two thousand rounds of ammunition, two gas masks, and some military literature to train one hundred men at a collective farm. Because the commanders did not normally live in the vicinity of their commands (they were quartered in the town where the battalion headquarters was located), they had to work through the local party committees to notify the transitory personnel and arrange dates for training.[68]

PUR required company *politruki* to spend between ten and fifteen days a month working with the *terrarmeitsy* in their local areas. Battalion and higher-level political people were supposed to spend at least seven to ten days per month with the troops during the time between assemblies.[69] Although mandated, training between assemblies was not always carried out. Many units slacked off after the summer assembly and did not begin their training until after the new year. Most of the responsibility for this lay at the higher levels of the military and political chains of command. Division commanders habitually gave only vague training guidance to subordinate units. A 1933 report on this practice stated, "The results of such 'instructing,' if we can call it that, were quickly noticed: many commanders went to their area [of manning] without well defined, definite plans of work, without aids and notes for training."[70] Company commanders received poor guidance because division commanders and their staffs and military district personnel responsible for this training did not inspect training at the *raion* level and had no appreciation for the tasks of their subordinates. The report also noted that "many [political] workers who are required to go to the area [of manning] do not go at all or go only for one or two days maximum, and their tasks are not fulfilled."

ELIMINATION OF THE TERRITORIAL SYSTEM

The agreement to have a mixed system was made before Stalin came to power. His consolidation of power saw the beginning of the demise of the mixed system. In 1931, the RKKA began the first major effort to convert territorial formations into regular army units. The Politburo authorized the remaining territorial divisions to transition into regular divisions in 1935. The party justified this change by focusing on the threat posed to the USSR by the "rise of militarism in capitalist countries" and asserted that the change was made possible by the economic advancement of the Soviet state as a result of the five-year plans.[71] It is not clear, however, that the stimulus for change originated in the Politburo. There were those in the military who had yearned for an all-regular army for some years. Foreign events also put pressure on the regime to reassess its military organization. Between 1929 and 1932, there was conflict with Japan in Manchuria, with the threat of more to come; and Hitler's rise to power in 1933, accompanied by anticommunist rhetoric, certainly caused the regime to take a second look at its defense capabilities.

Territorial units converted to regular footing by systematically increasing the numerical strength of their permanently assigned personnel, discharging *terrarmeitsy* at the end of their obligation, and creating regular units within their organizational structure. As regular subunits were formed, a division became part territorial and part regular until it reached the desired complement of permanent personnel and all territorial personnel had completed their service. Only then was it considered a true regular division. At the end of 1935, 77 percent of the army's divisions comprised regular divisions and only 23 percent were territorial. By 1939, all major territorial units had been transformed into regular units.[72]

Why eliminate the mixed system? True, the territorial system was created during a relatively peaceful time in Soviet history, and, as the thirties progressed, the prospect of conflict with either the Germans or the Japanese increased dramatically. Nonetheless, were these considerations sufficient justification for eliminating the admittedly inefficient territorial forces? After all, eliminating the system actually detracted from Soviet preparedness. By depriving the RKKA of a well-established, unionwide mobilization tool, the army would be less able to fight a total war. The territorial system had been the second echelon of defense. By transferring those units to the first line of defense, the RKKA deprived itself of an organized reserve, one that could send fairly cohesive units to supplement the regular army in a short time. If the object was to have a larger regular army, it does not follow that the territorial system needed to be abolished. At the time, untapped manpower abounded, and allocations for defense spending grew larger. By eliminating the territorial forces, the Red Army gambled that it could successfully fight a war solely with regular forces.

Eliminating the territorial force and subsequently increasing the size of the regular forces caused problems elsewhere. For one thing, it took more able-bodied men out of the fields and factories and put them in uniform at a time when the Soviet Union needed more agricultural and industrial production than ever before. It also added to the shortage of officers and political personnel. Previously, the platoon commanders were territorials; now they had to come from the regular officer corps.The Red Army therefore now needed roughly one hundred additional officers for every territorial regiment turned regular.

ORGANIZATION AFTER 1935

The reorganization of regiment and division structures during and after 1935 reflected the success of the first and second five-year plans. A direct comparison between the 1927, 1935, and 1941 rifle divisions and regiments reveals that in 1941 many more heavy weapons were available, as well as more sophisticated weapons and equipment, such as tanks and radios. The army obtained more and varied artillery, both horse-drawn and tractor-towed. In 1939, a heavy artillery battalion was added to the rifle division, giving it more than twice the cannon firepower of ten years earlier. Division engineer support was beefed up from a company to a battalion. The high command added an armor battalion in 1935, giving rifle divisions more shock power; these battalions, however, were taken away in 1939. As a result of the experience of Soviet forces at Khalkin-Gol, the authorized wartime strength of rifle divisions was raised from 13,000 to 18,000, although some on the General Staff wanted it as high as 22,000. The old Russian practice of overwhelming the enemy with numbers, rather than defeating him with tactical skill, had not died with the Revolution. Just before the war, the table of organization and equipment changed again, reducing the personnel of infantry divisions to 14,483 men. Even the number of horses authorized in a rifle division rose from 2,000 to over 3,000.[73]

The artillery also received new equipment in the form of bigger guns, mortars, and tractors for towing artillery. The High Command Reserve (RGK) had, in 1941, seventy-four regiments of heavy artillery, though the numbers are somewhat misleading because not all of these units were formed by June 1941. Due to the expansion of artillery, the RGK had guns for units it could not man. The number of heavy-artillery regiments at corps level increased from one to two, and an antitank artillery battalion was added. A problem arose for divisional medium-artillery battalions that was the reverse of the RGK heavy artillery; medium-artillery battalions had men but few guns.[74]

Although production of heavy artillery outpaced the army's ability to train artillery soldiers, tractor production could not match the army's needs. The army needed to equip new artillery units with tractors, especially those of mechanized and motorized divisions, and to replace its horses in horse-drawn artillery regiments. Supplying all units with the authorized number of tractors proved to be impossible because agriculture had for a decade received first priority for tractors; moreover, the army created units faster than it could supply them. The army assigned tractors first to the heavy artillery at corps and RGK level, then to mechanized units. Artillery regiments of rifle divisions remained horse-drawn through the war.[75]

Tank and mechanized forces expanded rapidly beginning in 1938. In 1939, the army planned to create four mechanized corps, twenty-one separate tank brigades, three separate armored-car brigades, and eleven tank instruction regiments by 1941. The army's appetite seemed to grow with the eating, and in 1940 it set its sights on forming at least twenty mechanized corps in the coming year, giving defense industries no time to plan, only to react. In 1938, a mechanized corps was authorized 12,710 men and 560 tanks. It consisted of two tank brigades and a mechanized brigade. The army, however, disbanded its tank corps in 1939, on the recommendation of a General Staff commission formed to study the reorganization of unit structure. The General Staff reassigned some tank brigades to the RGK and split the rest into tank battalions assigned individually to rifle divisions. Cavalry divisions gained mechanized brigades.[76]

As a result of the fall of France and the impressive success of Germany's panzer forces, the General Staff in 1940 reversed its decision and recreated armored corps, and for the first time authorized the formation of armored divisions. The army acted slowly on this decision, however, and did not begin to organize the majority of its armored corps until spring 1941, far too late for them to equip, train sufficiently, or develop unit cohesion before the war began.[77] At the end of 1940, the Red Army had nine tank corps. By June 1941, it had twenty-nine, each consisting of one motorized and two tank divisions. Each tank division was authorized 375 tanks, and the motorized division, 275; the minimum number of tanks needed for these corps was 29,725. The Red Army had half this number; one-tenth were of the most recent variety. Thus, at the beginning of the war, the majority of the tank corps were not at full strength in either men or vehicles because of organizational policies and because the army had set mid-1942 as its target date for full manning and equipping of its mechanized forces.[78]

Naturally, support and combat support branches had to keep pace with the growth of the rest of the army. Between 1940 and 1941, the army established eighteen engineer regiments and sixteen pontoon regiments, each authorized one thousand men. The number of railroad regiments also increased. The number of signal units grew dramatically, and were almost totally motorized. All of these branches called for men with above-average education but failed to get them in adequate numbers.[79]

The number of units in the Red Army in 1941 was staggering when compared with how many it had had fourteen years earlier. There were 198 rifle divisions in 1941, compared to fewer than thirty in 1927; thirty-one motorized rifle divisions in 1941 and none in 1927; sixty-one tank divisions in 1941 and none as late as 1939. The thirteen cavalry divisions in 1941 were roughly the same number as in 1927, but the 1941 divisions each had a mechanized brigade. Because of advances in technology, it was more complicated to command a regiment or larger organization in 1941 than it had been in the twenties. Commanders in 1941 had to rely more on their staffs, especially those in such specialties as armor, artillery, signal, and logistics.

Regiments and divisions grew in size as well as in the amounts of matériel, which was increasingly complex to use and maintain. Tactically, the units themselves took more expertise to handle if one was to get the maximum advantage from the new equipment. Therefore, the Red Army increasingly needed to recruit more educated individuals, to train them in using and maintaining the equipment, and to lead the organizations equipped with the new technology. The army continued to stress preconscription literacy training, even as the number of illiterates dwindled.

The Red Army's great strides in modernization did not affect all parts of the army equally. Mechanized and armored divisions benefited most from modernization, and their development was closely tied to advances in technology and industry. Technological advances, meanwhile, affected the infantry less. The Red Army liked to brag about the increase in mechanical horsepower per soldier, but, in fact, increased motorization and mechanization directly affected a minority of soldiers. In 1941, infantry divisions still relied on foot marches for tactical movement and horses to pull artillery and supply wagons. In concentrating the mechanical horsepower in tank and mechanized units, the Red Army proved no different from the German army, whose infantry divisions similarly relied on boot leather and horseshoes.

Because of their pride in industrial production, Soviet historians and memoirists liked to quote production figures showing increases in Soviet economic and military might. One should be careful, however, not to neglect the effect of agriculture on military preparedness. In the early thirties, during collectivization, many peasants had slaughtered their animals to avoid turning them over to collective farms. Between 1929 and 1935, the number of horses in the USSR dropped from 32.6 million to 14.9 million. By 1940, the number had recovered to only 17.7 million horses.[80] This slow repopulation adversely affected the army, which relied extensively on horses for mobility, especially the cavalry. The decline in the number of horses began just as the Red Army began to expand. Because of the importance of agriculture, especially during the famine years, 1932–1933, the military did not have priority in acquiring horses. At the beginning of the Second World War, the army still lacked sufficient numbers of horses, and those it did have were often of poor quality.[81]

Expansion and Partial Manning

The Red Army committed a grave error when it chose its method of expansion. It created more divisions, all partially manned, rather than filling its existing partially manned divisions or creating new fully manned divisions. Since the end of the Civil War, the Red Army's regular rifle and cavalry divisions had purposely been only partially manned with from six thousand to eight thousand men—between 40 and 60 percent of the authorized strength. To absorb the extra manpower created by the conscription of two draft cohorts and the elimination of the territorial system, the army could have easily filled existing divisions first, thus requiring many fewer new divisions. Partial manning created the need for a great many field and general grade officers. Had the RKKA brought its existing units to full strength, it would have eliminated the need for so many new corps, division and regiment commanders, and staffs. Many more regiment commanders would have been experienced colonels, and experienced majors and captains could have been sprinkled throughout the regiments, thereby avoiding the situation common in the late thirties, when a battalion's highest-ranking officer was a senior lieutenant.

Had divisions been manned fully from the beginning, the Red Army would have been at full strength on the first day of the war, and any disruption in mobilization caused by hostilities would not have affected them. As it was, the RKKA planned to use partially manned divisions as part of its mobilization scheme. Upon mobilization, reservists would report to divisions, bringing them to full strength. This plan presupposed ample time for reservists to travel to their units, and it ignored all considerations of unit cohesion and the need for refresher training. With five thousand to six thousand men joining a division overnight, existing cohesion in the companies was thrown into disarray; unit commanders knew the personalities and capabilities of only half of their men.

From beginning to end, the plan was flawed, as history had already proven: the tsarist army had used partial manning as its mobilization method, with disastrous results under conditions of rapid mobilization. What was especially damning about the Red Army's mobilization plan was that many of its senior officers and General Staff officers who wrote the mobilization plan had experienced the failure in 1914 as tsarist soldiers. In his book, *Strategiia* (1927), Aleksandr Svechin, a former tsarist officer and instructor at the Frunze General Staff Academy in the twenties, prophetically warned against repeating the mistakes of August 1914:

> We must avoid trying to set records for mobilization speed. If XIII Corps of Samsonov's army [in August 1914] proved unready for battle, this can partially be explained by the fact that it got its reserves just before boarding the rail cars and did not manage to become cohesive. The reinforcements remained nameless and unknown to their company commanders.[82]

Tukhachevskii, a participant in the First World War and a colleague of Svechin's at the academy, certainly should have known better, yet he had been an ardent proponent of ending the territorial system. A more timely example of the failure of this system, from which the Soviet high command should have learned, was the experience of the French army. The French mobilization plan in the interwar period was very similar to the RKKA's in that it used the active army as cadre for new units. Because there were so many new divisions in 1939 and 1940, they only had close to 15 percent regular officers and NCOs; the rest were reservists. In the years between the wars, the regular army had concentrated on the basic training of reserves rather than devoting time for more advanced training of its own forces. This created a system, much like that of the Red Army, of constant turnover of enlisted and officer personnel. According to Robert Doughty, the "active army for all practical purposes remained little more than a school for soldiers and a framework for mobilization."[83] What the NKO and General Staff failed to realize was the possibility of having both a large, though not huge, fully manned regular army and a territorial force. In time of war or imminent danger, the reserves could have reported to the territorial unit nearest their homes and brought them up to full strength. Or they could have been used for new divisions, while the regular army, on perpetual war footing, held back the enemy.

In June 1941, the Red Army had 170 divisions of all types in the western military districts. To bring these units up to full strength, nearly 1.2 million men would have had to have been mobilized, not including the men needed to bring the corps and support units up to strength. In fact, in May 1941, around 800,000 reservists were mobilized, but they were not all sent to the border areas or to the divisions. The Commissariat of Defense assigned many to the air force, fortified areas, and other interior military districts.[84] To bring the remaining regular divisions up to their authorized complement would have required another 950,000 men. If the reserves were sent to the regular units, who was left to cadre newly created divisions manned by new recruits?

The answer is that there were fewer reservists to go around for the new divisions than would have been the case if territorial divisions had been maintained.

Expansion put strains not only on personnel but also on equipment requirements. By creating so many divisions, the army actually hampered its modernization program. The original idea had been to replace aged and obsolete equipment and weapons, but because there were so many new units, the old matériel could not be discarded. Instead it remained in use, often alongside new equipment, creating a host of difficulties while the units waited for more equipment of recent production.

Newly formed armored units in particular suffered from equipment and personnel shortages. General K. K. Rokossovskii, arrested during the purge and released from the camps in 1939, took command of the IX Mechanized Corps at the end of 1940. It was a new corps consisting of two tank divisions and one motorized rifle division, all of which were still in the process of forming. Rokossovskii complained that his corps did not have the authorized number of tanks. Once again, the culprit was expansion, although the military liked to blame the defense industry. If fewer corps had been formed, more would have been at full strength and presumably more effective. The reasoning behind fielding so many mechanized corps at once was that there would be time to bring them all to full strength before war broke out with Germany. Stalin estimated that war could be avoided until at least 1942.[85] Rokossovskii also reported problems with training and cohesion. Because the divisions were new, the leaders had never worked together before, and large numbers of his officers had had no training in the use of tanks.[86]

Like the German, French, and American armies, the RKKA created new units by taking regiments from existing divisions and using them as the bases for new divisions. Each battalion of a regiment became the basis for a new regiment. In the years between 1937 and 1941, almost every rifle division gave up one regiment to create a new division. Some divisions even gave up two regiments. While the regiment that was forming the new division was hard at work conscripting and training the equivalent of two new regiments, the division that gave up the regiment busily replaced the unit it lost. The main drawback in this system was that while each division was building or rebuilding itself, major unit and advanced training suffered for an important part of the year. The demobilization of one cohort and the conscription of the next soon followed. Both the American and German armies had significant advantages, in terms of time and stability, over the Soviet and French armies. New units had many months or even years to train and develop cohesion before being committed to combat.[87]

The timing and implementation of organizational changes had a tremendous significance for the future success of a unit. Each time an organization changed, it affected the men of that organization and their ability to function. When the army modified organizations, it immediately affected hundreds or thousands of lives. Men and their families transferred from one post to another. Soldiers received extra technical training on certain items of equipment, as well as instruction on their tactical use—at least they were supposed to receive such training. In fact, every time a modification was made, the entire army was affected because it meant that more men needed to be conscripted, recruited, and trained. The armed forces required more well educated soldiers and more experienced officers than ever before. That these needs were not met played a significant role in the misfortunes of the Red Army in wartime.

SUMMARY

In some ways, the Red Army was a revolutionary army, but in many fundamental ways it was like any other army of the time. It faced the same basic tasks of organizing and training and met them in traditional fashion. The most revolutionary change from the old army to the new—aside from the social manipulations related to conscription and the work of PUR—was the Red Army's change to year-round training. This break from the past was brought on in part by the elimination of the old-style regimental economy utilized by the Imperial Russian Army. In comparison to European military systems, the Red Army was becoming a modern army. Western European armies had been training year-round for quite some time. Even the creation of the territorial forces was new to the Soviet Union, while reserve systems were commonplace in France, Germany, and England.

The Red Army did not successfully eliminate all of the nonmilitary activities that interfered with training. It continually had to sacrifice training time on behalf of the state. During the twenties and thirties, the state required the RKKA—during the first two five-year plans especially—to lend its men and units, both regular and territorial, to work on industrial and agricultural projects. Basic training in the form of preconscription training was not even a purely military function in the RKKA; it was a joint effort of the party, army, Komsomol, and Osoaviakhim, which created multiple opportunities for failure and assigning blame. As a consequence, the idea that training was the most important peacetime activity of the army seems never to have taken hold, with disastrous consequences once war broke out.

Another problem for the military until the very eve of the war was its limited budget, which reflected the low priority assigned defense once the military achieved a certain minimum size and low level of armament. The initial depressed level of industrial production and technology also influenced the army's structure and manning policies. There was little new technology and few sufficiently educated men to deal with existing technology. Therefore, the army concentrated on the use of the low technology forces of infantry and cavalry and only sparingly invested in the more sophisticated branches of armor, signal communications, and aviation. Emphasis on advanced technology only became possible in the mid-thirties, after the first five-year plan began to bear fruit. The army also relied on the territorial forces to train the majority of its men until the state could afford a large standing army. As industry developed, the army made more and more demands on it in terms of quality, quantity, and increased sophistication of weapons and matériel.

The elimination of the territorial forces in favor of a system of mobilizing reserves directly into regular divisions to bring them to a war footing proved to be a serious miscalculation. When war broke out with Germany in 1941, many partially manned units on the western border had to be thrown into battle immediately, with no time to receive reinforcements. Divisions in the west that were not placed at the front did have time to receive reservists but not to truly absorb them. Nor did they have time to retrain reservists or create cohesive units of men familiar with their equipment, each other, or their leaders before being sent into battle. Expansion also undermined the army's ability to fight because, without territorial forces, it had to create large numbers of partially manned units in order for mobilized reservists to have some place to go when called up. Thus, the RKKA found itself in a situation where newly created units did not have adequate equipment or leadership.

CHAPTER 2

Daily Life, Conditions of Service, and Discipline

Life in the army turned out to be rather less than promised for most *krasnoarmeitsy*. In many cases, the army neither fed him well nor housed him adequately. The state used him as a laborer in uniform. He farmed his own food and faced a disciplinary code that grew stricter every year. His officers often seemed indifferent to his welfare. Consequently, morale and military performance suffered. At times soldiers were so dissatisfied with army life and conditions of service that they committed crimes and infringed on regulations to such a degree that their officers seemed helpless to control them.

ARMY LIFE

Housing

From the first days of Soviet power, housing had been a problem for the Soviet armed forces as well as for Soviet urban society. In a speech to the Fourth All Union Congress of Soviets on 25 April 1927, Kliment Voroshilov discussed the poor state of military housing. He admitted that accommodations for the military were bad, even, in some instances, worse than they had been under the tsar. Many of the old army's barracks the Red Army needed were in Poland and the Baltic states. Even so, the number of old barracks under Red Army control would have been sufficient had they been in the right places. The USSR had different locational priorities in stationing its troops than had Imperial Russia. Many of the suitably located barracks had been damaged in the Revolution and Civil War, rendering them uninhabitable. Some dated from the reign of Catherine the Great. Voroshilov further lamented that the housing shortage for officers was particularly acute and that serious measures needed be taken by the Revolutionary Military Council (RVS) to mitigate the crisis. Officers' accommodations were often as poor as those for the rank and file. The army even pressed monasteries into use as regimental quarters.[1]

Five years after Voroshilov's speech, the Red Army was still trying to overcome its housing shortage and, like the civilian sector, came up short. Although the army constructed many barracks, they were not always first-rate. Many lacked indoor plumbing and electric lighting. After their completion, many of the barracks were found to be of rather low quality. Many of the minor finishing touches were not completed, making the dwellings uncomfortable and unappealing. The new barracks were a step up from living in tents, which many soldiers and officers had had to endure for months on end, but they were not as big an improvement as they would have liked.[2] Besides mismanagement and poor construction, the RKKA had to contend with the increase in manpower after 1928, which always exceeded the rate at which barracks were built.

Statistics on construction projects show the RKKA did try to address the housing situation. In 1930, 1,789 military construction projects were undertaken, and in 1935, 8,480. In 1933, the RVS created the Military Construction Administration to oversee all military construction from start to finish and rationalize the procurement of construction materials. The army realized that the construction of new garrisons and improvement of existing ones improved the culture, training, and discipline of the soldiers.[3]

Much time was needed to keep up the maintenance of the barracks, sometimes more than was regularly allocated. Regiments usually made a special effort to prepare the barracks for winter, to make up for the wear and tear of the previous winter and spring, and the neglect during the summer when the troops were away at camp. Army budget constraints made maintenance and upkeep difficult, however. In the twenties, military districts were not given separate building funds but had to provide money for barracks construction and upkeep out of their operating budgets. As a consequence, most of the money appropriated by the military districts went for maintenance, which was cheaper. The RVS recognized the cost-effectiveness of this as well and declared a "Red Barracks Month" in October 1925, which stressed barracks maintenance. This proved to be a recurrent theme in the years to come. October or November would be designated the month for cleaning and sprucing up the barracks. Prizes were awarded to the best barracks in a regiment or division.[4]

The Red Army set high standards for itself in providing living space for its men. By regulation, each soldier was supposed to have a living space of at least 14.6 cubic meters, preferably around 4.6 square meters of floor space and 3.5 meters of space above him. In addition to these individual requirements, the average company-sized unit was to have 1,474.91 square meters of building space for showers, laundries, club meeting rooms, a library, mess hall, offices, and so on.[5] These criteria were seldom met.

In contrast to rosy promises of fresh straw bedding and adequate floor space, the RKKA, in some situations, made no attempt to provide the men with housing. In the early thirties, for example, the men of the 10th and 17th air brigades stationed at the Khodynka aerodrome outside of Moscow had no barracks at all. They were expected to find their own accommodations in

Moscow and commute to the airfield, which often proved difficult and inconvenient.[6]

The situation of the 17th Territorial Rifle Division in 1925 and 1926 serves as an example of how budgetary constraints and priorities affected soldiers. The division was established in 1925 in the Moscow Military District (MVO) in the former camp of a tsarist rifle regiment. Obviously, a regimental camp could not hold a division, and therefore barracks space and officers' housing were in short supply. The camps also lacked enough rifle ranges, training areas, and artillery firing ranges. The division commander could only wrangle about thirty thousand rubles out of the MVO for construction of the necessary facilities. This amount proved to be insufficient to purchase all the needed materials to accomplish the work. A mess hall and twenty-four houses of four to six rooms each were constructed for officers and their families. By the commander's choice, the camp lacked bathing facilities for the men for another year.[7]

In his memoirs, Georgii Zhukov noted that his unit was forced by circumstances to build its own quarters from scratch:

In 1932 the division was rushed to the town of Slutsk in the Belorussian Military District. . . . Since these new quarters were totally unprepared, a point which must be emphasized, the division had to waste some 18 months building its own barracks, stables and other facilities, degenerating, as a result, into an inefficient labor force. Further, lack of building materials, the rains and other untoward factors prevented timely preparations for the winter. This disastrously affected morale and combat worthiness. Discipline grew lax and the incidence of sickness among the horses grew.[8]

Corps headquarters could offer no help, as the other formations of VI Cavalry Corps, likewise rushed to this same military district, learned when they found themselves in a similar plight. For all practical purposes, the division suspended combat training and political instruction while it built quarters. As a result, the division commander was fired, and Zhukov was assigned to his place.[9]

One can imagine the negative impact of this experience on the soldiers. The cavalry men spent most of their time building barracks instead of learning military skills. These eighteen months were three-quarters of a soldier's tour of duty. The men who joined the division during this time would have spent more of their service as laborers than as soldiers. While living in tents and uncompleted barracks, they were subject to the effects of the weather—extreme cold in winter, intense heat in summer. Vsevolod Garshin, writing in the 1870s, noted: "I frequently observed that the ordinary soldiers tended to be more affected by physical suffering than those from the so-called 'privileged classes.' The common soldiers perceived physical distress as a real calamity, which could cause them real anguish and depress them profoundly."[10] It is doubtful that the common peasant conscript had, over the intervening sixty years, come to appreciate his suffering at the hands of the state any more than his predecessors.

In May 1932, Zhukov's sister division was relocated to the Ukraine. It also had to build its camp from scratch. The soldiers set up their own lumber operation, felling trees and sawing them into boards or cutting them into shingles. Although they had plenty of wood, progress was slow because of the shortage of other building materials. Officers' wives helped by caulking chinks in the walls and painting. During the first few months, the soldiers spent many days and nights in the rain. The men of the 5th Cavalry Division spent an uncomfortable winter in 1932–1933 in partially constructed buildings, many lacking floors or pane windows. Some buildings had no roofs. When they arose on winter mornings, the men would shake off the snow that had accumulated on their overcoats and blankets. They finally finished the camp in spring 1933, except for the officers' housing, which was completed in the fall. The officers of this division put the needs of their men first, unlike the leaders of the 17th Territorial Rifle Division.[11]

As the Red Army grew, many of the units experienced dramatic changes in living conditions. When one of the regiments of the 14th Cavalry Division was first stationed in Tambov after the Civil War, it occupied the garrison of a former tsarist cavalry regiment. It had all the necessary buildings, including barracks, stables, mess halls, hospital, and storerooms, and of solid brick, no less. Because of this, the regiment began normal military training at once, unfettered by the need to make a home for itself. Later, in 1933, the division relocated to the Ukraine and had to give up its comfortable existence and build a new home for itself on the open steppes.[12]

Quality of life was greatly affected by the facilities the soldiers had at their disposal. For instance, although the Red Army promoted cleanliness, in practice soldiers did not bathe as often as the army stipulated, if for no other reason than that the necessary facilities did not exist. Boris Balinsky, an enlisted soldier, offers the following account:

> Once a fortnight the soldiers of our battery were taken for a wash in the *bania*—the . . . bathing establishment. The *bania* was in town, so we had to march quite a distance (perhaps half an hour) to get there. The wash was always in the evening, after supper. On arrival, each [man] was issued with a tub, a towel and a piece of soap. Hot and cold water was on the tap, and each washed himself in his tub. While we were washing our-

Soldiers relaxing in the barracks' literacy room.

selves, our underclothes were collected for a quick laundering. They were returned later, when it was time for us to dress. Although washing of the linen was done presumably by machines, there was not quite time enough to get the clothes dry, when we got them, they were still damp. There was no provision for anybody to get his own wear: one gave up an undershirt, underpants and cloth for the feet, and received back a shirt, underpants, and cloth for the feet. Who was wearing them before the wash was not questioned.[13]

In the main, infrequent bathing was a consequence of the state's continuing economic backwardness. Construction could not keep up with demand, and *bania* were few and far between.

In the early thirties, as new units formed, they went through the same housing ordeals as units that had been relocated. Units continued to relocate throughout the thirties with virtually no improvement in planning. Where a unit was stationed could make a world of difference. The best duty was, of course, in Moscow. The Moscow Proletarian Rifle Division was the show-piece of the Soviet regime, parading and conducting military demonstrations for foreign visitors. Ivan Boldin, a regiment commander in Moscow in 1924, described his unit as being at full strength, not only in soldiers but also in its complement of armorers, carpenters, tailors, and boot makers: "All the best that was available in the army at the time was here in the regiment." Their living quarters in a former tsarist barracks were not bad either.[14]

In comparison with workers' accommodations, the army did not have it as bad as it might seem, particularly after the start of the first five-year plan. John Scott, an American working in Soviet industry, reported that in Magnitogorsk lice infested the workers' barracks, and frequent shortages of coal and wood for heating made winters miserable. Construction of housing lagged because of shortages of materials and labor. The construction of workers' barracks was usually slipshod: roofs and water pipes leaked, foundations sank, and walls cracked. Some workers in Magnitogorsk even lived in tents because of a dearth of barracks. Life for students was on the same level as workers. Victor Kravchenko echoed Scott's observations, reporting that in his technological institute, barracks life was characterized by no heat, little food, and no conveniences. Students were packed five to a small room.[15] Unlike the workers, Red Army servicemen had a means of redress—the administration for soldiers' complaints and its chain of command. The administration could put pressure on higher authorities to rectify shortcomings. The workers had to rely on the often unresponsive local party administration.

Food and the Cooperative System

The Red Army went about feeding and supplying its men in a way that a Western soldier would not have considered unusual. The army had traditional mess halls and supply companies in every regiment. It also had dining facilities and departmentlike stores to provide amenities like tea and extra food, and services ranging from barbershops to canteens. Not all garrisons had the extra dining facilities and stores; they were usually found on the larger posts and were run by military cooperatives called *Zakrytyi Voennyi Kooperativnyi*, (ZVK). Soldiers ate free of charge at the military mess halls but had to pay to join the cooperative in order to enjoy its dining privileges. The cooperatives were roughly equivalent to the civilian concessions that Western armies allowed on posts to serve the soldiers of individual garrisons. At first these loosely associated cooperatives were organized on a geographical basis under the weak supervision of military district headquarters.[16]

The army had its own cooperatives, but the system of cooperatives was not unique to the military. Industry, too, had its cooperatives, called *zakrytye raspredeliteli*, which catered to factory workers and administrative personnel. Like those in the army, these cooperatives were particularly important in the more remote areas of the USSR. They offered not only goods and services but also maintained orchards, pigs, and cows to supply their dining rooms. Workers not included in cooperatives, or who desired to fend for themselves, were constrained by rationing. Bread was rationed until 1 January 1935, and such items as meat, fish, butter, oil, sugar, and potatoes were rationed up to October 1935. The soldier, then, had the advantage over the worker because his chain of command was responsible for feeding him. The civilian worker, by contrast, was entirely on his own and could not depend on the haphazard efforts of the trade unions or local party organs to improve his lot.[17]

In July 1931, after numerous complaints about food and services in the units, the party and government created an administration for the military cooperatives, the Central Military-Cooperative Administration of the RKKA. Cooperatives became a significant source of food and clothing for servicemen. The ZVK stores and dining facilities were distributed throughout the military districts but were in no way controlled by the commander and staff of the military units they served. The only real military influence over the operations of the ZVK came from the RVS. The ZVK was only partially supplied with foodstuffs by Red Army sources. To make up the shortfall in their needs, cooperatives raised their own livestock and ran farms, orchards, and dairies.[18]

The military newspaper *Krasnaia zvezda,* after receiving an avalanche of letters of complaint, sent a commission to investigate the military cooperatives unionwide in 1932. It reported that cooperatives worked well in Kiev, Smolensk, Odessa, Nizhni-Novgorod, Cheliabinsk, Volsk, and in parts of Moscow. In most places, however, the cooperatives were still performing poorly. In some, necessities were either in short supply or not available. Overall, it seems that the stores stocked insufficient wares for the number of patrons they were expected to serve. Yet, while some cooperatives went without, others had surpluses. Some enjoyed as much as a two-month supply during a period when the rest of the nation suffered a shortage of consumer goods and food. Soldiers accused the distribution centers of charging very high prices to the military cooperatives they supplied. Civilian workers leveled exactly the same complaints against their cooperatives.[19]

The ZVK also ran stores at the summer camps, with about the same results as experienced in garrison. For example, in summer 1934 in the camp at Krasnodar, the organization and service of the ZVK store were reported to be bad. The store lacked the basic items needed by a soldier in camp, such as sewing needles, uniform buttons, toothbrushes, pencils and paper, shaving gear, tobacco, and boot polish. In contrast, the ZVK store at Stavropol was well organized and well stocked. It had everything the Krasnodar store did not, plus cigarettes, matches, thread, clothes, boot brushes, and more.[20] There was no predicting how the ZVK would perform at any given site in any given year. A soldier never knew whether his unit would be well supported or to what degree he would be denied the necessities and minor luxuries of life.

Despite their poor accommodations, officers and soldiers generally had a slightly higher standard of living in the 1930s than the rest of Soviet society, not because of pay (which was very low for soldiers) but because of special food and clothing allowances. Even so, during the famine of 1932–1933 the army also did with less food. The army's central supply sources cut rations to the units by 30 percent, except in the Moscow Military District. However much the quantity and quality of food dropped in the military, it was still superior to that available to the general populace, which in many areas suffered famine conditions. The army tried to feed the soldiers adequate quantities of food, and, if official sources can be trusted, the number of calories in the Red Army daily rations were 3,329 in 1930. In 1929, the average worker consumed 2,338 calories per day. The worker or peasant who found himself in the army may have been well pleased by this turn of events. For example, Nikolai Iakovlev, an artillery battalion commander, reported that when the draftees of 1933 reported to his unit for duty, they were all suffering from malnutrition due to the famine and had to be put on a special diet. It took a month to prepare them for organized activity.[21]

Despite the army's apparent determination to supply adequate nutrition, the meals served were not necessarily well prepared. Kitchens in many units were said to have not improved in the ten years since the end of the Civil War. Dirty, unsanitary conditions often prevailed. One *Krasnaia zvezda* correspondent reported that in the Riazan mess hall, "there is always a kind of vapor and the air is constantly heavy with smoke. Dinner lasts over an hour as one attendant has to serve 50–60 persons."[22] This situation, he added, was not an isolated incident. The cooks wore dirty clothes and often had no aprons and towels. Additionally, the cooks were not well trained, which resulted in poorly prepared meals.[23]

To make matters worse, unit commanders sometimes did not care. They appeared indifferent to the problem of food supply, preparation, and distribution. In many units, the people in the chain of command responsible for such matters—the assistant regimental commander for supply, the mess hall inspectors (unit doctors), assistants to the inspector of rations (unit veterinarians), and others—neither inspected nor supervised mess operations. Officers could get by with such attitudes if their unit had separate messes for the commanding personnel. In some units, officers purchased all or nearly all of their rations from the military cooperatives, so they had no need to make the military supply system work. In other garrisons, cooperative stores could only provide about half the needs of the officers, so they, too, had to rely on the unit mess halls.[24]

In units where the leadership did not take an active role in insuring good and adequate food for their men, trouble often erupted. In July 1929 in a company of the 63d Rifle Regiment, soldiers complained so bitterly about the poor quality of their food that the regiment conducted an official investigation which resulted in the arrest of the company *starshina* and head cook. Both received time in the guardhouse as punishment.[25] Later the same year, there were two instances of collective refusal of soldiers in the 61st Rifle Regiment to eat because their food was so bad.[26]

Similarly poor conditions reigned in factory canteens. Because many food items were rationed in the years 1928–1935, many workers relied on subsidized factory canteens. In order to keep prices down, canteen operators would skimp on the quality of the meal; although the workers continued to pay the same prices, the food became less plentiful and nutritious. Dining rooms were in short supply, and most did not have enough dishes, tableware, tables, or chairs to serve the large numbers of workers who patronized them.[27]

In his book, *Boets-grazhdanin* (1937), S. M. Budennyi, the famed Civil War cavalry officer and crony of Stalin, addressed the criticisms of the poor conditions in the Red Army. He compared the old army to the Red Army and pointedly painted a bleak—and often inaccurate—picture of life in the tsarist army, making the Red Army look wonderful in contrast. Budennyi all but told the soldiers that if they thought it was bad in their unit, they should be thankful they had not served in the old army. He was very specific about bad living conditions in the Imperial Army barracks, and, because he had been in the old army, he was credited as an expert. Perhaps to deflect criticism of the poor quality and quantity of food in the Red Army, Budennyi detailed how bad it had been before the Revolution, when sometimes his own and his comrades' hunger was so bad that they thought they would die. This anecdote, perhaps, was designed to make *krasnoarmeitsy* feel less dissatisfied about their food situation.[28]

Unit Farms

In 1932, in response to the famine that prompted the 30 percent cut in rations, the RVS ordered all units to create supplementary farms (*podsobnoe khoziaistvo*) to bolster their rations. Self-sustaining measures by the army became very important from this time onward. It was, however, not a completely original idea; the tsarist army had depended on unit farms for survival in times of fiscal austerity.[29] Industry took similar measures. Factories organized their own farms, which employees worked themselves.

The army intended unit farms to compete with the ZVK in feeding the men and supplementing officers' diet. Officers bought food for themselves from the farms with money out of their pockets. Regimental supply officers used appropriated monies to buy food for the soldiers' mess from both unit farms and the ZVK, thus putting unit farms in direct competition with the cooperatives. Sometimes, however, greed overtook the operators of unit farms, who would sell primarily to local civilians instead of to their own units, thus defeating the purpose of the farms.[30]

Some units had already created farms on their own initiative, and those units that had not done so quickly acted once the order was promulgated. By late summer 1932, one regiment already had more than two hundred hogs, sixty cows, more than one hundred rabbits, and forty beehives. The RVS's standard was for every division to have four hundred cows, thirty-two hundred pigs, and twenty thousand rabbits, and to sow a thousand hectares with a combination of rye, wheat, and fruits.[31]

Although soldiers worked most farms, exceptions abounded. Some regiments hired civilians to work their farms and paid them out of profits from the sale of milk and produce. In one artillery battalion, the officers' wives tended the unit's gardens while the battalion was away at summer camp. In other regiments, officers' wives did the spring sowing. In some cases, demobilized soldiers stayed to work as hired hands on their former regiments' farms.[32]

In many instances, the regimental farms were more efficient and could undercut the price of the ZVK. The farm of the 87th Rifle Regiment sold its surplus potatoes to the regiment for five kopecks a kilogram; the local ZVK was selling theirs for ten kopecks a kilo. The efficiency of some farms was quite astounding. One rifle regiment, for example, spent 3,500 rubles to start its farm and by the end of the year had produced more than 200 thousand rubles worth of crops and livestock. Nikolai Voronov, of the MPSD, recalled that in 1932 his artillery regiment was given the holdings of a small defunct *sovkhoz*. His farm did so well that it could afford to sell its milk to the regiment's officers and those of the rest of the division for only thirty kopecks a liter, which was cheaper than the market price. It was fortunate that there was an alternative to the ZVK, because the state was clearly unable to provide all the victuals soldiers needed during the thirties.[33] Not all unit farms were successful, however. Sometimes much of the work went for nothing because harvesting was ill-timed or because not enough effort was put into gathering crops.[34]

Food became as important as training as the famine progressed during 1932–1933. One can only speculate how many man-hours were utilized in gardening instead of in training. The emphasis unit commanders placed on farming is illustrated by the example of the assistant regimental commander of the 87th Rifle Regiment, who was in charge of the regiment's farming operations. He was so involved in the unit's farm that he knew each of the regiment's thirty-eight cows by name.[35] The many unit farms, combined with the ZVK's system of military cooperatives, indicate that the army was preoccupied with feeding its men, especially during the famine years. Because neither the military supply system nor the ZVK could meet minimum requirements, the unit supplementary farms clearly made tremendous contributions in feeding the army. They were so important that the army kept using them and allowed diversion of soldiers' training time, even during the intensive expansion and rearmament in the late thirties and early forties, when training became all important. Eventually unit farms became institutionalized as part of the normal activity of major units and continue to operate at the present.[36]

Supplying the Soldiers

The Red Army, as did most armies, issued soldiers uniforms, boots, and overcoats, while officers paid for theirs. A soldier's equipment consisted of a small kettle, a Red Army token, a field bag, a bag for clothes, a bag for carrying biscuits, a strap for fastening the overcoat, a woolen flask cover, a bag for personal items, a rifle sling, cartridge boxes, and a cartridge belt. Officers were issued a revolver case and cord, a sword belt, a sword knot, spurs, a wristwatch, and a map case. When he finished his term of service, the soldier kept his clothes but not his equipment. While on active duty, soldiers kept a pay book in which they registered the receipt of clothing and equipment. Company commanders and unit supply representatives inspected it whenever they issued clothing and equipment.[37] Equipment could be exchanged when it became unusable. This was the ideal, but in reality, not everything was delivered on time or in the desired quantities. Despite the army's supply problems, soldiers were often better off than the average working man. The worker had to scrape and save his money and then compete with other workers to buy often scarce and expensive clothes, while the government issued the soldier his.

During the entire prewar period, the army's supply organs operated with regular inefficiency. According to one source, the army in 1928 received for the first time 100 percent of the clothes, boots, mattresses, blankets, and linen it ordered. Woolen clothes and warm winter clothing were still in short supply, however, and quality left much to be desired. By Soviet admission it was well below the quality of similar items in European armies.[38] As late as 1934, the Red Army was still using surplus Allied material from the First World War, such as French and British helmets and puttees.

Because of its own shortcomings, the military made heavy demands on the system of military cooperatives, not just for food but for everyday needs as well. This reliance came mostly in response to the needs of many units posted in remote locations that possessed very few amenities and whose needs the army supply organs could not meet. No matter what was available in the military cooperatives, a soldier could not expect to buy much because of his miniscule pay. In 1925, a soldier's pay amounted to one ruble and forty kopecks per month. This amount gradually increased to eight rubles monthly in 1937. A first-term junior commander's pay rose in the same time from one ruble and ninety kopecks to twenty-four rubles a month.[39]

Such low pay often burdened the families of men who had been the major breadwinners or who were helping parents get by. One soldier said that when he was at home he gave the money he earned to his parents, "but when I was in the Army, of course, I could not help them at all. All I got was . . . just about enough to buy tobacco."[40] Despite low pay, the army still expected soldiers to contribute to the many industrial and military loans.

Soldiers' Complaints

One of the keys to understanding the behavior of Soviet soldiers in the pre-war years lies in their complaints. The RKKA promised soldiers a high-quality life not only for themselves but for their families. The army guaranteed them adequate food, shelter, and rest, and though these were seldom provided, complaints on these issues were in the minority. Soldiers primarily and in overwhelming numbers complained about the plight of their families as they endured the Bolshevik social revolution, as well as about the state's failure to keep promises to families regarding tax exemptions, housing, jobs, loans, schooling, and so on. The Soviet government recognized the importance of addressing soldiers' grievances and established the Bureau of Red Army Men's Letters to handle soldiers' complaints. Officers and commissars were essential links in the problem-resolution chain. Outside the military, the party and government were supposed to resolve the problems of soldiers' families as they related to regime policy.[41]

Just because a soldier sent his complaint to an official agency did not guarantee its resolution. In 1929, for example, the procurator of the Novosibirsk *krai*, in response to complaints from soldiers, investigated the activities of the local party organs concerned with soldiers' privileges. He confirmed that the local organs had failed to provide the guaranteed privileges and services to the families of those serving in the Red Army. The procurator determined that the personnel in Novosibirsk did not know the appropriate laws, the privileges that were due to the servicemen, and who in their area was supposed to receive them. Unfortunately for many soldiers, Novosibirsk was not an exception among *krai* administrations.[42] Failures in fulfilling soldiers' rights and privileges did not stem from a breakdown in the system but from the underdevelopment of the national infrastructure and the weaknesses of the party and government structure at the local levels. In combination, these shortcomings made it incredibly difficult to communicate decisions, policies, and procedures in a fashion that could be understood by the rather poorly educated and often unmotivated people manning the party apparatus and government bureaucracy. The system to support the regime's promises to its soldiers was still in the process of being built in the twenties and thirties; prevailing conditions rendered it largely ineffective in many parts of the country for years.[43]

In 1932, the military press, acting as advocate for the men, reported that conditions of employment, domestic needs, and other issues affecting the soldiers' families frequently did not receive sufficient consideration.[44] On 7 July 1932, the party's Central Executive Committee (TsIK) published a decree stating that the laws relative to the privileges accorded families of military personnel should be carried out more thoroughly. An examination of the complaints of Red Army soldiers in the Middle Volga, Western, Moscow, and other military districts, in addition to information received from the People's Commissariats of Justice and of Social Welfare, showed that these laws had not been carried out satisfactorily. The TsIK noted that central party institutions exerted insufficient supervision over local executive committees and soviets. The report went on to document that subordinate organs delayed or arbitrarily decreased payments and occasionally failed to pay prescribed allowances for soldiers' dependents. State organs illegally taxed families of Red Army soldiers excessively and made illegal demands for delivery of fixed quantities of agricultural products, all the while exhibiting a careless attitude toward the complaints of the soldiers and their families and procrastinating in handling such complaints. The regime was very concerned that the promises to the soldiers be honored, because the enlisted men and their families were considered crucial to the socialist reconstruction of the countryside.[45]

If the situation in Belorussia was indicative of unionwide performance, it can be said that the orders of the Central Executive Committee failed to remedy the problem of poor local observance of the laws. In late autumn 1932, the social inspector of the Belorussian Central Control Commission formed a task force of inspectors to resolve the problems of servicemen's families. While addressing these problems, it discovered that the procurator of the Belorussian SSR had been slow to respond to complaints. Letters went unanswered for months, and some problems were never addressed. In addition, the procurator did not supervise other Belorussian organs that received complaints, such as *Kolkhoztsentr* Belorussian SSR, the Belorussian People's Commissariat of Land, and People's Commissariat of Labor.[46]

In the course of 1932, military procurators received 18,125 letters of complaint from Red Army servicemen. Of these, complaints about privileges not granted to families numbered 10,934. In the first quarter of 1933, they received 4,761 complaints, 2,500 of which were about privileges. Most of the complaints about privileges concerned the illegal actions of local organs of Soviet power with regard to taxes, guarantees to families, the illegal exclusion of soldiers and their families from collective farms, and the dekulakization of a relative.[47]

Part of the problem in addressing these complaints lay with the Bureaus of Red Army Men's Letters in the regiments, the first stop for letters of complaint. A 1933 inspection of twenty such bureaus in the Leningrad Military

District revealed many shortcomings in organization and personnel. To start with, the inspection disclosed that many bureau secretaries were ignorant of the appropriate statutes and codes governing actions concerning complaints. In the majority of cases, the bureaus did not even have the appropriate legal publications and codes on hand for reference. Many of the bureaus took no action but simply forwarded the inquiries to other agencies with requests for "compliance on the basis of existing resolutions of the party and government."[48]

The inspection also revealed a failure to keep records of soldiers' complaints. The time required to handle a complaint did not depend on when it was received but on the free time of the bureau secretary. For example, the 20th Artillery Regiment received from five to ten letters a day, while the 11th Rifle Regiment received between six and eleven. In both regiments, only one or two letters were processed each day by the bureau secretaries. At the time of the inspection, none of the twenty bureaus had taken any steps to speed up responses to complaints and petitions. As a result, most letters went unanswered.[49] Such inept handling of soldiers' problems—problems about which the soldiers felt strongly enough to warrant an official complaint—must surely have caused dismay in the ranks and may have contributed to discipline problems.

Complaints from the enlisted men continued to pour into the Bureau of Red Army Men's Letters at all of its various levels despite the efforts of the TsIK. So many problems remained in handling the letters and solving the complaints that the third plenum of the Commission of Soviet Control, held in May 1936, resolved that commanders and commissars be held responsible for seeing that their units properly addressed soldiers' complaints. Soldiers still were to send their letters off to the appropriate agencies, but it was now up to the commanders and commissars to follow up on complaints.[50]

In typical Russian fashion, there was a paradoxical limitation on complaints: they had to be submitted individually. If two or more soldiers jointly complained about a situation, either in person or in writing, the army considered it a breach of discipline. Soldiers were routinely punished, albeit lightly, for such collective action. Overwhelmingly, collective complaints concerned food and housing. One example concerned the complaint of fifty-five Uzbek conscripts stationed in the Ukraine. They were assigned to live in poorly constructed barracks without adequately warm clothing (by their estimation). In protest, they drew up a petition to the NKO asking to be transferred back to Uzbekistan. The regimental commissar censured them for their trouble and refused to reassign them. The NKO took the commissar to task for having allowed such a thing to happen; the military district political section then issued an order to its PUR functionaries to do more work integrating nationalities into the mainstream of the army. In another instance, a group of reservists who had been called up sent a letter to the Presidium of the Supreme Soviet protesting conditions in the 22d Motorized Pontoon Battalion. Their collective complaint was considered especially serious because they were well-educated and well-trained engineers, not typical malcontent conscripts.[51] Antipathy toward collective protest did not originate with the Red Army but was consistent with the outlook of the tsarist army, which often took brutal measures against any form of protest, justified or not.[52]

MILITARY DISCIPLINE, INDISCIPLINE, CRIME, AND PUNISHMENT IN THE RKKA

Instilling Discipline

The Red Army expected its soldiers to be loyal to the USSR, obedient to the orders of their superiors, respectful of friends and others in general and leaders in particular, and conscientious in fulfilling their service obligations. Moreover, the men were expected to behave in a manner worthy of a soldier. But unlike the Imperial Army, which had relied on class distinctions, privileges for higher-ranking officers, and the heavy hand of the noncommissioned officers, the army attempted to accomplish its goals through "revolutionary discipline." This concept was explained in the regulations:

'Revolutionary discipline' is understood as that discipline which . . . was formed from revolutionary enthusiasm with a clear understanding by the workers of their duty in relation to their class. In other words, revolutionary discipline is the discipline of the people, bound solidly with a revolutionary conscience, conscious of their socialist duty. . . . The discipline of the Red Army is a new discipline of the worker's and peasant's state. It is based not on class subordination but on a conscious understanding of . . . the goals and purpose of the Workers' and Peasants' Red Army. The more conscious the soldier of the Red Army is, the better he fulfills his revolutionary obligation to the socialist state, and the more combat ready is the Workers' and Peasants' Red Army.[53]

"Revolutionary discipline" had to be learned. It was not expected to come naturally to the conscript. According to RKKA doctrine, the foundation of discipline was education. Leaders were expected to train the soldier to submit to orders yet retain enough individualism to use initiative. Disciplinary education focused on the creation of self-discipline. This education was carried out on two levels. The army chain of command taught discipline through military training, such as teamwork and obedience, and PUR sought to instill discipline through a politically raised consciousness. In form, this revolutionary discipline was not revolutionary at all. All armies teach a balance of obedience and initiative. In content, raising political consciousness seems revolutionary but actually corresponds to the feelings of national loyalty that traditional armies reinforce and rely on for discipline and cohesion.[54]

Indiscipline

When one considers the conditions of poor housing and food, haphazard training, and the laxity officers sometimes displayed in their duties, it is not surprising that discipline suffered in the units. In the twenties and thirties, the party blamed discipline problems in the army on the "continuing class struggle and difficult material conditions." In 1928, the army averaged eight misdemeanors for every one hundred servicemen per month. Of these, 21 percent had a direct derogatory effect on the military capacity of the units. Fifteen percent resulted in arrest.[55] This high statistic averages out to about two crimes or violations of regulations a week for every company. Undoubtedly, "police" work, that is, keeping track of offenders and arranging hearings and punishments, distracted officers from training.

The number of serious crimes was also high, judging by the Soviet military press. In 1929, not a week went by when *Krasnaia zvezda* did not report at least one, if not a dozen, serious crimes by soldiers. The crime most often reported that required trial by military tribunal was money theft or selling supplies to civilians. Besides thievery, the military press each week reported selected crimes of indiscipline, desertion, and negligence. The 21st Rifle Division, for example, from fall 1927 to summer 1928, experienced 2,575 crimes and misdemeanors and 1,791 infringements of regulations. Enlisted men committed 1,717 of the crimes and misdemeanors; junior commanders, 694; and officers, 164. The following year, the number of reported infractions decreased among enlisted men (1,584) and junior commanders (443), but rose among officers (171), for a total of 2,198 infractions. Infringements of regulations (1,275) also declined. Of the crimes committed in 1927–1928, 355 resulted in arrest and trial by military tribunal. Although there were fewer crimes in 1928–1929, more (378) resulted in arrest.[56]

As early as 1926, Voroshilov had noted that peasants made up the majority of the army and called for raising the number of Komsomols in the RKKA to 300,000 to provide an example of self-discipline for the nonparty men.[57] Voroshilov implicitly suggested that he considered nonparty peasants to be undisciplined (or anti-Soviet by nature) and that their influence needed to be diluted by that of the Communists. Unless he was including the territorial forces, his figure of 300,000 was high because the RKKA only had 562,000 men.

Voroshilov's faith in Komsomols as examples of discipline may have been misplaced. Several years earlier, M. V. Frunze, chief of the RVS, had chastised a conference of Komsomols for their own lax discipline. He noted that in one rifle division in the Ukraine, between January and March 1925, one-third of the Komsomol soldiers had been punished for infractions of military discipline. During the same months in the entire North Caucasus Military District, 31 percent of the Komsomols received military punishments. In 1929, again in the North Caucasus, one brigade expelled seven men from the Komsomol, arrested five others, and gave sixty-seven punishments for indiscipline.[58]

Party membership did not guarantee better behavior. In periodic discipline campaigns, PUR held up Communist party members as examples for the rest of the army. In some cases the work of party cells was applauded as strengthening unit discipline. At other times, the press upbraided them for failing to be the models the party intended. In 1932, PUR roundly chastised several units for the conduct of their party cells. It accused the communist soldiers of letting down their commanders and fellow soldiers by committing breaches of discipline. In one company, ten of the twenty-five party members had committed misdemeanors. In another unit, fully half (eight out of sixteen) of the party members had been convicted of disciplinary infractions. Communist soldiers were reminded that as party members they were the "advance guard of discipline" and were to see to it that all of the commander's orders were carried out. Given that the army never ceased harping on this point, it seems that Komsomols and party members continually fell short of the mark.[59]

Each division had a detachment of men of the secret police (OGPU, renamed NKVD in 1934) called Special Sections (*Osobyi Otdel*). These sections watched over all members of a division, from private to general, and PUR to insure political reliability. They created networks of informers, relying heavily on PUR and party members to report on their fellow soldiers. What is not well known is that the Special Sections acted as the military police force of the RKKA, which had no separate military police. Special Sections investigated all crimes in the army, from murders and suicides to theft of government property and desertion. Under authority of the military prosecutor's office, they arrested and incarcerated suspects pending trial by military tribunal. In cases where the death penalty was imposed, Special Sections organized firing squads to carry out the sentence.[60]

In addition to the often poor conditions of life and slipshod leadership, lack of cohesion in the units may have contributed to discipline problems. Units experienced a high turnover of personnel because of the various terms of service. All conscripts in the army served for two years, so every year the army experienced roughly a 50 percent turnover. Volunteers could serve enlistments of three or four years, so every year one-third of the three-year men left and one-quarter of the four-year men left. There was also natural turnover of nearly 8 percent of military personnel annually for such reasons as medical discharges, death, desertion, misconduct, and imprisonment. Therefore, personal relationships and loyalties were harder to form than in armies with longer enlistment terms, such as the British and French armies, which had three-year enlistments, and the German army, which, in the Weimar period, had twelve-year enlistments.[61]

One company commander reported the following minor mutiny in his company. Every workday morning the men exercised under the supervision of their junior commanders. One morning they collectively refused to do the exercises. The commander reported that "it was because they just didn't feel like taking the exercises. There was a *starshina* who didn't want to take the men out to the physical exercises. Well it was just because the men wanted a holiday, and so they just did not go out." Even the *politruk* could not convince the men to obey because the [regular] *politruk* of the company "had gone on leave and was replaced by someone who was not liked by the men and so they did not listen to him." In the end, the men did not get punished, but the chain of command, including the *politruk*, was reprimanded for failing to control the men.[62]

In August 1932, *Krasnaia zvezda* reported on discipline problems in the RKKA and their sources. From an investigation of a railway regiment in the Moscow Military District came the following findings:

> It was discovered that defects in the interior guard duty were frequently caused by the nonobservation of regulations on the part of junior commanders. It appeared that duty rosters were kept very carelessly so that a soldier who had just been relieved from duty was immediately detailed again. Absence without leave was frequently caused by careless supervision and lack of control on the part of commanders over the return of the men from a club which was located outside the premises of the regiment.
>
> Sometimes the cause [of indiscipline] lies in the poor organization of the daily routine. Tents are dirty, boots are uncleaned owing to the lack of brushes and blacking, clothes are torn owing to the lack of needles, thread and repairing material. There is an inadequate quantity of crockery in the mess halls and the supervision over the preparation of food is insufficient.[63]

One cannot fail to notice that the findings of the investigation point out that conditions of life in the Red Army, shortcomings in supply, and poor leadership contributed to discipline problems.

The situation worsened as time went on. Foreign military attachés reported that, thanks to collectivization and dekulakization, dissatisfaction was rife in the RKKA, even among officers. One unconfirmed report said that nearly two thousand soldiers had been discharged in 1933–1934 because they proved to be of kulak origin or in sympathy with the kulaks and had actively agitated against the party. Possibly as a response to this unrest, the army began a discipline drive in 1933.[64]

Unrest in the army should not have come as a surprise, considering the turmoil in the countryside. By Soviet admission, peasants resisted collectivization in nearly all parts of the USSR. The regime ascribed this resistance to kulaks, a label given all peasants resisting collectivization, whether through sabotage, violence, or propaganda against collectivizers and representatives of Soviet power. Judging from the scale of opposition, there seems to have been a virtual war on. The significance for the army was that from 1929 to 1932, conscripts came to the army from a countryside in turmoil, and although those identified as kulaks were not allowed in the army, their relatives were. Conscripts from villages had seen the harsh treatment of "kulaks." They saw this label given to friends and family, to people they knew were not kulaks. Many conscripts may themselves have been opposed to collectivization. Therefore, strong grounds for anti-Soviet sentiment existed in the hearts and minds of many peasant conscripts.[65]

Many soldiers sympathized with the plight of the peasantry, and it is possible that whole units mutinied in protest of Soviet agrarian policies. Soviet sources are quiet on major outbreaks of indiscipline, such as mutinies, but, as early as 1929, *politruki* began reporting the existence of prokulak and anticollectivization trends among soldiers and officers. Individual acts of indiscipline constituted part of these trends.

The foreign press reported serious internal problems in the army in the early and mid-thirties. The French newspaper *Figaro* reported an anti-Soviet rebellion in Siberia in 1930, in which several army units and navy ships joined the rebels. The Japanese and Italian military attachés reported simultaneous unrest among units stationed in the Far East responding to a lack of food and arrears in pay. According to the Japanese military attaché, the OGPU was called in to handle things in case the men got out of control. TASS, the official Soviet news agency, regularly denied the veracity of these stories.[66] French and German newspapers reported a mutiny in an army unit at Riazan involving two regiments in summer 1932. After it was suppressed, some three hundred officers and men were said to have been executed. Foreign newspapers also asserted that during the same summer peasant revolts in the Ukraine were put down by troops.[67] All these reports remain unsubstantiated.

In his memoirs, Georgii Zhukov spoke of "misbehavior" by "politically backward" soldiers in his division. He believed that sometimes the men misbehaved in reaction to officers and political instructors who did not know or understand their men's characters and personal problems.[68] The term "politically backward," as used by Zhukov, meant men who did not agree with collectivization, were not party members, and, more than likely, were peasants.

The famine of 1932–1933 and the state's handling of the crisis also affected military morale and discipline. In 1932, Mikhail Soloviev, a reserve officer and military correspondent who later emigrated, went with his regiment to the Ukraine for summer maneuvers. When the soldiers saw mounds of emaciated corpses and the pitiable state of the living due to famine, their morale sank. Against orders, they gave food to the people, risking punishment if caught. Some sympathetic officers looked the other way when their men fed starving peasants. The peasant soldiers were especially concerned by what was happening in the Ukraine. Apparently the poor morale caused by the sight of ragged and starving peasants caused the army to call off the maneuvers and send the division out of the Ukraine. As the soldiers headed for the train to leave, the division's food warehouse caught fire and local peasants looted it. The soldiers were ordered to fight the fire but instead rushed into the burning warehouse, retrieved food, and gave it to the hungry peasants.[69] Clearly, their attitude was one of solidarity with the people rather than the regime.

Discipline and Morale in the Territorial Forces

Discipline proved to be as difficult to maintain in the territorial forces as in the regular forces. Territorial units had the same problems as regular units, plus the additional problem of absenteeism at assemblies. Territorial units not only had discipline problems with the transitory personnel when they were in uniform; the army sometimes had difficulty getting them into uniform. Peasant soldiers often failed to report for duty. Even the proletarian elements were sometimes uncooperative. In 1925, numerous workers did not attend the summer assembly; their excuse was that they were not notified. They claimed that although their workplace may have been notified of the assembly date, the word was not passed on. Such ignorance is highly suspect given the extensive propaganda associated with assemblies. Party members working in party organs also frequently failed to attend annual assembly because they considered themselves indispensable to their party work.[70]

U.S. military attachés reported that many territorial soldiers refused to report for duty in 1929 because of grain requisitioning and the onset of collectivization. They stated that discipline in many units, especially in the Ukraine, was shaky. They also reported that troops would not fire on revolting peasants in the Ukraine and that the OGPU had to be called in. The summer training of the territorial units in the Kuban was reported to have been suspended and the troops sent home because of their overt display of hostility.[71]

Territorial units were sometimes hotbeds of anti-Soviet activity. The OGPU was constantly on the alert for groups of "counterrevolutionary kulaks," said to be active throughout the RKKA. In the countryside, they sabotaged tractors; in the barracks, they undermined the political mood of their fellow soldiers. In September 1930, a "counterrevolutionary" group of five men was exposed in the 12th Territorial Rifle Division in Siberia. Others were found in Omsk and Tomsk. In August 1930, the Special Sections arrested a "counterrevolutionary" group in the regimental school of the 61st Territorial Rifle Regiment. The members were all peasant *terrarmeitsy*. To be considered counterrevolutionary one only needed be caught questioning the wisdom of the state in requisitioning grain or pushing peasants onto collective farms.[72]

From 1928 to 1932, PUR personnel and military cadre pressured the territorial soldiers to collectivize. Many *terrarmeitsy* resisted these efforts. The military requisitioned grain from transitory soldiers, their friends and neighbors, and the families of future conscripts. This requisitioning is something the transitory soldier would not have forgotten when he came to his assembly or when his cadre came around to do training between assemblies. One can easily imagine the strain on the relationship between soldiers and their officers and political leaders. Hostility from peasant soldiers surprised some in the party who thought collectivization and the reorganization of rural life would strengthen the territorial forces by making training easier and more efficient.[73]

Rewards and Punishments

As part of the Frunze reforms, the RKKA published a new set of discipline regulations in 1925. These regulations, updated almost every year thereafter, emulated tsarist regulations promulgated in 1916. They addressed the powers of platoon commanders, as well as company and battalion commanders, to reward and punish their men without recourse to military tribunals (courts-martial). The regulations provided administrative punishments such as extra fatigues and confinement in the guardhouse for several days. They were intended as tools for unit commanders to maintain order within the unit and were normally used only for minor infractions of discipline. Military tribunals tried serious crimes.[74]

The power to punish was held in varying degrees according to rank and position. A platoon commander could only send a man to the guardhouse for five days. A company commander could put a soldier in the guardhouse for ten days. The length of time a battalion commander could imprison a soldier rose from seven to fifteen days in 1925 under the new disciplinary regulations. The new rules did relax in one area. Previously, a man could be confined in the guardhouse for a maximum of thirty days per month. In 1925, this maximum was reduced to twenty days. The Red Army also used positive reinforcement to maintain discipline. The regulations called for specific rewards for soldiers, such as letters of commendation, prizes, and early promotion.[75] A notable difference from long-standing tsarist tradition, albeit one that the Imperial Army had made great strides in overcoming by the time of the First World War, was that corporal punishment was forbidden.

Serious crimes were brought before military tribunals for trial. The punishments that tribunals could hand down ranged from three months' deprivation of freedom to death with confiscation of property. Divisions, corps, and separate brigades could convene tribunals. They originally comprised three or four senior officers, but in the thirties an enlisted man was included as well. The original Statute on Military Crimes that governed military tribunals was passed in 1925. The army added to and strengthened it with more serious punishments in 1927, 1931, 1934, 1935, 1936, and again in 1940. Until 1936, deprivation of freedom could mean imprisonment or a term in a corrective labor camp. In 1936, the term imprisonment was introduced into the courts to specify prison terms for certain serious crimes.[76] For failure to carry out an order, for example, a soldier could be sentenced to up to five years' deprivation of freedom. If the infraction was committed in combat, he could be shot and his property confiscated. Absence without leave and desertion could result, in peacetime, in guardhouse punishment, or, in 1940, in assignment to a disciplinary battalion, or, in wartime, in death with confiscation of property. Breach of sentry and guard duties called for six months' confinement or, during wartime, death.[77]

The regulations anticipated a wide variety of behavior that, if not controlled, could negatively affect military operations. Some of the regulations, therefore, seem designed to deter certain actions that could happen in any army, such as draft evasion in wartime, which was punishable by a year or more in prison or death. Other regulations were uniquely Soviet, such as the penalty for *terrarmeitsy* of cavalry units who failed to bring their horses with them upon mobilization, which could lead to six months' deprivation of freedom. Also unique was a regulation stipulating that in combat situations, unit commanders could shoot on the spot soldiers who defied orders. Not only was an officer entitled to use arms against a soldier, but in certain circumstances the regulations compelled commanders to use them.[78]

EXPANSION, *EZHOVSHCHINA*, THE APPROACH OF WAR, AND DETERIORATION OF DISCIPLINE

Even before the *Ezhovshchina* (the terror purge), units suffered from poor discipline and morale. Criminal incidents, breaches of regulations, fatal training accidents, suicides, and desertion reflected this poor attitude. Between 1 January 1937 and 31 May 1937, the army recorded 400,000 disciplinary infractions.[79] During the *Ezhovshchina*, discipline eroded further as the men detected that their officers were in precarious and sometimes powerless positions. PUR personnel also lost prestige, authority, and influence. Before the end of the purge, the army began a discipline campaign to keep things from getting completely out of hand. The need for a discipline campaign during the purge is illustrated by an excerpt from Petro Grigorenko's *Memoir*: "The soldiers talked openly, not in defense of the commanders who had been arrested but just the opposite: 'Who is commanding us! Enemies of the people are intentionally putting us in danger of slaughter. All the officers [in the regiment] ought to be punished.'"[80] Indeed, some people believed that the *Ezhovshchina* was justified, and their attitudes often made it difficult for officers to control their units and do any meaningful training. In 1937 and 1938, supervisory personnel in industry had similar problems with discipline. John Scott reported that when a foreman issued an order, "The workers would sneer at him and say: 'Go on. You're a wrecker yourself. Tomorrow they'll come and arrest you. All you engineers and technicians are wreckers.'"[81]

In March 1938, *Krasnaia zvezda* announced the launching of a discipline campaign with a call for a return to "iron military discipline," which the officers and PUR had allowed to lapse. One captain, accused of allowing slack discipline in his unit, rebutted the charge, saying, "How can one accuse me of a weak fight for discipline when in my unit in [the first] three months of this year there were 132 punishments imposed and not less than 40 percent were imposed by me?" Indiscipline had escalated before this, however. In one battery of the 9th Artillery Regiment, the commander imposed 138 punishments in 1937. To appreciate the magnitude of these numbers, consider that there were only about one hundred men in a battery. Another artillery battery's reputation for indiscipline earned it the nickname of the "penal company."[82]

The military press spearheaded a campaign to restore the authority of officers as part of the discipline campaign. Numerous articles in autumn 1938 supported the authority of officers and junior commanders with such statements as: "No calling is higher than the calling of soldier in the Worker's and Peasant's Red Army. No profession is more honored than the profession of commander in this army."[83] Statements of this type—essentially untrue in the context of popular attitudes about the army—made little impression on the enlisted ranks.

Because indiscipline was rife before the purge, all discipline problems cannot be blamed on the purge alone. Discipline in the units deteriorated for a variety of interrelated reasons, including the youth and inexperience of commanding officers and political leaders in the companies and battalions; the loss of authority and status of officers; a lack of respect for *mladshii leit-*

enanty and *mladshii komvzvod* (junior commanders acting as platoon commanders) by officers, which undermined their authority with the men; the large numbers of *mladshii leitenanty* and *mladshii komvzvod*; the loss of status and authority of political leaders; and the conscripts' continued disaffection with the Soviet regime. The expansion of the army beyond the means of the military education system and the party to provide trained leaders also undermined discipline because there were simply too few officers and political leaders to adequately supervise the men. At the same time, the newer officers were barely trained, having been forced through military school at breakneck speed; and if they had been mobilized by the party, they were probably less motivated as well. Concurrent with the last phase of expansion of the RKKA in the years 1939–1941 came the call-ups of thousands of reservists, initially in anticipation of the invasion of Poland, later in response to heightened anxieties over the Soviet Union's relations with Nazi Germany. This convergence of expansion, calling up reserves, and the aggressive use of military force led to widespread disobedience on the part of soldiers.

Discipline in the officer ranks also lapsed during the purge. At the end of July 1938, *Krasnaia zvezda* again began reporting crimes by officers, presumably in the hope of deterring further crimes. In the late twenties and early thirties, the majority of reported crimes had been theft and embezzlement, rather than civil crimes and negligence. The reports in 1938 included many convictions for negligence of duties, which sent the message that officers would have to be more competent and conscientious or else suffer the consequences. The latest series of criminal reports were not related to the purge and never used the terms "wrecking" and "sabotage" characteristic of the *Ezhovshchina*.

Between 22 July and 23 December 1938, the press reported the convictions of twenty-six Red Army officers and one commissar by military tribunals. Of these, eleven officers were convicted of negligence and four of incompetence. Five officers were convicted of crimes committed while drunk. There was one instance each of stealing, embezzlement, misappropriation of government supplies, and abuse of authority. A military tribunal even tried a case of wife-beating and gave the offending officer thirteen years in the camps.[84] Between 8 January and 24 August 1939 (when the reporting of crimes by officers again ceased), *Krasnaia zvezda* reported that nineteen officers and one *politruk* had been arrested and tried by military tribunals. In this round, five officers stood accused of divulging military secrets and three of the illegal use of automobiles. Two officers were tried for disobedience. The remaining cases involved embezzlement and misappropriation, abuse of rank, negligence, disrespect, conduct unbecoming an officer, and drunkenness.

When indiscipline reached its peak in 1940, the most common serious infraction was desertion. Arrests for threatening the life of an officer were reported for the first time in 1940. Table 2.1 shows the figures for convictions by military tribunals conducted under the authority of the military procuracy. The military procuracy prosecuted a wide variety of criminal behavior, which included counterrevolutionary crimes, military crimes, official and property crimes, drunkenness, hooliganism, discrediting power, and miscellaneous. The category of military crimes includes military treason; evasion of military service, including absence without leave (AWOL) and desertion; insubordination and breach of military honor; crimes against military property; breach of rules of sentry, convoy, and guard duty; military official crimes, such as abuse of authority and negligent attitude toward service duties on the part of officers; disclosure of military secrets; battle crimes such as improper retreat or surrender; and crimes in violation of international conventions.[55] The figures indicate that discipline deteriorated in 1937 and 1938 during the purge; however, discipline was far better during the *Ezhovshchina* than it was in 1940. In a relative sense, the *Ezhovshchina* might have been considered the good old days with regard to military discipline by younger officers who joined the army between 1937 and 1939.

When interpreting the numbers presented in Table 2.1, one should keep in mind that the number of men in the army increased every year, so one would naturally expect a commensurate annual increase in crime. The years 1936 through 1938 are part of the second phase of expansion. The number of men did not double from 1936 to 1937, but the number of soldiers convicted of serious crimes did. This suggests a deterioration of discipline due to the assault on the officer corps in the purge. However, when one looks only at nonpolitical crimes, the picture changes dramatically. The increase in military

Table 2.1. Convictions for Serious Crimes by Military Tribunals, 1936–1940

	Officers	Jr. Commanders	Enlisted	Total
All Crimes				
1936	376	740	2,700	3,816
1937	1,559	1,488	5,634	8,681
1938	1,618	1,420	5,312	8,350
1939	1,277	1,347	5,203	7,827
1940	1,450	8,192	28,885	38,527
Crimes Excluding Political (Counterrevolutionary) Crimes				
1936	297	574	2,020	2,891
1937	602	910	2,090	4,602
1938	862	1,054	3,302	5,218
1939	912	1,259	4,567	6,738
1940	1,389	8,032	27,503	36,924

Source: A. T. Ukolov and V. I. Ivkin, "O Masshtabakh Repressii v Krasnoi Armii v predvoennye godu," *Voenno-istoricheskii zhurnal* no. 1 (1993), 57.

and ordinary crimes is much less dramatic than for crimes overall because the total number of crimes includes political arrests, most of which occurred during the purge. When these are taken out, a more accurate picture of military discipline emerges. Indeed, the increase in military crimes is more dramatic from 1938 to 1939, when the purge ended, than it was from 1936 to 1937, when the purge began. From 1936 to 1937, the number of serious crimes by enlisted men rose by less than 5 percent, a far cry from what the memoir literature leads us to expect. Indeed, crimes by those in authority escalated far more rapidly.

Most astounding is the wild jump in convictions for nonpolitical crimes in 1940, nearly two years after the purge. In 1939, the RKKA entered the third phase of expansion. During this phase, the Red Army called up hundreds of thousands of reservists and committed major forces to combat in the Far East (Khalkin-Gol), Poland, and Finland. In 1940, the army fought in Finland until March and was sent to invade (with little bloodshed) the Baltic states, Bessarabia, and North Bukovina in the spring. The combination of calling up reservists (many of whom were in their thirties and forties with families and established careers), combat, and the threat of further combat triggered the massive increase of indiscipline in the Red Army. Notification that a unit was to be transferred to the front in Finland would cause hundreds to desert overnight. The alert of the Kiev Special Military District to prepare to invade Bessarabia in June 1940 provoked scores of threats to officers' lives and large-scale desertions.[86]

The Disciplinary Code of 1940

In 1940, in an attempt to come to grips with skyrocketing discipline problems, the Commissariat of Defense, now headed by Marshal Semen K. Timoshenko, promulgated a new, stricter disciplinary code.[87] The rewritten definition of military discipline in 1940 made no mention of socialism or social-political duties. Instead, the army stressed unquestioning obedience to superiors and often referred to Lenin's admonishment, "Without discipline there is no army"[88]— altogether, quite a change from the comradely idealism of the 1920s.

The predominant infringements of military discipline the new code intended to enforce included arguing with officers; infringement of combat regulations; disobeying interior guard regulations; carelessness with weapons and ammunition; and unauthorized absences and desertion. During the war with Finland, rampant desertion plagued units at the front. Rather than admit that military service was a "privilege" that many young men would just as soon have avoided and acknowledge that the communist regime was still unpopular with a large segment of the population, the army blamed this behavior on improper upbringing and the youth of its soldiers. However, it was not only the rank and file that was disobedient; junior commanders were almost as undisciplined as *krasnoarmeitsy*.[89] Systemic indiscipline pervaded units with many young and "misguided" soldiers. Despite all the attempts of commanders and commissars to overcome it, "malicious hooliganism" persisted. Wherever undisciplined soldiers were assigned, they caused trouble and inevitably ended up in guardhouses.[90]

In discussions of discipline and morale, the military press frequently cited desertion as the most serious problem. The Red Army did not declare a man a deserter until he was gone for over six weeks, but a soldier AWOL for up to six weeks could only be punished by up to twenty days in the guardhouse. A junior commander could get the same punishment plus reduction in rank for an absence of thirty days.[91] Western armies punished men far more seriously for the same infraction. For example, thirty days was the norm for declaring a soldier a deserter, thus making him subject to court-martial and serious punishment when captured. In the Red Army, a soldier merely spent time in the guardhouse and then returned to duty. A PUR report prepared for the Central Committee in May 1940 lamented the lax treatment of deserters. The regulations called for captured deserters to be imprisoned for a year. In practice, commanders seldom imprisoned or punished deserters in any way unless they abandoned the front. After 1939, the RKKA treated all military districts on the western border as fronts, and the punishment for desertion there became very severe. In some cases, men received up to ten years in prison.[92]

The most important changes the army made in the regulations did not concern sentencing but the treatment of offenders in confinement. Guardhouse regulations governing confinement of arrested enlisted men were incredibly lax before the changes, if the examples Marshal Timoshenko offered are representative. He claimed that the regimen of garrison confinement was really a free and easy lifestyle. He likened guardhouses to hotels: prisoners had bunks with sheets and mattresses, and the detainees could sleep as much as they wanted. They frequently were allowed out on pass from the guardhouse to go to movies and cultural events, they could have friends visit, and they could mingle with other prisoners and fraternize with the guards. The men could take personal possessions to the guardhouse, and they were provided with games, such as checkers, chess, and dominoes, to pass the time.[93] In lamenting such soft conditions, PUR admitted, "We have guardhouses that do not seriously influence infringements of discipline." To substantiate this conclusion, PUR provided what it claimed was an accurate and representative example of attitudes toward guardhouse punishment in a letter by one detainee who wrote to his friends: "This is not a guardhouse, it is a rest home. Strive to get into the guardhouse. Raised voices that say 'attention' are not heard here. I attend to my many wants and afterwards read newspapers for a while or go play chess."[94] Western armies had no such thing as a pass from the guardhouse, and prisoners were not allowed personal possessions and fraternization with guards.

In his order setting forth new guardhouse regulations, which represented only one aspect of many disciplinary regulations issued between May and November 1940, Timoshenko stated that "the guardhouse is a place for isolation and reeducation of *krasnoarmeitsy* who have flagrantly infringed on military discipline, but has been confused, in particular, with vacation resorts." Timoshenko used the Tblisi garrison as an example. There, arrested men went into town under guard and returned to the guardhouse "for their night's lodging." Prisoners got plenty of sleep, getting up two or three hours later in the morning than the men of the regiments. They were well fed and acted like they were living in a health spa. No wonder Timoshenko was furious. He thought conditions in the guardhouses actually encouraged indiscipline.[95] Under the new regulations, life in the guardhouse became harsher. They allowed prisoners only six hours of sleep. Furthermore, soldiers would sleep on the floor. They could not have games or interact with the guards.[96]

The regulations had always provided for two types of confinement: light and hard. Ten days or less of confinement was light punishment; eleven to twenty days was hard punishment. The stipulations applied to both types, but there were different conditions in other matters. Soldiers under hard arrest were put in solitary confinement and were allowed no visitors. Men under light arrest could be housed several men to a cell and could have visitors. Now, both types of confinement called for only partial rations. Prisoners under hard arrest got only bread, water, and tea; the men on light arrest were fed meat, bread, and tea.[97]

If soft conditions were the norm during the previous two decades, it is easy to see why discipline had been hard to maintain. Commanders had no real coercive power; at any rate, they had not used their power to coerce good behavior, and it took the NKO to make the lower levels get tough with the men. Making confinement an unpleasant experience was a reasonable and realistic way to bolster the authority of the unit commander. Once men began to fear a stay in the guardhouse, the commander had more leverage to induce obedience. As always, he could order a man confined in the guardhouse for up to twenty days without recourse to a tribunal. Tribunals subjected convicts to terms in labor camps or penal battalions. Sentences in penal battalions could stretch from three months to two years.[98]

The Commissariat of Defense also increased punishments for officers under the new regulations. Arrested officers could forfeit up to half of their pay while under arrest, still extremely light punishment compared to that in Western armies. Any officer arrested and convicted in the German or French armies was either sent to prison or discharged from the service, or both. Provisions for extra details or house arrest as punishments did not normally exist in Western armies. Perhaps the lighter treatment of Red Army officers was a realistic response to the caliber of its men. If a hard line had been drawn, the army would have had to separate a larger number of men from the service than it already did for serious crimes.[99]

Overall, sentences handed down by military tribunals became far more severe in 1939 and 1940. In 1938, the army executed 52 officers and enlisted men for their crimes; in 1939, 112; and in 1940, 528. In 1938, 2,201 officers and enlisted men were sentenced to from one to three years in prison; in 1939, 3,292; but in 1940, none were given less than three years in prison or the camps. Instead, the RKKA created penal battalions. In 1940, 11,759 officers and soldiers were sentenced to serve in these battalions from six months to two years. In 1938, military tribunals sentenced 2,841 servicemen to three to five years in prison; in 1939, 2,283; and in 1940, 17,053. The number of men given more than five years in prison for their misdeeds also drastically increased in 1940 to 7,733, compared to only 812 in 1937. Conviction by military tribunal did not in all cases mean the forfeiture of either life or freedom. Every year, including 1940, several hundred servicemen would receive lesser consequences, such as fines, reprimands, or extra duties. No one, however, was allowed merely a censure in 1940.[100] The army raised disciplinary stakes in 1940, but it is not clear that they had the desired effect.

SUMMARY

The Red Army made many promises to its soldiers, promises that no typical Western army would make. It promised a brotherly feeling between officers and men, a standardized work day, decent housing, good and adequate food. Other armies would not promise such things for various reasons. They would not promise a brotherly comradeship between the ranks because of the tried-and-true dictum that familiarity between officers and men leads to disrespect, indiscipline, and a loss of authority for officers. Western armies did not promise good and adequate food and decent housing simply because they were a given. And no army made the ridiculous promise of a regulated work day. By their very nature, military life and duties do not lend themselves to regularity.

Why, then, did the Red Army make these promises, and what were the ramifications of its failure to keep them? The promises were an attempt to persuade the Soviet people that the Red Army was drastically different from the old army, which had a terrible reputation for brutality and harsh conditions. We must consider that the Red Army soldier would not have compared his situation to that of a soldier in a capitalist army, for his knowledge thereof would have been extremely limited or nonexistent. He would have compared his army experience to what he was told of service in the old army, to his civilian life, and to the ideals portrayed in Soviet propaganda.

Compared to service in the Imperial Army, service in the Red Army was better in some ways and worse in others. The most significant difference was the lack of corporal punishment. Although corporal punishment had diminished in the Imperial Army decades before the Revolution and was outlawed in 1904, it did not totally disappear from the ranks. Memories of it were still fresh in the collective peasant memory, and, of course, the men were reminded of it as part of their military indoctrination.

The soldier's preconceptions conditioned his assessment of his lot in the army. The Red Army raised the future soldier's expectations during his preconscription training. Even before he showed up at the assembly point for final processing, he had been led to expect good food and plenty of it, adequate housing and some personal space, a nondemanding work schedule (or at least one not out of the ordinary), and kind, caring treatment from his superiors. The only thing he stood a good chance of getting was decent treatment from his officers, but not necessarily their care. Whether or not a conscript really believed all the army's promises, whether he was sympathetic to the efforts, however unsuccessful, of his superiors to improve his lot, depended on his own attitudes toward military service and toward the new regime. Despite the army's many problems, the conscript would have recognized it as representative of Soviet society and would most likely have evaluated its performance on that basis.

The general failure to meet these expectations eroded the army's credibility in the eyes of soldiers. In the thirties, the central administration of the military was clearly unable to solve its food problem through central management and direction and had to let the units fend for themselves to supplement what little the army could provide. As the RKKA expanded, soldiers in new divisions were subjected to stays in overcrowded or decrepit barracks, which resulted in poor morale and often contributed to poor discipline. The Red Army genuinely did want its men to have a decent life while in service, but a host of factors, many outside its control, such as the military budget and the civilian economy, prevented it from delivering on its promises.

An undisciplined army was the price the army paid for its failure to live up to its promises to create decent conditions for service and provide competent leaders. In all fairness, the RKKA faced some daunting obstacles: the backwardness of the society from which both officers and soldiers came; the at first underdeveloped and then too rapidly developed but skewed economy; objectionable social policies promoted by government and party that alienated soldiers; and, finally, the uncontrolled expansion of the army that exacerbated an environment of shortages.

CHAPTER 3

PUR and the Army: The Nonmilitary Side of Military Service

The Red Army soldier experienced far more than military training during his service, and that was exactly what the Communist party intended. The party saw the Red Army as a vehicle for molding the young peasant and worker into the "new Soviet man," that is, for "modernizing" him. According to PUR doctrine, "Instilling in each Red Army man the discipline of a citizen-soldier and selfless devotion to our party, this is the basic task of all political work in the Red Army."[1] This was to be done through political and antireligious instruction, and through basic literacy and elementary education. As part of its support of regime policies, PUR encouraged Red Army men to volunteer to be trained for work in collective agriculture, form collective farms upon their discharge, and do volunteer work in the countryside while still on active duty. These activities were concurrent with their military training and duties. The Political Administration of the RKKA, not the military cadre, oversaw these activities. Mark von Hagen has suggested that the party and army were successful during the twenties in their endeavor to transform young Soviet men, but it would appear that their success was limited to that decade. The army was not a unique vehicle for achieving these results; each of its socialization programs was duplicated in other sectors of society. Yes, the army explicitly attempted to modernize Soviet youth, especially rural youth, but nearly all facets of Soviet social policy in the twenties and thirties acted as modernizing forces, particularly industrialization, which touched a much larger segment of the population. Even so, many peasants and even working-class soldiers rejected and resisted key elements of socialization in the thirties, especially collectivization.

THE ORGANIZATION OF THE POLITICAL ADMINISTRATION

In the overall organization of the RKKA, the Political Administration (PURKKA, normally referred to as PUR), was directly under the authority of the Revolutionary Military Council but also answered to the Central Committee. Subordinate to PUR's main administration was the military district political apparatus, which was responsible for supervising the political apparatus of subordinate corps, which in turn supervised division political sections. Within divisions, the real political work was done in the regiments, and the most important facilitator of this work was the regimental commissar.[2]

The regimental political apparatus comprised the military commissar; the regimental bureau of the party, headed by the secretary; a Komsomol organization; battalion commissars; company political leaders (*politruki*); literacy schools; and the regiment's assorted clubs and libraries. PUR personnel were assigned to all units, down to company level. The regimental party bureau was responsible for organizing and supervising the work of the VLKSM in the regiment. The regimental party bureau also admitted soldiers to party membership, though the actual recruiting was done by party cells.[3]

In 1925, PUR formally defined its tasks at the regiment level. It intended to firmly and clearly lead the Bolshevik line in all party work, give a correct Leninist education to all party members, candidates, and Komsomols, and promote the activity and initiative of cells. Regimental organs were to establish a close association with nonparty soldiers, taking the opportunity to discover and act on their feelings, needs, and questions. Finally, PUR sought to pay maximum attention to party organizations and their leadership, the problems of military life and instruction, and the reinforcement of discipline.[4]

Of all the political personnel, the company *politruk* interacted most closely with the soldiers. As part of his political education duties, the *politruk* ran the company's political discussions. As party representative, he was instrumental in recruiting new party members. The *politruk* was responsible for establishing a party cell in his unit. The cells consisted of party members and candidates and acted as the primary party organization in the army. Cells, it should be noted, were party organs, not PUR organs. A secretary, who was not a PUR functionary but just a member of the unit, headed the cell. PUR had the goal of having a party cell in every company. It did not succeed.[5]

The party was responsible for manning PUR and training its members. Formal training of political personnel in PUR was almost nonexistent. PUR's ivory tower, the Tolmachev Military-Political Academy, offered a three-year curriculum for political leaders; however, classes averaged only two hundred men a year, so it was impossible to expect many PUR men to have attended. In fact, PUR often assigned young novitiate party members or candidates to political duties with no special instruction. PUR expected commissars to learn through practical experience and self-instruction from Marxist classics. The majority of political workers brought into the army in the late twenties and after started out in this way. From these inauspicious beginnings, they rose through the Political Administration hierarchy. In the early twenties, the process worked satisfactorily because many party activists, still fired with revolutionary zeal, served in PUR. In the late twenties, these people seem to have moved on and were replaced by men for whom political work was just a job, not a calling.[6]

PUR had significant problems with manning throughout the twenties and thirties. Recruiting and retention both proved difficult. In 1929, for example, 1,144 *politruki* and commissars left PUR, an astounding 79.8 percent, or 913 of them, just quit or refused to stay on after they fulfilled their two-year obligation. Replacing these men in sufficient quantity proved impossible as the army expanded. At the beginning of 1931, PUR was short 1,641 men; by the end of the year it was lacking 2,485, due both to discharges and increased requirements. To cover the shortage, PUR planned to call up 1,500 of its reserves in 1932, and the VLKSM promised to mobilize 150 Komsomols for duty. PUR itself could only produce about 800 *politruki* from its schools.[7] As the army grew during the thirties, PUR's shortages increased and its representation was spread thin, consequently degrading its influence in the units.

Generally, as a result of poor preparation, political instructors could not always provide the most sophisticated instruction. Many were themselves unsophisticated and semi-educated, and they poorly understood what they taught. Political training was usually poor, and the efforts of the political leaders varied widely. Ian Gamarnik, head of PUR in 1932, lamented that because of the insufficient preparation of *politruki* little successful ideological work had been done in the army during the last several years.[8]

The lack of sophistication and intellectual preparedness of some *politruki* is illustrated by an example given by Mikhail Soloviev, a military correspondent for *Izvestiia* in the thirties. In his rounds of an infantry company, Soloviev, accompanied by a *politruk* named Gavriliuk, entertained the men with a story about a Russian explorer, freely inventing facts and description to better help the peasant soldiers relate to the old Russian explorers and to pique their interest as well. Afterward, he held a general discussion in which the men expressed opinions on a wide variety of topics. Through it all, Gavriliuk was as taken in and enthralled as the soldiers, and, according to Soloviev, "He genuinely believed that he and I were engaged in 'political educational work.'"[9] In Soloviev's personal assessment, the lower grades of *politruki* were just talking machines. Their instruction in Marxism-Leninism and its application to current events was well beyond the comprehension of most Communists and "what is left is not knowledge itself, but a stereotyped version of the particular subject in question." According to Soloviev:

The political instructor is thus perfectly capable of trotting out an answer to literally any question that comes up. If a soldier tells him: "My family at home is starving, they ought to be helped," the political instructor automatically retorts: "That, comrade soldier, is an ailment of growth. Now

we'll develop our industry, consolidate the collective farms, and everything will be O.K." After which the soldier doesn't even bother to point
out that while industry is being developed and the collective farms consolidated his family will die of starvation; or if he does dare to make such
a comment he is told that mortality is very low in the present socialist society and it will drop still more in the future. The soldier goes away angry
and disillusioned; but the political instructor enters in the appropriate
column that he has had a "personal conversation" on collective farm construction and the fall of the Soviet mortality rate. They [politruki] are
stuffed full with quotations, superficial information, and instructions, and
thus they do the work of the party.[10]

Another memoirist's opinion of PUR was that, "The vast majority of the
commissars consist of people who not only cannot be said to have no [sic]
outstanding intellectual gifts but in all matters of military knowledge . . . are
complete ignoramuses."[11] Their lack of military knowledge hurt their credibility with the men and the officers as well.

The preceding accounts contradict the conclusions drawn by many Western historians that PUR was efficient, influential, and powerful within the
military. John Erickson typifies such thinking with his statement: "At the senior levels, Gamarnik's men had become skilled political experts, with accent
on theoretical knowledge and a certain intellectualism. Lower down the
scale, the political assistant was trained to do an efficient job but was much
more a cog in a huge machine."[12] Indeed, some individuals were well versed
in Marxism, but by and large in the thirties the type of politruk represented
by Gavriliuk became more and more prevalent. By 1934, there were 15,000
political personnel in PUR responsible for educating some 700,000 soldiers.
One-third, with little or no training, had joined PUR after 1930 as a result of
party mobilizations. Social origins may also have been a barrier to indoctrination, in that most politruki were from the working class but most soldiers
were peasants.[13]

COMMUNIST SOLDIERS

Communist party members were always in the minority in the army, especially in the enlisted ranks. Krasnoarmeitsy and junior commanders usually
accounted for only a quarter of military party members; officers made up the
majority. The constant turnover of enlisted men and the growth of the army
were the main reasons why PUR had a difficult time maintaining company
party cells. As a result, in 1935, regimental party bureaus were designated
primary party organizations in cases where there were not enough Commu-

nists to establish company or battalion cells. In many divisions, it took a whole regiment of Communists to have a decent-sized party meeting.[14] Military party membership mirrored that of the party as a whole: most party members were from the working class, and workers were in the minority in the army. Of the peasants that did join the party, the majority were poor peasants (*bedniaki*). Landless peasants (*batraki*) were classified as workers. The big boost in the number of workers as a percentage of all party members came from the officer corps' party membership. In 1930, more officers were party members than ever before, and the majority of officers were of nonpeasant origin.[15]

Much more was expected of the Communist party member and Komsomol soldier than of the average nonparty soldier. They were exhorted to set the example in discipline and military bearing. Communists were expected to be active in the party cell and in the activities of political circles and associated clubs. Party members were to agitate among the non-Communists and involve them in political activities. During the Civil War, after a company of Red infantry had been routed, the commissar suggested that the Communists be shot as an example to the rest.[16] Such were the burdens of the communist soldier.

Communist soldiers were told that "Communists and Komsomols are the cement of the Red Army."[17] They were the first to be recruited for work on shock brigades. In the twenties, PUR expected them to help in grain requisitioning on weekends. In the thirties, they were the first enlisted to "help" the peasants collectivize. They were also called on to lead subscription drives for the various loans for industrialization and defense. Even in peacetime, being a communist soldier certainly had its drawbacks. Perhaps for these reasons, even as party and Komsomol membership grew, many men refused invitations to join the party or let their party and Komsomol memberships lapse.

Communist soldiers were supposed to watch their fellow soldiers and report anti-Soviet attitudes. Those Communists who actually followed this line were not well regarded by their peers. In his memoirs, Boris Balinsky, a rank-and-file soldier, described how the actions of the Communists in his artillery battery separated them from the average soldier.

The behavior of the soldiers in our squad was at all times watched by the Communists in our midsts, every word was noted. This became evident one day when there was held, in the evening, an "open meeting of the Communist party organization." Open meeting meant that non-Communists were allowed to attend, and of course it would have been very rash for anyone not to accept the invitation. At the meeting, apart from the general political situation internal affairs in the squad were aired, and accusations against some soldiers were made. The secretary of the Communist Youth League, Derevyanko, raised an accusation against me.

"Balinsky" he said, "was saying that he wants to go home, and intends to get a new flat from the Academy of Sciences." This was a crude misrepresentation and distortion of a conversation I did have.[18]

The party called other meetings for self-criticism (*samokritika*). At these meetings, the faults of everyone were supposed to be aired so that corrective measures could be taken. The word *samokritika* is misleading, because one did not actually offer serious criticism of oneself; rather, one criticized others in the unit. All ranks were supposedly open for criticism, but, according to one private, "It was very risky and dangerous for a man to criticize his superior at an open meeting."[19] Not all enlisted men were intimidated, however, and officers sometimes complained that at party cell meetings enlisted men often acted as though they had the right to give orders. Even enlisted party leaders tried to squash criticism of their actions or at least keep knowledge of their shortcomings from getting outside the cell. These practices were not unknown to the PUR hierarchy and were often criticized.[20]

PUR considered *samokritika* a serious matter, especially when a *chistka* (purging the party rolls of those deemed unfit) was in progress. At these times, the military press took great pains to encourage and even demand self-criticism as necessary for keeping party members in tune with the party line and active in their cells. *Chistka* commissions used information gained from *samokritika* sessions to weed out the less disciplined and less serious card-carrying party members.

What were the advantages of being a communist soldier, and why would anyone consent to nomination to the party? The complaints of nonparty members give a clue. Soldiers complained that when uniforms were issued, some old and some new, the party members received the new ones. They accused party members of using their status to get the softer duties. In the regiments Communists usually got the library and newspaper jobs, thereby avoiding their military duties and such unpleasant activities as going to the field in winter and washing horses and cleaning stables. For special supplies, equipment, or privileges, Communists could bypass military procedures and use party channels to get what they wanted. The party criticized such practices to no avail. There were also many postservice advantages associated with party membership.[21]

CHISTKA IN THE ARMY

Along with the party's stress on recruitment within the military, the Red Army was subjected to party purges called *chistki*, which were designed to expel undeserving people from the party. These purges did not come in the dead of night as a surprise to unwitting victims. Quite the opposite. They were announced months in advance in the military press and in memorandums to the military's party organs. Regimental party bureaus were told to prepare for certification commissions, and they in turn instructed company cells to engage in self-criticism to identify the unfit beforehand, to facilitate the work of the commissions. In 1933, PUR published explicit instructions on the preparation and conduct of *chistki*.[22]

Reasons for being purged included holding Menshevik or Trotskyite ideas; knowing Nepmen (in the twenties); failing to adhere to the party line; party passivity; isolating oneself from the party masses; having no value to the political apparatus; sexual depravity; military indiscipline; associating with kulaks or other enemies of the people; having been married by the church; and other infractions along these lines. Soldiers expelled from the party were not, however, always ousted from the military. Until 1937, it was unusual for soldiers or officers to be discharged solely for party matters. When soldiers were discharged as a result of *chistki*, it was usually for a combination of political and moral factors.[23]

The party conducted *chistki* simultaneously in the army (including the territorial units) and in civilian party organizations. Military and civilian *chistki* were not always conducted according to a uniform pattern. Victor Kravchenko described a *chistka* at his technical institute in 1933 that was a public affair. In the presence of a large audience, the party member to be examined stood before the *chistka* verification committee, which was armed with information supplied by the primary party organization. After handing over his party card, he recited his political life history. The commission gave back the party cards to those who passed the subsequent examination of their social origins and political behavior. People suspected of being in trouble were often taunted by members of the audience who urged the commission to expel them. Those who failed the test were expelled from the party on the spot.[24]

Civilians in managerial positions who were expelled from the party often lost their jobs, or, if they were students in higher education, were expelled from their school, because it usually took party credentials to attain a managerial position or to enter higher education from the period of the first five-year plan and thereafter. The trauma could be so great that those purged sometimes committed suicide.[25]

Chistki procedures in the Red Army differed somewhat from those in civilian party organs. There were normally two methods of determining who would be expelled. Both involved the use of verification commissions formed by the military district headquarters on orders from the RVS and PUR. One method was for the verification commission to ask regiments and higher political sections to prepare a list of party members, candidates, and Komsomols they recommended for expulsion. Then the commission would simply read the reports about each individual and either endorse the recommendation or overturn it. Party members were able to appeal their expulsion to the verification commission, which would normally then hold a hearing to decide the man's fate.[26]

The other method required the verification commission to do all the examining and decision making regarding expulsion. Prior to the arrival of the verification commission, regimental party bureaus prepared by having party cells engage in *samokritika*. The commission then met with the party bureau, composed of the regimental party secretary, his assistants, and the regimental commissar, and read the results of the self-criticism sessions. Seated at a table, they would call individuals to be examined into a private room one at a time. The person being examined usually stood alone facing his interrogators. After listening to his story, the commission asked him questions and then delivered a verdict on his membership in the party, sometimes immediately but often after short deliberations.[27] The army's *chistki* seem to have been well organized and private, which helped maintain discipline in the unit and the authority of the officers during the proceedings. If there was a point at which proceedings were unstructured, it was at the *samokritika* sessions, where members' faults were laid out and candidates for expulsion identified; but cells often closed these sessions to nonparty members and even Communists from other units.[28]

Communists who served in the army were generally quite lenient toward each other when it came to *chistki*. For example, between December 1929 and August 1930, during the upheaval of collectivization and dekulakization that created a "right opportunist deviation," the XVIII Rifle Corps purged itself and found only thirty-three men to expel, of whom twelve were also recommended for discharge. After appeals, thirty-two men were expelled and ten discharged—a small number, indeed, for a corps comprising three divisions and supporting elements. Similarly the 21st Rifle Division conducted a *chistki* in 1929 and expelled 63 of the 837 party members examined. The top three reasons for expulsion were association with class enemies (seventeen cases), alienation from the party masses (eleven cases), and indiscipline (ten cases).[29] In two battalions of the XI Territorial Rifle Corps, forty-eight officers were examined and only two expelled in the 1933 *chistka*. Three of the officers examined proved to be masquerading as party members and were disciplined for their fraud.[30]

The basis on which army Communists judged each other is evidenced by the 1929 *chistka* in the 35th Rifle Division. In this division, only nine men, all officers, were purged, and two of them were discharged from the army. The final report of the 35th Rifle Division cited party passivity and distance from the Red Army masses for the expulsion of most of the officers. Some of the more serious reasons for expulsion were having fought on the side of the

Whites in the Civil War, being a former Trotskyite, sexual perversion, disagreeing with party policies, and being the son of a kulak. Of the two officers discharged from the army, one was a sexually dissolute pervert who had served in Kolchak's army, so it is quite understandable why he was let go, but the other was merely labeled a squabbler who was "distant from the Red Army masses."[31] Because the army had no party membership requirements, there was no reason to discharge men for no longer being in the party. Yet expulsion from the party could have serious consequences for officers, for promotions to the higher levels of the army were often linked to party membership. Losing one's party card could mean the stifling of a career. It was, paradoxically, actually worse for an officer to have been a Communist and been expelled from the party than never to have been in the party at all. Officers who lost their party cards carried the stigma of being distrusted by the party. Those who had never joined the party had the potential of becoming members.

The military purge had a special twist: men were purged not only for political reasons but also if they were deficient militarily. *Chistki,* therefore, served as a means of reinforcing military discipline among party members.[32] Thus, failure in one's military duties could mean being booted out of the party; however, the true purpose of *chistki* was to preserve political conformity and the power of the Communist party in the army.

POLITICAL INSTRUCTION

In the late twenties, the purpose of political instruction was not to explain Marxism-Leninism to illiterate peasants but to emphasize the benefits of Soviet power and to convince them of the necessity of obeying the Soviet regime. According to one high-ranking PUR leader in 1928, "The real backbone of the worker and peasant army is the young peasant, who comes into the ranks of the Red Army with all the prejudices which exist in the countryside, [and] who receives letters from the countryside fostering these prejudices."[33] Such was the rationale for two of the primary concepts conveyed to the soldiers, Soviet patriotism and proletarian internationalism, which were intended to loosen the peasant's ties to the village and give him a broader outlook.

Political instruction was always haphazard and conducted inconsistently from unit to unit. In units of one-man command, political training sometimes died a rapid death. Commanders occasionally ran roughshod over their *politruki* and their duties. In the 17th Artillery Regiment, for example, the battery *politruk* Mikhailev was conducting political instruction with young soldiers on the theme "How the Workers' and Peasants' Red Army Was Built." During the first ten minutes of instruction, five men left to do a fatigue detail on the orders of the battery commander. Several minutes later a new order came for the release of six more soldiers. Nine men remained in the group. Not yet halfway through the hour of instruction, a third order came from the commander to release another two men for fatigues. This scenario was considered normal in the regiment. PUR argued that this situation was not desirable, that political instruction should be respected by small unit commanders, and that political instructors and commanders should better coordinate training time to minimize conflicts.[34] Such practices made a mockery of K. Voroshilov's statement, "The Red Army is a first-class school of military-political and cultural education of men."[35]

Cultural development of the soldier, also an aspect of political instruction, was thus the responsibility of PUR. *Politruki* showed films, organized cultural excursions, and encouraged the men to form clubs, such as literature and music circles and groups organized around sports, art, nature, agriculture, and drama. Exactly how active these clubs and circles were is open to question. Some units had none. Efforts to increase the sophistication of the Soviet citizen were not unique to the Red Army but pervaded Soviet society. Because of PUR's concentrated efforts, the peasant soldier, depending on his unit, more than likely received more real exposure to culture than the average peasant and maybe even as much or more than the average worker.

THE CAMPAIGN TO ELIMINATE ILLITERACY

An essential part of turning conscripts into new Soviet men was teaching them to read and write. For the most part, this task fell to the political workers and military officers in the units and was officially sponsored by PUR. Initially, this was a huge task, considering that an overwhelming percentage of *krasnoarmeitsy* were peasants who represented the least educated segment of Soviet society. In 1927, for example, 70 to 80 percent of the rural poor were illiterate.[36]

The idea to use the military as a locus for literacy instruction did not originate with the Red Army. As part of the Miliutin reforms in the latter half of the nineteenth century, the Imperial Army had endeavored to use the military as an agent of modernization through literacy. Forrestt Miller, an historian of reform-era Russia, claims that "the army had become even at this early date [1868] the school of the nation and was proving more effective at the dissemination of primary education than was the Ministry of Public Education."[37] The British army, in comparison, had been teaching literacy since the 1840s. In the 1930s, the British reported that nearly one-quarter of their annual intake of recruits required instruction. The difference between the British and Red armies was their criteria of semi-literate and illiterate. The

Meeting of a party cell.

British considered any man who had four years or less of schooling to be semi-literate and in need of further education.[38] A *krasnoarmeets* who could but sign his name was labeled semi-literate. The Red Army considered men with only four years of schooling potential officer candidates. The Red Army claimed to do an extremely fine job of literacy instruction until the task was eventually obviated by the spread of public education in the USSR. The British army continues to instruct its undereducated soldiers.

One Soviet source from the twenties claimed that between 1 January 1926 and the end of October 1926, 33,795 illiterate *krasnoarmeitsy* achieved literacy. The Leningrad Military District claimed that its units instructed almost the same number (30,000) of illiterate and semi-literate men, but over a five-year time period, 1924–1929. Not all of the men given literacy instruction actually achieved literacy, but the RKKA asserted that most did. Voroshilov went so far as to claim in 1933 that "after nearly ten years not one Red Army man leaves the ranks of the army illiterate."[39] This was an especially bold claim considering that for the duration of the literacy campaign many party cells and officers charged by PUR to give instruction sloughed off this task despite frequent admonishment.[40]

The army combined its campaign to combat illiteracy with an effort to give soldiers an elementary education. At the end of 1928, regiments began offering evening education classes. The teachers were often fellow soldiers, officers, or local civilians hired by the army. Besides reading and writing, they taught basic mathematics skills. These classes stepped up their work in 1929 through the end of the first five-year plan.[41]

One of the army's many slogans of 1933 was "Not one illiterate man is to enter the RKKA." This stipulation did not mean that illiteracy was a way to evade military service; rather it meant that literacy instruction was to become part of preconscription training. Conscription commissions identified preconscription-age males as literate or illiterate, and sent the latter to "literacy points" for intensive instruction. As the stress shifted to preconscription literacy training, the formal campaign to eliminate illiteracy in the regular army trailed off in 1934 and seemed to end in 1935, although literacy classes continued to be held in the units for several more years.[42]

The main difference between the Red Army's literacy campaign and the tsarist army's literacy movement was that the Imperial Army *wanted* to teach its soldiers to read and write while the Red Army *needed* to teach its men to read and write. For the Imperial Army, it was a luxury to have literate men; for the Red Army, it was a necessity because of the increased mechanization and technological sophistication of the armed forces. Increasingly more tasks required basic literacy and elementary mathematics. As the years went by, there were greater numbers of artillerymen, tankers, aviators, mechanics, signalmen and other support personnel who had a great need to be able to read and write. For this reason, the Red Army could not treat the literacy campaign as an inconvenience or distraction from training, as many officials had done in the Imperial Army. The Red Army had an easier time sustaining literacy instruction because all of Soviet society made literacy a priority. Party activists and Komsomols working through soviets, trade unions, and cooperatives taught in factories, cooperatives, and villages across the USSR. Thus, adult literacy instruction in the twenties and thirties in Soviet society was not unique to the Red Army.[43]

THE ANTIRELIGIOUS CAMPAIGN

The new culture of the Soviet Republic was intended to be not only socialist but atheist as well. For this reason, the League of the Militant Godless (*Soiuz Voinstvuiushchikh Bezbozhnikov*, SVB), which had been active in civilian society since 1925, began an antireligious campaign within the RKKA under the auspices of PUR. The SVB took soldiers on excursions to antireligious and secular museums, electrical power stations, former monasteries, observatories, factories, and nearby *sovkhozes* to promote a scientific understanding of the world and the secular accomplishments of the

Soviet state. The settings served as backdrops for atheistic speeches and lectures and were usually followed by question-and-answer periods. The goal of the League of the Militant Godless was to expose Red Army men to as much antireligious propaganda as possible. The general theme of antireligious instruction was that religion was superstition, a drug that prevented cultural development. The league labeled church and clergy class-based tools of capitalists and imperialists.[44]

With approval of unit commissars, the SVB sought to establish cells in every unit to assist PUR and officers in antireligious work. Some basic tasks of the SVB were to develop antireligious work in companies, Lenin corners, among the rank-and-file soldiers in general, and especially among Komsomols and leading Red Army men. The SVB people conducted their work through talks; dissemination of the league's newspaper, *Bezbozhnik;* speeches; lectures; parties; excursions; and participation in corners and circles.[45]

The SVB's work in the army did not go uncontested. Some soldiers actively resisted atheism and clandestinely preached Christianity while antireligious campaigning was in progress. In fact, in the twenties and early thirties, believers were in the majority in the average rifle division. The army estimated that about 4,500 to 6,500 men within a regular division of from 6,000 to 8,000 men were believers. The SVB, meanwhile, boasted 137,199 members in the army in 1932. Although this represents less than one-fifth of the regular army, it is rather a strong showing when compared with the weak performance of the civilian godless.[46] Yet even this number is most likely an exaggeration. Many SVB cell leaders, in order to show progress in their work, asked their comrades if they could enroll them but did no antireligious work. There were jokes in the Red Army that many SVB cells did not do any antireligious work but, in an effort to create the necessary statistics the party craved, simply handed out membership cards.[47] Some of the men may indeed have allowed the SVB to sign them up out of antireligious conviction, but others may have done so just to get the SVB off their back or to do a friend a favor.

The antireligious campaign is an important example of the forms of indoctrination imposed upon soldiers. Genuine believers were offended. According to Nicholas Timasheff, "Persecution of religion bred hostility in large masses of the people towards the Soviet regime."[48] Others did not care, while some may have thought it was reasonable. In the end, the soldiers associated the antireligious campaigns with the new regime, for better or worse. The final result was that religion was suppressed but not eliminated. The antireligious campaign fizzled as the first five-year plan progressed, and, after 1932, antireligion was seldom mentioned in the military press; indeed, little mention of the antireligious campaign ever made it into the military press—that subject seems to have been consigned to *Bezbozhnik.*

PUR AND COLLECTIVIZATION

Under Stalin, the Soviet regime was intent on changing the existing system of private capitalist agriculture to socialized agriculture through collectivization. The party intended to collectivize all peasants, so it made sense to organize peasant soldiers while they were in the army. PUR took on the task of organizing everything in the army associated with collectivization. The movement to involve soldiers in collectivization was multifaceted. It encouraged peasant soldiers to establish collective farms on land given them by the state after they were discharged; it encouraged soldiers who owned independent farms to join their village collectives upon their discharge; while still in the service, politicized soldiers were encouraged to persuade civilians to join collectives; and, finally, it called for training peasant soldiers in various trades associated with agriculture so they could work on collective farms, machine tractor stations (MTSs), or in rural administration upon their discharge.

PUR did not form teams of soldiers to go out and dekulakize rich peasants or force unwilling peasants to join *kolkhozes*. There were such teams, but the Special Sections of the OGPU in the army organized and led them. PUR officials often assisted by actively recruiting soldiers, both party and nonparty members, to participate. Most of the collectivization effort that PUR supervised was geared to what soldiers would do when they returned to their villages after their stint in the army.

PUR perhaps suffered its greatest failure in the socialist reconstruction of the countryside. Not only did PUR fail to win over a sizable number of peasant soldiers to the idea of collectivization or dekulakization in the manner envisioned by the state, but it aggravated an already tense discipline and morale situation in the army. Most peasants conscripted into the army in 1929–1930, when the Urals-Siberian method of coercive grain procurement was in practice and massive collectivization and dekulakization were begun, did not favor the goals of the regime or the means employed to achieve them. Being forced to choose between joining collectives and maintaining their individual holdings created conflict within and between individuals, families, and whole villages and, consequently, between those entities and the Soviet state.

The first facet of the movement to collectivize soldiers was called the soldiers' collectivization movement. It encouraged peasant soldiers to form special "initiative collective farms" to show other peasants the benefits of collectivization in the hope that they would form *kolkhozes* on their own. Soldiers who participated would not return to their home villages after their discharge but would start anew wherever they established their *kolkhoz*. This movement attracted soldiers who had little hope of being reintegrated in the

PUR-sponsored entertainment for the soldiers during a break in summer training.

life of their old villages, namely, poor and landless peasants. There was a high correlation between party membership and joining or forming these agricultural collectives.[49]

On 2 February 1929, the Central Executive Committee and Council of Peoples Commissars (SNK) approved the founding of the collectives. In April of that year, PUR began to prepare the prospective collective farmers for *kolkhoz* life while still on active duty. For the rest of the year, the military press filled its pages with stories about soldiers forming collectives upon discharge and the support given them by their former units, PUR, and local party organs.[50]

Soldiers formed most collectives in the districts where they served. Their units, PUR, and the local party organs were supposed to support the soldiers' collectives. Despite the prominence given the movement in the military press, the party and government did not always hold up their end. Many collectives folded before their first harvest due to poor organization and lack of

support from the state. Some farms never got off the ground because of dis-
agreements between soldiers. There was even an instance where the head of
the farm wasted the start-up funds on drink and debauchery.[51]

PUR criticized its *politruki* for distorting portrayals of collective farm life.
In their zeal to recruit soldiers, the *politruki* often related only the good
things about collective farming, failing to mention that there would be much
hard work to do.[52] Because of poor preparation, lack of support, and miscon-
ceptions about collective farming, many soldiers' collectives failed rather
quickly and did not serve as the shining examples the party had intended.

PUR exerted a more intense effort to get soldiers to form or join collective farms among the territorial forces, and for good reason. More peasants
served in the territorial forces, and greater results could presumably be
obtained more quickly. Therefore, the political administration made a
major effort between 1929 and 1931 to draw peasant *terrarmeitsy* into the
collectivization movement.[53] First PUR encouraged landless peasant soldiers to found collectives on government land. Next came a campaign to
enlist middle peasants in local *kolkhozes*. In the first years of the collectivization drive and liquidation of kulaks, the party realized that "the middle peasants were still waiting with regard to the idea of collectivization."
For example, PUR surveyed the mostly middle peasant new recruits of a
territorial artillery regiment in 1929. They were asked if they approved of
collectivization and if they were willing to join a collective. Of the seventy
respondents, twenty-three approved, forty were undecided, and seven
were adamantly opposed.[54]

Not only did PUR have trouble with reluctant territorial soldiers, but it
also had difficulty with *vnevoiskoviki*. At one training assembly in the Siberian Military District in 1929, not one of several hundred peasant trainees
agreed to join collective farms. PUR's response to this was to say that these
men had a "kulak stench" about them. Even in an assembly of nonpeasant
soldiers, the *politruki* reported that the men had developed a "peasant sentiment" because of the close relationship many had to the countryside and
their support of the peasants in their resistance to PUR's coercion, openly
questioning the party's policies in the countryside.[55] Both the terms "kulak
stench" and "peasant sentiment" refer to attitudes hostile to collectivization.

The emphasis on collectivization continued the next year. In summer
1930, PUR ordered *politruki* of territorial units to intensify their work among
the soldiers during both the assembly and periods between assemblies, with
the goal of having them found *kolkhozes* in their villages. The *politruki* did
not always meet with success. For example, the 61st Rifle Regiment held
training between assemblies over Easter, and during the training the commissar announced that at the end of the assembly all the peasant soldiers would
have to join *kolkhozes*. This caused twenty-one *terrarmeitsy* to desert at their

first opportunity. Everywhere in the RKKA in 1930 reports filtered in of the "peasant sentiments" of territorial soldiers, new recruits, and even officers.[56]

Even though PUR's work of collectivizing *terrarmeitsy* involved collecting mere promises, it created much trouble for the army. The Political Administration of the Leningrad Military District reported in the summer of 1930: "There is active resistance by Red Army men, especially among those who have family with a kulak sentiment. . . . Parallel with this observation is the well-known spreading of kulak sentiments, which is most highly developed in the territorial units and only a little less so in regular divisions."[57] Throughout 1929 and 1930, political sections throughout the RKKA reported the development of "peasant sentiments," among regular and territorial units, even among the select recruits picked to be junior commanders. When *politruki* fully explained collectivization policy, soldiers often reacted in the extreme, as exemplified by one soldier's exclamation, "I would sooner shoot myself than join a *kolkhoz*."[58]

PUR not only put pressure on soldiers to form or join collective farms upon their discharge, but it attempted to use soldiers still in service to pressure civilians. During fall 1929 and spring 1930, when mass forced collectivization began, PUR sponsored a letter-writing campaign. *Politruki* urged soldiers to write to their relatives in the village touting the advantages of socialized agriculture and encouraging them to form collective farms.[59] For the most part, the only soldiers who agreed to do this were those who had already decided to form or join collective farms upon their discharge. In some cases, these letters seem to have worked. A letter from a Red Army soldier and future *kolkhoznik* sometimes convinced the rest of the family to support the collectivization of their village. In many cases, however, there was considerable and sharp backlash against soldiers who wrote such letters. One soldier received letters from his uncle and wife denouncing his decision to join a *kolkhoz*. His wife wrote, "Because you have joined a *kolkhoz* you are no longer my husband and I am no longer your wife." Another soldier got a letter saying, "You are a hooligan, an enemy of the whole village, to the devil with *kolkhozes* and Soviet power."[60] Whether these men reconsidered their decisions is not known, but it certainly illustrates the conflicts collectivization forced on the men.

Civilian peasants spontaneously conducted a counter letter-writing campaign against collectivization. As the mass collectivization drive grew in intensity, families wrote more frequently to their soldier relatives of the difficulties in the countryside. In sympathy with their families, many soldiers wrote home swearing they would never join a *kolkhoz* and went so far as to agitate against collectivization among their military peers. One soldier told his friends: "My mother left the *kolkhoz* she was in and I will not volunteer to join one. The party is worse than the kulaks in its exploitation of the peasants." His mother had informed him that the *kolkhoz* leadership were all party members who only gave orders and did no work. Another soldier, hearing of the ongoing disaster in the villages, not only forbade his wife to sign them up in the *kolkhoz* being formed in their village but ordered her to leave the countryside altogether, abandon their holdings, and seek work in the city.[61] Such letters were common, and the anticollectivization talk they engendered prevailed in the barracks at this time despite PUR's efforts.

A coincidental campaign by the regime "to eliminate the kulaks as a class," created even more serious problems than the collectivization campaign. The question of what to do with kulaks, which translated into anyone excluded from the *kolkhozes*, became very divisive, tearing the party cells apart and causing confusion in PUR's ranks. The fundamental problem was that the average soldier, peasant or worker, party member or nonmember, enlisted man or officer, thought kulaks should be eliminated as a class through confiscation of their wealth but not persecuted by the state. The consensus was that former kulaks should be allowed to join *kolkhozes*. A large number of soldiers objected immediately, openly, and unequivocally to the party's self-proclaimed "new policy." The policy split the party cells into opposing factions and indeed created what the party labeled a "right opportunist deviation" in the party organs and PUR. It was a rightist trend in that it represented a soft attitude toward class enemies, like Bukharin's Right Opposition in 1928–1929—in this case, treating kulaks as though they were no longer class enemies after their dispossession. It was considered opportunist in that it supposedly represented an attempt to create a political faction that could bid for power, in the manner of Bukharin in the last round of the power struggle. And it was deviant in that it strayed from the party's general line. A parallel "deviation" arose in rural civilian party organs as well.[62]

Soldiers challenged their *politruki* and commissars with some powerful logic, questioning the party's self-proclaimed "new policy in the countryside." At a meeting of his party cell, one soldier asked, "Why is it impossible to accept good Soviet kulaks in *kolkhozes*; if we can keep old officers who were former class enemies in our army, then just why is it impossible for kulaks to enter *kolkhozes*?" At a similar meeting, another soldier said, "The kulaks do not need to be annihilated, they need to be taken into the *kolkhozes* so they can show the poor people how they ought to work." Such opinions were common and were roundly reproved by higher officials in PUR during fall and winter 1929–1930. "Right deviationists" were condemned as lackeys of the discredited Bukharin, Rykov, and Tomskii faction that Stalin had defeated in 1928.[63] In the cells, vehement arguments ensued and members' political status was challenged; some were even threatened with the loss of their party cards for being "soft on kulaks." One communist soldier, opposing such threats, termed them "political hooliganism."[64]

Not surprising, with the party organs in disagreement over the appropriateness of the party line, PUR's effectiveness suffered in communicating a coherent message to the soldiers justifying collectivization. According to one *starshina*, among the one hundred peasants in his company, only one understood the socialist reconstruction of the countryside. The rest who did not "understand" presumably were in opposition to party policy. In many units, the political organs and unit leaders proved reluctant to push collectivization after meeting resistance from their men. In many cases, they could not even get their own cell members to agree to join *kolkhozes* upon discharge. That PUR could not depend on the party cells to conform is amply illustrated by the case of the assistant commander of the 36th Rifle Regiment who was sent to his home area to agitate for the party's policies but ended up denouncing the new policies while drinking with a group of kulaks, one of whom was his brother. For this episode, he was expelled from the party and discharged from the army. Cases abounded of party members and Komsomols refusing to join *kolkhozes* and forbidding wives to join.[65]

As a result of their "ignorance," and despite the possibility of arrest by the Special Sections, soldiers were quite brazen in their criticism of dekulakization as practiced and of collectivization in general. In many instances, soldiers opposed to collectivization harangued and even threatened procollectivization soldiers with bodily harm or even death. Two middle income peasants (*seredniak*) soldiers attempted to murder their party cell leader over the issue of dekulakization. There was also class-based antagonism. One *politruk* quoted a soldier as saying, "Workers love to walk around with their briefcases giving orders. Workers have no right to be in the countryside dekulakizing working peasants, taking everything. Now, because of it, people are facing starvation." The peasants most hostile to collectivization and dekulakization were the middle peasants, but even many poor peasants voiced opposition.[66]

In an effort to eliminate opposition to the party's rural policies, the army discharged nearly ten thousand soldiers and officers from the regular and territorial forces in 1929–1930. Reasons for discharge ranged from being a kulak or the son of a kulak; having relatives who were boycotting state grain purchases or state goods or both; associating with class enemies; and exhibiting counter-revolutionary tendencies.[67] The party also conducted a general *chistka* with the aim of cleaning out all class aliens, specifically kulaks and speculators. Overall, however, the party did not expel many men, and *politruki* reported a reluctance among soldiers to accuse each other of infractions or recommend people for expulsion. Some of those expelled were labeled kulaks or friends of kulaks, and some were "exposed" as relatives of kulaks. Others did not have to be exposed or expelled but quit the party or Komsomol out of conviction. Two students of the Tomsk Artillery School, one a *batrak*, submitted resignations from the party because "they did not understand the new policies of the party in the countryside."[68]

The most active and least publicized participation in collectivization by soldiers was that of teams, otherwise known as brigades (*brigady*), that went out to dekulakize and force peasants to collectivize. The Special Sections of the OGPU temporarily assembled these brigades. Volunteers for the brigades were overwhelmingly party members or Komsomols. When on assignment to dekulakize, they were completely under the control of the Special Sections, even to the exclusion of the military chain of command. Brigades kept the identities of their members secret, and for good reason. In cases where their fellow soldiers found out they had been out dekulakizing or collectivizing, brigade workers often received rather harsh treatment.[69]

In some instances, however, soldiers pursued dekulakization with a vengeance, but with particularly selfish motives. A battalion of the 29th Rifle Regiment in the Leningrad Military District formed a brigade of fourteen men, most of them officers, to assist the Special Sections in dekulakizing a nearby village. In the process, the officers stole six divans, fifty chairs, four lamps, and four horse collars on behalf of the battalion. This theft created a terrific row between the brigade and the *kolkhozniks*. It was only settled when the officers relented and turned the horse collars over to the collective farmers. To make matters worse, after dividing the property, two members of the brigade, a company commander and his *starshina*, began ransacking the former kulaks' houses in search of gold and silver—presumably for themselves. This was the last straw for the battalion commissar, who made a formal complaint against the two for setting a bad example for their subordinates.[70]

Brigades of military school students worked in the countryside during school vacations and holidays. The Omsk infantry school, for example, sent eleven brigades to help collectivize *bedniak* and *seredniak* farms in winter 1930. Seven of these brigades consisted exclusively of Komsomols. Although the Omsk infantry school was very active in collectivization, the territorial regiment stationed there was not. In contrast to the enthusiasm shown by the students of the infantry school, the entire Omsk Territorial Rifle Regiment could only organize one brigade of sixteen men for collectivization work in Omsk *raion* in the winter of 1930. Obviously, the average peasant *terrarmeitsy* showed a great reluctance to participate in such activities.[71]

One of the most dangerous things soldiers did was to agitate for collectivization among the peasants. Again, this activity was purely voluntary and almost exclusively engaged in by party members. Angry peasants killed or wounded many agitators on their rounds. The soldiers were particularly vulnerable because they worked alone or in very small groups, as did civilian agitators, of whom many hundreds, if not thousands, were killed by peasants.[72]

In the end, neither the Communist party nor PUR were able to bring the "right deviationists" into line or squash the anticollectivization sentiments of many of the soldiers, despite major ideological efforts. What finally brought the crisis to a close was Stalin's "Dizzy with Success" speech of March 1930. With this speech, which blamed the excesses of mass collectivizing and dekulakization on the local party organs, Stalin called for a relaxation of the tempo of collectivization, leading the peasant masses to think it would in the future be voluntary. The immediate effect of the speech in the army was for thousands of soldiers who had promised to join collectives to cross their names off those lists. Similarly, thousands of *kolkhozes* broke up as civilian peasants left them in droves.[73] For the rest of 1930, collectivization seemed almost to have been a taboo topic. There was little mention of it the military press or in political reports from the regiment level to military district. The collectivization campaign in the army did pick up again in 1931, but at a much lower key.

Another major PUR program was training men for work in agriculture after their discharge. The party hoped to use the army as a vehicle for the socialist reconstruction of the countryside. All categories of men participated in this training: *batraki, bedniaki,* and *seredniaki,* workers and white-collar employees, and *kolkhozniks* and independent farmers.[74] The party expected that these specially trained men, when they left the army, would give collective agriculture a boost and carry the party line into the rural areas. The program to send trained cadres to the countryside started long before collectivization but picked up momentum as collectivization began. In 1925, PUR trained 12,000 men for work in the countryside. In 1927, another 30,000 soldiers were trained. On the eve of collectivization in 1928, PUR prepared nearly 68,000 men for work in the countryside. The next year an additional 71,000 men were trained for rural work.[75]

Soldiers who volunteered for training for work in the countryside received instruction from PUR personnel or local party organs, beginning six to eight months before their discharge. The courses usually consisted of between 150 and 200 hours of instruction. This program was centrally directed by *Kolkhoztsentr* SSSR and was administered within the RKKA by PUR, which assigned each military district quotas of men to train and particular skills to teach them.[76]

In 1930, as part of the massive effort to make collectivization work, PUR set a goal of one hundred thousand soldiers to be trained for socialist reconstruction of the countryside and relied heavily on Komsomols and party members to make it happen. PUR expected all peasant Komsomols, party members, and junior commanders to participate in the program. PUR trained the bulk of these men for working on *kolkhozes*; 20,409, for example, were trained in *kolkhoz* management to become *kolkhoz* chairmen. The regime expected the 25,805 Red Army men trained to be tractor operators and mechanics to work on *sovkhozes, kolkhozes,* and machine tractor stations.[77] Training for work in the countryside continued until 1935, although in 1931 this effort subsided greatly, mainly as a result of the soldiers' dissatisfaction with the pace and violence of collectivization and the high command's concern about the time it took away from military training.

The effort to train one hundred thousand soldiers for postservice work in the countryside should not be confused with, or too closely compared to, the party's civilian training movement, which also began in 1930. Like the agricultural training in the army, *Kolkhozcentr* SSSR sponsored this movement. Twenty-five thousand working-class civilians, many of whom were party members, volunteered to go to the countryside to collectivize the peasantry and later return to their factories. They had only a week or two of training before going to the villages, where they were supposed to work in *kolkhoz* administration, helping to organize and run the collective farms.[78] In contrast, the army's one hundred thousand volunteers were nearly all peasants, many of them nonparty men, who were taught practical skills to use back in their villages—which the party hoped would already be collectivized by the time they got there.

The civilian volunteers descended upon the countryside in January and February 1930 and were in the very forefront of collectivization. The soldier contingent did not get back to their villages until the late summer and fall of 1930, in the regular conscription and demobilization cycle. Because many of the soldiers had been trained in *kolkhoz* management, it seems more likely that they were intended to make collectivization work, whereas the civilians were supposed to create collectivization. The demobilized peasant soldiers were theoretically committed to working for the success of the regime's collectivization policy for the duration of their lives, while the civilians were the energetic, politically conscious, and enthusiastic, but nonetheless temporary, spearhead of collectivization.

PUR after Collectivization

For the remainder of the decade, political training, like military training, received tremendous emphasis from the top but was haphazardly administered at the bottom, and by 1941 it was officially relegated to secondary status behind military training. In 1934, in its annual plan for political instruction, the army cut back the number of class hours to only eighteen (it had been as high as sixty hours a year in the twenties). Finally, in 1939, Lev Mekhlis formally acknowledged the primacy of military training over political training. He blamed past problems in this area on Gamarnik, the former PUR chief, and the Tukhachevskii "gang of wreckers." At the Eighteenth Party Congress, Mekhlis explained:

There used to be a practice of taking commanders . . . from their unit for a whole month on end, on the pretext of giving them a course in Marxism-Leninism. During the height of the military training season, commanders would be taken from their units and sent to school. This of course had a detrimental effect on military training. Furthermore, Red Armymen were kept for many hours from military exercises on the pretext of improving their education. Lastly, the work of the divisional party schools was so arranged as to tear Communists and Young Communist League members from their military exercises. All this was put to a stop on the instructions of comrade Voroshilov.[79]

By saying that political training would now be considered wrecking if it interfered with military training, Mekhlis sent a mixed signal to PUR that certainly could not have helped its performance. PUR still required units to conduct political instruction and imposed penalties for failure, but commissars had to be careful not to do too much or to appear as though they were interfering with military training. This tension created an interesting situation in the late thirties: the commissar watched over the unit commander but was discouraged from overdoing political work. PUR's reduction of political training mirrored the state's curtailment of political education in the public schools at this time.[80]

Political instruction now became more systematized through planning by higher political organs, resulting in less need for input by lower-level political leaders. As before, however, implementation varied widely. Not until 1939 did the party issue its basic tool for instruction, *History of the KPSS(b)—Short Course (Istoriia VKP(b). Kratkii kurs)*, which was supposed to systematize the content of political instruction for all of Soviet society. Effective use of this book nevertheless depended on the abilities of the individual political leader, which by 1939 were generally minimal.[81]

In 1937, on the eve of the purge, PUR's performance came increasingly under fire for failure to train its personnel and to further develop the education of party members. PUR chastised the primary party organizations for not aggressively recruiting men into the party. Actually, the quality of political work had been deteriorating for years, despite all efforts to reverse the trend. As a result, PUR launched a 1937 campaign to use the "schools of the party active" to better train PUR leaders and thus raise the quality of political education in the units. Every division had a school of the party active, which consisted of occasional instruction by high-ranking political officers of the lower-echelon men (battalion commissars and *politruki*) and the party active within the companies. The party active were supposed to be the cutting edge of the Communist party in the battalions, and here in the school of the party active members learned the literal party line. Soon after PUR initiated the campaign, criticisms of units failing to live up to standards began. The most common accusations were failure of division political sections to plan and supervise training of the party active within their divisions; poor preparation of instructors; failure to teach appropriate subject matter, or worse, failure to teach at all; and lax enforcement of attendance. Commonly less than half of those required to attend did so. This in fact was not a new phenomenon. Attendance by party members at political instruction and meetings had historically been a problem that seems never to have been solved.[82]

Commissars and *politruki* did not sit still for this criticism. Many fired back that they were not receiving support from their superiors. They complained that they were not being properly trained and that they should not be condemned for failing as a consequence. In general, such responses indicate a lack of dedication to political education and party work by all levels of PUR below the NKO. Corps political detachments routinely let down division political sections, which in turn neglected their regimental political organs. Even regimental political sections did not adequately support their battalion commissars who begged for guidance and aid.[83] PUR criticized many regiments for poor planning and disorganization, which was a catch-all phrase for

Soldiers enjoying some evening entertainment with collective farmers after having helped bring in the harvest.

unsatisfactory performance in all areas.[84] The situation worsened as the army expanded and the level of experience declined in the political organs. With such disorganization in PUR at the unit level, it should come as no surprise that many ordinary party members and Komsomols would not live up to their responsibilities as role models for other soldiers. Just as in the twenties and early thirties, PUR continued to complain that many party cells had undisciplined members who tarnished the party's reputation, did not reinforce the discipline of nonparty soldiers, and undermined the strength of the Red Army. The question remains how much influence PUR actually had over the men and just how much value party members and Komsomols really had as party representatives, especially since so many PUR personnel stayed in the service for only short periods.

All in all, *politruki* and commissars proved to be equally as transient as soldiers and junior officers, despite PUR's attempts to create an organization manned by professional political workers dedicated to service in the army.[85] The goal was, however, unrealistic given PUR's inability to recruit and retain adequate numbers of leaders and its reliance at the end of the decade on conscription of civilian party officials to temporarily fill PUR positions. In sum, the purge and the imposition of a new PUR regime under Mekhlis, the reinstitution of dual command, and the creation of new political positions in the companies in 1937 did not increase PUR's efficiency and power but in fact seem to have reduced it.

ESTIMATING PUR'S EFFECTIVENESS

As we have seen, the Red Army soldier was subjected to far more than military influences during his service. PUR had a great deal of interaction with the soldier, which colored his impression of military service. Because of the political work and literacy, antireligious, and agricultural skills instruction, the Red Army soldier's military experience was truly unique in comparison with that of his tsarist predecessor or his counterpart in any other army. This is not to say that his experiences made him a better soldier. The regime attacked the soldier's lifestyle and values from all sides, which may have caused disorientation and aversion both to the military and to political authorities. Lives were changed by the newly acquired ability to read and write. Religious beliefs were assaulted by the antireligious campaign, and the economic and social lives of the peasants were altered by collectivization. One of PUR's goals was to inspire "Soviet patriotism," yet in the process it created the conditions for backlash, not only with the programs mentioned but also with the promises, often unkept, of privileges for soldiers and their families. The Red Army soldier was supposed to be a "new Soviet man" by the time he was discharged. Many probably were, but not necessarily in the form the party desired.

The reflections of several expatriate Soviet citizens offer insight into the impact of military service on the individual. The first, Boris Balinsky, a Ukrainian, was a thirty-year-old university instructor when conscripted in 1936. He only served a short while because his university petitioned to have him released. His experiences are nonetheless illuminating:

> My character . . . changed. I believe I became hardened. I learned to swear, using the vile vocabulary of a soldier. I do it even now, when I am vexed or frustrated, but now I do it under my breath, so that nobody can hear. My attitude to women had been very soft and romantic, in spite of my having been married for over six years. This was now invaded by the cynical attitude of a soldier.
>
> My social and political attitudes were changed. The patriotic sentiments cultivated in the army are very pervasive—after all, we were in the army to defend and strengthen our homeland. Being a member of the armed forces made me feel part of the establishment. It was my regiment, my army, thus also it was my country and my government. I came to identify myself with the existing social order.[86]

Despite his changed social and political attitudes, the arrest, imprisonment, and death of his wife at the hands of the NKVD during the terror finally convinced him that life would be better outside the Soviet Union. When he got the chance, he fled with the Germans during their retreat from the Ukraine in 1944.

Another expatriate was an officer, a *voenspets*, who had been a captain in the old army; he had risen to the rank of colonel in the Red Army and never became a party member, though he was invited to apply. During the Second World War, he was captured by the Germans and afterwards refused to be repatriated. His service in the Red Army actually turned him against the party and state. He observed: "A party man even if he were against the policies of the Soviets and of the Communist party had outwardly to be devoted. He came to feel himself as the master of the situation, as a wheel of the government. Whereas others thought themselves as a cog in the whole depressive machinery."[87] Because he was surrounded by PUR men, the NKVD, and people he could not trust, he "avoided all talks which would bring out my antigovernmental views or my views on the party."[88]

Still another soldier was an enlisted man, first drafted in 1931. After his term of compulsory service expired in 1933, he went back to his village. Several months later, he reenlisted. He was demobilized in 1935, only to reenlist again in 1936. He was offered the chance for higher schooling and a commission in 1938 and took it, becoming a quartermaster 2d class (equivalent to a junior lieutenant) in 1939. Captured by the Germans during the war, he refused to go back to the Soviet Union in 1945.

His parents were not happy about his conscription, but, in his words, "While I was in the army they simply regarded it as inevitable."[89] He professed that he had no great love for the army. Why, then, did he reenlist?

> In 1933 my term was over. As you know in that year there was a terrible famine in the Soviet Union. In August of that year my father died, in September my mother. I returned to the village on the Volga, in which we had lived. We had a little house there, but when I entered it, I found it empty. You can imagine how terrible I felt. I didn't know what to do. The famine continued. My situation was so terrible that I simply felt I had to get out of that village.
>
> While there, I got to know a man who was organizing a regiment, which was to go to the Far East. . . . So I joined and went. I spent two years there, thinking that in that length of time, far away from home— 7,000 kilometers from the village where I had been brought up— I would forget this catastrophe. In 1935 I was discharged. . . .
>
> I returned to the village once more. Now I had no place to live, no money and it was hard to find work, because I had no particular specialty. I worked there for perhaps six months, earning 180 rubles per month. It was impossible to live on that, so I decided to go back into the army. I met a friend there, with whom I had been in the Far East. He was just joining a regiment which was to leave for Leningrad. I joined the regiment and went.[90]

Once a member of the Komsomol, this soldier quit because of what he saw the party doing to the peasants during dekulakization. He later refused to rejoin. He had no respect for the party or its policies. He summed up his attitude toward service in two sentences: "I am not especially a military man and the military life doesn't please me. But it was hard for me to do anything else."[91] After nearly ten years of service, he was not much of a "new Soviet man."

In evaluating these testimonies, we have to recognize that the university-educated man and the *voenspets* were distinctly in the minority in military service. The enlisted man from the village was the most representative. All three are exceptional in that they chose to stay in the West after the war. Taking all that into consideration, we can conclude that their experience of military service was not significant enough to convince them to remain Soviet citizens. In fact, the actions of the party and government provided the critical impetus for abandoning their country. The university man, whose service had engendered proregime sentiments, left with the Germans because of the arrest and execution of his wife by the NKVD. The *voenspets* felt alienated by the stigma attached to his social origins, which he could not overcome even through military service. The enlisted man-turned-officer was ultimately repelled by the party's actions at the local level during the famine and dekulakization, and by his later treatment at the hands of a Special Section.

The military's success in promoting Soviet patriotism is difficult to gauge and cannot be measured simply by counting how many prisoners refused to come back. Men could enjoy and appreciate their service and still, in the long run, not feel loyal to the party and regime. In fact, they could even be turned against the regime. The *voenspets,* for example, was dedicated to the army but not to the regime, which he considered responsible for his social discrimination. The quartermaster was dedicated to neither the army nor the state; he just wanted a job.

Former soldiers were supposed to be exempt from punitive taxation, dekulakization, and forced collectivization. Yet, party activists forcibly collectivized and dekulakized thousands of former Red Army men in the thirties.[92] These men had children who would someday be liable to serve in the army, and they themselves were the reservists who were called to the colors in 1939–1941. Countless thousands of future Red Army men were victimized in the same manner between 1928 and 1933. Is it any wonder that indiscipline was rife among soldiers in these years and that, when given the chance in the Second World War, many men took the first opportunity to shoot their leaders and surrender? Can two years of military service and amateurish political indoctrination be expected to have been enough to prevent disaffection with the state?

Mark von Hagen argues that military service was an effective means of establishing regime support among some peasants in the twenties.[93] Collectivization and dekulakization from 1929 to 1933, however, proved to be a turning point in PUR's ability to influence soldiers. During collectivization, family, social, and economic concerns overpowered most PUR attempts to indoctrinate peasant soldiers. The military high command and its Politburo allies urged Stalin to slow the pace of collectivization in 1930 because they could not be sure the troops would remain loyal if collectivization continued at its rapid and violent pace. This is the ultimate irony. The regime saw the army as an opportunity to mold the peasant, but the peasant turned the tables in 1930–1931 and, through the army, modified the behavior of the state, albeit temporarily. The Soviet Union was not the only country to use its army to instill patriotism and loyalty. In the nineteenth century, both the French and German armies made purposeful attempts to teach patriotism and civic duty. In Allan Wildman's assessment, these efforts failed, and it was eventually the public school systems that succeeded in the task.[94] The same assessment may very well apply to the USSR.

SUMMARY

The Soviet soldier's military experience was quite different from that of soldiers in other armies, but his life was not very different from that of Soviet civilians. Conditions in the army were a mirror of conditions in civilian society, although they may have been better in many instances. The soldier's life was not particularly different from the civilian's with respect to the party's attempt to modernize and socialize him into the new socialist society. Literacy, antireligious, and cultural campaigns all were conducted in civilian society and even preceded the military movements. Collectivization was overwhelmingly a civilian peasant undertaking, although nonpeasant party members from industry, government, and the party apparatus participated in the movement. Civilians participated in brigade work just as did soldiers and officers. Although the Soviet military experience was unique, then, perhaps too much has been made of its uniqueness in Soviet society with respect to politicization.

What we can say about the army, PUR, and its influence on a soldier is this: military service could shape the individual's attitude toward the Soviet regime either negatively or positively, but its influence must be assessed within the context of the soldier's life experience and what was happening in the larger society around him. Some far more critical things could happen to the peasant or worker during his life, events that could shape his attitudes toward Soviet power, for example, grain requisitioning, dekulakization, collectivization, working under harsh and primitive conditions for low pay in the USSR's crash industrialization, or the loss of a close friend or family member during the terror. We must consider that these experiences could have weighed more heavily than a mere two years of early morning hikes, field training exercises, and political lectures. After all, until 1936, the average age of army conscripts was 23. They were not callow, impressionable teenagers but fairly mature men.

CHAPTER 4

The Red Army Officer Corps

In the years between the Civil War and the Second World War, the Soviet military failed to create a competent, well-trained, self-confident, cohesive, and motivated professional officer corps. Perhaps no other mistake contributed more to the sufferings of the Soviet state in the early years of the war. The primary causes of this failure were the inability to recruit sufficient numbers of officers and extraordinary methods of procurement; the lack of a professional noncommissioned officers corps; insufficient training; recruitment of unsuitable and undereducated men; and the confused interrelationships of responsibility and authority within PUR. What resulted was an officer corps with little cohesion, talent, ability, respect, and or status— an officer corps unprepared to fight a major war. The blame rests with a regime that wanted an army larger than its society could man with volunteer officers.

BEFORE THE DELUGE: OFFICER PROCUREMENT POLICY

The Bolshevik party considered it a progressive measure to derive the bulk of society's leadership from the working class and poor and middle peasants. The army was no exception. In direct contrast to the army of the old regime, in which on the eve of the First World War hereditary nobles accounted for nearly half of the officer corps, the Bolsheviks forbade nobles, kulaks, and sons of clergy from performing military service. Although some men who had actually opposed the Revolution and its values joined the armed forces and became officers to hide their prerevolutionary association with autocracy, they did not adopt a new sense of loyalty.[1] Some former tsarist officers who did not embrace bolshevism were allowed, or in many cases were forced during the Civil War, to serve as military specialists under the watchful eyes of a Bolshevik commissar. Other exceptions included former tsarist officers who became party members and were given positions of great responsibility. Unlike the old army, the Red Army considered all enlisted men potential officers.[2] Before the Second World War, recruiting men from the ranks to military schools was the army's preferred means of officer procurement.

From the founding of Soviet power until the Second World War, the Red Army officer corps could be divided into the following categories: former officers, sergeants, and enlisted men of the Imperial Army; professional revolutionaries; the products of Soviet military schools; mobilized party members; reservists called to short terms of active duty; junior commanders promoted to officer rank after passing a qualifying examination; and political officers given military rank and assignments under varying conditions. Curiously enough, the Bolsheviks also allowed several thousand former officers of the White armies of the Civil War to serve in the Red Army well into the 1930s.[3] It was a rather heterogeneous group of men of varied nationalities, social origins, education, and motivations for serving. Consequently, the military leadership lacked strong cohesion.

There were two subgroups of officers within the commanding personnel (*nachal'sostav*)[4]: Red Commanders (*kraskomy*) and military specialists (*voenspetsy*). The title *kraskom* referred both to men who had served as Imperial Army officers but later embraced the Revolution and to those who first joined the military and became officers during or after the Revolution. *Voenspetsy* were tsarist holdovers who did not adopt communist politics but were willing to serve in the Red Army. The term *kraskom* was officially dropped in 1927, and all officers were then known simply as commanders, although the idea that there were two kinds of officers lingered in the collective consciousness of the army for years to come.

During the twenties and thirties, the army acceded to the party's wishes in attempting to recruit its officer candidates as well as enlisted men primarily from the youth of the working class and poor peasantry. Those formerly from the middle class, kulaks, and the majority of Cossacks, as well as their offspring, were neither conscripted nor allowed to join the military until 1936. In establishing this criterion, the party automatically eliminated the most educated sector of society and the ethnic group with the greatest military heritage. This policy clearly indicates that the rational desire for political reliability came before efficiency, an example the young Weimar Republic might have done well to follow, yet it was a policy that deprived the military of the freedom to recruit freely from society as a whole.[5]

Early Attempts to Create a Professional Officer Corps

In the late twenties, as a result of attempts to bring order to the system of military leadership, an ideal career path began to emerge. A qualified potential officer would attend a military school of his future branch of service. These military schools were to function as the equivalent of a college education, with a heavy emphasis on the military arts on the order of Britain's Sandhurst, France's St. Cyr, and the United States' West Point. The regime intended the graduates to become career officers. Upon graduation, the former cadet was officially designated a middle commander with the right to hold positions at platoon and company level.[6]

After at least two years in a line unit, junior officers could go on to advanced courses or schools to receive instruction in a particular military specialty. Upon graduation, or after six years of service, they were eligible to hold command or staff positions at the battalion and regiment levels. Officers desiring to further their careers could attend military academies or civilian universities after they had attended a military school, served at least two years in the units, or reached thirty-three years of age and passed an entrance examination. An officer was supposed to have eleven years of service to be promoted to serve at the division level and sixteen to be promoted beyond that.[7]

Training Officers: The Military Education System

The single most important stage in an officer's professional development—regardless of his nation—is his initial training at a military school. It is there that the military formally transmits its ethos and values and creates the common ground necessary for the development of professional loyalty and comradeship between officers. Additionally, schools impart the special knowledge and skills that separate officers from civilians. The military education system also serves to upgrade standards of performance.

Ideally, the Red Army officer was given the bulk of his training through a three-tiered military education system—the Soviets used the term military instruction faculties (*Voennouchebnykh Zavedenii*, VUZy)—however, the RKKA never experienced ideal conditions at any point before the Second World War. The first level consisted of military schools, the second of short courses of specialized instruction for officers with several years' experience. The highest tier was the academy level, where, originally, the best officers were sent to get several years of instruction in technical or tactical matters. All three levels provided not just opportunities for training but also for instilling or reinforcing military values and breaking down barriers between party-recruited and army-recruited officer candidates.

Each branch of the armed services had its own military schools. For the infantry and cavalry the course of study lasted three years. For other branches, training spanned four years, although, after 1928, the curriculum was usually condensed, comprising military and general education subjects. The regulations stipulated that to qualify for officer training at a military school, applicants had to be from seventeen to twenty-five years of age, be recommended by two people of authority (preferably Communist party members), be physically fit, and have had at least seven years of general education.[8] Any of these requirements could be waived. The most commonly waived requirements were age and education. The army, like civilian higher-education establishments, usually settled for young men with approximately four years education, provided that they could pass the entrance examination. Despite low standards, the requirements did bar many potential officers and greatly limited the enrollment of military schools. In 1928, the party was forced to address the problem of too few qualified applicants for military schools. Using trade unions and Komsomol organizations in some of the larger cities, the party established preparatory courses for military school aspirants. Nearly four thousand workers and *batraki* attended these schools in 1929. This definitely helped. Of all students admitted to military schools in 1930, one-third had attended preparatory schools.[9]

The advanced military training courses that comprised the second level of officer education were called *kursy usovershenstvovaniia komandnogo sostava* (KUKS), and courses specifically for higher officers were called *kursy usovershenstvovaniia vyshego nachsostava* (KUVNAS). The majority of KUKS courses introduced new equipment and were conducted under the aegis of the military academy of the particular branch of service offering the training. After completing the courses, officers returned to their garrisons to teach their units what they had learned. For example, from 1930 to 1932, KUKS courses prepared thousands of men—mostly infantry and cavalry officers—for work in the newly formed mechanized formations and in the air force. KUVNAS courses, by contrast, generally served as finishing schools or short courses of specialized military instruction and were part of an attempt to upgrade military performance primarily of the higher-ranking officers who had had little or no military education but had achieved their rank during the Civil War. They also prepared officers for higher levels of command.[10]

Initially, only senior officers attended military academies. The first few classes purposely trained men to replace many of the military specialists teaching in the VUZy and prepared selected commanders to receive regimental and higher commands.[11] After 1929, academies also became sources of commissions. Student officers received technical schooling in medicine, electrical engineering, veterinary medicine, armored warfare, artillery, engineering, aviation, and chemistry, to name the most prominent. The Frunze Academy, the only academy to provide advanced instruction on tactics and staff skills, never became a source of commission but remained a center for advanced military instruction. Graduation from a military academy was sure to help a career, but the advancement of an officer's career still depended on other variables. Party membership, patronage, and personal ability still counted for quite a bit.[12] Few officers had the necessary general education to enable them to meet the entrance requirements of the military academies, so the army established a preparation school in 1928 to prepare promising officers to attend military academies.[13]

The acquisition of higher military instruction by officers was very uneven in the Red Army's initial years but grew year by year. The most revealing statistic on military education and expertise is that in 1935 the Soviets boasted that half of their corps and division commanders possessed some higher military education, though regiment commanders lagged behind at only 15 percent.[14] The Soviets are justified in their pride in this level of military training, considering they virtually started from scratch with an uneducated population. Nonetheless, it is far from impressive in comparison to Western armies, which normally had all their higher officers trained in advanced military schools, and this after a complete secondary education and university training or its equivalent as well.

The Revolutionary Military Council recognized the undesirability of the low level of education and took steps to improve the basic education of officers. In 1932, the RVS introduced a two-year program to give officers lacking a general education some instruction in the Russian language, mathematics, algebra, geometry, and physics to be taught in the divisions. In June 1935, the Commissariat of Defense passed a resolution that all officers who had not completed their general education by 1 January 1939 would have to enroll in public schools and complete their educations.[15]

OFFICERS AND THE PARTY

From the founding days of the Red Army, there was a dichotomous relationship between the party and the army. The party had introduced commissars and political instructors into the army during the Civil War. The duties of commissars changed several times in the twenties and thirties. At times they were responsible for countersigning military orders to ensure the political loyalty of the commanders; at other times they were relegated to the role of political instructors. At all times they shared responsibility for the welfare of the men but did not answer directly to the military chain of command. Thus, there existed side by side two separate chains of command and shared responsibility. After the Civil War, officers began to agitate for *edinonachlie*, that is, the right to command their units without political supervision and under the sole charge of the military officer. Mikhail Frunze championed the transition from dual command to *edinonachalie*. Under *edinonachalie*, commissars no longer shared command but simply oversaw political affairs. Nonetheless, Frunze accepted PUR and its role in the army. He thought that the party could play a positive role in enforcing military discipline. He encouraged and expected Communists and Komsomols to set an example of self-discipline for nonparty soldiers. Frunze perceived that this "army of a new type" could base its discipline on political awareness, and he expected

PUR and unit commanders to see to it that the men received the appropriate political knowledge.[16]

To extend its influence over and ensure the creation of a class-conscious and loyal army, the party manipulated the social composition of the army as a whole and leadership cadres in particular. To accomplish this, the party sought to recruit to the officer corps more men with working-class backgrounds. Toward this end, the Central Committee decreed, on 30 March 1928, that 50 percent of students in military schools were to be workers. On 6 February 1929, it increased the requirement to 60 percent. This increase was to be achieved by recruiting young workers, preferably factory school (*rabfak*) graduates, those with seven years of education, graduates of secondary schools, party members, and Komsomols, and by classifying *batraki* as workers. The trend to "proletarianize" was not exclusive to the military but was general policy throughout the Soviet Union.[17]

After 1929, the army was indeed successful in increasing the number of students of working-class origins in military schools to the decreed 60 percent or more, but it failed to increase the representation of workers in the officer corps to a similar level because the RKKA consistently commissioned officers by means other than military schools. Commissioning officers outside the military school system invariably produced a large peasant contingent. In 1933, for example, workers represented 63.1 percent of all students in military school but only 43.5 percent of all army officers. The number of working-class officers actually decreased to 42.3 percent in 1934 before rising to 44.2 percent in 1936.[18]

The party sought to increase its membership among officers as another way to extend control over the army. In 1926, fewer than half of all officers were party members. Throughout the thirties, the percentage of communist officers rose steadily. The party accomplished this primarily by recruiting officers into the party, not by recruiting Communists into the army. In civil society, however, the party recruited members to leading positions in all areas of work. The party also did intensive work among the *voenspetsy*, and by 1930 over half of those still in the army had joined the party.[19]

PUR and Officer Relations

Western historians and military experts have long assumed the relationship between army officers and the political personnel of PUR to be antagonistic, but this assumption is based on an exaggerated generalization of a few extreme cases. In the twenties and thirties, most military men in the West believed that the party, through PUR and its *politruki* and commissars, controlled every aspect of military life and was like a millstone around the neck of each and every commander. This view was originally fostered by contemporary reports of most military attachés, especially the American, British, and German military attachés in Moscow. Years later, emigré literature and studies that relied on emigrés as sources reinforced this perception. These works also suggest that in any conflict of wills, PUR had the upper hand because of its political status.[20] Certainly, commissars sometimes proved to be irritating to unit commanders, especially when they overstepped their political duties and presumed to involve themselves in military activities, yet they had a vested interest in the performance of the unit. If something went wrong, serious enough for the commander to be punished, the commissar often got the axe as well. With the system set up this way, the possibility for friction existed, yet mutual dependence and cooperation could result if the personalities of the leaders lent themselves to it, as quite often they did.

Beginning in 1925, trusted unit commanders were allowed the privilege of *edinonachalie*. There were two types of *edinonachalie*. The first type separated military and political duties as noted earlier. In this arrangement, the military commander did not need his orders reviewed and signed by the commissar before they became official. In the second type of *edinonachalie*, the commander was in charge of both the military and political training of the unit, and the commissar, if he had one, was his assistant in political affairs. This version was allowed in cases when the commander was an exceptional party member; not all commanders who were party members were granted this status. It represented a radical reversal of roles from the Civil War origins of the commissar. This situation was rather rare and was usually granted to Civil War veterans and political leaders who took military command. A man with this status was referred to as a "commander-commissar." In 1929, one-third of all commander-commissars were former commissars and *politruki* who had become army officers. It was not until the early thirties that all commanders had *edinonachalie*. To achieve such status, one first had to be nominated and then attend an *edinonachalie* preparation course sponsored by PUR.[21] It is important to remember that commissars remained at battalion level and higher, whether or not the commander had one-man command, unless he was a commander-commissar. When a commissar was present, all that changed with *edinonachalie* were the commander's and commissar's functional areas of responsibility. Normally commander-commissars acted as the commissar, and the company *politruki* answered to them.

Although to some participants the transition to unified command seemed to be evolving at a snail's pace, others in PUR considered it far too rapid. In spring 1928, an opposition group formed in a section of the staff of the Tolmachev Main Military-Political Academy that protested the rapid pace of reform. In particular, it criticized the "tendency to belittle the role of the party organs and a muddying of the functions of party-political work in the army." This group, later labeled the "inner-Army opposition," blamed many of the disciplinary ills of the army on the loss of influence of the political apparatus in the army since 1925. The "opposition" did not oppose the idea of *edinonachalie*, only the speed of its implementation. They felt that, in the rush to turn control of political training over to army officers, many unqualified commanders received *edinonachalie;* consequently, political education and discipline had suffered. The senior leadership of the army and PUR reacted (perhaps overreacted) severely to this challenge to their decision making and forced men of the "opposition" to quit their posts, compelled them to recant in public, and expelled them from the party. Lev Mekhlis, in 1938, singled out the Tolmachev "oppositionists" still serving in the army for thorough repression.[22]

Personality problems caused the most friction between PUR and commanders. The principle of whether political personnel belonged in the army or not seldom caused disputes. Conflicts most often arose when political officers strayed into military matters, or officers cut into PUR's instruction time. Temperament determined how men handled transgressions. Commanders and their commissars occasionally even became close friends.[23]

Although cooperation between officers and political leaders produced many benefits, some officers, in order to avoid potential conflict, tried to avoid their PUR counterparts whenever possible. One battalion commander noted: "I came in contact with them [PUR men] especially at meetings. I didn't have it too bad because the secretary of the party cell was a good fellow. But other party people were bastards and they would report to the commissar everything that happened in the companies."[24]

The occasional differences between PUR and the army leadership did not seem to negatively affect officers' outlook toward the party. Indeed, party membership among officers grew at a steady rate throughout the twenties and thirties. Some officers joined out of belief in the party and the Revolution, others as an opportunistic move to further their careers. The higher the military rank, the higher the frequency of membership in the party proved to be. Party membership did not necessarily come before promotion, but because a commissar also had to sign promotion orders, the potential to use party membership as a carrot or stick existed.[25] There was a perception among some men (in both military and civilian life) that swift and high promotion only came with party membership. One officer, a nonparty quartermaster 2d class, who rose from the ranks to his position, said: "Well, everyone has an opportunity to get ahead, depending on how he does his work and what his political position is. If the man belongs to the Communist party, he can move often and fast and just as high as he wants. If he is not a member of the party, but does good work and is well disciplined, he can also get ahead, but it will be slowly and he will never get up as high as if he was a party member."[26] Indeed, officers sometimes misrepresented themselves as party members hoping to secure an advantage they otherwise might not have.[27] It comes as no surprise that successful officers seldom gave credit for their advancement to their party membership.

Vladimir Unishevsky, an air force pilot, relates that two opposing groups of students formed in his flying school: nonparty officers and party officers. The nonparty officers loathed the party members because they regarded them as neither true Marxists nor politically oriented but as opportunists who at every turn used their party membership to get ahead, to get out of trouble, or even to set PUR or the Special Section against nonparty officers.[28] Whether a party member used his membership for personal gain depended on personality, yet the very existence of alternate avenues of success available only to a few created tension. It also created conditions under which back stabbing and petty quarrels could create more serious consequences than in normal bureaucratic organizations.

PROBLEMS WITHIN THE OFFICER CORPS

From 1928 to 1941, the Red Army officer corps suffered from four major problems that would negatively affect its performance in battle: an inability to recruit sufficient number of officer candidates to keep up with increasing needs, which resulted in a permanent shortage of officers; an inability to retain many of the officers it did recruit; poor discipline among officers; and an inability to raise the level of competence of the officer corps as a whole. Instead of looking upon their service as a high calling, some officers saw it as an opportunity to enrich themselves illegally, others saw it as a temporary inconvenience, but only a minority saw it as a worthy career. Time after time, training and even combat operations were bungled because the same things went wrong, suggesting that a great many Soviet officers did not become experts at their jobs and were neither externally nor internally motivated to become so.

The Shortage of Officers

The army's most serious problem, its irremediable shortage of officers, led to its being a hollow force on 22 June 1941. Attempts to overcome the shortages led to deleterious compromises in training, rendering much of the midlevel leadership functionally unfit to fulfill its duties. Beginning in the late twenties, the Red Army failed to recruit and retain sufficient numbers of officers to man its administration, schools, and units. The army expanded so quickly that it could neither recruit enough officers nor thoroughly train the officers it did have. The subsequent purge of the officer corps in 1937–1938 deprived the corps of many experienced officers who would have facilitated the expansion. The purges resulted in even more vacancies that could only be filled by less experienced and inadequately trained men.

The Red Army also had a hard time retaining its officers. The turnover, especially among school-trained officers, created a void of experienced field-grade officers. The army never made good its shortages dating from the mass dismissals of leaders in the twenties. In the fervor of the Revolution and the Civil War an abundance of adventurous men gladly served as military leaders, but, after peacetime reductions of the entire Soviet armed forces, Soviet men seem to have been reluctant to make their careers in the military. A huge number of nonparty officers and even party members serving as officers at the request of the party served only two years, having no desire whatsoever to serve longer.[29]

Like industry and agriculture, the military embarked on huge expansion projects without first considering its leadership needs, although they were easily forseeable. Thus, the military's need for leaders always outstripped its ability to produce them. Moshe Lewin's studies of the Soviet economy during the first five-year plan provide insight into the Red Army's dilemma. Lewin notes that the Soviet government had a propensity for undertaking large-scale projects without providing beforehand for training the necessary cadres. This inexcusable defect resulted in incalculable losses. The root of this problem, according to Lewin, was the tendency of the Stalinist dictatorship to act first and think later.[30] With large-scale recruiting problems hampering efforts even before expansion, surely the RKKA leadership must have known that growth would only exacerbate its difficulties.

The First Officer Recruitment Campaign

In 1926, the RVS discharged sixteen thousand officers and PUR personnel. This, the last of the massive post–Civil War dismissals of officers and political personnel, heralded the beginning of the Red Army's continual shortage of leaders. In 1928, the army had 45,867 regular officers in the line units. That same year, in a speech to the Sixteenth Conference of the All-Union Communist party (VKP(b)), Marshal Voroshilov spoke of recruiting more leaders and asked the party to make manning military schools a top priority.[31] The next year, Voroshilov pushed for still more officers. In a 1929 speech, he said, "One of the most important problems of our military development is training new commanding-political leaders for the RKKA. This is a real problem . . . the basis of the problem concerning officers is still to be determined."[32] The problem was recruiting and retaining officers.

The Central Committee agreed that there were not enough officers to provide adequate leadership and ordered that more be recruited and that the number of military education facilities be increased. The following year,

1930, the army issued a report showing its current strength in officers, its needs through 1933, and a plan for meeting those needs. The report identified a current shortage of 3,103 officers and projected that, if no changes were made in recruiting, the army would be short 8,600 officers in 1931 and 11,300 in 1932, but, if its plan were followed, the ground forces would have a surplus of some 1,100 officers in 1933. This was a very ambitious plan, because in the preceding three years the army had only managed to grow by about three thousand officers each year.[33]

The basis of the shortage, as stated in the report, was the creation of new units. The RKKA estimated that in 1931 it would need a total of 15,513 new officers: 8,046 to fill newly created units; 2,474 to compensate for natural attrition; 3,103 to make up the shortage from the year before; and 1,890 to replace men transferred out of the RKKA to other duties. To meet these needs, the RKKA counted on the military schools to graduate 6,850 new platoon commanders and planned to ask 4,030 reservists already serving a year of active duty to stay on another year while calling up an additional 440. It also planned to have eight hundred junior commanders serve as platoon commanders. This would give the army 12,120 new officers, leaving a shortfall for 1931 of 3,393 officers. The plan for 1932 was similar. The RKKA planned to increase the output of military schools to over ten thousand graduates, call up more reservists, ask about two thousand reservists to stay on for an additional year, and have an additional one thousand junior commanders serve as platoon commanders. This strategy would still leave a shortage of 2,050 officers because attrition, transfers out of the RKKA, and the shortage from the previous year were all greater than before and created a need for 7,105 additional officers to fill positions in new units.

In contrast to the preceding years, the outlook for 1933 was rosy indeed. The army expected to need 14,095 new officers in 1933, based on natural attrition of 3,325 officers, the need to cover the shortage of 2,050 carried over from 1932, 1,880 officers to replace the junior commanders who had served as platoon commanders but were to be reassigned to normal junior commander responsibilities, and 6,930 officers to fill in for the reservists who would be sent home. (The army did not plan to create more units, so the personnel section projected no requirement for officers to fill new positions.) To meet these requirements, the army planned to graduate 15,233 officers from military schools, thus creating a surplus of 1,138 officers. The planners were so confident of success that they even went so far as to divide the surplus among the branches of the ground forces.[34] The army then launched a campaign to increase the recruitment of officer candidates to its military schools.

The army aimed to quadruple the number of officers it had in military schools as of 1930. This proved to be an impossible task, as Table 4.1 illustrates. The essence of the difficulty in recruiting proved to be Soviet society able 4.1. Graduates of Ground Forces Military Schools, 1928–1947

	1928	1929	1930	1931	1932	1933	1934	1935	1936	1937	Total
ıfantry	2,395	1,926	2,420	3,474	3,044	3,087	2,091	1,635	1,546	1,953	23,571
rtillery	787	700	846	796	2,046	3,862	2,741	1,228	3,067	2,075	18,148
avalry	453	225	419	683	482	690	578	146	354	329	4,359
ırmor		10		187	1,433	863	1,376		803	1,067	5,739
ıgnal	171	108	287	276	417	696	888	10	677	639	4,169
ngineer	130	92	108	102	519	416	286	164	299		2,116
OSO°	63	85	77	129	265	199	140	68	281	284	1,591
hemical						17	100	36	175		328
echnical and other specialties	336	95	144	418	992	263	612	473	814	1,918	6,065
ıedical								145		143	288
eterinary	140	119	99	72	122	74	73	74	231	109	1,113
ıotal	4,475	3,360	4,400	6,137	9,320	10,167	8,885	3,979	8,247	8,517	67,487

Military Communications Service.

ıurce: "O Nakoplenii Nachal'stvuiushchego sostava i popolnenii im Raboche'-Krest'ianskaia Krasnoi Armii: Iz ıravki-doklada nachal'nika Upravleniia po nachal'stvuiushchemu sostavu RKKA Narkomata Oborony SSSR . A. Shchadenko, 20 Marta 1940 g," *Izvestiia TsK KPSS* no. 1 (1990), 178.

itself. The peasant- and worker-dominated society did not readily provide willing career officers. Tsarism had left a cumbersome military legacy for the Red Army. Before the First World War, careers as military officers were open only to a small segment of the population. The option to choose a military career was a new development for the common person. Service as an enlisted man was old hat and extremely unpopular, but the masses of peasants and workers had no frame of reference for service as an officer. In other words, the lack of a tradition of professional, long-term, voluntary military service among the masses made recruiting volunteers to the officer corps very difficult.[35]

Young men's impressions of the army a decade after the Civil War were often negative. During the military school recruitment drive of 1930, recruiters reported the word in the factories to be, "Don't join the army, the pay is measly," and "officers have no personal life."[36] The Soviet high command did not understand the depth of this problem, and therefore, miscalculated its ability to recruit for military schools. Not once during the 1930s did the RKKA meet its goals in recruiting to military schools. Table 4.1 shows that ground forces military schools produced only 67,487 officers in ten years.

The army rather quickly abandoned the plans it had devised in 1930, and, under pressure of circumstances, the RKKA deviated greatly from its self-defined ideal process of officer training. To make it easier to fill the demand for officers, the NKO modified the commissioning process in 1931, making it no longer necessary for prospective officers to complete or even attend mili-

Officers studying at a military academy.

tary school. Promising young junior commanders were given exams and, if they passed, were made officers. Regulations stated that a junior commander who wanted to become an officer first had to serve a full year in the ranks. Military districts, however, did not consistently observe this rule, and often allowed new junior commanders to become officers by examination.[37]

Special Mobilizations

In 1931, in response to the army's request for help in increasing the number of officers, the Central Committee ordered party organizations to make a special effort to recruit Communists into the ranks of the officer corps. This "special mobilization," as the party called it, became a regular occurrence in the thirties. It should not be surprising that this directive produced results, because in effect it resembled a draft. As a result, many young Communists and Komsomols were sent directly to military schools and academies to become officers in the technical branches (artillery, engineers, signal, and aviation, mostly). In 1931, seven thousand party members and Komsomols entered the RKKA, three thousand to the ground forces and four thousand to pilot training in the air force.[38] Again, in 1932, ten thousand communists were mobilized for military technical institutes, academies, and schools. Between 1931 and 1935, approximately twenty-seven thousand specially mobilized party members became students in the military school system. The party mobilized mostly workers and few peasants.[39]

That the party placed a high priority on the mobilizations is obvious, yet one has to wonder how effectively the *raikom* party organizations fulfilled these requirements. In the 1933 special mobilization in Smolensk Oblast, for example, the *raikom* received its instructions on 10 June 1933 and had to be through by 1 July. In an effort to guarantee quality, the *raikom* secretaries were directed to personally interview all selectees. The instructions never mentioned the word volunteer; rather, the words select and selected predominated.[40]

Such examples illustrate how the party and army abused the military school system. Schools shortened curricula from three years to eighteen months, exceptions were made in duration of attendance, and some men were forced to attend. These modifications resulted in the sacrifice of quality training and cohesion among officers. In 1933, Voroshilov admitted, "In general the training of the commanding personnel is not as good as it ought to be."[41] If it was not good at that time, it could not have improved by flooding military schools with men who did not desire military careers. Nor did abbreviating training at the point most critical for professional development and socialization into the military improve the situation.

Besides promoting Communists from the ranks, PUR made many of its people available to serve as officers. The army tested selected political officers on their military knowledge and commissioned as company-grade officers those who passed. In the course of 1931 and 1932, PUR transferred 1,244 political workers into the military. Simultaneously, in a move that completely contradicted its manning needs, the army transferred twenty-five hundred officers and five hundred junior commanders to PUR to serve as political leaders, negating the effect of transferring PUR men to military duties.[42]

Intensified Recruitment from the Enlisted Ranks

While the civilian party organs recruited party members for the officer corps, the army renewed its efforts to recruit leaders from within its enlisted ranks. The army initiated a major campaign in the training year 1931–1932 to convince soldiers and junior commanders to volunteer for military schools, primarily for infantry and cavalry officer training. The RKKA planned to man the VUZy on a district basis. Each military district had a quota, and in turn set quotas for its divisions and regiments. The deadline for fulfilling the plan was 1 March 1932, but when that date rolled around, several military districts had failed to meet their goals.[43] The majority of volunteers were party members or Komsomols. The party likely used its leverage to encourage volunteerism, as with "special mobilizations" of civilians.

Once a regiment identified its officer candidates, it was supposed to give them special instruction to prepare them for military school. Not all units, however, provided this training. Later, the army dropped the requirement that soldiers go to military school, and junior commanders could become officers after as little as two months special training in a locally organized course. The army specifically identified second-term junior commanders, that is, junior commanders who had reenlisted after fulfilling their initial conscription obligation, for this privilege. In 1935, for instance, of thirty-three junior commanders recruited within the 17th Red Banner Rifle Division for special officer training, eighteen had already spent between one and three years commanding platoons.[44] That these junior commanders had been holding officer positions in the first place reveals the seriousness of the officer shortage and its effect on reducing the general level of military education among the army's leadership.

The special recruitment of junior commanders meant that regiments plucked many of their best and brightest enlisted men from the ranks, and it exacerbated an already critical shortage of second-term junior commanders. In 1930, the ground forces suffered a shortfall of 12,678 second-year junior commanders. In 1931, the shortage had grown to 14,041. As a short-term solution, units assigned first-term junior commanders to duties and responsibilities of second-termers, creating some five thousand vacant positions normally filled by first-term junior commanders.

Only two months after the end of the special recruitment for officer training, the army began another campaign to encourage junior commanders still in the ranks to reenlist. Each unit was assigned a quota of men to be reenlisted. Some units more than fulfilled their quotas; some failed to realize even half. Again, party members and Komsomols led the way in reenlistments, suggesting pressure from PUR to reenlist. The NKO sponsored other campaigns to reenlist junior commanders in 1933, 1934, and 1935, but with much less fanfare. In 1933, Komsomols or party members constituted three quarters of the reenlisted men.[45] Some of the junior commanders who reenlisted and stayed in the ranks actually served as platoon leaders during their second tour of duty. The army denied them commissions but gave them the rank of *starshina*. Having enlisted men serve as platoon commanders, unprecedented in peacetime Imperial Russia, represented a dramatic break from the past on the part of the Red Army. Later, the military allowed many of these men to become officers by examination with no specialized training whatsoever. That is to say, the high command made no organized effort to promote a psychological transition from the enlisted ranks to the officer corps.

ISSUES OF COMPETENCE

One significant by-product of the shortage of officers and the compromises made to acquire more was a decrease in the overall level of competence of the officer corps. Although there were many outstanding officers who mastered their responsibilities or even showed brilliance in tactical or strategic command of troops, they were, especially at the company and battalion levels, the exception. The larger the army became, the lower the level of basic military skill sank, until, by the outbreak of war, the truly capable leaders and thinkers had been so thinly spread among the divisions and regiments that they could in most cases make only a temporary and local contribution to the national defense.

From early on, officers' attitudes toward their daily responsibilities reflected a deep-seated lack of concern for raising standards and military self-improvement. Their lack of responsibility affected all areas of military life, but nowhere was it more harmful than in training and the health and welfare of the men. For example, in 1927, officer irresponsibility reached such proportions at the summer camp of the 27th Rifle Division that a general order was issued to address it. In "Order No. 12" the camp commander noted that attendance at training was minimal, that many of the officers and political personnel were absent, and that some of the officers were sneaking into the nearby town of Polotsk to go whoring. He issued a general order requiring commanders to keep track of their personnel, stay at their posts, and supervise their units. Finally, he forbade officers to go to Polotsk without permission and promised dire consequences for infringements.[46] That officers had to be ordered to be at their posts and to know what their men were up to is appalling.

The camp commander not only had trouble with his officers missing training, he also had difficulty getting them to supervise the daily routine of their men. In "Order No. 8" he had stipulated:

Notwithstanding frequent orders that the sanitary regulations should be strictly followed in order to prevent the spread of infectious diseases among the troops, the sanitary conditions in some of the units in the training area are so bad as to cause serious fear for their future welfare. Particularly serious faults are to be noticed in the 80th Regiment. The camping ground of the regiment is not kept sufficiently clean. The back portion of the camp is in the highest degree dirty, rubbish is lying about in various places, the cook-houses are dirty, the cooks are slovenly, the fatigue men there do not know their duty, the mess rooms are not properly cleaned, the tables are not washed and are covered with layers of grease and fat, the well is uncovered and dirty, the bread of the men in the supply company was found in a dirty box under the sleeping bunks. All these faults may easily cause outbreaks of acute stomach diseases which would be difficult to cope with under camp conditions.[47]

It is unclear whether the root cause of these problems was sheer negligence, lack of training, or a combination of both on the part of the officers, yet as leaders in positions of responsibility none should have needed such reminders. The sanitary conditions in the camp speak loudly of the officers' neglect. In all armies, officers are responsible for ensuring the health and welfare of their men and enforcing regulations. The Red Army officers' failure to do so often resulted in unhealthy situations for soldiers and for themselves. Such incidents recurred regularly and did not cease before the German invasion, and surely must have made a negative impression on the soldiers.

Those with power guarded it jealously and regarded any challenge of their decisions as a personal affront and threat to their standing. It is not hard to imagine a former *batrak*, now serving as company commander and party member, lording over men once considered his social superiors. One pilot reported in his memoirs:

> The leaders of the Red Army lose no opportunity of proclaiming loudly that personal interests play no part in its ranks. A palpable lie! Personal jealousies and animosities are more widespread and more deeply seated there than anywhere. Anyone accusing a superior officer of unfair punishment has that punishment doubled. And personal quarrels are settled more cruelly here than elsewhere. This makes the moral conditions of service in the Red Army often unbearable. One of my friends, a robust and energetic young man, was driven to such lengths by "C" that he barely escaped being sent to a lunatic asylum with persecution mania.[48]

The party and the army inadvertently brought about such unbearable conditions of morale by their response to the shortage of quality officers.

Discipline: Criminal Activity of Officers

Officers engaged in an astoundingly high degree of criminal activity. Whether this was related to low pay and poor living standards is not clear. The most frequently reported crime committed by an officer was the embezzlement of pay and appropriated funds. The military press published only a few select crimes each week, but between 1925 and 1929, a week seldom passed in which military tribunals did not sentence at least one officer to death or imprisonment.

In the four-month period from September through December 1929, military tribunals convicted forty-two officers of criminal activity. Embezzlement, stealing, and selling government property for personal gain accounted for twenty-two of these convictions. Negligence and inefficiency accounted for eight convictions. The remaining thirteen crimes included indiscipline, protecting Nepmen, taking bribes, and stealing from enlisted men.[49]

The most frequently abused position in these years was that of supply company commander of regiments, divisions, and even military schools. Because these men were in charge of the supplies and bookkeeping, the opportunities for making money illicitly were many. Officers most often stole and sold fodder but would even sell weapons and ammunition to civilians. Supply officers committed most embezzlement, but ordinary line officers often used temporary appointments as paymasters to line their pockets. With the end of the NEP, economic crimes tapered off, to be replaced primarily by crimes involving the use of alcohol. In the early thirties, the party cited drunkenness and drunken debauchery as reasons for arrest or expulsion from the party for a large number of officers.

Murders, suicides, AWOLs, and desertions kept the Special Sections busy. Misdemeanors and crimes by officers usually numbered in the hundreds annually at the corps level. There were also a good many crimes serious enough to warrant arrest.[50] As shown in Table 4.2, the onset of combat operations and calling up of reserves led to a drastic deterioration of discipline in the officer corps, particularly in the category of military crimes and drunkenness.

Part of the responsibility for such aberrant behavior must lie in the method of recruitment of officers. Because the army was short of officers, it may not have been choosy about recruits—not that recruiters let in known criminals. One advantage of the military school system was its ability to weed out ne'er-do-wells; unfortunately, quite a number of men did not go through this system, either before or after the special party mobilizations in 1932 and 1933. Therefore, the army could not closely scrutinize the characters of candidates until after commissioning. To be fair, however, one must acknowledge that everyone in Soviet society was stealing something. According to Moshe

Table 4.2. Convictions of Officers by Military Tribunals, 1936–1940

	1936	1937	1938	1939	1940
Military Crimes	40	82	109	128	1,019
Counterrevolutionary Crimes	79	957	756	365	61
Official and Property Crimes	149	327	599	597	44
Drunkenness, Hooliganism, etc.	112	193	156	186	326
Total	380	1,559	1,620	1,276	1,450

Source: A. T. Ukolov and V. I. Ivkin, "O Masshtabakh Repressii v Krasnoi Armii v predvoennye godu," *Voenno-istoricheskii zhurnal*, no. 1 (1993), 56–57.

Lewin, civilian society during NEP and later experienced large-scale corruption, and sometimes the party purged the whole leadership of a district or even a republic for having tolerated or participated in such affairs.[51]

The end of the NEP did not dramatically change things. On August 7, 1932, the state passed a fiercely repressive law against theft in *kolkhozy*, and later broadened it to embrace all other sectors and serve as its main weapon for protecting its property. Mass thefts were in fact taking place as the economic situation, especially food supplies, deteriorated. According to Lewin, in an environment of deteriorating economies, Soviet society seemed to have been transformed into a nation of thieves.[52] Therefore, the army recruited its leaders from a society actively involved in looking out for itself at the expense of the state. Overcoming immoral and selfish attitudes in civil society and the military became harder as shortages became more acute. The high number of officers commiting crimes should have dismayed all military personnel. There is no comparable behavior in any major Western army in this century.

Off-duty Conduct

It was bad enough that officers conducted themselves "unprofessionally" on military bases, but it did not stop there. Officers often acted as irresponsibly off duty as they did on. Their behavior reflected the backward and coarse social origins of almost all the officers, with the exception of the *voenspetsy*. The most pervasive problem that negatively affected the performance of the corps and tainted the public's impression of Red Army officers was alcohol abuse. Public drunkenness of officers of all ranks in and out of garrison, alone or in groups and even in the company of enlisted men perpetually plagued the officer corps. On one occasion, for example, two officers sent to conduct preconscription training in the countryside never conducted a bit of training but stayed drunk for two months. They were finally turned in to the authorities by townspeople when they staged a duel in the street.

Drunkenness and debauchery, often cited as one charge, were cause for expulsion from the party. The army regularly cashiered men for being incurable and unrepentant alcoholics. One Lebedev, commander of the Baikal Rifle Division in 1932, for example, asked that his new assistant division commander be relieved for alcoholism. The assistant, Atsapov, reported for his first day of duty dead drunk. It took three days before he sobered up enough to do a decent day's work. After that, Lebedev complained, Atsapov was always drinking or drunk. In another instance, a regiment commander requested the relief and replacement of one of his doctors for having stayed drunk during the entire Polish campaign in 1939.[53] The negative effects this officer's behavior had on soldiers' morale is incalculable.

The military press publicized the following incident, decrying the backward and unsophisticated behavior of army officers.

In the quarters of the commanding personnel of the Chongarsk Regiment the fatigue duty roster in the corridor had disappeared. A search was made for the offender and for some reason the wife of the assistant company commander was suspected. M. (also [an] assistant company commander and occupant of the same building) undertook to clear up the case. An actual cause of suspicion against K's wife did not exist. Nevertheless, an order was issued that she had to do two extra fatigue duties by cleaning the corridor. This "disciplinary punishment" convinced everybody of her guilt. In the quarters she was called "thief" and other names. After the wives had quarreled with one another, the commanders started doing so. If that were not enough, the kerosene cooker of M. (who investigated the case) suddenly disappeared. The inference was that, if K's wife had taken the roster, she had also taken it. A search was made [of] her room but the cooker was not found there. Then to Mrs. K's name "prostitute" was added. The annoyance was carried on so violently that Mrs. K. became mentally deranged and had to be taken to an infirmary. The cooker had been hidden "just for fun" by the assistant company commander.[54]

This incident indicates not only a certain lack of sophistication but also the general immaturity and pettiness of a great many officers fresh from peasant life or from first-generation working-class families. With such puerile behavior characterizing their off-duty hours, can one wonder that their official duties suffered? The situation did not improve when, in the 1930s and early 1940s, the army and party gave officer status to increasing numbers of men who had little or no training or socialization in the corps.

CONTINUING SHORTAGE OF PROFESSIONAL LEADERS

In the years from 1933 to 1936, the RKKA became predominantly a standing army and nearly doubled in size. At first glance, this growth might appear a boon to the military, giving it potentially more political power and influence. In reality, expansion caused many difficulties, and procuring officers continued to be a strain.

The shortage of officers continued into the mid-thirties. The problem consisted of inadequate recruitment and the larger than normal—by Western standards—number of officers needed by the Red Army. Between 1928 and 1937, officers represented approximately 9 percent of the armed forces personnel in the Red Army. Previously, during the years of reform and demobilization (1924–1926), officers had comprised over 15 percent of military personnel.[55] In comparison, the German army had only 4 percent officers, the French army had 4.5 percent, and the British territorial forces had 6 percent during this same period. Professional noncommissioned officer corps, however, bolstered their effectiveness.[56]

The officer in the Soviet Armed Forces filled a post of enormous importance, especially when compared to officers in other armies. Officers and a small number of enlisted specialists form the backbone of mass conscript armies. The RKKA was no exception. Most other personnel were conscripts and stayed in the services only for the duration of their conscription. A minor exception to this was in the famine years, 1932–1933, when many soldiers reenlisted to secure the basic necessities of life.[57]

In Western professional and conscript armies, officers and NCOs formed the backbone of the armed forces. The Soviet military, like the Imperial Russian Army, did not have a professional noncommissioned officer corps to provide stability and continuity. Some Western historians have mislabeled Soviet junior commanders noncommissioned officers. In fact, junior commanders were conscripts, not professionals, and normally only served for the duration of their conscription. The connotation of professionalism that goes with the term NCO is not applicable to the junior commander in the Red Army. Some in the army recognized this fact but tried unsuccessfully to convince the officer corps of the need to train junior commanders more thoroughly and retain as many as possible as career soldiers.[58]

The function of the career NCO in traditional armies is to act as the bearer of institutional knowledge and to serve as intermediary between the officer and the enlisted man, much as the foreman in a factory mediates between the supervisor and the workers on the shop floor. The NCO, with his wealth of experience, acts as a stabilizing element in the unit and is the primary enforcer of discipline in the barracks. He also passes on tradition as officers rotate through assignments and enlisted men finish their tours of duty. In the RKKA, in place of the traditional long-serving NCO, each regiment selected and trained some conscripts from its allotment of the annual draft to serve as junior commanders for the duration of their conscription. These junior commanders served in the same capacity as NCOs in Western armies but without the experience and esprit de corps of their Western counterparts. They did not have to work their way up through the ranks, that is, prove their worth and "pay their dues" as privates. This meant that Red Army officers performed many tasks that Western armies traditionally delegated to NCOs. Even in the Imperial Army, the NCOs, variously known as *unter-ofitseri* and *serzhanty*, had two years of service and training before assuming their positions.[59]

Not only did junior commanders seldom stay in the service longer than their obligatory two years but while they served they were often not used to their full potential. Once in their companies, after completing their training in the regimental school, platoon and company commanders seem to have had little interest in training them further. By and large, unit commanders made no conscientious effort to improve junior commanders' leadership and military skills. From the time of the Frunze reforms to the German invasion, the army leadership rather hypocritically criticized this point in the military press. The NKO could have created schools to instruct junior commanders at more advanced levels but never did so. The high command evidently found it easier to blame and harangue unit commanders than take action itself.

Consequently, Red Army officers did much of the rudimentary training of the draftees, making them an essential link in the lower levels of training. This function detracted from their ability to develop the skills appropriate to their position and to conduct the supervisory and administrative duties related to unit combat readiness. For example, Karl Aru, an artillery officer, noted that, in his artillery regiment, young officers trained the squads and gun crews, chores that in Western armies are traditionally delegated to sergeants.[60] This shortsighted mentality on the part of the officers may have been due to the constant turnover of junior commanders: they did not want to spend the time to train junior commanders who would be leaving in a year or so. But, why then, would a junior commander want to reenlist if he was not taken seriously as a leader?

The larger percentage of officers in the RKKA may have been a reflection of its lack of a professional NCO corps. In 1928, when the Red Army had 529,000 men, 48,000 were officers. In 1933, to satisfy the 9 percent figure, the Red Army and Air Force would have needed over 81,000 officers because the army had expanded to over 900,000 men. The armed forces did not meet the number of leaders needed to keep the officer corps at 9 percent. Success would have meant producing a minimum of 33,000 officers in the space of four years, if no officers left the army during that time. The four years after 1933 represent the worst years for recruiting officer candidates—the military schools produced only 23,217 officers. Recall that in 1928 Voroshilov first made public the military's shortfall of officers, and only several years later the "special mobilizations" began. By 1937, it would have required at least 117,000 line officers to lead the 1.3 million man Red Army, yet it had only 107,000.[61]

From 1932 to 1938, the NKO called 49,113 reserve officers to serve for one year to alleviate the officer shortage. Some even served an additional year to help the army through crisis periods. The army frowned on this practice because it deemed reservists' training insufficient with regard to the new technology then being introduced. Not only that, but 19,147 of the reservists were *mladshie leitenanty*, whose training had been even more perfunctory than that of other reserve officers. The many men who left the service further aggravated the officer shortage before the purge. Between 1928 and 1938, the army lost 62,000 officers, some due to death, injury, judicial action, and so forth, but the most common loss was among those who quit the service for civilian life. The army transferred another 5,670 officers from the ground forces to the air force. Thus 183 more men left the ground forces than were produced by the military schools in the same years.[62]

After 1935, the Red Army attracted better-educated officer candidates than it had a decade earlier. Among the entrants to ground forces military schools in 1937, half had completed high school. In contrast, 87 percent of military school students had only six years or less of education in 1928.[63] The quality of the recruits rose with regard to education if not behavior, although both fell below those of comparable Western armies. Despite their seemingly better quality, officers continued to perform poorly. In June 1940, Marshal Timoshenko, the new commissar of defense, proclaimed that in general officer training was inadequate. In particular, military schools did not train officers as thoroughly as they ought to. He said, "The sharp growth in the number of officers from military schools with insufficient capacity and insufficient cadre has required the accelerated graduation of officers from schools and the training of junior commanders—[as] *mladshie leitenanty*, that cannot match the quality of regular officers." Even the experienced higher officers "have good military qualities, but they do not have sufficient military educations."[64]

OFFICERS' EVERYDAY LIFE

When one considers how Red Army officers lived, what they were paid, and how they were treated in relation to leaders in other sectors of society, it becomes clearer why the military had trouble attracting and keeping officers. The massive changes in pay and privileges enacted in 1935 are understandable in a practical rather than a political sense.

In December 1926, in a speech to senior officers of the Moscow Military District, Voroshilov tried to explain away the discharge of nearly 16,000 officers and political personnel as an economy measure. While the impetus for the discharges may indeed have been economic, it turned out to be a convenient means of purging Trotskyites. To the remaining officers, Voroshilov made less than reassuring remarks in an attempt to mitigate the negative effect of the mass discharge on morale: "These extensive discharges have of course seriously affected the morale of our commanders and have led to a great deal of uncertainty. I can give the assurance that the RVS does not intend in the near future to take any further action of this sort and will do its best to avoid similar large-scale reductions of officers."[65] He went on to admit that officers did endure substandard living conditions and hinted that they would not get much better in the near future:

> The ordinary living conditions of our commanders are not at all satisfactory, but are no worse than the conditions of life of similarly placed personnel in other branches of the government. . . . Nevertheless, these conditions in the Red Army must be improved. With the limited funds available it will be impracticable to bring about a general improvement at once for all grades and duties, therefore we intend to give first consideration to improving the material status of commanders of troops; improvements for subordinate commanders and for staff personnel will follow.[66]

Many men chose to leave the army to seek better employment. Statistics from 1928 and 1929 provide a profile of those who gave up on the army. In those two years, the RKKA discharged 4,426 officers from line units. Of these officers, 1,825 quit because they just did not like the army enough to stay. The army arrested and imprisoned another 643 and forcibly separated the rest from the service due to age or medical problems. The majority of the officers discharged (80 percent) were working-class or white-collar employees—exactly the types of people the army most hoped to retain. The technical branches, such as artillery, engineer and signal, lost the most men. Company-grade officers comprised the majority of discharges, totaling 3,168; most of the men who were discharged had six years or less of service and about half had military school educations. Three-quarters of all dischargees were between the ages of twenty-five and thirty-five. Party members, candidates, or Komsomols represented less than half, 1,777.[67] In 1930, the ground forces discharged a smaller number of officers, 1,691, of whom 35 percent quit because they did not like the army. Another 10.4 percent were arrested, and 5.4 percent were discharged for negligence or incompetence.[68] These numbers tell us that the voluntary request of officers to be released from active duty because of some disaffection with the army constituted the single greatest cause for discharge. The RKKA lost a good number of trained and educated men every year—men who thought they could do better elsewhere.

Pay

For the first sixteen years of the Red Army's existence, officers received extremely low pay. It drove out many of the most talented, and the poor remuneration seems to have discouraged many capable men from joining.[69] Table 4.3 shows the increases in Red Army officer pay. Pay differed for the various branches of the RKKA, just as in the civilian workplace, where wages differed according to skills. The RKKA gave members of the artillery, engineers, and air force pilots higher pay than infantry officers. Not until 1934 did an infantry platoon commander make more than a blue-collar worker. Thus, it is not surprising that the factory floor may have looked more appealing to young men than a hard military life.

Foremen and supervisory personnel earned slightly more money than officers in the twenties and early thirties. An engineer or supervisor made 134 rubles, which was more than a company commander made in 1931. During the first five-year plan, wages for supervisory personnel and technicians rose dramatically. In 1934, factory foremen could make from 250 to 350 rubles a month—equivalent to the pay of a rifle battalion commander—and supervisors could make from 450 to 650 rubles a month, the wages of division and corps commanders.[70] Industrial wages went up again in 1935: foremen now made around 550 rubles a month, and superintendents, 1,200, which was well ahead of military pay raises. By the system of bonuses for production, wages of ordinary factory workers and management personnel went up considerably more than monthly wages indicate. Despite raises, officers' financial position improved only marginally because of inflation, which lowered their purchasing power.[71] Clearly, for many years the Soviet state put more stock in industry and in its workers than it put in the military and its leadership. Unfortunately for the military, potential officers understood the states' priorities all too well.

Service-related expenses further diminished officers' pay. Unlike enlisted men, they had to provide their own uniforms and food as well as furnish their quarters. Some uniform items, such as boots, could cost as much as four hundred rubles. Even with the raise, officers could not be considered handsomely paid. True, officers did get additional pay for housing, but so too did

Table 4.3. Infantry Officer Monthly Pay in Rubles, 1926–1939

	1926	1928	1931	1934	1936	1939
Plt. Cdr. (Lt.)	75	100	110	260	350	623
Co. Cdr. (Cpt.)		123	130	285	425	750
Bn. Cdr. (Maj.)		130	140	335	475	833
Rgt. Cdr. (Col.)	140	180	195	400	600	1,200
Div. Cdr. (Gen.)		195	210	475	700	1,600
Corps Cdr. (Gen.)	200	220	275	550	800	2,000

Source: RGVA f. 37837, op. 21, d. 23, ll. 15, 77; "Pay in the Red Army, February 10, 1933," U.S. MID Reports, Reel 3, 548, 549; "Pay in the Red Army, January 3, 1936," U.S. MID Reports, Reel 3, 554–559; B. F. O. 371, 1939, vol. 23688, 241–245.

civilians sometimes receive assistance for housing from their places of employment. Moreover, workers, like military men, had cooperatives for food and goods. In this respect, officers really had no advantages over their civilian counterparts.[72]

Living Conditions

Poor housing for officers did not help the image of the Red Army and may have hindered its ability to recruit. Even before the first five-year plan, housing was a critical problem, not only for the army but for the whole of Soviet society. In 1931, for example, the RKKA could not provide nearly five thousand of its officers with military quarters.[73] What housing existed often was in a pitiful state. Even the living quarters for senior officers were as overcrowded and dilapidated as that for civilians. Throughout the twenties, thirties, and even into the forties, officers complained bitterly about substandard accommodations. Because the overall quality of life for the officer corps was often lower than that of the equivalent sector in civilian society, it is not surprising that people were reluctant to take responsibility for defending a society that would not provide them with even basic comforts. Once again, this shows continuity from the prerevolutionary army. When Alexander III ordered a mass redeployment of units from Moscow and St. Petersburg to the western frontier, officers accustomed to decent housing were forced to live in "miserable little hamlets in western Poland and the Ukraine"; a mass exodus of officers from the army ensued.[74] These same conditions replicated themselves in the thirties, when the army created numerous units in the Ukraine and transferred others there; all had no choice but to build their own quarters. The army had an even more difficult time getting officers to serve in the remote and inhospitable Far East.[75]

Officers often lived in communal apartments, as did most urban dwellers. For example, a 1932 *Krasnaia zvezda* article offered the following description of officers' housing in an aviation brigade: "The officers' apartment house is in a dilapidated state; the plaster is coming down, and the doors and windows do not shut properly; and no sink is provided for a block of three buildings."[76] This was typical. In a letter to the military press, an officer complained that when it rained, the officers' apartments filled with water from the leaky roof. The water, he said, flowed freely from the top floor to the lower ones. The windows had no glass; it had fallen out because the windows had been constructed so poorly. The doors were made of cheap plywood, making heating the buildings almost pointless. The quarters had no running water. The previous winter, officers, their families, and enlisted men had crammed into the soldiers' barracks together because officers had no separate quarters. Overcrowding required that even classrooms be used for sleeping spaces. It was not unusual for housing to have insufficient heat or even none at all, which in a typically frigid Russian winter was a real health hazard.[77]

Officers with families—the most adversely affected by the primitive living conditions—expressed considerable anger and anguish over the plight of their wives and children. The married officers of the Ukrainian Military District complained that two families had to share a two- or three-room apartment. They also claimed the facilities for their children, such as day care, kindergartens, and playgrounds, were inadequate.[78] In the early thirties in the Leningrad Military District, many officers lived in their offices because there simply were not enough quarters and civilian housing was also hard to get. In 1931, for example, the Moscow garrison could not provide 1,730 officers and their families with quarters, and another 529 had what the army classified as "bad" quarters.[79] The fact that officers and their wives complained so bitterly indicates that they expected to live better. They were not appeased by the knowledge that civilians often lived under identical conditions.

Housing conditions may have been a factor in the composition of the officer corps, because they influenced who volunteered for the army and who stayed. Opportunities abounded for educated men during the prewar five-year plans. Many may have left the army for other work and better conditions, while those who lacked sufficient education for civilian work became officers, no matter what the conditions, to get educations, which, ironically, they hoped would enable them to improve their lives. For example, Sergei Shtemenko relates the conditions he experienced in Moscow in 1933 as a student at the Academy of Motorization and Mechanization:

> I lived near the Academy, in Lefortovo. During my first year, I was in a hostel. In my second year they gave me a room measuring nine square metres and I brought my family up from Kiev. Mother slept on the bed, my wife and I on the floor, and our baby girl in a tub next to us. So a year later, when we moved to a larger room in a house we ourselves had helped to build on the grounds of the Academy, we felt we were living in the lap of luxury.[80]

What may have made all of this acceptable to Shtemenko and others like him was that he had been a poor peasant with only a second-grade education who had been forced to leave home as a teenager to look for work because his family could no longer afford to feed him. Failing to get into agronomy school, he joined the military after a friend from his village who had become an officer sent word that Shtemenko could probably get into a military school, even with his low qualifications. As a result, Shtemenko entered the Moscow Horse Artillery School in 1926, at the age of nineteen. Whatever the army had to offer had to be better than what he had experienced since he left home (working as a porter, carrying bricks on construction sites and chopping wood, and living in the attic of a store and later in a little room above a state-run pawnshop).[81] No wonder Shtemenko stayed in the army; it was the best thing that had ever happened to him. Because the army and party recruited heavily among poor peasants and young workers, this story must have been repeated many times.

The Red Army was not the only army in the interwar period that struggled to recruit officers under conditions of low pay and low social status. The French army also had a great deal of trouble retaining good officers, and for much the same reasons. Many officers left the service in the thirties because the French government consistently refused to improve the salary compensation and living conditions.[82] The British army also suffered from officer shortages, partly because promotions in the officer corps came so slowly it was hard to recruit qualified men. One could spend fourteen years as a subaltern, six as captain, and nine as major before being faced with mandatory retirement. Like the Soviets, the British had a problem with the public's perception of military service. According to Brian Bond and Williamson Murray, the public perception that the unrewarding profession of officer in the army was adequate only for men of second-rate qualities or the fool of the family was the primary cause for the shortage of suitable officer candidates.[83] In Britain, France, and the Soviet Union, society's highest rewards continued to come in the civilian and political sectors. In contrast, the revived German army retained its pre–First World War social status and enjoyed good pay. According to Siegfried Knappe, a young German army officer in 1937, a lieutenant's salary enabled him to own an inexpensive car and a horse and generally maintain a fairly good standard of living.[84] Consequently, the German army had little trouble recruiting officers in the prewar years.

TOWARD A TRADITIONAL ARMY

In the mid-thirties, the RKKA made a concerted effort to enhance the social status and professional appearance of its leaders. The army raised officers' pay, came out with dress uniforms, assigned officers the privilege of being tried by military courts for civil infractions, and brought into use many of the old tsarist titles of rank. Contrary to the idea that the changes were the result of Communist party capitulation to the military in some behind-the-scenes deal in which the high command acquiesced to the ruthless pace of collectivization in return for the trappings of a traditional army, the reason for the changes was far more simple: the regime needed to make a career in the armed forces more appealing in order to recruit more officers.

The RKKA made its changes as part of an ongoing process of reestablishing traditional authority, which occurred throughout Soviet society in the early thirties. The process consisted of measures taken by the Communist party to end and replace those radical policies that undermined the power and purposes of the regime. In the army, this undertaking entailed the restoration of some privileges and trappings of the Imperial Russian Army to the Soviet officer corps and pay raises.[85] The military was a latecomer to the process, which began in civilian society in 1934.

Introduction of Ranks

The Commissariat of Defense announced the decision to introduce titles of rank on 23 September 1935. The change did not come as a complete surprise; a commission had studied the question for a year prior to the announcement. *Krasnaia zvezda* offered the following official explanation:

> For the great bulk of officers . . . service in the Workers' and Peasants' Red Army is becoming a life profession the peculiarities of which call for strictly stipulated regulations on this branch of service. In the training and education of the masses of Red Army men, particularly responsible tasks devolve on officers as a whole, while the leading role of the commander in the field calls for the establishment of military titles which clearly express the military and special qualifications of each commander and member of the officer corps.[86]

The Central Executive Committee, which made the decision to introduce rank, intended to "raise the authority of officers" and "enhance the prestige of commanders and strengthen discipline."[87] This goal marked quite a change from 1926, when Voroshilov, in response to grumblings from officers who did not share the egalitarian ideals of 1917 and wanted ranks restored, had said, "An officer who depends on the prestige of rank is unable to fulfill his proper functions as a leader of the masses."[88] Reality had proven the contrary.

The introduction of personal titles of rank meant that an officer kept his rank until promoted to the next higher rank. In the previous system, duty positions had titles, which were a form of rank. Not only did positions have titles but they also had insignia to identify them. When an officer received a new duty position, he took the title and insignia of that position. With the introduction of ranks, an officer kept his rank until promoted, no matter what position he held, which was the way it was in European armies and had been in the Imperial Army.

Creating personal ranks had some interesting and rather counterproductive consequences: the army used the new rank structure to discriminate against those who rose through the ranks to become officers. After the Civil War and prior to the introduction of ranks, all officers in the combat arms entered the military as platoon commanders with the designation *komvzvod,* the lowest officer rank. Beginning with the class of officer candidates that graduated from military schools and academies in May 1936, school-trained officers became lieutenants (*leitenanty*), the next to the lowest officer rank; but, beginning in August 1937, junior commanders who rose through the ranks and received commissions after special training became *mladshie leit-enanty*, now the lowest officer rank. They both held identical positions—platoon commanders—but the school-trained officer was awarded higher rank and pay, and, consequently, higher status. Identifying those individuals who did not attend military school as inferior in title, rank, and pay implied that military school attendance was the preferred route for a career officer. The army commissioned junior lieutenants as reserve officers, not regular officers; they did not have as long a service obligation as military school graduates and were generally not expected to make the military their career. Thus, the army increased the group identity of school-trained officers but simultaneously decreased overall cohesion among officers.

Because the army depended on a tremendous number of *mladshie leit-enanty* to keep the units going but treated them as second-class officers, it inhibited their full integration into the leadership. The title *mladshii leitenant* was similar to the title given junior platoon commanders (*mladshii kom-vzvod*). This label, most likely, was intended to identify them with their former peers rather than their new ones.

There was more to rank than just the title. Officers held their rank for life, and could only be deprived of it by a court-martial confirmed by the commissar of defense. The length of service before promotion was now formally regulated, and the rules for retirement were modified.[89] The privilege of being tried by military courts for civil crimes rather than by civil courts indicated that the Red Army was becoming more traditional and less revolutionary. Like their aristocratic predecessors, some Red Army officers began to see themselves as a caste separate from society at large.

Witnesses to these changes, such as the British and American military attachés, came to the conclusion that the Red Army officer corps was being bought off by the regime in return for their acquiescence to such unpopular policies as collectivization and dekulakization. Another assessment might well be that these changes were simply part of Stalin's attempt to restore order and predictability to Soviet society. After all, similar changes were made in civil society. Moreover, it is clear that the party and government now wanted service as an officer to become a profession. The past failure in recruiting may have helped shape the nature of the military's modification because it was obvious that changes were in order if the army was to attract officer candidates. By creating a more orderly environment and by adding prestige to the job, perhaps they would succeed in providing the necessary cadres for the army. I do not mean to suggest that all these changes were merely a recruiting ploy; they certainly were not. There had long been a movement within the military to stress the acquisition of professional military attributes; Stalin's social conservatism created an environment in which this movement finally bore fruit.

SUMMARY

It is logical to expect the Red Army to have adopted a peacetime routine and to have settled into a regular pattern of professional development of its officer corps after the Frunze reforms and the demobilization of millions of soldiers and leaders. This expectation never materialized, however. From 1925 to 1941, the Red Army remained in a state of flux regarding tactical and strategic doctrine, equipment, and personnel. The officer corps was particularly beset by constant change. This instability stemmed primarily from recruiting policies and an insufficient number of officer personnel. Unsuccessful attempts by both the party and the army to address the officer shortage further aggravated instability. From 1928 onward, the Red Army was shorthanded in officers.

The Red Army could neither recruit enough officer candidates nor keep many of its officers past their initial obligations, for several reasons. For one, the pay and housing of an officer were often not any better than that of an industrial worker. Moreover, the army could not recruit from the nobility and bourgeoisie, the sectors of society that had supplied the majority of officers for the Imperial Army. The peasantry and working classes, the sectors of society from which the RKKA could recruit, had no tradition of professional military service. The higher status afforded industrial workers and managers and civilian party apparatchiks also hindered recruiting. Although the Soviet press lauded the military, its status in society's eyes remained relatively low. Furthermore, the army suffered from high turnover, although this problem was not unique, for all of Soviet society felt the same flux. The Red Army experienced fully the social upheaval of the twenties and thirties.

As a result of the officer shortage, the Red Army resorted to extraordinary and unorthodox recruiting methods, such as directly commissioning large numbers of enlisted men and junior commanders; transferring political personnel from PUR to military duties; recruiting women; and relying on the party to bring military schools to full strength through "special mobilizations" of party members and Komsomols. The army also relied on reserve officers serving short terms of service to fill the gaps. The diverse methods of procuring officers interfered with the army's ability to educate its leaders and raise standards.

Based on the number of crimes committed by officers, there seems to have been a lack of ethics, a lack of honor, and little sense of duty among many in the officer corps. Ineptitude occurs in all cultures and every part of society, but the amount of criminal activity perpetrated by Red Army officers is astonishing when compared to that in Western armies and the Imperial Russian Army. The plethora of criminal activity indicates that the Red Army did not get the best society had to offer, which was a function of its recruiting policies. These practical problems helped shape the reforms of 1935, which were designed to foster prestige and social status, thereby enhancing cohesion and recruitment efforts; because of flawed implementation, however, they failed to do so. Daily life changed very little.

On the eve of the 1937 purges, the Soviet armed forces can be described in both positive and negative terms: positive in potential and negative in results. Through the rearmament programs instituted during the first and second five-year plans, the RKKA had emerged as a technologically improved mass army of almost 1.5 million men. At the same time, the capability of the leadership to employ its men and equipment effectively had not advanced nearly as far as circumstances warranted. By the mid-thirties, the army and the party both wanted the officer corps to truly become a profession. The army had a well-established education system and procedure for selecting a potential corps of career officers, but because it could not produce them fast enough, the army and the party created officers in such a way and in such numbers as to actually defeat measures to increase quality. The military had no recourse; if the army was to expand it had to have leaders immediately.

CHAPTER 5

The Purge and Further Expansion

The 1937–1938 purge of the Red Army officer corps is commonly and mistakenly viewed exclusively as a blood purge characterized by arrest and execution of officers by the NKVD, headed by Nikolai Ezhov, for whom the period is named. This purge is said to have decimated the Red Army leadership and terrorized it so badly that it was unable to recover before Hitler's invasion. The *Ezhovshchina*, then, supposedly is the root cause of the Red Army's failure in battle in 1941. Westerners have only recently gained access to published Russian archival materials revealing that the purge did not eliminate as many officers as heretofore believed. The simultaneous expansion of the army caused at least as much (if not more) havoc in the officer corps as the purge did. The expansion was the greater cause in limiting the effectiveness of the officer corps in leading soldiers and in degrading the RKKA's efforts to rearm and reorganize for war. The RKKA increased its expansion at a dizzying rate even as the purge tore bloodily through its ranks. This new round of growth required the party and army to recruit and train more officers than ever before.

The *Ezhovshchina* has also been misrepresented as coming primarily from above, inflicted on the army by the Communist party and regime. It is now time to consider that much of the mayhem of the *Ezhovshchina* came from below, that is, from within the army. Soldiers, officers, the military procuracy, and the high command willingly facilitated and participated in the decimation of the officer corps in a process of personal and institutional conformity and adaptation that predated the terror.

THE PURGE

It has been widely assumed that practically all officers removed from the armed forces in 1937 and 1938 were arrested for political reasons and suffered either execution or imprisonment. This assumption is false. Thousands of officers thought to have been lost in the purge due to arrest turned out not to have been arrested but discharged from the army for having been expelled from the Communist party. Primary party organizations, in an orgy of denunciations well beyond Moscow's control, independently expelled thousands of officers for their associations with "enemies of the people" and foreigners. The army almost always subsequently discharged expelled officers. The processes of arrest, expulsion, and discharge became interrelated, adding confusion to fear and magnifying the psychological effects of the terror.

The damage these losses caused the RKKA was somewhat mitigated, for the Commissariat of Defense simultaneously reinstated thousands of discharged officers and commissioned tens of thousands of new officers. These reinstatements and additions numerically more than made up for the permanently purged officers. Nonetheless, the loss of officers hurt and the regime criminally and stupidly wasted a wealth of irretrievable experience, loyalty, and intellect. The influx of new officers, combined with the complex nature of the purge, make it difficult to assess the impact of the *Ezhovshchina* on military cadres.

Based on data compiled by E. A. Shchadenko, chief of the officer personnel section of the People's Commissariat of Defense, arrests accounted for the minority of removals of army officers and political leaders (see Table 5.1). The army discharged the majority for having been expelled from the party. Further information reveals that not all of those listed as arrested by the NKVD's Special Sections were arrested for political crimes. The NKVD arrested about one-third of its victims for other crimes relating to military service or for criminal behavior, such as drunkenness, hooliganism, abuse of power, murder, and other crimes commonly associated with the officer corps. A total of 4,474 officers were reported arrested in 1937, and 5,032 in 1938; however, of these 9,506 arrests, the army instigated only 3,177. Not having its own military police corps, the army requested that the Special Sections arrest these men for various and sundry crimes, of which 1,713 were politically related. The NKVD, of its own accord, arrested 6,300, not 9,500 officers in its melee of political repression, but rather a number closer to 6,300.[1]

The process of cleaning the army of "enemies of the people" actually was part of an informal party membership purge, or *chistka*. The NKVD, which arrested officers for allegedly being enemies of the people, was not directly involved in the membership purge of the party; however, in some cases it did feed information on individuals to PUR and to party cells to elicit denunciations.[2] The Special Sections did arrest some expelled officers, but many officers just lost their party cards and were summarily discharged from the army.

The data do not reveal the subsequent fate of the men who were expelled from the party and discharged from the army but not later reinstated. In the civilian sector, expulsion from the party sometimes preceded arrest. The same held true for the armed forces. The data only allow assessment of the number of leaders eliminated from the army between 1937 and May 1940; they are not a basis for determining how many men the NKVD ar-

Table 5.1. Army Officers Removed from the Rolls, 1937–1939

Reason for Discharge	Discharged in 1937	Discharged in 1938	Reinstated 1938–39	Total Discharges
Arrested by NKVD	4,474	5,032	1,431	8,075
Expelled from KPSS for associations with conspirators	11,104	3,580	7,202	7,482
By directive of NKO of 24 June 1938 for associations with Poles, Germans, Latvians, and other foreigners		4,138	1,919	2,219
Political-moral reasons (drunkenness, moral depravity)	1,139	2,671	430	3,380
Medical discharge or death	1,941	941	12	2,870
Total	18,658	16,362	10,994	24,026
Percent of *nachal'sostav**°	13.1	9.2		

°Includes officers and political leaders.
Source: "O rabote za 1939 god: Iz otcheta nachal'nika Upravleniia po nachal' stvuiushchemu sostavu RKKA Narkomata Oborony SSSR, E. A. Shchadenko, 5 Maia 1940," *Izvestiia TsK KPSS,* no. 1 (1990), 188.

rested in the *Ezhovshchina.* All told, 34,301 army, air force, and PUR leaders were discharged either through arrest or expulsion from the party. The number of enlisted men arrested and discharged is still unknown. The RKKA reinstated 11,596 officers by May 1940. These data leave the fate of 22,705 men unknown. At best, those discharged would have been free to choose new careers and lead normal civilian lives. Those arrested and convicted (not all cases resulted in conviction) were either executed or sentenced to the Gulag. Those expelled and not rehabilitated may later have been arrested and possibly convicted of some political crime and sent to the Gulag or possibly executed. Certainly not all the arrested officers were executed—large numbers were released and rehabilitated after May 1940. In November 1941, the Gulag administration reported approximately 18,000 servicemen of all ranks in confinement.[3]

Shchadenko's data show that in absolute numbers and percentages of the officer corps, the purge had a more limited effect on the military than previously thought. Early Western estimates suggested that between 25 and 50 percent of the Red Army officer corps was repressed in the *Ezhovshchina.* Conveniently, Shchadenko's office gave the percentage of the leadership permanently discharged as of May 1940, which allows a calculation of the total strength of the *nachal'sostav* in the purge years. In 1937, the *nachal'sostav* numbered 144,300; of those discharged in 1937, 11,034 remained discharged as of May 1940—7.7 percent of the *nachal'sostav.* In 1938, of 179,000 leaders, 6,742 became purge victims and were still discharged in May 1940—3.7

percent of the *nachal'sostav*. Because the Red Army stepped up officer procurement during the *Ezhovshchina* at a rate that outpaced discharges, it is extremely difficult to determine the cumulative numerical impact of the purge on the military. Shchadenko's annual figures are probably the most definitive we will ever have. The same situation holds true for the Red Air Force (VVS) and PUR. The VVS had approximately 13,000 officers in 1937, lost 4,724 in the purge, and numbered about 60,000 officers in 1940.[4] PUR began 1937 with about 31,000 personnel, lost 5,000 in the terror, grew to 41,000 in 1941, yet remained short of its authorized strength.[5] The reason for the earlier high estimates by Western historians of the percentage of repressed officers and PUR men is not so much the erroneous estimates of the number of repressed officers but the tremendously low estimates of the size of the *nachal'sostav*. Most estimates put Red Army officer strength at between 70,000 and 80,000 men.[6]

The Purge as a Deadly *Chistka*

It appears that in 1937 and 1938 the call to unmask enemies of the people, a function of the *Ezhovshchina,* was accompanied by an informal *chistka* organized neither by the People's Commissariat of Defense nor by PUR but rather by the primary party organizations themselves. There were important differences between this informal *chistka* and normal membership purges. The primary party organs from company cell to regimental party bureau now looked for enemies of the people (wreckers and spies) instead of politically errant, morally corrupt, or incompetent individuals. Of course, it is conceivable that party cells classified some of the incompetent and corrupt as enemies of the people, yet a large number of officers (although fewer than in previous years) continued to be discharged by the NKO under the category "political-moral reasons." Anyone discharged, other than for moral or medical reasons, was expelled from the party without benefit of a hearing. And, of course, anyone arrested by the NKVD was immediately expelled from the party. More than paralleling each other, the two processes of expulsion and arrest became intertwined.

To better appreciate the dynamics of the *Ezhovshchina*, it is useful to compare and contrast it with the *chistki* of previous years. Like *chistki*, the terror did not come unannounced, and there was some attempt to mentally condition the intended victims beforehand. Certain clues should have tipped off the astute observer—the highly publicized show trials of the former Right Oppositionists Grigory Zinoviev and Lev Kamenev in 1936, for example. Earlier, in 1935, Zinoviev and Kamenev had been held indirectly responsible for the murder of Kirov, and in the initial crackdown that followed, the NKVD arrested forty-three officers in the Moscow Military District. At the same time, PUR expelled 131 men in the Military Political Academy from both the academy and party. Many of them were subsequently arrested.[7] These incidents served to alert the Soviet population that enemies of the people, namely "Trotskyites" and "fascists," could be found at the highest levels of the party, government, and army. The trials alerted observers that even seemingly impeccable revolutionary and Bolshevik credentials provided no immunity from suspicion. Then Field Marshal Mikhail Tukhachevskii's name was ominously brought out in the Karl Radek-Iuri Piatakov trial in January 1937. In March, the NKVD began to selectively arrest Red Army officers serving as advisors to the Republican forces in Spain.[8]

In the two weeks before the arrests of the first officers in the Soviet Union proper, numerous articles in the military press called for more vigilance against enemies of the people. Therefore, when the regime announced the arrests of high-ranking military officers—Mikhail Tukhachevskii, Iona Iakir, Ieronim Uborevich, August Kork, Robert Eideman, Boris Feld'man, Vitaly Primakov, and Vitovt Putna—the shock was less than it might otherwise have been.[9] Another factor that led some people to accept that the generals may have been traitors was that the "traitors" were said to have been tried by a military tribunal of high-ranking officers, which, except for the secrecy of the trials, was normal for serious military crimes.

The mass of the military, led by the PUR, accordingly called for the death penalty for fascist-Trotskyite traitors, just as they had after Zinoviev's and Kamenev's trials. Three days after the press announced the arrests, all units battalion-sized and larger in the Red Army, Navy, and Air Force had passed resolutions calling for the traitors to be shot.[10] During Bukharin's trial in 1938, PUR organized the party cells to pass resolutions to root out "fascist-Trotskyite" centers everywhere. The politruki and commissars announced that death was the only just punishment for such traitors. The rank-and-file soldiers vowed increased vigilance in uncovering enemies of the people.

Unlike a chistka, the Ezhovshchina had no unit hearings. Arrested men were tried in secret, and although some were cleared of wrongdoing and released, many simply disappeared into the Gulag or the grave after interrogation by the NKVD. Another important distinction is that the Ezhovshchina was not limited to Communists. Although it caught up mostly party members, some non-Communists were repressed in the terror as well, although nonparty servicemen were less likely to be denounced in primary party organization meetings. A third difference is that, in previous chistki, enlisted men and officers seem to have been equally susceptible to expulsion, whereas in the Ezhovshchina the targets for expulsion were overwhelmingly officers. Just as it had done after each chistka, the party claimed that it was strengthened; the RKKA claimed to be bolstered by the purge of fascist-Trotskyite traitors, which enabled it to promote younger, loyal, and deserving Communist and nonparty officers.[11]

Communist party members suffered most in the *Ezhovshchina* because party organs, initially encouraged to expose enemies of the people, turned inward to examine themselves as they had been conditioned to do. People of high rank and responsibility (almost always party members) suffered the most. Because associations with such people became grounds for expulsion and discharge, their associates— other party members and ranking officers— were more vulnerable to terror and expulsion than lower-ranking nonparty members.

An especially important difference between the informal *chistka* of 1937– 1938 and previous formal *chistki* was the consequence of expulsion. Prior to June 1937, servicemen expelled from the party as a rule only lost their party cards, but, during the *Ezhovshchina,* they were most often, but not always, discharged from the military and marked as likely candidates for arrest. The worst result of the purge was no longer simply a stifled career but a ruined career and possibly personal doom. Beyond that, the expulsion proceedings contributed to a feeling of helplessness among victims and potential victims. Meetings of the primary party organization were characterized by a lack of formal procedures and by emotional discussions in which the accused had little chance to defend themselves. Nevertheless, some men discharged for being "associates of enemies of the people" did quite well, such as one military procurator expelled in 1937 for having been a member of a Trotskyite deviation back in 1923. While appealing his discharge, he was allowed to live in Moscow and work as a consultant to the People's Commissariat of Justice RSFSR.[12] Generally, the drop in morale among officers at this time has been attributed solely to the terror. However, the threat of discharge added to the psychological torment and must be considered when assessing the total impact of the purge years.[13]

The manner in which expulsions became part of the *Ezhovshchina* is revealed in accounts by Lev Mekhlis, appointed head of PUR in 1938 after Ian Gamarnik headed off arrest by committing suicide. Mekhlis prefaced his report to the Central Committee by relating the following incident, which he labeled absurd: "The party organization of the 301st Transport Company of the 48th Rifle Division submitted the following resolution. 'Our horses are in a poor state, they do not have cover, their oats are poured out on the ground, and they appear ill on account of it, do we not have here, on the part of the officers, enemies of the people?'"[14] The resolution said nothing about expelling or arresting the company's leaders, but was submitted to the regimental party bureau for consideration. Mekhlis complained that the party cells, by failing to understand what was intended by the terms criticism (*kritika*) and self-criticism (*samokritika*), had actually undermined the authority of the officers.

Primary party organizations apparently felt pressured to make denunciations of some sort; when ideological bases were lacking, they based their accusations on performance.[15] Because of the rapid expansion, terror, and discharges, many men found themselves elevated to positions for which they were not prepared and naturally made errors in judgment and performed poorly before mastering their responsibilities. Individuals in the primary party organizations sometimes labeled such mistakes "wrecking" and used them to have their leaders either expelled or arrested.

In a speech to the Eighteenth Party Congress in March 1939, as part of Moscow's move to end the *Ezhovshchina,* Mekhlis described the following instance of unjust and hasty expulsion:

There was even a bizarre case of expulsion like the following. The representative of the special department in a certain regiment told the commissar, Gashinsky, that he was after the club superintendent, a *politruk* by the name of Rybnikov. Gashinsky passed this on in confidence to the party organization, and Rybnikov was expelled by the primary party organization. It soon turned out that Rybnikov was not a bad bolshevik and that the special department was after him . . . to get him to work in their department. The mistake was corrected, but only after comrade Rybnikov had been put to a lot of mental suffering.[16]

The two examples offered by Mekhlis show a contrast in purge procedures of primary party organizations. The 301st Transport Company referred their finding to the next higher level for action, just as often happened in the purge of civilian society.[17] In the Gashinsky case, however, the primary party organization itself expelled the "enemy of the people," suggesting that there were local variations in the *Ezhovshchina,* just as in *chistki;* however, it reinforces the argument that the primary party organizations, not the Special Sections, were responsible for the major losses in 1937 and 1938.

The connection between expelling party members and exposing enemies of the people is reflected in an internal document of the military soviet of the Kiev Military District (KVO), which provides details of both expulsions and terror in the district. The document refers to an earlier directive from Stalin and Voroshilov that the Kiev Military District was to "clean the army of enemies of the people." It also orders members of the district's military soviet to make lists of candidates, both party and nonparty, to fill positions vacated by purged officers.[18] Therefore, it would appear that the center, by the use of vague phrases, encouraged the lower levels to stir things up in the units (but to what extent is unknown) and then left them to their own devices.

The orders to the military districts to stir things up were preceded by an article in *Krasnaia zvezda* on 14 June 1937 calling on all army party organs to assist the NKVD in "exposing enemies of the people." Yet, after the military purge was under way, only the arrests of Marshal Tukhachevskii and his cohort were ever mentioned in the military press. The military press did not encourage denunciations or witch hunts. This restraint was quite unlike the civilian press, which was full of exhortations for uncovering enemies of the people, spies, wreckers, and their protectors. Because the military press virtually never mentioned the *Ezhovshchina* after June 1937, it would seem that their reading of the civilian press kept the primary party organizations active in expelling their members, sometimes in conjunction with, but often independently of, directives from PUR, the People's Commissariat of Defense, and the NKVD.

Just as the NKVD's net widened to include associates of enemies of the people, party cells also expelled officers accused of associating with enemies of the people. For example, I. T. Starinov, a field-grade officer, reported:

> Soon after my arrival Dmitrii Ivanovich Vorob'ev, my assistant for material and technical supplies, was accused of having connections with Trotskyites. The only pretext for this accusation was Vorob'ev's friendship with Colonel N. M. Ipatov . . . who had been declared an enemy of the people not long before. Engineer P. I. Martsinkevich and Vorob'ev's assistant, V. N. Nikitin . . . tried to defend him at the party meeting. But there were ill-wishers present; Vorob'ev was expelled from the party.[19]

What makes this a particularly apt example is that the party reinstated Vorob'ev nine months later, indicating that his association with an enemy of the people was inconsequential and that the primary party organization had overstepped its bounds. It seems that being an associate of an enemy of the people soon became regarded as a less serious offense, often meriting rehabilitation.

Not every primary party organization got caught up in the whirlwind of denunciations. A. T. Stuchenko, a student officer in the Frunze Military Academy during the *Ezhovshchina,* said: "Our party group held together. We did not look for 'enemies of the people' among ourselves and firmly resisted all attacks from outside. We even began to be accused of a loss of revolutionary vigilance, and our sectional party organization was threatened with disbandment." Their lack of "vigilance" did not sit very well with the school's commissar, but the section leader staunchly resisted denouncing men in his group. When the purge ended, he and his group were praised. The same school commissar then said: "Now those are fine Communists in the cavalry section! A close-knit bunch, they held together."[20] It seems that membership in a close-knit group proved one of the better ways of avoiding denunciation. It also seems that it was largely the average party member who contributed to the unpredictability of the *Ezhovshchina* .

The terminology used in official documents reflected the ambiguities of the purge. The aforementioned KVO report reveals that, as of 25 March

1938, of 2,922 men dismissed from their positions and discharged from the RKKA, 1,066 had been arrested by the NKVD. This is an important indicator that terror and expulsions were part of the same process. The report referred to the operation in the Kiev Military District as a *chistka*, not of the party but of the army. This characterization parallels Shchadenko's report, which labeled the purge "cleaning out the army" (*Ochistka armii i peresmotr uvalennykh*). The use of the word *chistka* in the KVO military soviet report may have created confusion about Moscow's intentions and thus led to a familiar membership purge (*chistka*) in which the party was cleaned through expulsion.

A third example of the convergence of terror and party purge is a report by Mekhlis to the Central Committee in May 1940 in which he gave the status of postpurge PUR. The report included discussions and figures on arrests and expulsions from the party and discharges from the army in exactly the same format as Shchadenko's report. Thus, Mekhlis presented the whole cataclysm of 1937–1938 as one event, whereas in fact it was two. This anomaly, coupled with the fact that only 265 of the 3,176 men discharged from PUR in 1938 were discharged as a result of arrest, suggests that NKVD involvement was more limited than previously thought.[21] Mekhlis lamented the "gross errors" that occurred, again blaming the excesses on the primary party organizations and holding the center blameless.

Not until Khrushchev's "Secret Speech" of 1956 did anyone describe the purge as unjustified. In memoirs published afterward, many of the survivors told how they for a long time believed the purge was justified. They described the abuses of the purge in terms of a man-against-man conflict. In other words, many genuinely thought that enemies of the people served in the armed forces—as earlier *chistki* had proved—and that the system was not to blame for the injustice that arose from human error at the local level. Petro Grigorenko, who experienced the purge firsthand as an engineer officer, viewed the terror as a plot established at the highest levels that worked all too well because of the ability of evil people, meaning the NKVD, to use unrestricted power for their own ends. Stepan Kalinin, also an army officer, observed in his memoirs that abuses were attributable to political true believers and self-promoters in the military.[22] These opinions are very nearly correct but too limited in those they blame. Initiated at the center, the terror was bolstered at the local level by some who saw it as a means of settling personal rivalries, but it became too widespread to have been limited to a few "evil people." These memoirists conform to the idea that the army was blameless, a victim rather than an accomplice. Still unacknowledged by survivors and Russian military historians, the breadth of the purge was established not in a smoke-filled room in the Kremlin but in the units, by soldiers and officers attempting to conform to the latest shift in the political wind. The process relied on the convictions of the Special Sections and party organizations that the purge was just and necessary. Individual credulity fueled the excess.

Denunciations and expulsions may have spread so quickly because officers and the rank and file had been conditioned through two decades of *chistki* to see class enemies and wreckers in all walks of life. The *chistki* of the late twenties and early thirties proved that the Red Army could be penetrated by class aliens in all categories of personnel—enlisted men, officers, and political leaders—and that anyone could become a class enemy overnight as the party introduced new policies and changed the general line on old policies. The purposefulness, thoroughness, and apparent impartiality of the *chistka* attestation committees legitimized the process and results. The *chistki* may well have created trust in party-sponsored "cleansing" activities in the minds of future victims. When the blood purge came along, they were helpless before it. Their trust in the system was so strong that some of the victims still professed faith in it and believed for years afterwards that, even though their arrest was a mistake, the *Ezhovshchina* itself was just and necessary.[23] I. T. Starinov gives an example of such faith in his memoir. When he questioned the guilt of some arrested officers, a friend said: "Not another word Il'ia! Comrade Stalin has taken charge of cadres himself . . . and he will not let innocent people be wronged. It is not for nothing that he made Ezhov head of the NKVD."[24]

Indeed, the *Ezhovshchina* does not seem to have alienated the army from the party. During 1937, 10,341 military party members were expelled from the Communist party. At the same time, 23,599 officers and men gained admitance to the party, 17,496 of them after the purge began. The party admitted over 100,000 soldiers and officers in 1938; and more than 10,000 joined the party in the first month of 1939. Civilian party admissions also picked up.[25] A great many people appear to have retained faith in the party as a positive force, or at least as a means for personal advancement.

The Role of the Military Procuracy

By Soviet military law, servicemen could only be arrested on the orders of the military procurator's office, and, for officers to be arrested, the procurator's office had to petition the Commissariat of Defense. During the purge, the regime subverted the military judiciary. First, the Central Committee invested military district soviets comprised of representatives of the district commander, PUR, and the NKVD through the Special Sections with the authority to arrest and discharge military personnel. Second, the Special Sections adopted the technically illegal practice of arresting soldiers and officers administratively, without permission from the military soviets or military procuracy. Oleg Suvenirov, Russia's most recent standard bearer of the idea that Stalin's cult of personality was the root of all the RKKA's ills, maintains that the Special Sections' circumvention of the military procuracy is the key to understanding how the army was done in by the NKVD.[26]

There is no doubt that the NKVD illegally circumvented the military judicial system and then proceeded to act arbitrarily in arresting, imprisoning, torturing, and killing thousands of officers, but we must acknowledge the role of the army in preparing the way for this. From the beginning, the army acknowledged the supremacy of the Communist party and the political and social order it was creating. It should be noted that expulsion and discharge on political grounds began in 1931 and were seldom related to *chistki*. Equally important, the army established the precedent of discharging soldiers and officers for political deviance. In the first year that this went into effect, the military procuracy discharged 1,166 officers—883 for political considerations and 283 for moral reasons—but arrested none.[27]

In 1935, the army went further and established the precedent of arresting officers for even the most minor political irregularities, though not all officers who made political missteps were arrested. The best examples include the case of a veterinarian who was arrested in September 1935 on charges of anti-Soviet agitation for expressing the opinion that the Ukraine would be better off independent of the USSR. The procuracy built the case against him on letters from soldiers and officers of his unit who denounced him not only as anti-Soviet but also as a bad veterinarian. In another case, a battalion commander was arrested in August 1935 for saying of Sergei Kirov's murder, "It was the death of a scum." He, too, was turned in by members of his unit. The army added other charges after his arrest, such as having been a member of Kolchak's White Army, having been expelled from the party in 1933 for his service with Kolchak, and having a brother who was censured by the Special Sections in 1932—charges that, by themselves, had not led to arrest or dismissal until the political climate changed in 1935. A final example of the army's self-subordination to the primacy of politics was the military procurator's authorization in November 1935 for the Special Sections to arrest a company commander charged with being a member of a Trotskyite counterrevolutionary movement. Ironically, Deputy Commissar of Defense Marshal Tukhachevskii, who was falsely accused of the same charge only two years later, gave the authorization for this arrest.[28] The army, then, had tacitly agreed, years before the purge, that politically unsuitable officers should be arrested or discharged and that it would lend a hand, even take a leading role, in the process. The RKKA gradually but surely fell into line with the trend in civil society to hunt for wreckers, diversionists, spies, Trotskyites, and so on. It was neither the first nor the last societal trend that would be reflected in the army.

The notion that there would not have been political repression of the officer corps without the machinations of the Special Sections is unfounded.

During the *Ezhovshchina*, the military procuracy, in conjunction with the NKO, had 1,713 officers arrested for purely political reasons. The military procuracy was guilty of cleaning its own ranks of enemies of the people with less than diligent attention to truth and justice. As merely one example, Rozovskii, chief military procurator in 1938 and 1939, petitioned the NKO for the discharge of a military procurator for having been born in America and being a practicing Jew. He based his petition on an accusation made by an arrested man who smuggled the information out of prison in a letter to his wife who passed it on to Rozovskii.[29] Here the army's highest legal representative adopted a favorite tactic of the NKVD, basing accusations on the testimony of prisoners.

Rehabilitation

By 1 May 1940, 11,596 discharged officers had been reinstated. In all, 30 percent of army officers arrested or discharged in 1937 and 1938 were reinstated. In the air force, the odds were distinctly greater against purge victims. Of the 5,616 air force officers victimized by the purge, only 892, or less than 16 percent, were reinstated by the end of 1939.[30] In 1937, less than 5 percent of those arrested were reinstated, indicating that the NKVD was initially methodical about targeting "enemies of the people." Higher reinstatement figures of officers arrested in 1938 (24 percent) suggest that the NKVD had truly gone beyond the bounds of legality. By comparison, in 1937, nearly 40 percent of those expelled and discharged but not arrested were reinstated, and in 1938, 80 percent, which suggests that the primary party organizations had gotten completely out of control and acted in a manner contrary to the wishes of the party. It also suggests that the higher political organs in the army had much more authority and independence at this time than previously accepted. Had the army been thoroughly cowed by the party and secret police, it would not been so vigorous in overruling the actions of the cells and making appeals to the NKVD. Such appeals and overrulings could have been dangerous because people such as military procurators who made appeals on behalf of arrested men and overturned decisions of the primary party organizations became vulnerable to charges of aiding enemies of the people—yet this does not seem to have deterred many officers from doing what they thought was right.

Most rehabilitations took place at the local level and were granted by the primary party organizations, the political and military chain of command, and special appeals commissions. Still other officers, though fewer and mainly of higher rank, were rehabilitated by higher authorities, whose approval was required before an inmate could be released from the Gulag.[31] Reinstatement came rather quickly for some. In the KVO, a special appeals commission reinstated thirty officers even as the purge progressed. At the same time, Moscow failed to enforce central control of the purge. In the KVO, denunciations were still common in the autumn of 1938, the commission having failed to achieve its assigned completion deadline of May.[32]

In 1939, the RKKA's military procuracy routinely requested that men charged and arrested as enemies of the people have the charges against them changed to associates of enemies of the people and then be released from the Gulag and reinstated in the army. This tactic was often successful.[33] To a lesser extent, the chief procurator's office argued for rehabilitation on the basis of facts. One case in particular provides insight on the purge. In 1939, Chief Military Procurator Rozovskii appealed to the NKO for the rehabilitation of Sergei Skalon, military procurator of the 9th Rifle Division, who had been discharged for associations with foreigners. The case against Skalon was based on the fact that he had been born in Latvia. Rozovskii argued that although Skalon had indeed been born in Latvia, he was not Latvian nor did he know anyone in Latvia. Skalon had been born in Latvia to Russian parents because his father was a railroad worker and had been assigned to work in Latvia. The family left Latvia in 1911 with ties to no one when Sergei was four or five years old.[34] Skalon must have made this argument when he was arrested but was not believed, and it took intervention by a higher body to reopen his case. Skalon's discharge was not completely groundless; he fell into a category that made him susceptible to punitive action by the state. Rozovskii appealed many other similar cases in which a past, and sometimes long past, deviance had come back to haunt officers. Many were indeed political, such as the case of M. Savitskii and others who had been expelled from the party for Trotskyite deviance as far back as 1923 but had been allowed to continue to serve the army until 1937, when the rules were temporarily suspended.[35] Once their names were cleared, they picked up where they left off, notwithstanding the physical and psychological scars they may have incurred.

REINTRODUCTION OF DUAL COMMAND

During the *Ezhovshchina,* Mekhlis strengthened his power over the newly reconstituted PUR. On 15 August 1937, PUR reintroduced the title *voennyi komissar,* commonly rendered as military commissar. The term, which might better be translated as war commissar, was originally introduced during the Civil War and had not been used since 1925. Simultaneously, the Commissariat of Defense reinstituted dual command at regiment level and higher, meaning that all military orders had to be countersigned by a commissar. Mekhlis defined the role of commisars in the purge years using language reminiscent of wartime: "They should know all that is going on in every corner of the Red Army; they must be faithful instruments of the general line of the Stalinist Central Committee, and, together with the party organizations, nip all treason in the bud, safeguard our beloved army from spies, and see to it that no enemy penetrates into our ranks."[36]

In the postwar years, the Soviet military asserted that the reimposition of dual command hamstrung the army and put it under the control of the political organs, but this suggestion does not hold up well to close scrutiny. In general, if a commissar attempted to control a unit, his success would depend, as before, on personality; in part because of the terms of dual command: "The military commissar answers together with the commander for all spheres of the military, political, and economic life of the unit."[37] If anything went wrong, the commissar stood to be included in any punishment. Before dual command, the commissar could not be blamed for shortcomings in unit military activities. Dual command, then, gave the commissar more authority, but it also made him more responsible for results and personally vulnerable in case of failure.[38]

In many cases, the relationship between commander and commissar did not change with the reversion to dual command. Commissars just signed whatever the unit commander asked of them, recognizing that they knew little of military affairs, trusting the commander not to get them both in trouble. Mekhlis deemed this passive relationship unhealthy. He truly wanted PUR to provide oversight, and those who acted passively were taken to task. One commissar was criticized for justifying his actions by saying, "Why should the commissar worry about the plans for combat training? This is the unit commander's business. The commissar has enough work without it."[39]

In 1938, PUR created two new political positions to enable it to do more political training and bolster discipline at the company level: deputy political instructor (*zamestitel' politruk*), to assist the platoon commander; and assistant political instructor (*pomeshchnik politruk*), to assist the company politruk. Komsomol junior commanders filled these positions. As political assistants, these men no longer filled military positions but came under the control of the political apparatus.[40]

RETURNING TO "NORMAL"

By the end of 1938, Stalin and company sought to halt the *Ezhovshchina* and bring conditions in the army back to normal. It took some effort by the center to end the purge in the Red Army, indicating that Moscow had indeed allowed the purge to run amok in the units. It could, with the proper pressure, have stopped the process at any time, yet this does not seem to have defined the center's role. It could start and stop the *Ezhovshchina* and eliminate selected victims, but it could not effectively guide the primary party organs.

Officers who had been expelled from the party in 1937 and 1938 intensified their petitioning for reinstatement in 1938, blaming their unjust expulsions on true enemies of the people, namely those who had been arrested in the terror. Party organizations held meetings in the units to discuss unjust expulsions and, in the words of Mekhlis, "to act on the basis of facts and documents, not rumors and whispers."[41]

In assessing the *Ezhovshchina*, extreme judgments must be tempered by the consideration that the loss of large numbers of men from the service was not unusual for the RKKA. The purge years were not the only period in which the officer corps lost significant numbers: in 1927, 16,000 officers and commissars (possibly 20 percent of the officer corps) were discharged from the army; in 1935, 6,198 officers, or 4.9 percent of the total army ground forces officer corps, were discharged for political, moral, and other reasons; in 1936, 5,677 leaders (4.2 percent) were discharged.[42] Simultaneously, thousands more officers quit the service of their own volition. Moreover, the reputation of the party was not destroyed, and party-army relations remained strong.

Restoring Party Discipline

The party and the army worked together to restore military discipline to an acceptable level, but the party alone had to get the political organs back on track. The immediate task, once the hierarchy decided to end the purge, was to get the party bureaus and cells to stop the denunciations and expulsions. In early 1939, in an effort to make it unmistakably clear to the regimental political and party organs that the regime desired an end to the purge, Mekhlis railed at the Eighteenth Congress, saying, "The work of our party commissions suffer from many defects. Political organs and party organizations often expel party members far too light-heartedly. The party commissions of the Political Administration of the Red Army finds it necessary to reinstate about 50 percent of the expelled men because the expulsions were unjustified."[43]

As part of the return to normalcy, an interesting story made the pages of *Krasnaia zvezda* in January and February 1939. It concerned the trial of a *politruk* charged with falsely accusing a Red Army officer of being an enemy of the people. The trial was noteworthy because it was the only trial covered extensively in the military press. The *politruk* was found guilty of slander and sentenced to five years in prison.[44] It is very likely that the purpose of this trial, and the publicity assigned it, was to give notice of the end of the purge. Anyone who could read between the lines knew that from now on anybody denouncing someone had better be sure of the facts and of support from the party organs. These two examples illustrate that the primary party organs played an extensive role in the *Ezhovshchina* and that ending the purge required more than calling off the NKVD; PUR had to stifle the power and initiative of the lower party organs in the army.

Whether the army returned to "normal" or not after 1938 is an open question. Thereafter, the experience could never have been far from the thoughts of the officers and men involved. The scars on the psyche of the army remained at least as long as Stalin was alive. Many officers retained physical and emotional scars from their interrogations and imprisonment, despite their rehabilitation. No doubt a certain inhibition characterized their actions thereafter.[45] But the army did not stop in its tracks, and the failure of the army to overcome the dysfunctions of the prepurge years does not permit the assumption that those problems would have been cured had there been no purge.

A NEW CRISIS IN OFFICER MANNING

During the *Ezhovshchina*, the shortage of officers reached crisis proportions. The army failed to solve this problem before the German invasion. The new crisis in officer manning between 1937 and 1941 was the result of expansion in conjunction with the purge that created a tremendous need for additional leaders at the battalion level—a need that could be met neither by normal nor by extraordinary recruiting methods.

Although Marshal Tukhachevskii's announcement to a group of military officers of the decision to again expand the regular forces in 1936 was greeted with stormy applause and shouts of "Hurrah!" there proved to be little to cheer about and many difficulties in the ensuing years.[46] The most significant strain was procuring the necessary number of officers to lead the Red Army. For example, on 1 January 1938, the Red Army experienced a shortage of 39,100 officers. By the end of the year, the army was short 93,000 officers. One-third of the shortfall was due to the purge; the rest was caused by the increased requirement for officers resulting from the creation of new units during the year.[47]

Blaming the shortage of officers on the purge actually dates from the *Ezhovshchina*, when military district commanders met with Peoples' Commissar of Defense Voroshilov, in November 1937, to report on the progress of the purge in their districts. The commanders bitterly decried the shortage of officers resulting from discharges and arrests. N. V. Kuibyshev, commander of the Transcaucasus Military District, complained that one of his divisions was commanded by a major, that he was short 23 percent of unit commanders and 40 to 50 percent of officers in the technical branches, all due to the purge. He said this amounted to 1,312 men.[48] However, his district had been purged of just 533 officers that he knew of. Of the other 779, some had been transferred, some quit the army when their obligations expired, and the rest quite simply had never been there; expansion had created positions that had gone unfilled. One can only speculate that he and the other district commanders tried to make Voroshilov believe all their personnel problems stemmed from the purge, seeking to make the terror look worse than it was in order to put pressure on Stalin to bring the *Ezhovschina* to an end as soon as possible.

Not only is the officer shortage mistakenly blamed exclusively on the purge, but so is the poor state of military proficiency in the years 1939–1941. It is widely believed that poor performance stemmed from the execution of the best leaders, which left only the inept and incompetent to carry on. The professional competence of the prepurge officer corps may have been overestimated, inasmuch as it went hand in hand with making martyrs of the purged. There are a number of other explanations. Expansion of the armed forces from 1.5 million to nearly five million men by the spring of 1941 cannot be dismissed as a source of "incompetence." One recent Russian biographer of Stalin, Dmitrii Volkogonov, in perpetuating the idea that all the army's problems were Stalin's fault, reports that at the beginning of 1941, just 7.1 percent of the military leadership had higher military education, 55.9 percent had military school education or its equivalent, 24.6 percent had special short courses of instruction, and 12.4 percent had no military education whatsoever. In addition, by summer 1941, about 75 percent of officers and 70 percent of political personnel had been in their assignments for less than a year. All this, Volkogonov claims, resulted from the purge.[49] Yet it is not valid to use the purge as an excuse for officers' lack of command experience two and a half years later. As devastating as the purges were, the loss of about 22,000 officers should not have caused such a downturn in training or left open so many leadership positions. A greater appreciation of the effects of expansion on officer assignments helps illustrate other significant personnel problems of the RKKA.

Expansion and Officer Procurement 1937–1941

The number of units created by the RKKA increased dramatically on the eve of the war, and consequently, the need for more officers became more acute. Between 1 January 1939 and 1 May 1941, the army created 111 new rifle divisions and at least 50 new armored and motorized divisions. By June 1941, the RKKA had 303 divisions; 81 of which were still in the process of forming when the war broke out.[50] Therefore, all officers serving in units created after June 1940 would de facto have less than a year in their position. This explains why 75 percent of officers were in their positions for so short a time. The creation of every new battalion, brigade, division, and corps meant new command positions to be filled, regardless of the qualifications of the available officers. Here is the reason why 68 percent of platoon and company-level officers only had a five-month course of instruction.[51] A great many were junior commanders trained as *mladshie leitenanty* to fill positions in new units, not to replace purged lieutenants and captains. The increase of new assignments over five years contributed to upward and lateral mobility, as well as overall instability in officer assignments in units, as shown in Table 5.2.

The large number of new assignments and reassignments illustrate that the instability in officer assignments cannot be solely attributed to the purge. Not including reinstatements, at most 23,500 officers would have needed to be reassigned to cover the losses of the *Ezhovshchina*. Reassignments far exceeded this number during the purge years. The army's creation of new units and the termination of the territorial system contributed most to this phenomenon.[52]

In addition to attributing the instability in assignments to the purge, Soviet historians incorrectly blamed the purges for the decline in military schooling among officers. At the beginning of the German invasion, 37 percent of Soviet officers did not have military school educations. The implication is that educated men were purged while unschooled men were untouched. A close inspection of the numbers, however, shows that by 1941 those lacking education were at the bottom echelons; in contrast, almost all battalion commanders and above had mid-level or higher military schooling, including KUKS courses. Most unschooled officers were *mladshie leitenanty* promoted from the ranks, as shown in Table 5.3. The vast number of undertrained officers served at battalion level, where they were responsible for training and leading the masses of the Red Army and incorporating new technologies. The consequences should be obvious.

Another indication that more than the purge was at work in degrading the army's capabilities is that nearly a year before the onslaught of the *Ezhovshchina,* many officers held positions normally reserved for men at one or two

Table 5.2. Number of Officers Reassigned by Promotion or First Duty, 1935–1939

	1935	1936	1937	1938	1939
Division or higher level	105	567	585	1,620	1,674
Regiment level	2,750	8,960	7,602	31,760	37,671
Battalion level	23,422	28,555	26,351	109,843	159,105
Total	26,277	37,782	34,538	143,223	198,450
Percent officers assigned to new units	21.5	29.1	23.8	59.9	55.4

Source: "O rabote za 1939 god: Iz otcheta nachal'nika Upravleniia po nachal'stvuiushchemu sostava RKKA Narkomata Oborony SSSR, E. A. Shchadenko, 5 Maia 1940," *Izvestiia TsK KPSS*, no. 1 (1990), 186.

Table 5.3. Sources of Procurement for Active Duty Offices, 1935–1939

	1935	1936	1937	1938	1939
Academies	1,359	2,311	2,803	2,762	4,432
Military schools	3,979	8,247	8,517	20,316	35,290
Courses for *ml. lty.*				26,750	51,221
Readmitted or called up from reserves	9,642	2,834	2,675	7,172	10,204
Total	14,980	13,392	13,995	57,000	101,147

Source: "O rabote za 1939 god: Iz otcheta nachal'nika Upravleniia po nachal'stvuiushchemu sostavu RKKA Narkomata Oborony SSSR, E. A. Shchadenko, 5 Maia 1940," *Izvestiia TsK KPSS*, no. 1 (1990), 186.

ranks higher. Due to expansion, many majors instead of colonels commanded regiments, numerous captains rather than majors commanded battalions, and lieutenants and senior lieutenants commanded companies, batteries, and squadrons in place of captains. There were even instances of *kombrigs* commanding divisions and *komdivs* commanding corps. In the summer maneuvers held in September 1936, only four of eighteen brigade- and larger-sized units had commanders of the appropriate rank. Officers with ranks at least one level below the authorized rank commanded the others.[53]

The elevation of men to higher positions did not follow a strict pattern. Some men became battalion commanders after only three or four years of service, while other men with as much as seventeen years of service were kept in their battalions instead of being promoted. In the preexpansion Red Army, it took at least ten years of service before an officer assumed a battalion command (unless he achieved it during the Civil War). In the days of expansion, men with as little as three years service received such commands.[54]

PUR, too, was shorthanded and had to turn to the civilian party organs for help. In 1937, the party mobilized several thousand men for PUR. Many were strictly civilian Komsomol and party members thrust into the army to fill slots. Others were both experienced party members and former soldiers who often proved to be of great value to PUR. In August 1939, the Central Executive Committee ordered local party organs to induce four thousand Communists to serve at all levels of PUR. Some were senior party personnel whom PUR assigned positions at corps level and higher. The August mobilization brought the number of PUR personnel to 34,000. Although many of the mobilized party members had political experience, they were not familiar with PUR's policies and procedures, nor did they know anything about the military and thus needed special training.[55]

The measures taken in 1939 did not keep pace with PUR's growing requirements, which increased in tandem with the army's, and, in 1940, the party drafted another fifteen hundred Communists for PUR. Between 1938 and 1941, PUR's rolls expanded to include nearly 41,000 political workers of all ranks. Nonetheless, PUR was not able to fill all vacancies, and many officers became de facto commander-commissars without the perquisite political qualifications. Party work in the ranks suffered accordingly.[56]

THE GERMAN EXPERIENCE

The Soviet military's experience of rapid expansion had its parallels. The total mobilizations of the British, French, German, and American armies in both world wars required many officers to assume positions above their ranks. For the most part, they limited it to lower levels of command. The most common situation was for first lieutenants to command companies and for majors to command battalions. Rarely did commands at the regiment level or higher go to those without the proper rank or professional training.

The experience of the German army during the thirties offers a useful comparison: when the Reichswehr made the transformation to Wehrmacht as Hitler prepared for war, the German armed forces underwent the same type of expansion the RKKA experienced. In 1933 and 1934, the German army grew from one hundred thousand to three hundred thousand men. Between 1934 and 1936, it increased to six hundred thousand men against the wishes of military planners who had envisioned reaching a force of this size (thirty-six infantry divisions and three armored divisions, an increase from seven infantry divisions and three cavalry divisions) only by 1939.[57] By 1 September 1939, the active army was 730,000 men strong. The size of the Luftwaffe rose from 18,000 in 1935 to 370,000 in 1939. The greatest single problem the Germans claim to have had in this expansion was procuring adequate numbers of officers.[58]

Between the wars, the German army, like the Red Army, preferred to recruit its officer candidates from the ranks. Men were identified in the first few months of their first year of service as potential officers and offered the opportunity to attend *kriegsschule*. Those who accepted received six months of special prepatory training while in their units. One difference between the Soviet and German systems was the caliber of men recruited. Officer candidates for the German army had to have completed *gymnasium* and passed the *abitur* in preparation for attending university. Other differences were that the *kriegsschule* lasted only nine months and offered only military instruction and intense socialization to the mores of the traditional German (or perhaps Prussian) officer corps.[59] Through the military schools, the Wehrmacht produced 4,000 officers per year.

The Germans addressed the procurement problem with a variety of measures. Like the Red Army, they expanded their military school system and cut back the curriculum. Between 1936 and 1938, they drafted and commissioned 2,500 police officials, reactivated 1,800 retired officers, commissioned 1,500 NCOs and acquired 1,800 officers from the annexation of Austria. When this did not prove sufficient, the army took steps to commission more NCOs in 1938.[60] Beginning in 1939, the German army routinely commissioned NCOs without additional formal instruction.

During the course of this expansion, General von Schwedler, head of the Army Personnel Office, and General Beck, chief of the General Staff, debated the wisdom of maintaining the rapid rate of growth. General Schwedler resisted any further increase in the number of Wehrmacht formations because, in 1935, he considered the officer corps to be already so diluted by recruits from nontraditional sources that there was no longer "an officer corps in the true sense." Beck overrode Schwedler's objections, according to historian Wilhelm Deist, at the risk of impairing the efficiency of the officers, considered the most important functional element in the military hierarchy.[61] No such voice of caution was raised in the RKKA.

When the Wehrmacht mobilized for the war with Poland, it numbered 3.7 million men and maintained its officer corps at 4 percent of the total. The state of the Wehrmacht's leadership on the eve of the war was comparable to that of the Red Army. In September 1939, only about one in six officers was a fully trained professional by German peacetime standards. Because five-sixths of the officer corps had neither the knowledge nor, more important, the experience required for effective military leadership, standards of professionalism inevitably deteriorated. Some German generals even feared that the abilities of many officers were being overtaxed by promotion beyond their capabilities. One General Staff officer, General von Leeb, went so far in 1939 as to describe the new German army as a "blunt sword."[62] Although von Leeb seems to have exaggerated the decline of officer skills, it is only logical to conclude that the Red Army suffered from exactly the same training problems and inexperience, though undoubtedly on an even larger scale.

How, then, can one explain the great successes of the Wehrmacht from 1939 to 1942, when it had the same problems as the Red Army, which went from calamity to calamity? First, we have to realize that the German army officer corps had extremely high standards of civilian and military education and a very strict code of conduct, both rooted in its aristocratic heritage. Therefore, any decline in these standards did not necessarily mean that incompetent men were commissioned; rather, the Wehrmacht commissioned men that by its standards were less than ideal. Moreover, the German army—unlike the Red Army—had a well-trained and experienced noncommissioned officer corps to help take up the slack in leadership. Finally, the population from which the German army recruited its officers and NCOs was better educated, more in sync with the technology of the time, and more socially and culturally cohesive. German society provided better raw material for military leaders in the industrial age than Soviet society could muster. The German army did not have an actual problem recruiting officers—there was never a shortage of volunteers—just a reluctance to lower its standards below a certain point.

RENEWED EFFORT TO PROCURE MORE OFFICERS

Expansion and purge produced many vacancies at the lowest levels of the Soviet officer corps—more than the military school system could fill. In response, the RKKA expanded the military school system, but a stopgap measure had to be employed while it organized schools and increased their output of officers. The Commissariat of Defense thus chose to commission enlisted men to be *mladshie leitenanty.*

Plugging the Gap with *Mladshie Leitenanty*

Recognizing the great need for still more leaders, the Commissariat of Defense instituted a program to expand military education and commissioning facilities. In August 1937, when the purge began picking up steam, Voroshilov ordered the military soviet of each district and separate army to set up special short courses for training junior commanders to become officers. The candidates were to be recruited from the best reenlisted junior commanders. The courses were to last from 15 September 1937 to 15 January 1938. The army awarded the rank of *mladshii leitenant* to those who passed. This response proved no more than a quick fix, because the NKO did not expect these new officers to make the military a career. That option was open to them, however, and they could become lieutenants by examination at a later date.[63]

Corps set up the schools, which did not run uniformly from September to January as directed. Varying from corps to corps, some were condensed to three months. They taught general education subjects (basic mathematics and literacy), as well as military topics. Many of the officer candidates in these courses were senior junior commanders (*starshina*) and *mladshii komvzvod,* so the best of the enlisted men were taken from the ranks. What Voroshilov had intended as a one-time event quickly became institutionalized for the simple reason that the army's continued growth outpaced the production of military schools. Well after January 1938, these short courses continued to turn out *mladshie leitenanty* every three to six months.[64] The schools did not stick to the original criteria of recruiting only reenlisted junior commanders, but recruited first-term junior commanders as well.

Although the NKO gave the order establishing training for junior commanders to become platoon commanders in 1937, not all districts acted at once. In the Urals, courses did not start until 1939. The 1939 graduating class of the Sverdlovsk Infantry School in the Urals numbered only 147 students. According to a history of the district, "The output of infantry schools was insufficient compared to the growth in the numbers of the infantry forces. Therefore, in 1939, the district began to train the best junior commanders to command platoons. All the divisions organized courses for *mladshie leitenanty* with this goal."[65] One cannot help noting that if the district had obeyed the order earlier, it might not have fallen so short of officers. Certainly the district was as busy as any other, organizing, supplying, and housing new units, but it had procrastinated until the situation became acute.

Commissioning men from the ranks was not unique to the Red Army. The French, British, German, and American armies all had procedures for training and commissioning qualified enlisted men and noncommissioned officers. The major differences between the Red Army and others were the qualifications and circumstances under which enlisted men were allowed to become officers. In the thirties and during the war, the British, French, German, and American standards for prospective officer candidates all exceeded those of the Red Army.

In the French army, NCOs could take a competitive examination upon completion of the NCO course. No one could even apply for the NCO course without first completing two years of service. Moreover, only a small percentage of the top scorers were commissioned. Just as in the Red Army, men commissioned in this way were discriminated against and had little chance of getting past the rank of captain. A board of officers decided all promotions above captain; here, military school graduates conspired to monopolize promotions.[66] The British army opened its military academies, Sandhurst and Woolwich, to NCOs after the First World War. Educational qualifications for applicants were quite high and the standards rigorously enforced. Training lasted eighteen months. By 1938, former NCOs accounted for 17 percent of the officer corps.[67]

The German army also commissioned enlisted men and NCOs. In peacetime, such commissions were extremely rare and limited to NCOs; the expansion during the thirties, when large numbers of NCOs were commissioned, was a major exception. In wartime the Wehrmacht gave special training to and commissioned enlisted men, but standards were very high, and prospective officers had to meet the same qualifications as military school candidates. The army did not expect these men to make the military a career but only to serve for the duration of the war. In both the German and French armies, the professionals frowned upon commissioning men from the ranks.[68] The British army responded to the crisis of officer manning and expansion in 1939 in radical egalitarian fashion: it closed its two military academies and in their place established thirty-five Officer Cadet Training Units. Entrance was open to all enlisted men simply by recommendation of commanding officers and subsequent interview by a board. Training lasted a total of six months.[69]

In the U.S. army, Officer Candidate School (OCS) provided an opportunity for an enlisted man or NCO to earn a commission during peace and war. In sharp contrast to the low but realistic educational expectations of the Red Army, the American army required officer candidates to have at least two years of college and pass a competitive examination. There was no minimum time of service required for application to OCS. Senior NCOs were not allowed to apply because once a man had served long enough to achieve senior NCO status, the army considered him more valuable as an NCO than as a junior officer. Like the Red Army, the training time in the U.S. army's OCS was short. It lasted only four months, but the curriculum was strictly military, the students having mastered general educational subjects as a condition of acceptance. The training was very intense, and a high attrition rate was purposely maintained to weed out the less capable and unmotivated. After graduating from OCS, the soldier was commissioned a second lieutenant and sent to an officers' basic course for several months of specialized branch training. The army established OCS only in July 1941, not to meet the needs of an expanding army (the War Department thought the Reserve Officer Training Corps programs could meet the need for officers), but as an egalitarian measure to give conscripts an opportunity for upward social mobility in hope of making the peacetime draft more palatable.[70]

As brief as the Red Army's courses were, not all prospective *mladshie leitenanty* attended them. Enlisted men could become *mladshie leitenanty* simply by examination. One junior commander proudly told a *Krasnaia zvezda* correspondent that he was semi-literate when conscripted, became a candidate to the party, was secretary of his Komsomol bureau, and then, with the help of a friend, passed the test for *mladshii leitenant*.[71] This anecdote tells something about the low quality of newly promoted *mladshie leitenanty* and helps explain why they were identified as different from school-trained lieutenants. Junior commanders could be recommended for officer rank by their regiment and, if approved, could be given direct commissions to junior lieutenants within their units without taking a test.[72] These innovations indicate that the RKKA had a desperate need for leaders at the lower levels of command.

In exceptional cases, junior commanders did not have to become officers to hold officer positions. Junior commanders frequently commanded platoons, but as the pace of expansion quickened, they were also given company commands. In these companies, platoon commanders must have been junior commanders, too, because an officer would not have been placed under the command of an enlisted man.[73] Again, the acute shortage of officers at the lower ranks in the regiments, as well as the varied and extreme measures taken to address the shortage, lowered the cohesion and level of expertise of the army's leadership.

In 1939, the first nineteen-year-olds were conscripted, and, as a matter of course, some of them became junior commanders. Thus the age and maturity level of the enlisted ranks sank lower than ever before. This factor must be taken into account when assessing the quality of the leadership at the lowest levels in the companies and batteries. Although there is no way to measure the effect of placement in leadership positions on younger men, it is reasonable to assume that the less mature would be the least effective. Many of these young junior commanders found their way into the ranks of *mladshie leitenanty* not long after 1939, thus lowering the experience and maturity of the officer corps at the company level.

The army experienced a shortage not only of officers during this period but also of junior commanders. Normally junior commanders led squads in the ground forces, but by 1938 the Red Army had resorted to allowing second-year enlisted men to lead squads after passing an examination. The regiments gave these men no special training comparable to that of junior commanders before they became squad leaders.[74] The shortage of junior commanders resulted from three causes: expansion, intensive recruitment of junior commanders for the officer corps, and the army's failure to reenlist large numbers of junior commanders whose service obligation expired. In 1938, the Commissariat of Defense launched a particularly intense drive to reenlist junior commanders. However, company commanders and *politruki,* supposedly the cutting edge of reenlistment recruiting, did not uniformly pursue this drive with vigor. Thus, many commanders had no one but themselves to blame for their shortage of qualified junior commanders.[75]

The lack of trained men in leadership positions in the enlisted ranks further hindered the effectiveness of officers in the regiments. Not only did a new dividing line arise between school-trained officers and those who rose through the ranks, but now an increased stratification within the ranks of junior commanders emerged. Junior commanders on reenlisted service had higher rank, pay, and status than other junior commanders. In addition, ordinary first-term junior commanders trained in the regimental schools and ordinary enlisted men served in junior commander positions with no special preparation. Thus, cohesion among junior commanders suffered for many of the same reasons it suffered among officers.

FURTHER EXPANSION OF THE MILITARY SCHOOL SYSTEM

In March 1938, the NKO officially shortened the course of instruction in military schools for training officer candidates from three to two years. This move merely acknowledged a practice that had been in effect for several years. Simultaneously, the RKKA raised entrance requirements: the infantry required an eighth-grade education, and artillery and flight schools stipulated a tenth-grade education. At the beginning of the military school year in the fall of 1939, the army claimed that many of its students were high school graduates.[76]

Between 1937 and 1940, the ground forces increased the number of their schools from 49 to a total of 133. The number of air force schools increased from 18 in 1937 to 90 in 1941. Under normal circumstances, the larger number of graduates from military schools would have increased the quality of leadership and military proficiency in the army, but these were not normal times. The increased number of military school graduates seems not to have added to the overall capacity of the officer corps. The number of training facilities appears impressive, but the quality of instruction and number of officers actually produced through this system were lower than one might expect. Shortening the duration of schooling from three to two years, or more commonly to eighteen months, reduced the quality of instruction.[77] This diminution is especially important considering that the army intended military schools to be institutions of higher education, not simply courses in particular military skills. Second, to assist in filling these schools, the party conducted another "special mobilization" in 1937, which netted thousands more nonvolunteer communist and Komsomol officers. In 1938–1939, the army asked for 210,000 new officers. Of this number, the NKO wanted 85,455 to be school-trained officers.[78] As it turns out, military schools produced only about 63,000 officers. The military school system actually provided a minority of new leaders in stark contrast to the 1930 plan to produce an officer corps trained and commissioned entirely through the military school system.

As one might suspect, the rate of expansion did not bode well for the quality of training in military schools. By 1939, many of the instructors were senior lieutenants, whereas before the expansion most instructors had been captains. The performance of military schools reflected the declining level of experience in the officer corps. At the end of the first month of instruction in the fall of 1939, the NKO singled out the Minsk Infantry School and the Sevastopol Antiaircraft School as examples of ill preparation for instruction. The Commissariat of Defense accused them of not having thoroughly prepared plans for instruction and of not completing their curricula, a situation common to nearly all military schools.[79]

Part of the problem was the magnitude of the task given the military schools. From 1928 to 1937, the entire military school system had commissioned 67,487 officers for the ground forces. In the following two years, they commissioned an astounding 62,800 officers, partly by increasing class sizes, which reduced the effectiveness of instruction, and partly by creating new schools, which invariably had difficulty establishing themselves due to shortages of instructors, weapons, billets, office and classroom buildings, and prepared training areas.[80]

The problems in the Sevastopol Antiaircraft School illustrate the effects of expansion on military schools. In fall 1938, the school doubled its two instruction battalions in order to train more students. The four battalions were expected to train 1,200 students, whereas before, when the school had two battalions, it usually had fewer than three hundred students. The introduction of new antiaircraft guns in 1938 and 1939 further complicated training; the instructors had to train themselves on the new guns before they could train students. As it turned out, because recruitment still lagged behind quotas, the combined graduating classes of 1939 and 1940 numbered only about one thousand antiaircraft lieutenants.[81]

The expansion of the Sevastopol Antiaircraft School reflects the demise of quality instruction throughout the military school system. During the thirties, the antiaircraft school graduated sixty-one classes with a total of 4,586 graduates. In 1941, however, the school graduated ten classes and 2,277 graduates. In one year, the school trained half as many men as it had in a decade. The school had begun with a three-year curriculum in the twenties, reduced it to two in the thirties, and finally to less than one year on the eve of the war. With such a compressed training schedule and overburdened faculty, the quality of training had to suffer.[82]

Despite efforts to raise competence through schooling, military proficiency continued to falter, partly because of the increasingly short time officers spent in assignments. In the twenties and early thirties, a unit commander might have held his position for anywhere between four and eight years. But during expansion, commanders were rapidly promoted to higher commands, with less time at each level. By mid-1938, the average regiment commander was between twenty-nine and thirty-three years old. Before 1936, this had been the average age for battalion commanders.[83] The youth and inexperience of the commanders must have affected their ability to train and lead their subordinates.

GENERAL ASSESSMENT OF THE OFFICER CORPS ON THE EVE OF THE WAR

According to the Red Army's ideal career progression, an officer could expect to be a platoon commander or assistant company commander for his first four years of service, then move on to become a company commander or work on a battalion staff up to the ninth year of service, when he became eligible to command a battalion. Regimental command was supposed to be possible after twelve years, brigade or division command after fifteen, and corps command and higher after seventeen. Compared to the Imperial Army and the major European armies, this was extremely rapid promotion after the company command. In the German army, few men could aspire to become battalion commanders until they had served at least twelve years. Regiment commands came after nearly twenty years of service. Division commands for the lucky few came even later.

The careers of most RKKA regiment, division, and corps commanders and senior staff officers on the eve of the war do not closely fit the ideal pattern. Many had earned their commissions in the military schools. Few had held commands at all levels—to provide experience and confidence—before the one they held at the outbreak of the Second World War. The level of command most often not held was battalion command. Acquisition of higher military schooling was inconsistent. The length of time it took to get to their wartime command also varied greatly: some officers attained regimental command after only eleven years, while others took as many as nineteen. Some officers reached division command in seventeen years and corps command in nineteen, but without having been awarded the appropriate rank. It was not unusual, in 1940, for high-ranking officers to have actually served more time as enlisted men than as officers before taking on the responsibilities of major unit command or staff work.[84]

In 1941, officers at and above the regiment level shared the fact that they started their careers in the twenties as volunteers and party members, and most of those who assumed division commands had a total of at least sixteen years of service. Some took less time than the ideal to get promoted; others took more. Many were military school graduates, and most had attended KUKS or military academies or both. Some had even been arrested during the purge and later rehabilitated. In comparison to European armies, most senior Soviet officers received promotion to high positions of responsibility at younger ages, with less experience and less military schooling.

Men who rose to positions higher than corps level before the war had even more diverse career experiences. None of their careers come close to the ideal career pattern. This is typical of nearly all of the very highest commanders and leaders of the RKKA in 1941. Even after the purge, many of the top leaders had revolutionary and political origins, as well as prior experience in the Imperial Army as soldiers or even junior officers. Nearly all the top Red Army commanders, that is, men who commanded armies, army groups, military districts, and fronts, had made great leaps to the top. Their careers were not built step by step. For some, the highest unit they commanded was a battalion or regiment before leaping to the top. Their other assignments, with the exception of schooling and service in Spain, consisted of staff positions. Some spent many years in the military as commissars before becoming officers, with little or no military experience below the regimental level. Their military education was limited to KUKS and sometimes the Frunze Academy.

Few generals had a well-rounded experience, with time in regiments and staff experience at various levels.[85]

Not only did senior officers take various and unusual routes to the top, but, despite the purge, the Red Army had many senior officers available to fill the top slots, although some were less prepared than others for their assignments. In June 1941, for example, all military districts (many of which became fronts at the beginning of the war) were commanded by generals who were veterans of the Civil War and had at least twenty years of military service. The majority had higher military education, all were party members, and more than half were in their forties.[86] The most serious weakness in the Red Army officer corps was in the ranks below general. This weakness was somewhat evident at the regimental level but was particularly acute at the battalion and company levels, where commanders lacked the thorough tactical training and leadership skills so vital in combat.

In early 1937, those who entered the army through "special mobilizations" made up almost one-quarter of the officer corps. A majority of military school graduates, plus Civil War veterans and a handful of *voenspetsy*, comprised the remainder. In 1941, the number of military school graduates dropped as a percentage of the total because of the enormous number of enlisted men promoted to *mladshii leitenant* between 1937 and 1941. *Mladshie leitenanty* accounted for nearly 50 percent of all platoon commanders in the war with Finland. Many *mladshie komvzvody* also led platoons in combat. Lieutenants trained in military schools constituted the minority.[87] In other words, the Red Army spread thinly its pool of educated and experienced men, with very few in the fighting battalions. By the end of 1939, the absolute majority of officers had been in the armed forces for five years or less—strictly due to the growth of the army.[88] The majority of officers commissioned between 1939 and 1941 were *mladshie leitenanty*.

A significant number of infantry company and even battalion commanders were senior lieutenants who had never commanded platoons. Many began their careers as conscripts before going on to military schools or courses for junior commanders. Few had been in the army long enough to attend a KUKS before the war, and nearly all held positions above their rank soon after commissioning. Most were peasants, for the support branches had first claim on the more educated men.

To avoid seeing an overly bleak picture, one should keep in mind that many young officers were indeed good men, although overall the caliber of men taken into the officer corps in the thirties continued to be mixed. But, having been placed in midlevel leadership positions straight out of school, they lacked the experience necessary to train their subordinate leaders thoroughly. Never having served in platoons, they could not pass down any lessons of experience to their own platoon commanders, creating the void in training Trotsky had prophetically warned against.

Disciplinary actions against officers resulting in demotions and discharges numbered in the thousands annually. Problems with alcohol continued to be severe. A 1940 report of the Central Committee concerning officers stated, "Drunkenness continues to remain the scourge of the army." The report noted that drunkenness not only interfered with the functioning of the army, but, because large numbers of officers and men got drunk in public, it also tarnished its image.[89] Assigning semi-trained men great responsibility exacerbated the problem.

Contradictory manning policies hindered the already serious problem of training and expanding the number of officers. During 1938 and 1939, the ground forces, especially the infantry, had the greatest need for additional officers. Nonetheless, in these two years, they were robbed of twenty-three thousand officers to provide leaders for other branches and services. At the same time, the army did not fully exploit its reserves. In 1938, the NKO proposed to call up thirty thousand reserve officers to "mitigate the acute shortage" of officers. This voluntary summons netted only 4,600 officers, a far cry from the requirements. In 1939, the army mobilized thousands more reservists, yet because reserve training was haphazard, even nonexistent in some localities, the reservists' effectiveness was limited—at least in the short term.[90]

SUMMARY

For too long it has been easy to blame Stalin and the *Ezhovshchina* for undermining Soviet military leadership during the first phase of the German-Soviet war. This explanation is no longer tenable when one considers the chaotic conditions created by the expansion of the military. The instances of officers commanding units above their rank and the use of junior commanders as platoon commanders began before the purge. Certainly, no one can deny that many valuable people were senselessly and forever lost in the purge. The only certain effects of the *Ezhovshchina* on the officer corps, however, were the destruction of trained cadres and the degradation of morale within the officer corps and PUR. Slack discipline in the units and early promotion may seem to have been associated with the purge, but they actually predated it. Like the purge, the expansion created thousands of new command positions at all levels, which facilitated the rapid promotion of many men to heights they previously could only dream of. Because it coincided with the beginning of the expansion, the loss of experienced men hindered the implementation of the army's measures for coping with the effects of continuing large-scale growth. This is not to say, however, that had there been no purge there would not have been problems with expansion or manning.

Among the things we can conclude about the purge is that it was a collaborative effort of the party, army, and security organs. It was not something inflicted upon the army exclusively from the outside. The *Ezhovshchina* originated in the Kremlin, but the military willingly and avidly pursued the party's policy. The army itself convicted nearly two thousand of its own officers of being enemies of the people, and it was soldiers and officers of the primary party organizations who denounced and expelled their peers from the party. The military procuracy and army personnel administration on their own arrested and discharged men for their political difficulties. The military had set the precedent of discharge for minor political deviance in 1931 and arrest in 1935.

Between 1937 and 1941, the purge and expansion almost totally disrupted the officer procurement system that had been developing since 1925. Military schools and academies still trained and commissioned many men, but enlisted men with little formal training increasingly obtained officer rank. The majority of enlisted men who became officers did so through courses for junior commanders that lasted only several months, and the army even gave some enlisted men officer rank through direct commissions with no special training. In the prevailing military culture, school-trained officers did not treat commissioned enlisted men as equals, which consequently worked against their assimilation. PUR transferred still more of its men into the officer corps without benefit of special preparation. Further erosion of the influence of the officer corps resulted from increasing instances of enlisted men commanding platoons and even companies without officer rank.

The Red Army in 1939 was an army whose leadership possessed vastly varied training and experience. Some corps and division commanders had received all the military schooling available in the nearly two decades of their service. Others had had only one five- or six-month course. Some were professional military officers from before the Revolution; others were Red commanders from the Civil War, revolutionaries with political connections, or political men in military assignments. Unqualified men led units that had an almost 50 percent annual turnover in enlisted strength, meaning that at best half of a unit's men would be only semi-trained, and those who were fully trained would soon be finishing their service. Equally transient were the leaders' primary assistants, the junior commanders. Under these circumstances, proficiency remained low—many soldiers never acquired more than basic skills, if that—and the rank and file had little confidence in their officers.

CHAPTER 6

The Last Eighteen Months of the Red Army: November 1939 to June 1941

Between 1 January 1939 and 22 June 1941, the Red Army created 111 infantry divisions and scores of tank divisions. It increased its manpower by over 1.5 million men.[1] This last leap of growth sealed the fate of the army in the initial phase of the German invasion. Because this vast growth paralleled the phasing out of the territorial system, structural changes in the organization of divisions and regiments, as well as the introduction of new equipment, training and small unit leadership became more important than ever. Nonetheless, neither training nor leadership improved. Procurement of officers still lagged behind ever-growing needs. The method the RKKA used in its attempt to become a bigger and better fighting force turned out to have made it less capable of performing its missions, and, ironically, it seems that the Soviets followed its policy of rapid expansion based on false information. In 1940, the Commissariat of Defense estimated the strength the German army could deploy against the USSR at around eight million men—more than twice the actual number.[2] Therefore, expansion in 1939 and thereafter was pursued at a frantic if not altogether paranoid pace, especially after alarming difficulties developed in the war with Finland in winter 1939–1940. In the process, the RKKA inconsistently changed unit organization and reshuffled its leaders, creating a great deal of confusion, instability, and systemic incoherence.

THE OFFICER CORPS ON THE EVE OF THE WAR

Twenty years after the end of the Civil War, the officer corps was further away than ever from being a cohesive social group. It had experienced its high point of cohesion and homogeneity in 1930; thereafter, the army never ceased to use unorthodox measures to procure additional officers, thus reducing existing cohesion. The purge and expansion further reduced cohesion by forcing men through the ranks quickly. On the eve of the German invasion, career patterns had become more varied than ever, so varied that it became impossible to assume that any given officer had had the civilian education, military training, and command experience requisite to his post.

Training New Officers

In the late thirties, officer training became more abbreviated, and new officers were sent to the units with less preparation than ever before. To help fill newly created officer positions and some left vacant by the purge, Marshal Voroshilov, in June 1938, ordered ten thousand officer cadets commissioned before they completed their courses at military schools. This step could only have had a negative affect on their proficiency. Not having finished their already compressed formal schooling, they were less prepared to function at peak capacity in the units, or perhaps their highest capability was at a lower level. Graduating the students early proved to be no solution at all, for it created a deficit in officer procurement for the next year and was simply a case of robbing Peter to pay Paul.

The younger officers' lack of practical experience and inability to train their platoons during field training constituted the gravest problem for line units.[3] The practical inexperience can be attributed to the hasty and incomplete training of officer candidates. Most of the military schools and academies abbreviated their courses and graduated their students early before covering the entire curriculum. Those that did try to cover the entire curriculum kept students in classrooms eighteen hours a day, six days a week, with few if any field exercises to reinforce their lessons. *Mladshie leitenanty* generally had a year or more in the ranks, yet it was not thoroughly reinforced because their formal training, if any, lasted only three to six months.

The training of junior commanders, *mladshie leitenanty,* and lieutenants continued to suffer right up to the time of the German invasion. Because of the inadequate preparation of the men who would lead the platoons, leadership, training, and cohesion were weak. By 1940, most rifle and cavalry company commanders and artillery battery commanders had started out as ill-trained platoon commanders, so their leadership was also poor. The battalions, too, were weak. Composed of poorly led companies, they were often assigned to young officers commanding above their capacity: Built on such flimsy foundations, the regiments suffered in their ability to train and care for their soldiers, even when commanded by experienced commanders. As the Red Army became overwhelmed by the task of expanding and creating more regiments and divisions, it gave short shrift to the platoons and the platoon leaders, to the detriment of the entire army.

At the end of the Civil War, Leon Trotsky had argued for the importance of the platoon leader and his training against those who wanted to focus or even limit the energy of the General Staff to issues of strategic theory. The General Staff would have done well to heed his advice. Trotsky's 1922 discourse hints at the resistance higher commanders displayed toward giving the platoon central importance, an attitude transmitted from the tsarist officers to the Red commanders.

Everybody of course recognizes the importance and meaning of a platoon commander but not everybody is willing to see in him the central point of our military program in the period immediately ahead. Some comrades even express themselves somewhat condescendingly on the question. . . . The remarks of our charming Comrade Muralov smacked a little of this spirit. He said: "Naturally, it is necessary to grease boots, sew on buttons and educate good platoon commanders, but this is far from everything." For some unknown reason, the platoon commander is here lumped together with buttons and boots. In vain! Buttons, boots and the like pertain to those "trifles" which in their totality are of enormous importance. But the platoon commander is in no case a trifle. No, this is the most important lever of our military mechanics.

"But," some object, "aren't you forgetting about the senior commanding staff?" No, I am not forgetting it and it is precisely to the senior commanding staff that I set the task of educating the platoon commander. There can be no better school for a commander of a regiment, or a brigade, or a division than the work of educating the platoon commander. Our post-graduate courses, our academies, and academic courses are very important and useful, but the best training of all is received by a teacher in teaching his pupils; best trained of all will be the commander of a regiment, the commander of a brigade and the commander of a division who centers his attention in the immediate future on the training and education of platoon commanders. For this cannot be done without clarifying more and more in one's mind all the questions of Red Army organization and tactics without a single exception. . . .

The platoon commander—this is now the central task. General phrases about educating the commanding personnel in the spirit of maneuverability offer very little in essence, distracting attention away from the most important task of the present period. . . . The new epoch advances to the fore a new task: to set in order the basic cell of the army—the platoon; to sum up our military experience for the individual platoon commander, raise his knowledge, his self-esteem. Everything now centers about this point. It is necessary to understand this, and to get firmly to work.[4]

Trotsky's words had not lost their relevance seventeen years later; indeed, they were almost prophetic. The Red Army was building an edifice on sand, an edifice that was to be shaken badly by the Finns and then toppled by the Germans, only to be imperfectly rebuilt in a cauldron of fire.

THE BUDGET AND QUESTIONS OF ARMAMENTS

Under the Soviet regime, historians of the Great Patriotic War often posed this question: Was the Soviet Union materially prepared to engage in war in 1941, and to what degree was Soviet industry responsible for the matériel supply status of the armed forces? They most commonly answered that the armed forces were not properly equipped, relied on obsolete equipment and suffered from shortages of military hardware. The military stressed that the Germans overpowered it with matériel, but the defense industry refused to take the blame. The army's claim that it was not adequately supplied with weaponry and up-to-date equipment is questionable. Missing from this argument are the role and method of expansion and their effect on the sufficiency and efficacy of rearmament. There is evidence that the defense industry produced sufficient war matériel for the armed forces, but problems in supply grew out of the army's manning and reequipping policies, which prevented it from realizing the true potential of its equipment and weapons.

The Defense Budget

Initially, the army's problem with rearmament did not arise from the defense industry but with the Politburo. Since the end of the Civil War, the Politburo had relegated defense spending to a low priority, well behind industrial and agricultural recovery. Even in the first two five-year plans, which were in part billed as efforts to increase the military capacity of the USSR, the portion of the budget and resources devoted to defense, including the war industries, indicate that armaments, in comparison with civilian needs, were a low priority. Table 6.1 shows the growth in the defense budget. The military's share of

Table 6.1. Defense Budget of the USSR, 1929–1940

	Defense Budget (million rubles)	National Budget (million rubles)	Defense as Percent of Total
1929	916.5	7,331	1.25
1930	1,182		
1933	1,421	42,080	3.4
1934	5,019	55,444	9.1
1935	8,186	73,571	11.1
1936	14,883	92,480	16.1
1937	17,481	106,238	16.5
1938	23,200	124,038	18.7
1939	39,200	153,299	25.6
1940	56,800	174,350	32.6

Source: "Military Budget, 1929, 1930," *U.S. MID Reports,* Reel 4, 110; data for 1933–1940, Alex Nove, *An Economic History of the USSR,* 3d ed. (Penguin Press, 1992), 230.

Students of an artillery military school.

the budget at first increased gradually, then escalated only as preparation for war became the order of the day.

The increases in military expenditures up to and including 1938 are best interpreted as normal housekeeping expenses. These necessary expenses increased to keep up with the requirements imposed upon the armaments industry by the increase in military formations. For every new infantry division, cavalry division, and tank brigade, hundreds of tanks, artillery pieces, and machine guns, thousands of additional rifles, and tens of thousands of uniforms and boots were required, as were factories to produce them. In comparison to the tsarist army, which rearmed in the two decades before the Russo-Japanese War and annually received as much as 30 percent and never less than 17 percent of the national budget, the Soviet armed forces seem either woefully underfunded or not serious about rearming until 1939.[5]

Table 6.1 shows the correlation between the increase in size of the armed forces and the increase in defense expenditures. In 1934, the RKKA added 400,000 men, which represented an 80 percent increase in strength. This drove the defense share of the budget from 3.4 to 9.1 percent. In 1936, when the size of the RKKA increased by 50 percent to 1.3 million, the defense share of the budget rose accordingly from 11.1 to 16.1 percent. And, in 1939, when RKKA manpower rose beyond the three million mark, the defense share of the budget rose from 18.7 to 25.6 percent.

Armaments

The single most important reason for the military's shortage of up-to-date equipment on the eve of the Second World War was the defense industry's late start in gearing up design and production of improved armaments. Not until the Soviet military tested its equipment in combat against foreign weapons did the modernization program become truly efficacious. Throughout the 1930s, however, Soviet industry produced new and ever larger quantities of equipment for the expanding RKKA, but not in the quantity and quality necessary for the coming war. The defense industry tremendously increased its output of military weaponry as it shifted into high gear in the late thirties, annually producing rifles by the millions, machine guns and artillery pieces by the tens of thousands, and tanks and aircraft by the thousands.[6] The defense industry produced enough military hardware for the army and air force to arm all their men and equip most, but not all, of their regular formations. Whether industry had produced enough to arm the reserves of an army mobilized for total war is an entirely different question.

After the fact, in trying to shift responsibility for the defeats of 1941, the military disparaged the quality of the weapons and blamed the defense industry for not having provided modern equipment. On the eve of the war, the Red Army had an estimated fifteen to twenty thousand tanks—more tanks than all the world's other armies combined; however, only 1,475 were of the new medium T-34 and KV-1 types, most of which were produced in the first half of 1941. In the post-Stalin period, the military claimed that before the war it had only 1,475 tanks; the rest, apparently, it considered to be of no consequence. Clearly, the armor situation was not nearly as bad as the military has suggested. The armored forces consisted mostly of light tanks with a smattering of lumbering heavy tanks, yet the light tanks of the BT-5, BT-7, and the T-26 and T-28 types were well armed (the BT-5, BT-7, and T-26 had 45mm guns and the T-28 was armed with the same 76.2mm gun as the T-34 and KV-1), fast and maneuverable.[7] The Germans also had primarily light tanks, but these were armed with smaller 37mm and 50mm guns. Though lightly armored, the Soviet tanks were not outclassed or out of place on the battlefield in 1941, if put to proper use. The medium tanks introduced in 1940 outperformed any tanks the Germans had.

The military had a genuine complaint concerning its inferior aircraft. The number of combat aircraft on hand in 1941 is estimated at roughly nine thousand, 1,540 of which were newer types designed since 1937. Compared to

German aircraft, the old Soviet fighter planes were slower, less maneuverable, and undergunned. Soviet bombers also flew slower and carried a smaller bomb load than their German counterparts—in contrast to the first-rate design of the new aircraft introduced into the air force in limited numbers on the eve of the war.[8]

The experiences gained in Spain, the continued expansion of German military might, and the German-Soviet invasion of Poland convinced the Soviet leadership to begin a serious rearmament program. The second five-year plan (1932–1936) attempted to raise the technological level of the RKKA as well as to complete a general rearmament, yet achieved only modest results. The third five-year plan (1937–1941) aimed at further rearmament, focusing on aircraft, armor, and artillery. The regime did not take significant steps to implement the plan until 1939. The Commissariat of Defense paid special attention to producing more antitank guns and new regimental and divisional artillery. It stepped up production of light and heavy machine guns, and moved forward production timetables for the new tanks.[9] Specifically, as a result of the Soviet experience in the Spanish civil war, the VVS requested better aircraft in large quantities. In September 1939, the Central Committee ordered that eighteen more aircraft plants be constructed no later than December 1941. The Central Committee went so far as to authorize a group of aircraft production managers to travel to Germany to buy airplanes from the Luftwaffe to study. Several Soviet aircraft designed subsequently, such as the IL-4 and PE-2 bombers, owed much to these German airplanes.[10]

The Shock of the Winter War

In winter 1939–1940, the Red Army experienced a Pyrrhic victory over the Finns that finally awakened it to the need for drastic reform. The fact that it took such a catastrophe as the Winter War to convince the military hierarchy it needed to change says little for the high command's ability to adapt in the absence of calamity, for the Red Army had had several warning signals that serious problems existed. In July 1938, in the Far East, the Japanese and Soviet armies clashed at Lake Khasan. The Japanese precipitated the battle as a test of the Soviets' ability and resolve to defend contested areas of Manchuria. In this nine-day battle, one Soviet corps comprising two rifle divisions and one mechanized brigade succeeded in restoring the original border after initially being pushed back some distance. The RKKA incurred 717 deaths (129 officers) and 3,279 wounded.[11] In its post-action report of the battle, the Special Red Banner Far East Army (OKDVA) staff brought to light numerous shortcomings, including, but not limited to, the complete lack of coordination between battalion-sized elements; the lack of coordination between infantry and armor units; and the failure of the units to communicate in code, despite the fact that the corps had been alerted for combat a month ahead of time. The report also stated that during the initial retreat, soldiers had abandoned backpacks, machine guns, and other equipment. Soldiers had also avoided closing with the enemy to engage in combat with bayonets. The underlying problem was that the XXXIV Corps had given the men little training, concentrating instead on such matters as cultivating hay, chopping firewood, growing vegetables, managing construction, washing underclothes, and similar tasks. Not long after the Battle of Lake Khasan, Marshal Bliukher, commander of the OKDVA, was arrested and the OKDVA divided into the First and Second Far East Armies.[12] Hailed officially as a victory, the deficiencies exhibited by the corps in battle did not lead to any special introspection on the part of the army.

The Battle of Khalkin-Gol, which lasted from May to September 1939 and cost the Red Army 6,831 dead (including 1,063 officers) and 16,394 wounded, provided additional evidence of the Red Army's unpreparedness for war.[13] The conflict was marked by poor organization at the top, which led to mass confusion among and between units for much of the battle; arbitrary punishment of commanders during the operation at the personal orders of Georgi Zhukov, the Soviet commander; lack of supplies and equipment; and an obvious willingness on Zhukov's part to accept enormous casualties to ensure victory. For the most part, the men had atrocious morale. Just as at Lake Khasan, men fleeing the battle abandoned their rifles and equipment. Reservists assigned to the front were more of a detriment than an asset. In one instance, a regiment abandoned its position in front of the Japanese and moved away from the battle in the form of a mob rather than a military formation. Most of the men had thrown their weapons away. According to Petro Grigorenko, who had been assigned to Zhukov's staff, a staff officer stopped the retreat and reorganized the regiment. All of the surviving officers were reservists and were greatly confused as to what to do. They had been in the regiment for so short a time, they could not even remember the names or faces of the soldiers assigned to their units.[14]

The General Staff made a study of the battle, but never circulated it.[15] Just as the battle ended in the Far East, other units of the RKKA invaded Poland to "liberate" the western Ukraine. Two weeks earlier, the Germans had attacked from the west, as agreed in the Nonaggression Pact between Germany and the Soviet Union concluded the month before. Although numerous problems of coordination and efficiency surfaced in the hurried campaign, the army accomplished its mission with only 1,139 killed and missing (including 180 officers) and 2,383 wounded.[16]

Before the army could do anything to correct the deficiencies that had been exposed during its engagements in Spain and Poland, Stalin ordered it to attack Finland in November 1939. The RKKA expected a quick and easy victory. With an unsound strategy and poor coordination of units, the Red Army blundered into the Finnish defensive line on the Karelian isthmus only to be decimated by the outnumbered Finns. Only when the RKKA assembled a huge infantry and artillery "steamroller" did the Red Army manage to overwhelm the Finnish defense by sheer weight of men and matériel.[17]

The Red Army suffered horrendous casualties. Recently published archival sources list 126,875 dead and missing and 264,908 wounded. The casualties including 29,000 officers, 14,372 of whom were killed or missing.[18] According to one Soviet source, the war's long duration (three and a half months) and high number of casualties was due to the "lack of professionalism of the Soviet commanders at all ranks, their inability to coordinate actions on the battlefield, and their unconcern for the life and health of Red Army soldiers."[19] Some of these problems were a direct result of expansion: poor training of junior officers; lack of cohesion; and disorganization. It is also certain that the purge of officers of the Leningrad Military District greatly hindered the efficiency of the war effort. At the last minute, to bolster the resources of the Leningrad Military District for the operation, the NKO called in units from all over the Soviet Union. In some instances, whole divisions mobilized; in other cases, a division would send just one regiment to operate under the control of another headquarters. The regime even threw individual regiments and battalions of the border guards haphazardly into the fray. All told, the RKKA used forty-six rifle divisions, or the equivalent thereof, against twelve Finnish divisions.[20]

During the war, the Red Army proved to be its own worst enemy, throwing some of its newest divisions into the fight without allowing time for the regiments and battalions to train together and develop the teamwork and cohesion necessary for success. Of the forty-six divisions, thirteen had been formed just that year and several other divisions had given up the regiments to form them. The army further handicapped itself by bringing its units to full strength just days before sending them to the front. To make matters worse, according to a postwar report, "the combat units at the front were brought to full strength with completely untrained cadre." A large number of these men were newly commissioned *mladshie leitenanty* fresh from their brief officer training courses. PUR also hastily assigned semi-trained personnel to fill political positions in front-line units.[21]

The 136th Rifle Division, formed in September 1939, was one of these new units sent to Finland only three months after its formation. Not only was the division inexperienced at working as a unit, but it was led by men who lacked experience in their positions. The division commander was a colonel; one of the regiment commanders was a major; numerous *mladshie leitenanty* commanded companies in one regiment; and the other regiments had lieutenants and *mladshie leitenanty* leading platoons. The artillery battalion had both lieutenants and *mladshie leitenanty* commanding batteries.[22] Without doubt, the expansion of the army was to blame for the lack of majors to lead battalions, which left the lieutenants to command companies and batteries, and for the absence of a general to command the division.

The war with Finland led to a major reevaluation of military policy and some important personnel changes at higher levels. Stalin replaced Commissar of Defense Marshal Voroshilov, whose true organizational and leadership talents were revealed in the Winter War, with Marshal Timoshenko, whom he charged with getting the RKKA into fighting condition for a war against the next potential enemy—Nazi Germany. As he left, Voroshilov compiled a lengthy report for his successor detailing the shortcomings of the RKKA. This sobering report revealed inadequacies from the highest to the lowest levels of such dimensions that they could potentially render the army useless against a prepared enemy. As of the date of the report, 8 May 1940, only two days before the awesomely successful German invasion of France, the Red Army did not have an operational plan for war, neither in the west nor in the east. It did not have an up-to-date mobilization plan, and its reserves consisted of over three million men who were for all practical purposes untrained. Worse yet, it had no plan to train them in the event they were called up for war. The army was short of officers, especially in the infantry, which lacked fully one-fifth of its authorized officers. Military schools failed to produce sufficient numbers of graduates, and they could not train them to meet minimal standards of competence. Simultaneously, the army allowed trained, experienced officers to leave active service. The report bluntly stated, "The quality of officer training is poor, especially in the platoons and companies." Junior commanders received especially poor training. In the field and in combat, the various arms were unskilled in working together: artillery did not know how to support tanks, and aviation did not know how to support the ground forces. The infantry was not resolute in pressing home attacks and did not know how to disengage from enemy contact when necessary. Nor did the infantry know how to attack fortified positions, construct and overcome obstacles, or forge rivers. Soldiers did not know how to ski, and their use of camouflage was amateurish. The armored forces had a serious problem with maintenance procedures and suffered a shortage of trained mechanics. The rear services were totally unprepared to support the army in combat. It had been over two years since there had been any planning for the rear services, and the army's situation in 1940 called for an entirely new plan.[23] Timoshenko had his work cut out for him.

In spring 1940, the RKKA applied the lessons learned from the invasion of Poland and the war with Finland in the areas of tactical doctrine and equipment. Infantry training was revamped, and the army gave special emphasis to the task of perfecting assault techniques against fixed fortifications, such as those they had had to overcome in southern Finland. The Red Army became fixated with the lessons of the Winter War, as though these were universal. They ignored the special conditions of terrain, climate, and national characteristics of the opposing forces in their application of the lessons. Of particular note in this matter was the army's attempt to pass on lessons applicable to armor. Veterans of the war were sent to teach these lessons to armor units throughout the USSR. The General Staff ordered new field service regulations drawn up incorporating the lessons learned from the recent combat experiences of the Red Army, but due to bureaucratism and institutional inertia, they never were.[24]

In the summer of 1940, the Commissariat of Defense, seemingly bent on training the entire army at one fell swoop, ordered major maneuvers to be held in the Moscow, Western Special (formerly the Belorussian Military District), Kiev Special, Odessa, Siberian, Transcaucasus, and Leningrad military districts, involving most of their divisions. Previously, only one or two major maneuvers had been scheduled each summer. These maneuvers stretched into October and the conscription season. During these maneuvers, Marshal Timoshenko attempted to raise morale by giving on-the-spot promotions and awards to soldiers, officers, and political personnel who had done good jobs or shown potential for higher leadership responsibilities.[25] Unfortunately for the soldiers, that was about the extent of the individual attention they received. Timoshenko concentrated training in 1940 at the army and corps level, and the Red Army continued its tradition of neglecting the training of individual soldiers and small units.[26] This tendency contrasted starkly with the way the German army, faced with similar circumstances after the Polish campaign, prepared for a campaign in the west.

Like the Red Army, the German army underwent rapid expansion in 1939 and 1940. It called up reservists and untrained conscripts and formed new divisions. In the process, it siphoned off handfuls of experienced officers and NCOs from the units that had participated in the Polish campaign. Inexperienced men replaced veterans, leaving virtually the whole army in flux. Most important, from fall 1939 to spring 1940, the Wehrmacht focused nearly all its efforts on individual and small-unit training that incorporated the lessons learned from the invasion of Poland. Divisions only undertook large-unit training when companies and battalions were thoroughly prepared and the men had achieved what the army considered a minimal acceptable level of competence. At times, divisions suspended unit training and reverted to individual training when units received large numbers of new personnel, or when inspection uncovered serious deficiencies. During the entire period, the German army high command took an active role in monitoring and assessing training, ensuring that commanders focused on small-unit training as long as necessary and that training was as realistic as possible. The high command also mandated special training for junior officers and NCOs, which included going off for several weeks of intense leadership and tactical training. By concentrating training at the lower levels, the German army, in a matter of six months or even less in the case of some divisions, efficiently and effectively prepared reserve and newly created divisions for the war in the west.[27]

The RKKA was no better prepared for combat in June 1941 than it had been in November 1939, judging by the example of the Fourth Army stationed in the Western Special Military District (ZOVO). Its training in 1940 and 1941 was far from realistic, and it conducted little or no combined-arms training within its divisions. Timoshenko himself admitted in 1940: "We have spent a very long time in the classrooms, we have become accustomed to learning by verbal explanations, without bothering ourselves with the difficult conditions of a combat situation or difficult terrain conditions, in a word, everything that rests on the shoulders of a fighter, commander and political worker during a war and in combat."[28] The little time allocated to training was often cut short by the construction of defensive works along the western border, the establishment of ammunition and supply dumps, and, as in the early thirties, when units had been shifted about willy-nilly, the construction of housing, messes, stables, rifle and artillery ranges, tank driving ranges, sports facilities, and so on. The Fourth Army lost much of the experience it had gained in the major maneuvers of 1940 to the massive discharge of soldiers and officers who had fulfilled their military obligations at year's end.[29]

The Kiev Special Military District (KOVO), Odessa Military District (OVO), Western Special Military District (ZOVO), and Baltic Military District (PriBVO), all of which were on the border with Germany or its allies, experienced similar training conditions. An additional problem experienced in the KOVO, and quite likely in the other border districts as well, was the recalcitrant and uncooperative local population. The KOVO and OVO faced hostile Moldavians; the PriBVO faced Estonians, Latvians, and Lithuanians; the ZOVO and KOVO, Poles and Polish-Ukrainians.[30]

The Soviet high command did call for improvements in training but exerted little effort to ensure that units followed instructions. In fact, the high command failed to learn crucial lessons from the war with Finland, namely the negative consequences of partial manning and rapid expansion. The NKO did, however, end dual command in August 1940, because it suspected that the system had interfered with the smooth conduct of military operations. Commissars reverted to their roles as head of unit political activities and no longer had to countersign orders of the unit commanders. Simultaneously, the armed forces proceeded to expand to the five million mark, which did not help the officer manning situation. At the beginning of 1940, sixty thousand officer positions were vacant.[31]

In the midst of its personnel turmoil, the army began to modernize and reorganize its forces, but often in an incoherent manner. The army's lack of coherence in its modernization program and organizational restructuring is shown in the way it introduced into its structure nearly nineteen hundred medium T-34 and KV-1 tanks and heavy KV-2 tanks. Instead of assigning the tanks as large units (they could have completely outfitted three armored divisions and two separate tank brigades), they were doled out in battalion strength or less to replace aging tanks that were then withdrawn from service. The RGK reserved several hundred new tanks for itself.[32] This distribution not only deprived the front-line divisions of the advantage of the shock value of superior vehicles operating in large tactical units, but it actually hampered their use. If the tanks had been massed together, their support units would have needed to only carry parts and ammunition for the new weapons; yet because they were mixed in with other types of tanks, both ammunition supply and maintenance systems were more complicated. Mechanics had to be trained to work on the new vehicles as well as the old. It also complicated training. Since only a handful of persons were familiar with the new tank, replacing casualties required on-the-spot training of new drivers and gunners.

Because the tanks had different capabilities, combining the new tanks with the old complicated the tactical use of the new armored vehicles in unison with the other tanks. Using the T-34, KV-1, or KV-2 to full advantage would expose the older, more thinly armored tanks to higher risk. Using the new tanks at the performance level of the others would sacrifice the advantages built into the new tanks. As a consequence, in the first months of the war, the Red Army often used T-34s, KV-1s, and KV-2s separately or in very small numbers, usually three or four in a group. The Germans initially were shocked to see these excellent medium and heavy tanks, which, owing to their long-range guns, could destroy German panzers before they could retaliate. Moreover, the armor of Soviet medium and heavy tanks was impervious to most German antitank guns. Because the Soviet tanks were used ineffectively, the Germans quickly adopted countermeasures that robbed the Red Army of the technical advantage it might have had.

The Kiev Special Military District in 1940: A Case Study

On the eve of the clash of arms with Hitler's Wehrmacht, the Kiev Special Military District manifested all the ills afflicting the RKKA. The majority of the problems stemmed from expansion within the military. They centered on indiscipline, shortages of officers and materials, poor training, relocation westward into the Polish Ukraine, and the imminent invasion of Bessarabia and North Bukovina in spring 1940. All of these problems were interrelated, and none can be discussed in isolation.

Beginning in September 1939, the KOVO experienced profound changes that its leadership failed to adequately address. The conquest of the western Ukraine caused a major relocation of units westward. In addition to problems concerning housing and training facilities, supplying the troops with food, necessities, and personal items became more difficult. The move disrupted operations of the KOVO's cooperatives, which were slow to recover; consequently food prices went up for officers' families. Soldiers' personal items, such as tobacco and tea, also cost more. Morale suffered accordingly.[33]

Housing was a serious problem. The district quartered many units among the population in a very unsatisfactory manner. In February 1940, the 130th Rifle Division complained that its units were spread out all over the countryside. One of its regiments was divided among three different villages; another regiment among four. Even then, the villages did not always satisfy the needs of the units. One village commandant complained that 120 of his men had no place to stay.[34] This lack of coherence made communications, command, and control difficult for the division and regiment staffs.

The so-called liberation of the Western Ukraine turned the RKKA into an army of occupation, despised by many Poles. They subsequently worked to harass and obstruct the Red Army's efforts to create a state of peacetime normalcy while it licked its wounds.[35] Such an atmosphere contributed to discipline problems. In May 1940, for example, a mob of soldiers from various subunits of the 3d Cavalry Division ransacked a village. The Special Sections arrested the soldiers, and the II Cavalry Corps commander punished the commander and deputy commander of the 44th Cavalry Regiment, as well as the commander of an engineer detachment, for failing to control their men.[36]

Before it finished settling into its new location, the KOVO sent eight rifle divisions and forty-one regiment-sized and smaller units and the district commander Timoshenko to fight in the war against Finland. Some left in November 1939, others in January and February 1940. When these units returned in spring 1940, they had to reorient themselves to their environment and reconstitute their battle-worn ranks and equipment. Simultaneously, the KOVO was ordered to establish several more rifle and tank divisions and numerous artillery regiments and specialized units, and to prepare to conduct maneuvers in the late summer or fall. In the midst of these activities, the district was assigned the task of invading Bessarabia in fulfillment of some hard-nosed diplomacy conducted by Stalin.[37]

Many of the major difficulties the KOVO would face in accomplishing its tasks were rooted in the events preceding the invasion of Poland. In preparation for the invasion, the NKO had called up tens or possibly hundreds of thousands of rank-and-file reservists to flesh out the partially manned divisions.[38] The problem was that they did not do so until late August and early September. Thus, many of these men reported to units only days or weeks before they engaged in armed combat. Furthermore, roughly one-third were over the age of thirty, having served their tours of duty ten or more years earlier. This situation created several problems: the men were, for all practical purposes, untrained and they were no longer in top physical shape. Their reserve service had consisted of having their name on lists maintained by the NKO and *raikom* military commissions. Most serious of all, they made no attempt to disguise their recalcitrance and anger about being mobilized. The majority of the men called up had families and careers they had to leave behind. An engineer battalion commander complained in January 1940, "Of the people sent to me, many soldiers are of older ages, for example: 31 percent were born between 1898 and 1905. Of the arrivals 30 percent have four or more dependants." Of his 408 men, then, 126 were between the ages of thirty-four and forty-one. He complained that discipline had gone to hell. The men argued with their officers and showed them no respect. Of the 388 new recruits he had just received, 34 were physically unfit for service in the RKKA. He summed it up by saying that "the political-moral situation of the personnel of the [entire] 18th Special Sapper Brigade is a boiling pot."[39]

The commander of the 135th Rifle Division complained to his corps commander that more than one-third of the enlisted men (700 out of 2,007) in the newly formed 656th Reserve Artillery Regiment assigned to his division were between twenty-nine and thirty-nine years old. The regiment, which had only recently begun to form, suffered ninety-one desertions by the last week in January. The corps' other reserve artillery regiment reported identical problems. Older reservists barraged their commanders and higher military and political authorities with verbal and written petitions to be sent home. They most often complained of the financial strains their families suffered without them.[40] A private's pay could not support a family with children; it barely subsidized the soldier's own needs. While they waited to be sent home, reservists disrupted the daily activities of their units and were insubordinate to their officers, most of whom were their juniors in age.

By spring 1940, the reservists' behavior had apparently become so serious and uncontrollable that their officers gave up trying to bring them to heel; instead, they appealed to their superiors to discharge reservists who were thirty or older. In March 1940, the commissar of the 6th Special Sapper Battalion asked the KOVO Military Soviet to discharge all the reservists called up in September 1939 who were older than average and had families. For his battalion, this number amounted to more than ninety men. All of them, he said, had from four to seven children and their families were in dire economic straits. Other battalion commanders echoed his plea.[41] This question was deemed serious enough to finally be taken up at the highest levels of the

KOVO. Nikita Khrushchev, in his capacity as first secretary of the Ukrainian Communist party and member of the KOVO Military Soviet, questioned why the NKO Reserve Personnel Section had called up these men in the first place. The NKO justified its action as a response to military necessity. It refused to release the reservists on the grounds that they needed the training and many brought engineering and mechanical skills that the army needed.[42] Consequently, discipline was not restored and the units remained in turmoil.

Simultaneously, the district formed many new units, which it manned with new conscripts and older reservists. This proved to be an unhealthy combination, and many of these new units got off to a bad start. The problems the older reservists created had been foreseen over a decade before. In *Strategiia* (1927), Aleksandr Svechin had warned that "a company composed of both strong and weak troops should . . . be considered equivalent to its weaker members. It cannot be led at a fast pace but must accommodate the slower pace of its older members. Discipline and training techniques also vary with age. We cannot handle the fathers of families in the same way as rascally, exuberant schoolboys."[43]

Some men did secure discharges, but not because of family problems. Industrial enterprises petitioned the army to release men crucial for their operations, and the party simply ordered the army to return men it needed for civilian party work. The director of a chain factory petitioned the commander of the KOVO in February 1940 for the return of one of its employees, a reservist who had been called up in September. The factory deemed him not merely invaluable to production but also legally exempt from military recall. The power of the party is illustrated by the case of a reservist called up in September 1939 who, in March 1940, was in the midst of training to become an officer. The party forbade him to become an officer and ordered him to return to his job in the Dnepropetrovsk *oblast*.[44]

An example of the personnel problems that beset new units is offered by the experience of the 61st Motorized Division, which began to form in December 1939. It started with 2,715 men conscripted in 1937 and 1938 and transferred from other units. In January 1940, it began receiving men drafted in 1939: 225 in January, 5,900 in February, 2,710 in March, and 1,100 in April. These men represented forty different non-Russian nationalities, and few could speak Russian. By the end of April, the division was nearly at full strength in *krasnoarmeitsy*. It had only 70 percent of its authorized junior commanders, nearly half of whom were reservists who harbored negative attitudes. It almost goes without saying that the division did not have enough officers. The greatest shortage was among company-level officers. Thirty percent of company commanders were either *mladshie leitenanty* or lieutenants straight out of military school. A report by the division staff lamented that "they do not have the experience to command companies."[45] Equipment and weapons dribbled in irregularly. By the end of April, the division still had not received training guidance from corps or conducted unit training.

New and old units alike suffered from equipment and officer shortages. The army established many of the new units long before it had equipment available for them. This meant that little or no training could be done in the meantime. In the established units, equipment problems stemmed from losses suffered in the Polish invasion and the Winter War that had not yet been made good, and from attempts to bring the number of enlisted personnel closer to wartime strength.

Some units experienced shortages of the most elemental supplies, particularly boots. The 139th Rifle Division is a case in point. It had been detached from the KOVO to fight in the Winter War. It spent the entire war, from November 1939 to March 1940, at the front and returned to the Ukraine at the end of March. Prior to and during the war, the division had requested resupply of standard necessities but had received nothing. As of June 1940, 5,500 soldiers had no serviceable boots. The men had worn out their boots during the war and did not have the means to repair them. The division commissar, in pleading with the commissar of the KOVO for resupply, observed that the shortage of necessities, particularly boots and greatcoats (the division was short 3,700 greatcoats and winter was not over), had a bad effect on morale and the leadership was fast losing credibility with the soldiers. An investigation turned up several interesting bits of information. First, the division commander, Colonel Glushkov, had not actually ordered new boots and such and neither had his staff. Consequently, the district staff denounced the 139th Rifle Division for being disorganized. Second, the entire military district suffered from a scarcity of boots and other essential personal items. Units of XXXIV Rifle Corps, for example, needed 9,000 pairs of boots, 8,900 raincoats, and 15,082 pairs of *letportianki* (foot cloths the Red Army substituted for socks). Pleading and complaining finally did yield results for the 139th Rifle Division; between 18 and 22 June, the division received 4,800 pairs of boots. Seven hundred men still lacked footwear, but it was a start.[46]

The lack of military purposefulness (the division did not conduct training from the time it returned from the war until the middle of June) and meaningful tasks to occupy the men (except for work on the unit's farm), as well as the dearth of footwear, coats, and such, further depressed morale and exacerbated discipline problems. The commissar of the 139th Rifle Division's admitted in mid-June that discipline had reached the lowest level he had ever seen. Rampant drunkenness caused chaos in the ranks. The head of the district Special Section reported that in a fifteen-day period, between 25 April and 10 May 1940, the 139th Rifle Division had more than four hundred cases of drunkenness, which had resulted in four seriously injured soldiers and junior commanders, one battered wife, and a suicide.[47]

The men complained about everything, and PUR made virtually no effort to counteract the negative atmosphere. The 718th Rifle Regiment was singled out as the worst within the division. Its commander, Pavlov, had been discharged in 1932 for drunkenness and then recalled to active duty in 1939. Within months of being recalled, he and the 718th had been sent to the front in Finland, where his personal problems mounted and the regiment's condition deteriorated.[48]

Some divisions of the KOVO suffered equipment shortages of more substantial items (though, if one agrees with Trotsky, not necessarily more essential than footwear) such as tanks, tractors and horses, artillery pieces, and machine guns, which hindered unit training and preparedness. For example, XLIX Rifle Corps, just days before the invasion of Bessarabia and North Bukovina, had 103 percent of its authorized rifles but only 78.6 percent of its authorized number of heavy machine guns. It had 68 percent of its 45mm antitank guns, 68 percent of its 122mm howitzers, 75 percent of its 152mm guns, and 94 percent of its 76mm guns. It was well stocked in light mortars, having 96.2 percent of its 50mm mortars and a superabundance of 82mm mortars (155 percent), but it had only one-third of its authorized heavy mortars. Most serious, its armor battalions had only 14.2 percent of their authorized tanks.[49]

In spring 1940, VI Rifle Corps, which participated in the occupation of Bessarabia, was in some respects worse off than XLIX Rifle Corps. Its 41st, 97th, and 99th rifle divisions had tank battalions that were authorized fifty-four tanks each. Neither the 41st nor 97th rifle divisions had a single tank; the 99th had one lone tank. None of the three divisions had received any of the armored cars it had been authorized. Not only was the striking power of the corps diminished but a lack of horses also affected its mobility. The 41st Rifle Division was missing 244 horses, the 97th was short 328, and the 99th was lacking 246. The corps' two supporting artillery regiments were short a total of 533 horses. In addition, one of the regiments had only 8 of its 144 authorized artillery tractors, and the other had but 11 of its 210.[50] Not only was VI Rifle Corps not ready for combat, but with such equipment shortcomings it was in no condition to train.

Heavy equipment seems to have been in the shortest supply everywhere. The 135th Rifle Division was supposed to have twenty of the newer 76mm cannons but had only four; it was authorized sixteen 122mm mortars but had only eight. Even special units under the direct control of the KOVO suffered shortages. The KOVO's artillery tractor park had 264 tractors fewer than it was authorized, its tank brigades were equipped at 70 percent, and its cavalry regiments' tank battalions at 60 percent. The 140th Rifle Division was authorized 325 trucks but only had 43, which completely undermined its ability to move men and supplies. The district's 303d Separate Antiaircraft Artillery

Battalion was authorized three batteries, one of 76mm guns and two of 37mm guns, but had only one 76mm antiaircraft gun and no 37mm guns.[51] Consequently, air defense and training were at a minimum. Every division in the KOVO was below its authorized strength in artillery, and most suffered shortages of tanks, tractors, and horses as well. Even binoculars were universally scarce. On the bright side, only one division reported not having enough rifles.[52]

Lack of necessary equipment hindered and sometimes prevented training and so did the shortage of officers. Of course, discipline and morale suffered as well. That the shortage of officers made maintaining discipline that much more difficult was the subject of a report by the VI Corps commander to the commander of the KOVO in early June. The corps staff itself was short eighty-three officers, its 97th Rifle Division was short 259 officers, the 99th Rifle Division was short 115, and the 41st Rifle Division lacked 266. All told, the corps had around 80 percent of its authorized officers but nearly 90 percent of its enlisted men.[53] Some division commanders jealously guarded their officers, and it seems there was little cross-leveling among units to establish a district average of officers. Thus, within corps there could be vast discrepancies between the number officers; for example, the 80th Rifle Division was short 199 officers, yet its sister division, the 130th, was only 29 officers below full complement.[54]

On the other hand, the commander of XIII Rifle Corps, in order to have at least one full-strength division, forced three of his divisions to give up officers to the 62d Rifle Division, which at the time was closest to having its full complement of enlisted men. The corps staff itself provided several officers to bring the 62d Rifle Division to full strength. This was a rational move on the part of the commander because the other divisions were at half strength in enlisted men but had more than half their complement of officers. The 72d Rifle Division had only 6,789 enlisted men, which was one thousand less than half strength, but had 806 officers, only fourteen shy of its authorization.[55] Thus, the corps commander created one battle-ready division (in number of personnel at least) without significantly weakening the three other divisions. The negative side of such lateral transferring was that it weakened unit cohesion.

Expansion also required the transfer of enlisted men between formations, which created a different set of problems. Commanders used the opportunity to send their troublemakers and malcontents to the new units as a way to shore up discipline in their own, making things hard for commanders forming new units who were already seriously short of qualified and experienced leaders. They complained bitterly but without noticeable effect.[56] The annual turnover of enlisted men continued unabated and threw training and cohesion into ever more serious confusion. The 130th Rifle Division, for example, received six thousand reservists in October 1939, and then turned around and discharged three thousand regular conscripts in February 1940. Although by this time only about one-third of the men left the army every year, new conscripts were not assigned in neat draft cohort packages equal to one-third to make up the difference. Units formed in the mid- and late thirties sometimes received up to 70 percent of their personnel from one year group.[57]

Even as the KOVO expanded and attempted to absorb and tame its reservists and to replenish and reconstitute some battleworn units, the Commissariat of Defense issued orders to prepare to invade Bessarabia. As the district prepared for this latest offensive, discipline began to unravel to a degree never before seen in the Red Army; desertions rose to crisis proportions, and soldiers made and sometimes carried out death threats on their officers. A few threats were related to the reservists' desire to go home, but most were in reaction to the impending war with Bessarabia and the soldiers' lack of confidence in their officers in particular and the RKKA as a whole. One soldier in a tank battalion came out and said, "Our army is not prepared for war. People are poorly informed of this. If we were called on to attack we would just be human targets." A tank soldier of the 44th Rifle Division, and presumably a veteran of the Winter War, remarked to his comrades, "If I were to get an order like that in combat I would kill all the leaders in the platoon and company."[58]

The leadership of the KOVO was equally concerned about the quality of its leadership in the face of impending battle. Just two weeks before the invasion of Bessarabia, Marshal Timoshenko, at the urging of the KOVO staff, relieved the commander of the 1st Motorized Division for poor leadership and failure to fulfill orders. What comes across very clearly is that the men seemed to think that war would present an opportunity for them to shoot their officers and get away with it. Many men expressed the sentiment that if they were sent to the front and issued ammunition, the first one they would shoot would be their platoon or company commander. After being denied permission to go home, a reservist who was extremely upset by the plight of his family and his failure to get anyone to help them went so far as to threaten to kill his regiment commander if the unit was sent to the front. Another soldier told his unit commander, "All right then, you had better be quick in battle because I'll be there to shoot [you]." Another said, "When I get my first chance I will shoot the detachment commander."[59]

In June 1940, in order to get the men under control, the KOVO Military Soviet ordered the execution of two soldiers who had threatened their commanding officer. Another was executed for failure to obey an order.[60] This had no effect on the men, and threats actually increased in July. One soldier was arrested for telling his commander, pistol in hand, "At the front the first round is for you." Another soldier actually bayonetted his platoon commander to death.[61] Still another soldier warned his tank platoon commander that his pistol would not do him any good in combat because, "I will be in my tank and I will have a weapon too."[62] In the 34th Cavalry Division, a soldier who felt oppressed by his platoon commander's orders asked, "Do you want me to shoot you?" In another unit, during a discussion of training in which the men were being difficult, a lieutenant asked a soldier, "Really, how will you carry out orders in combat?" The soldier replied, "There it will be seen who gets whom" (kto-kogo).[63] Such cases of indiscipline were not limited to enlisted men. In June, a mladshii leitenant shot his regiment commander and promptly deserted.[64] Not until the invasion had been carried out successfully without resort to armed conflict did the death threats to officers cease.

Desertions and AWOLs also proved to be major discipline problems for the KOVO in 1940. They had been a problem in 1939, but the threat of being killed in war escalated the rate of occurrence. In January 1940, when it was rumored that XIII Rifle Corps would be sent to the front in Finland, the number of AWOLs, desertions, attempted desertions, and cases of excessive drinking skyrocketed. The men openly sang songs about not wanting to be sent to Finland. As it turned out, the 62d Rifle Division of the corps was sent to the front. In the days preceding its movement to the front, 240 men deserted. Others deserted en route, jumping from the trains or running away at railway stations.[65] According to a report of the Sixth Army Military Soviet, at the end of January 1940 a large number of soldiers deserted from the Sixth Army as a whole but especially from a division on its way to Finland. The report stated that the men more frequently resorted to self-inflicted wounds to avoid service at the front or to secure a discharge. Drunkenness among soldiers and officers escalated, and many men consorted with prostitutes. The reported also mentioned a higher than normal incidence of venereal disease.[66]

Desertion plagued both line and support units destined for the front. In a two-day period, 24–25 January 1940, 292 men deserted from six different support units, equaling 8 percent of those units' personnel. In June, units slated to take part in the invasion of Bessarabia experienced similar increases in the rate of desertion.[67] Some men went so far as to desert to the Germans in Poland. Ten men of the 136th Rifle Regiment did so in March 1940. When the KOVO asked that the soldiers be sent back, the Germans gave them the opportunity to return; all declined.[68] The army even had officers desert. A senior lieutenant of the 80th Rifle Division deserted from the front while the division was in Finland and was finally caught and arrested in June 1940. Between October and December 1940, five more officers deserted.[69] As with death threats, only in the aftermath of the move into Bessarabia did the rate of desertion lessen. In the fourth quarter of 1940, three months after the operation in Bessarabia, the KOVO military procurator reported the desertions of fourteen junior commanders and 168 *krasnoarmeitsy*.[70] The decrease in desertions reflects a substantial improvement over January 1940 but still cannot be considered healthy.

The relationship between imminent combat and crime in the KOVO is very interesting. In the fourth quarter of 1939, as the word spread about the pending deployment to Finland, there were 1,011 serious crimes subject to military tribunal (not including AWOL and desertion) committed by all ranks. One year later, after the Winter War had been won and the troops had returned to the Ukraine, and after Bessarabia and North Bukovina had successfully been occupied, there were only 466 serious crimes.[71] Clearly, many troops were not motivated to support the foreign policy of the USSR. The officers and junior commanders lacked the ability to control their troops, and perhaps they also lacked confidence in their unit's ability to survive in combat. One can only speculate that the rank and file's confidence on the eve of the invasion of Bessarabia was extremely low because it had the recent experience of the Winter War as an object lesson. Many of the men were veterans of that war and, fearing a repetition of the slaughter, probably passed their anxiety on to their comrades.

The move into Bessarabia caused the dislocation of many units that once again had to establish housing, training facilities, and so on. Many were quartered on the population. Like the Poles, the Bessarabian population proved fairly hostile to the presence of Red Army troops, making conditions that much more difficult. As a military operation, the invasion of Bessarabia and Northern Bukhovina showed serious weaknesses in the Red Army. Marshal Zhukov, commander of the district since May 1940, made a special note of the lack of discipline in the afteraction report.[72] He relieved several division commanders of their duties as a result of their poor performance and court-martialed one. The court-martialed commander had lost control of his division in the movement into Bessarabia and the men had run amok. The military tribunal accused him of being ineffective and a discredit to the RKKA.[73]

The KOVO magnified every ill of the RKKA: shortages of officers, transfers of officers between units, infrequent training, equipment shortages, poor morale, indiscipline, relocation of units, and so on. It is reasonable to expect that all the border districts shared similar experiences. The Odessa Military District in the southern Ukraine and newly occupied Moldavia, the Western Special Military District in eastern Poland, the Leningrad Military District, and the Baltic Military District had all expanded the number of new units and personnel; had sent units to Finland and got them back in bad shape; were bolstered by recalcitrant older reservists; and had relocated westward into territories inhabited by populations hostile to the RKKA. By the end of 1940, equipment and personnel shortages had still not been made good, even as war clouds again began to gather. The army mobilized another 800,000 reservists in the spring of 1941 and sent them to the western border districts.

Discipline and morale were at an all-time low in the Red Army in fall 1940. Poorly trained men and officers contributed greatly to this phenomenon. It would be an exaggeration to say that morale was the decisive factor in the events of summer 1941; yet Svechin, who propounded a doctrine for preparing for a major war, highlights the extreme importance of morale:

> A well-trained soldier with good weapons has enormous advantages over a poorly trained and equipped soldier. It is particularly important . . . to avoid pursuing quantity at the expense of quality. A bad soldier has the same stomach, takes up just as much room in a railcar and requires the same number of noncombatants as a good soldier. But he is much more expensive when a war begins. . . . All items of supply are destroyed with surprising mercilessness in a bad company, because a bad company is a leaky sieve which is always ragged and weaponless because it sells its equipment and loses overcoats and shoes, leaves weapons and telephones in the battlefield, and it is more gluttonous, because it falsifies its strength and demands excess rations. It expends just as much effort as a good company in kicking up mud on the roads or shivering in the rain but fills the hospitals with many more wounded, completely exhausts local resources, disgusts the local population, and suffers heavy casualties in battle. . . . A bad company can melt away like ice in the summer, and while it expends a vast amount of lives, health, and effort, it does very little useful work. Everything is spent on overcoming internal frictions and fighting figments of a sick imagination rather than the actual enemy. What are troops who have bad attitudes and are poorly trained worth in war?[74]

Without a doubt the Red Army was plagued with bad soldiers and bad companies. Inevitably bad soldiering will undo good generalship more surely than good soldiering will overcome bad generalship.

SUMMARY

Between 1939 and 1941, the RKKA faced greater problems than ever before of cohesion, equipment supply, training, and personnel due to ongoing expansion in the service of foreign policy. Divisions were unstable because of the transfer of regiments out of the divisions and the creation of new regiments, the constant turnover of officers, and geographical relocation. Rearmament with new weapons and equipment that the commanders had not

A tank detachment commander instructing his men during a training exercise.

been trained to use furthered instability. The officer corps, for the most part, was preoccupied with keeping its head above water as it struggled with an ocean of daily administrative tasks imposed by constant change and modernization. For many it was a task well beyond their training. Because many officers obviously lacked competence, the enlisted men lost faith in their leaders, especially after the examples of Lake Khasan, Khalkin-Gol, and Finland. The events of 1939–1941 overloaded even the many high-ranking officers with years of experience. Nothing had prepared them for the task at hand. Questions of mass expansion, occupation of territories with hostile populations, rearmament, and new methods of mechanized warfare overwhelmed them. Discipline deteriorated, particularly among the older reservists who served against their will. The mere threat of going to war propelled many to desert or to threaten the lives of their officers. Such was likely the case in all military districts on the Soviet western border in 1940. Conditions worsened in 1941, as the RKKA continued to expand and call up more reservists.

CHAPTER 7

The Predictable Disaster and the End of the Red Army: 22 June to December 1941

The eve of the German invasion found the Red Army, for the most part, unprepared for war. Many of its units were not on a war footing either organizationally or mentally. As a social unit, the army was riven by fault lines, some of its own making, others not. Poorly trained officers led unmotivated men. The army had begun reequipping, but in such a way as to disorganize training and maintenance. The RKKA continued to expand, furthering the breakdown of cohesion and continuity in major units. Finally, the regime had not clearly stated the mission of the armed forces in the newly acquired western territories, thus leaving the army leadership, as well as the rank and file, to assume that normal peacetime laxity, complacency, and incompetence remained the order of the day. After the war, the Soviet army refused to acknowledge that its prewar condition contributed to the disaster that ensued between June and December 1941—at least those aspects under its control. Instead, it focused on external causes for its failures. This concluding chapter examines some of the most prominent Soviet excuses and, in so doing, establishes the importance of the social causes of the Red Army's 1941 disaster.

22 June 1941: The German Invasion of the Soviet Union

On the morning of 22 June 1941, Adolf Hitler reneged on his promise of nonaggression, made to Stalin in 1939, and set his armed forces against the most powerful Russian army ever assembled. Despite colossal victories by the Germans and often fanatical heroism by the common Soviet soldier, the year ended in failure for both the Wehrmacht and the Workers' and Peasants' Red Army. The Germans had failed to take Leningrad and Moscow, had failed to destroy the capacity of the Soviet Union to fight, and had failed to cause the collapse of the Soviet government. As of late November, the Germans had killed, captured, and wounded close to 4.5 million Soviet soldiers while suffering 743,000 casualties of their own.[1] Still, there were always more *krasnoarmeitsy* to fight the next day. The Red Army, the world's largest armed force, had failed to successfully defend its borders from invasion and had allowed an enemy to conquer most of European Russia, all at a much greater cost to itself than to the enemy. Why?

THE EXCUSES

The Soviet regime's answer to this question has changed several times in the past fifty years. Initially, it denied that there had been a problem at all. The Red Army had not suffered a humiliating rout; rather Stalin had skillfully lured the fascist invaders deep into Soviet territory, weakening them as they advanced until the moment was right for the inevitable and irreversible counterstroke that would not only doom the invading force but end in the destruction of the Nazi regime. After Stalin's death, as part of Khrushchev's de-Stalinization campaign, a new explanation arose: indeed, the Red Army had suffered military reverses, but they were all Stalin's fault. Stalin had forced the army to adopt an offensive strategy when a defensive one would have been more appropriate; Stalin had purged the army of the best and brightest and depleted the numbers of officers; Stalin was responsible for the attack having been a "strategic surprise"; and Stalin's interference in tactical matters had greatly interfered with the conduct of the defense in the first phase of the war, especially in the Kiev encirclement in September 1941. Even problems within the army were attributed to Stalin. Poor training and low officer morale were all deemed a result of his cult of personality.

Moreover, Soviet scholars exaggerated the strength and skill of the Axis forces. They credited the Axis with numerical, technical, and tactical superiority, so even had there been no Stalin, the Red Army could not have been expected to do well in the face of such an overwhelmingly superior enemy. But the technical superiority of the Wehrmacht was also Stalin's fault, because he was responsible for the failure of the defense industry to provide sufficient quantities of modern equipment. The *krasnoarmeitsy* were merely victims and their leaders blameless; together they performed heroically, not only against the Germans but in overcoming the obstacles Stalin placed before them.[2] The Soviet military initiated most of the attacks on Stalin and the definition of the nature of the setbacks in 1941. Their one aim seems clear: to avoid responsibility for the disaster. Many of their arguments do not stand up to close examination, despite occasional elements of truth.

TESTING THE EXCUSES

The effect of the purge on the army already has been examined at length, and it will suffice to reiterate that, although the purge did deprive the army of some good leaders, it did not cause a great shortage of officers, as Soviet historians have claimed. In fact, the purge helped propel to the top many officers who would eventually become great commanders in the victory over Germany. The excuse that Stalin forced an offensive strategy on the army is false—it had been the dominant mode of thinking since the Civil War—and is entirely irrelevant. The French army had a highly developed defensive strategy and mentality since 1918, and it did not work against the blitzkrieg. And ultimately, the German army's offensive strategy did not succeed against the Soviet military, who turned the tables and beat them on the offensive.[3]

Were the Soviet military and regime really surprised, and of what importance was the surprise? Was Stalin really to blame? For many, yes, the invasion came as a bolt from the blue. The army seemed to be caught off guard despite many obvious signs of German preparation along the Russo-German border in Poland. Stalin had been warned well in advance of the invasion by various sources, such as his own spies, the British government, and German Communists. He disregarded all warnings, thinking them false or an attempt by the Germans to get him to provoke a war. He evidently truly believed that if he maintained good relations with Hitler he would not be attacked.[4] Not all of Stalin's generals were as trusting. In fact, many Soviet commanders suspected that the German attack would come when it actually did. Some even took precautionary measures on their own initiative—at risk to themselves if Stalin should disapprove.[5]

Even though many front-line commanders suspected an imminent attack,[6] the Germans did achieve tactical surprise sufficient to give them momentary advantage. The claim that Hitler achieved "strategic surprise," that is, a degree of surprise that gave the Germans far-reaching and long-lasting advantages, was made to cover up Red Army mistakes such as partial manning. The element of surprise does help explain why units on the border initially suffered from confusion that put them at a disadvantage. It in no way explains why corps and armies from the interior that had had weeks to prepare before their first engagements failed in battle. Surprise can also explain why the German air force caught hundreds of aircraft on the ground and destroyed them the first day of the war. It cannot explain why they caught Soviet airplanes on the ground on the third and fourth days.[7]

Stalin's interference in operations after the fighting had begun has also been used to shield the Soviet generals from blame. One explanation is that Stalin had an unrealistic picture of the war because of poor reporting from the field. Stalin, therefore, gave unrealistic orders to commanders in the field: he ordered counterattacks when units should have stayed on the defensive and improved their positions; he gave orders to stand fast when retreat would have saved men and matériel; he ordered reserves thrown into battle piecemeal straight from the march when they would better have been used as concentrated forces in a second echelon of defense. Although Stalin may be responsible for the debacle at Kiev in 1941, when he refused to grant the generals' request for permission to retreat and hundreds of thousands of men were needlessly lost, along with the city,[8] he had nothing to do with the other great encirclements, and he cannot be charged with the plethora of significant and costly tactical mistakes by the army.

The claim that poor training and low officer morale were by-products of Stalin's cult of personality and the purge is contradicted by evidence that these shortcomings existed not only before the purge but even before Stalin consolidated his power. In addition, one would also suspect that the lower-ranking officers, those in the battalions, would not have had the persecution mania often attributed to officers because the majority of them entered the army after 1937.

The army's attempt to shift some blame to the defense industry is also shot full of holes. Not only did the RKKA use its weapons ineffectively because of improper training, but it inadequately maintained and supplied them, so that a great deal of weaponry could not be employed at all. There are reports that in June 1941, 73 percent of the older tanks and 88.4 percent of the aircraft were inoperable due to maintenance problems.[9] This was a result of the military's failure to sufficiently organize its maintenance service and supply system, as well as its weapons and ammunition supply systems, for peacetime training and wartime operations. Given these circumstances, there are no grounds for the military to blame the defense industry for shortcomings in military matériel. A close look at the weapon procurement process and army supply process does not exonerate Stalin, but it further discredits the army.

Stalin and Armaments

Stalin's involvement in the armaments procurement process is universally condemned in Soviet memoirs as detrimental to the smooth functioning of the procurement system. Memoirists give the impression that the better an idea, the less chance it had of being adopted. No correct choices were ever made the first time around. Rather, Stalin often decided on whim the proposals brought before the Politburo. According to B. L. Vannikov, commissar of armaments, "A remark casually dropped by Stalin usually determined the outcome of a matter," and the atmosphere at meetings was not conducive to free discussion or dissension from the choice adopted by Stalin.[10] In other situations, however, Stalin sided with the majority opinion, expressing none of his own. Sometimes he listened closely to the various proposals and counter-proposals and chose the one he thought was better, for which he was criticized much later by those whose proposals he rejected.[11] Still other industrial managers portray Stalin favorably as a facilitator of military production, whose intervention was invaluable in overcoming bottlenecks and securing hard-to-get resources.[12]

Focusing on Stalin and his part in weapons procurement is not helpful in gaining a deeper understanding of the problems in the defense industry because it diverts attention from the role of the defense industry in designing and adopting weapons. Before Stalin could make a decision between good and bad designs, the defense industry had to present them. The military had the initiative in the process. First it had to identify a needed weapon or piece of equipment or a modification to an existing item and establish a project. Then the Main Military Council of the army or navy had to establish its position on the particular weapon before taking it to the Defense Committee, where the Politburo and Stalin finally became involved.[13] In other words, people farther down the chain of responsibility sent up designs that, in hindsight, were later labeled unsound propositions. Stalin could and did make arbitrary and uninformed decisions that caused problems in the production and development of weapons, but, at the same time, he could be circumvented by those intent on getting their way. Stalin reserved the right to decide between the arguments presented, while emphasizing the role of midlevel officials, armaments administrators, and users in the weapons development process.[14]

Other economic and bureaucratic factors played their role in arms procurement and production. The Central Committee, for one, was much involved in arms production between 1939 and 1941. Although the defense industry had top priority for resources and investment capital in the final years before the war, the efficient use of inputs was far from assured. The rapid and often incoherent expansion of industry, and the purges and problems in planning and transportation, negatively affected the quality and quantity of production.[15] Certainly the Soviet defense industry had enough problems without Stalin's interference, but, because of the nature of the system, it is not clear that things would have been significantly better had Stalin not interfered. A more thorough explanation of the difficulties in weapons procurement involves a combination of three main factors: central planning, the purges, and the procurement system.

Procurement and Allocation of New Weapons

It is true that the regime included armaments modernization in each five-year plan, but the armed forces consistently grew faster than projected. Consequently, the army's needs always outpaced industry's ability to deliver. The third five-year plan was supposed to begin in 1937 but did not get under way until 1939, probably as a result of purges in the planning organs. In the interim, industry followed annual plans based on the second five-year plan. Because of this, the RKKA lost two years of modernization and the high command changed its mind on the types of weapons it wanted, forcing industrial planners to begin all over again.[16]

The production of essential strategic war materials, such as ferrous metals, all types of steel, pig iron, coal and petroleum, chemical products, and electricity, slowed down concurrent with the disruption of planning. Even the volume of freight traffic fell. The defense industry, not independent of the rest of the economy, suffered from the same investment crisis that affected all heavy industry in the late thirties. In addition, the purges removed experienced factory managers and promoted untrained, inexperienced replacements, causing an across-the-board productive downturn in the USSR. The expansion of the Red Army, which took workers out of the factories and mines, caused production to slow. Beginning in 1938, as the armed forces grew, the urban work force began to shrink. The manpower pool continued to shrink through 1941, causing multiple problems for labor-intensive industry.[17]

As noted, the armament procurement system in the USSR depended on input from the military, the designers, and the producers. The military had to tell the designers what kind of weapons it wanted and then had to convince the producers to make them. The designers had to create feasible and competitive designs, and the industrialists had to create the means to produce the weapons. The military was the driving force behind weapons modernization and acquisition, yet it did not have full control of the arms procurement process. Once designs passed the scrutiny of the Main Military Soviet, the Committee of Defense and finally the Politburo could either approve or disapprove them. In the Committee of Defense, the military bargained with the industrialists on specifications, materials, quantities, and costs. The most important problems arose here. The industrialists had to deal with quotas set by the state planning commission (Gosplan), and naturally they wanted to make the weapons that were easiest and cheapest to manufacture. They also hesitated to switch from one product to another because it incurred additional costs and caused quotas to go unfulfilled until new production lines could be established.[18]

Military planners often turned out to be the weak link in the procurement chain. They vacillated in choosing designs. They changed their minds about quantities or put in orders too late to be included in the latest annual or semiannual plan. Such problems occasionally prevented production altogether and more often delayed it.[19] Plans and priorities became disordered, which created ill will between the military and industry. Due to indecision in the Red Army, industry did not produce any antitank guns in 1941. The army's last-minute decision to ask for more automatic rifles in 1941 meant cessation of current rifle production and several months of dead time while factories retooled.[20]

The example of democratic France demonstrates that armaments procurement operates in many ways independent of the influence of the political order. Like its Soviet counterpart, the French air force in 1938 lacked first-line fighter aircraft capable of matching the performance of the Germans, despite the fact that the aircraft industry had produced several excellent prototypes and the leadership was fully aware of the British development of the Spitfire and Hurricane fighters. Only in 1939 did production of more modern warplanes begin. The French also had trouble deciding which type of antitank gun to produce for the army, despite their acknowledgement of its great importance. It took the French from 1934 to 1937 to develop a 47mm antitank gun prototype because the army could not resolve whether it should be an infantry or artillery weapon. As a result, the line units still had woefully inadequate 25mm antitank guns when war broke out.[21]

Failure in the Transport System

Stalin is also held responsible for the forward displacement of the military units in Poland and for the forward stockpiling of military supplies and strategic reserves of industrial raw materials in the western USSR beginning in 1940. Further, he is blamed for overruling his experts' advice in doing so. Official Soviet histories maintain that it was a mistake to stockpile raw materials west of the Urals near industrial centers and war matériel near the frontier because they were thus vulnerable to enemy action.[22] These judgments ignore the realities of the inadequate Soviet transportation network in 1941 and assume that the German successes of 1941–1942 were inevitable, implying that the General Staff and Stalin should have known that they were going to be pushed back hundreds of kilometers.

Though the Germans did overrun much of the western USSR and captured many of the supply depots and raw material dumps, their success does not detract from the soundness of the decision to put them where they were. The forward deployment of war supplies and raw materials was actually a sound decision, given the wholly inadequate state of the Soviet transportation and military supply network. The example of the Northern Front is representative of the whole: in East Prussia up to the Lithuanian border, the Germans could run 228 trains a day to support their troops; the Red Army, from the border of the RSFSR through Lithuania to the East Prussian border, could only run eighty-four trains a day. In the western border regions, the railway network remained essentially the same as it had been on the eve of the First World War.[23] Suspecting that the USSR would soon be at war and that the railway system would be taxed to the limit with wartime requirements, strategists were prudent to stockpile as much as possible within easy reach of the units before hostilities commenced.

The military organized its prewar planning for supply along the same lines as the central planning of the economy. The General Staff determined the demand of the fronts and then told the various subordinate supply services to whom they should deliver particular supplies. The transport administration was to haul the supplies to the front-level supply units, which would then distribute the materials to the armies. During peacetime, the service and supply units were only partially manned, like the rest of the RKKA, and were to come to full strength upon mobilization immediately before the outbreak of war. The Soviet historians Skryabin and Medvedev report that the army assumed that at the outset of the war, each front would have a ready-to-go base for logistic support of the troops including railroads, waterways, highway and air routes, local and specially established supplies, dumps, repair shops, and medical and veterinary facilities.[24] This supporting infrastructure, however, did not exist in peacetime, and the service and supply units were still at half-strength when the war began. It is not surprising, then, that the supply services failed utterly to deliver their goods once the war started. By 26 June 1941, only five days after the invasion, the entire front suffered an acute shortage of ammunition, fuels, lubricants, and food.[25] The chaos in transportation, particularly railroad transport, that followed the outbreak of war lasted months. The regime, not the military, remedied the situation in late February 1942 when the State Defense Committee (GKO) set up a Transport Committee that coordinated planning and basic transportation of military and civilian shipments.[26] During the winter offensive of 1941–1942, which Stalin hoped would decimate the Germans, the Main Artillery Directorate could not fulfill its function because it had not worked out accounting and reporting procedures for the artillery supply service for wartime conditions and did not have the means to deliver ammunition to the fronts in accordance with General Staff directives.[27]

If commanders could not get adequate ammunition and supplies from supply centers only a few kilometers away, they undoubtedly could not have gotten them more easily had they been stored safely behind the Urals. The problem of moving supplies in wartime was aptly demonstrated by the French in 1940. They had plenty of supplies but had serious difficulty in delivering them to the troops under wartime conditions of rapid movement and enemy air attack.[28]

The shocking part of this transportation malady is that it should have been foreseen. Long before the war, foreign observers predicted the effect that the shortcomings in the railway system, combined with the deplorable roads, would have on military operations. In 1936, British military historian B. H. Liddell-Hart, after viewing Soviet military exercises, wrote: "If the Red Army attempts to concentrate its immense forces to act in any particular theatre there will be an inevitable congestion of the routes of supply in that area. Herein lies a continual danger of breakdown."[29] In early 1941, the U.S. military attaché in Moscow wrote: "Couple the lack of good highways and inefficient railroads with the slow antiquated horse transport, it is almost a foregone conclusion that the supply system of the Red Army will break down. The army cannot move much faster than it could thirty years ago."[30] The

Commissariat of Defense knew of these problems but did not act on them. In 1940, the Commissariat of Transport had drafted a seven-year plan to reconstruct western railways. The army, though, did not send a commission to investigate transportation capabilities until February 1941. G. K. Zhukov participated on this commission and noted many deficiencies. He did not think that any of the projects scheduled for 1941 would be completed by the end of the year but did not recommend that any special measures be taken.[31] Apparently, the Soviet military did not take the situation seriously.

The very idea of coordinating transportation, not just of supplies but of men as well, seems to have been alien to a vast number of Red Army leaders. This deficiency seriously hindered their tactical movement at the beginning of the war. In a letter to Stalin several months into the war, one lieutenant wrote, "Use of auto transport is poor, most of it is driven about on unnecessary chores and not used for transferring soldiers, which would create mobility in maneuver." As a consequence, people in his unit suffered unnecessary fatigue from marching on their almost daily moves. This put them at a disadvantage to the Germans, who quickly moved their soldiers by truck so they arrived in combat with energy left to fight.[32] Surely Stalin cannot be blamed for the military's failure to properly plan the use of its resources.

MYTH OF GERMAN SUPERIORITY

Contrary to what Soviet historians would have the world believe, the Germans did not have advantages in numbers and equipment. In fact, the Soviet army outnumbered and outgunned the Germans during most of the war. For Operation Barbarossa, the Germans and their allies numbered some three million men and had 3,200 tanks and 2,000 aircraft. The Soviet armed forces in the western regions also numbered approximately three million men, 10,400 tanks and 9,500 aircraft.[33] Official Soviet histories, however, inflated the size of the German forces to 5.5 million men, 4,300 tanks and assault guns, and nearly 5,000 aircraft. At the same time, they minimized their own numbers, reporting only the 2.68 million men in the 170 divisions along the border and not including the hundreds of thousands of men manning the fortified areas and the one hundred thousand NKVD border guards. As late as the mid-1980s, Soviet historians tended not to divulge the number of earlier model tanks and only reported the new tanks (1,871) and aircraft (1,540). When counting men and machines, they failed to include the thirty-two divisions displaced west of the Dvina and Dnepr rivers from interior military districts in May and June, and though they were not all combat-ready by 22 June, they were able to deploy behind the front and prepare for imminent engagement.[34]

A comparison of the armament of the standard German and Soviet tanks shows how even the quality of armor really was. The 76mm gun of the Soviet T-28, T-34, and KV-1 tanks had longer range and penetrating power than any of the German guns. The 45mm gun of the Soviet BT-5, BT-7, and T-26 was equivalent to the German 50mm tank gun and superior to the German 37mm guns. The Wehrmacht's 50mm and 37mm guns were effective only at close range against the majority of Soviet tanks and hardly at all against T-34 and KV-1 medium tanks and the KV-2 heavy tank.[35] The Germans clearly did not have a technical superiority in armor. Their tactical use of tanks, coupled with good training, gave them their advantage. If the Red Army had used its light tanks as proficiently as the Germans, things would have been very different.[36]

In addition to claiming that the Germans had a numerical advantage in airplanes, Soviet historians claimed that the surprise attack on the airfields the first day of the invasion, which destroyed thousands of aircraft on the ground, factored significantly in the German successes of 1941. This assertion is disputed by German generals who note that the front was far too wide for the Luftwaffe to cover the whole of it, and air superiority was always local rather than general. Often, the German spearheads had no air cover at all because the armor moved forward out of the range of supporting fighter aircraft. The VVS shot down or damaged 1,284 of the 2,000 German aircraft committed between 22 June and 19 July. On 29 June, the Luftwaffe had only 960 operable airplanes, and it did not reach 1,000 again until 3 July. The Luftwaffe did achieve notable successes against the VVS, which it attributed to the superior training of its pilots, not to numbers. In air-to-air combat, the Luftwaffe was devastatingly effective against Soviet pilots.[37] The excuse that the VVS was outnumbered in aircraft does not hold much water, especially when one considers that in the Battle of France the French air force outnumbered the German air force in modern airplanes 3,289 to 1,600, not including the hundreds of aircraft the British contributed, yet Germany prevailed.[38]

Soviet historians also claimed that the Wehrmacht had the advantage of experience from the campaigns in Europe just months previously. This theory incorrectly assumes that all the German divisions participated in the invasions of Poland, Western Europe, and southeast Europe in fact, a significant number had never seen combat and many had been in existence for less than a year.[39] Even for those with combat experience, the Russian campaign posed new and unexpected challenges. A postwar study of German small-unit actions in the Soviet theater of operations concluded:

Even the best trained German troops had to learn many new tricks when war broke out and when they were shifted from one theater to another. In each instance they were faced with problems for which they were not sufficiently prepared. Occasionally a combat efficient unit without previous experience in Russia failed completely or suffered heavy losses in accomplishing a difficult mission that presented no problems to another unit familiar with the Russian theater even though [it] had been depleted by previous engagements.[40]

The initial period of the Russian campaign was as much a learning experience for the Wehrmacht as for the RKKA, but it appears the Germans learned more quickly. In fact, the attack on the USSR surprised many German soldiers as much as it did their Soviet counterparts. For secrecy's sake, the soldiers were not told of the invasion until the night of 21 June, just hours before the opening assault. Many of these soldiers had arrived in Poland only two or three days before the invasion, and it was invasion of England that was uppermost in their minds, not an attack on Russia.[41]

Even so, the German soldier was far from the inhuman Hitlerite automaton pictured by the Soviet media. There were problems with morale, fatigue, and battle weariness, as one would expect in any army subjected to prolonged combat. Very likely, as a result of the strain of war and in particular the extremely harsh conditions in Russia, desertions and self-mutilations among German soldiers were not uncommon.[42]

Furthermore, Soviet memoirs and official histories give the impression that the German army was entirely mechanized and simply overpowered the RKKA with massed panzer formations. In reality, the Germans used only nineteen panzer divisions in Operation Barbarossa—seventeen on 22 June. The vast majority of German divisions were infantry divisions—just as with the Red Army—which relied on foot marches and horse-drawn artillery and supply wagons. Most of the combat, not only in 1941 but in the course of the entire war, was between infantry divisions in which the Germans had no inherent advantages materially or numerically. If the Wehrmacht was not so powerful, if Stalin was not so culpable, and many commanders not so surprised, then the fault for the debacle of 1941 must lie with the Red Army itself. Clues to just what was wrong with the Red Army as a fighting organization are evident in its battle performance.

RED ARMY COMBAT BEHAVIOR

In the opening days of the German invasion, the Red Army performed unevenly. Some units fought hard but ineffectively, some fought with desperate heroism, and some did not fight at all. Between June and December, most combat behavior, however, seems to reflect desperation rather than either cowardice or valor. Eyewitness accounts of Red Army combat in 1941 reveal an almost complete lack of combined-arms coordination, lower-level initiative, and imagination in adapting to German tactics. Instead they show a rigid, centralized command structure and an inflexible mentality that relied on masses of men and matériel to compensate for inadequate military proficiency, especially on the part of the officers. For example, in one afternoon on the second day of the war, a German battery of three self-propelled guns, which had never seen combat before, in one afternoon destroyed a battalion of forty Soviet tanks with no losses of its own.[43]

Its tactics, primarily that of hitting the enemy head-on in massed formations, greatly contributed to the destruction of the Red Army. Between 20 August and 3 September 1941, six divisions of the Twenty-second Army were ground to dust, not so much by the Germans as by their own commanders. On 20 August, the 186th Rifle Division entered combat with 7,900 men and 386 vehicles. On 3 September, when it was withdrawn to regroup, it had only 2,778 men and 36 vehicles. The 174th Rifle Division had 9,360 men and 145 vehicles on 20 August, but only 2,363 men and 85 vehicles two weeks later. The 179th Rifle Division suffered the heaviest casualties of all. On 3 September, only 1,617 men had survived out of an initial 8,903, more than 7,280 men having perished at the front. The 214th Rifle Division lost 4,334 of 6,194 men and 198 of 222 vehicles in the same action. The 126th Rifle Division fared the best, losing only about half of its manpower (4,455 of 8,764 men) and two-thirds of its 62 vehicles. The only armored force, the 48th Tank Division, began the fight with 6,574 men and 318 vehicles but suffered 3,799 men killed and 246 tanks, armored cars, and trucks destroyed or abandoned. The units were so badly mauled that the army commander deemed them beyond salvage. Instead, he parceled out the surviving men and equipment among three other ravaged divisions and sent them back into battle.[44] These casualties took a heavy psychological toll on the surviving *krasnoarmeitsy*, not all of whom were able to withstand the stress brought on by the incredible carnage. Consequently, desertion, panic, and cowardice proved significant problems.[45]

The army's disorganization reflects poor decision-making powers from corps level up to the Commissariat of Defense. This weakness is illustrated by the initial combat experiences of the 7th Tank Division of VI Mechanized Corps, XV Mechanized Corps, VIII Mechanized Corps, and a report by Major General Volskii to Lieutenant General Fedorenko, deputy people's commissar of defense, on 5 August 1941. One can readily identify the problems lower-level commanders had as a result of the bungling of their superiors.

The 7th Tank Division of VI Mechanized Corps began the war in relatively good order. It had 98 percent of its authorized rank and file, 60 percent of its junior commanders, and 80 percent of its officers. It had 51 KV tanks, 150 T-34s, 125 BT-5s and BT-7s, and 42 T-26s. The usefulness of the KV and T-34 tanks was somewhat limited in that they had not been supplied 76mm armor-piercing shells.[46] The 7th Tank Division, then, was equipped and manned at nearly full strength—far more completely than official Soviet histories would lead one to expect of any division.

On 21 June, the division's units continued to conduct training according to plan. Several units were in their assigned positions, while others were scattered among numerous training areas and firing ranges. The division commander, Major General Borzilov, claimed to have had no knowledge of the impending attack by the German army, even though the corps commander had conducted a meeting with the division commanders on 20 June 1941, at which time he instructed them to increase combat readiness by issuing ammunition to the tanks and increasing security at vehicle parks and supply dumps. At the meeting, the corps commander warned that these measures were to be carried out without making a sensation; to tell no one and to continue normal daily activities as usual.[47]

At 0200 hours on 22 June, the 7th Tank Division received word through a field liaison officer of a combat alert. Ten minutes later, the division staff announced a combat alert, and by 0430 hours the division's units had concentrated at its assembly point. At 0400 hours, enemy aviation bombed the division's area, and one of its regiments saw twenty-six of its men wounded and four killed but suffered no equipment damage. The division saw no action on 22 June but corps headquarters ordered it numerous times to move to different locations that night and the next day in anticipation of engaging the enemy, who proved consistently elusive. As a result of the division's road marches, the Luftwaffe subjected it to numerous air attacks, destroying sixty-three tanks. The division finally went into action on 24 June and claimed to have destroyed two German infantry battalions and two artillery batteries. From then on, the division was in constant battle, and by 29 June, while covering the disorderly retreat of the cavalry and motorized rifle division of its corps, it had been reduced to three T-34 tanks. It finally abandoned these on the night of 30 June due to lack of fuel and lubricants.[48]

As for XV Mechanized Corps, it spent the entire time between 22 and 28 June traveling back and forth behind the front responding to changing orders. The corps never once engaged the enemy but suffered numerous mechanical breakdowns that cost it a large number of tanks. The same fate befell VIII Mechanized Corps, which was transferred between armies and then shifted from one area to another without joining battle. In the course of its journeys, the corps, without seeing combat, lost 50 percent of its vehicles, all to mechanical failure brought on by "super forced marches," which did not allow time for routine maintenance.[49] Tables 7.1 and 7.2 show that the German army was not the greatest enemy of Soviet tanks; rather, the Red Army was. Both the 8th and 10th tank divisions began the war at nearly full strength but lost roughly three-quarters of their tanks between 22 June and 1 August 1941. Of the tanks they lost, however, battle accounted for only about

Table 7.1. Combat Vehicles in the 8th Tank Division, 22 June–1 August 1941

Type	Strength on 22 June	Lost in Battle	Missing in Action	Abandoned by Crew	Evacuated to Depot	Other Causes
KV	50	13		25	5	2
T-34	140	54	8	31	32	15
T-28	68	10		2		1
BT-7	31	2	1	12	3	1
T-26	36	6	1	13	5	
BA-10	57	7		14	5	13
Total	382	92	10	97	50	45

Source: V. P. Krikunov, "Kuda delis' tanki?" Voenno-istoricheskii zhurnal, no. 11 (1988), 33.

one-third; the rest were either stuck in swamps, abandoned by their crews, or evacuated to the rear for maintenance. Many broke down before they ever reached the battlefield.

In all, the 8th Tank Division, after forty days of war, had 88 of its original 382 armored fighting vehicles left fit for action. Of the 292 vehicles it lost, only 92 were lost to enemy action. The 10th Tank Division, which started with 448 combat vehicles had, as of 1 August, only 141 tanks and armored cars at its disposal, assuming that those that did not make the alert were subsequently repaired. Of the vehicles lost between 22 June and 1 August, fewer than half were destroyed in combat.

On 5 August 1941, Major General Volskii submitted a report to Deputy People's Commissar of Defense Fedorenko detailing the reasons, as he saw them, for the rapid breakdown of tank units in the first month and a half of war. Volskii argued that the mechanized corps had been wrongly assigned to armies rather than to fronts. The army commanders had no idea how to use them, and the striking power of the corps were of strategic rather than tactical nature, thus more effectively employed by the higher command. Mechanized corps had in several instances been ordered to pull back and occupy fortified areas, which was a misuse of their mobility. In practice, when mechanized corps fell back, the Germans pursued them so closely that they were unable to man the fortified areas in time, and most were thus lost. Army commanders did not know how to combine infantry and armor operations and therefore employed them separately, thereby reducing the effectiveness of both. Army commanders usually sent tank units into battle with no reconnaissance, putting them at a disadvantage to the Germans. Even corps commanders used their forces improperly, sending tanks into the fray not only in small groups but also as individual vehicles. [50]

The lack of familiarity with armored formations by higher commanders proved devastating to the armored vehicles themselves. Volskii reported:

The army staffs completely forgot that the equipment had a certain running life, that it would require inspection, minor repairs as well as an additional replenishment of fuel and ammunition, while the technical personnel and chiefs of the army ABTO [motor vehicle and armored section] did not suggest this to them and instead of, after carrying out a task, pulling back the mechanized corps, giving it time necessary for this purpose, the combined-arms commanders demanded that they "come out fighting" and nothing more.[51]

When the tank units did "come out fighting" the army staffs did not provide them with timely intelligence or information on adjacent units. Army commanders, unschooled in mobile armored warfare, often tried to use tank and motorized units in linear defenses rather than as mobile striking groups, again depriving themselves of inherent advantages.[52]

Volskii also had severe criticism of the lower-level commanders. He complained that mechanized corps, tank division, and tank regiment commanders and staffs still had not mastered the "operational-tactical viewpoint" required of armored unit commanders. They did not exercise initiative, did not use all the mobile means at their disposal, and did not exploit their maneuverability. Moreover, as a rule, they employed frontal attacks and neglected reconnaissance at all levels. Command and control, from platoon commanders up through corps commanders, were extremely poor, and the use of radios was especially inept. Many officers did not have maps, which frequently caused units to get lost on the way to battle. He leveled his harshest criticism at commanders in the mechanized corps who "were not up to their job and had completely no idea of how to command [their units]."[53]

The lack of support services took almost as great a toll on Soviet armor as did the enemy. Tank crews were poorly trained in maintenance. Units did not have salvage equipment to retrieve and repair damaged vehicles. Mechanized

Table 7.2. Combat Vehicles in the 10th Tank Division, 22 June–1 August 1941

Type	Strength on 22 June	Arriving on Alert	Lost in Battle	Missing in Action	Abandoned in Retreat
KV	63	63	22		34
T-34	38	37	23		9
T-28	61	44	4	3	37
BT-7	181	147	54		46
T-26	22	19	7	3	14
Armored Cars	83	72	24		27
Total	448	382	134	6	167

Source: V. P. Krikunov, "Kuda delis' tanki?" *Voenno-istoricheskii zhurnal*, no. 11 (1988), 33.

corps lacked higher-level maintenance units in the rear echelon to assist them. No one seemed to take the initiative to designate collecting points for damaged vehicles. The Sixth Army commander, for example, deemed his ABTO chief to be so incompetent that he was removed from his position. The root of these problems, according to Volskii, was improper officer training. Before the war, in the military schools, academies, and KUKS (advanced military training course), no one had carefully considered what the mechanized forces might encounter, not only in the way of combat maneuver but also in terms of support needs and interarms coordination. This lack of foresight extended to the highest levels of the government and Commissariat of Defense, where there was a complete lack of appreciation of the particular needs of large armored formations. The NKO had failed to plan production and distribution of such a basic necessity as fuel, the lifeblood of mechanized corps, relative to the expansion of mechanized forces. In the first months of war, lack of fuel was a significant problem for the fronts.[54]

SOCIAL AND SOCIETAL CAUSES OF THE DISASTER

By 22 June 1941, the Workers' and Peasants' Red Army of the Soviet Union had become, as Trotsky had warned, "an edifice built on loose sand."[55] The primary reason for this was rapid and incoherent expansion. A secondary reason was the social disruption of civil society characteristic of the Stalin era.

The effects of the massive, rapid industrialization on Soviet society are best summed up by Moshe Lewin: "A series of furious economic, educational, and military undertakings shook up and restructured society, affected all its social classes, and thereby caused havoc in the system. Sudden changes of social position, occupation, status, and location operated on such a scale as to create a 'quicksand society' characterized by flux, uncertainty, mobility, high turnover, and anomie."[56] Without a doubt, the Stalinist thirties wreaked havoc on the RKKA as a social system. As in civilian society, the military experienced enormous flux, uncertainty, mobility, high turnover, and anomie. Much of the chaos came into the army from its connections to civilian society, which the army then exacerbated by its expansion. Lewin identifies "the cadres of these years, with some notable exceptions, basically as *praktiki*, that is, responsible, often top-level cadres in political, social, technological, and even cultural positions whose training was inadequate or nonexistent. They learned as they went along."[57] This describes almost exactly the military cadres of the thirties, both the officer corps and PUR. The army thrust men into situations and positions for which they were unprepared, not only by lack of training but culturally as well, and that they often did not want. The armed forces simply grew too large too fast and introduced more new technology than its leaders could master. The USSR, as a predominantly backward rural society with peasant values, was in most respects unable to create a modern mass army that required people with urban skills and values.

Leading, supplying, and training a mass army simply overwhelmed the individual officers. In 1941, the army still had many officers of peasant origin. They came from homes with no electricity or plumbing. Growing up, they had had little or no exposure to automotive or other complex machinery. As officers they were thrust into a quasi-urban social setting, with responsibility for supervising others in doing things that they themselves had not been prepared for. It seems as though every officer wanted results from his subordinates, while he fended off his superiors as he attended his tasks. The result: low morale, high turnover, and many duties performed poorly or not at all.

The army was in a constant state of emergency from 1928 to the beginning of the war. The first crisis was officer manning; second, the long-standing discipline problem among both officers and men, which was exacerbated by collectivization in 1929–1933 and by calling up older reservists in 1939–1941; third, the food crisis; fourth, the ever-present housing crisis; fifth, a perpetual training crisis; sixth, the great purge of 1937–1938; and subsequent crises were the three phases of expansion. The first phase led to unorthodox recruiting of officers, which disrupted cohesion in the officer corps; the elimination of the territorial system marked the second; and the last major phase of expansion coincided with the purge, the casualties from the war with Finland, and intensified demand for more equipment.

The Soviet Union's "successful" foreign policy and rearmament programs were responsible for three additional major crises: first, the reevaluations of doctrine, but without arriving at consistent or definitive solutions, following the series of conflicts with Japan, Poland, and Finland; second, the expansion of the mechanized forces in 1940–1941 and subsequent rearmament; and, third, the relocation of units to the western borders in 1939–1941, which disrupted training, added to the housing problem, created a need for new war plans, and sowed the seeds for intensified supply problems in wartime. Many of these crises overlapped and coexisted, creating a situation beyond the control not only of the high command but of the platoon commander, his company commander, and on up to the regiment and division commanders.

To make matters worse, the enlisted men were disinterested in soldiering at best. Soldiers often proved uncooperative and sometimes demonstrated outright hostility to their leaders. This resulted primarily from their disaffection with the communist regime and anyone identified as its agents. The recall of hundreds of thousands of reservists who were angered at having to leave jobs and families created another important source of disaffection. The large number of men who eventually joined the Germans attests to the festering anger over collectivization and dekulakization. The distribution of scarce food supplies among the urban population and the party at the expense of the peasantry further alienated the rural population from the regime. The experience of collectivization, which was not complete until 1938, lingered fresh in their minds as they struggled to meet their high delivery quotas.[58] Ukrainians in particular welcomed the Germans as liberators from the collective farm system. Still others, such as families of purge victims, saw the Germans as liberators from communist oppression. The army never adequately trained the junior commanders to competently assist their officers and generally underutilized them. The army regularly siphoned off the best to become officers, thus decreasing the level of effectiveness of those who remained.

In the twenties, Aleksandr A. Svechin had described the preconditions for preparing the army for protracted warfare:

> The basic source of a soldier's morale is the conscientious attitude toward war of the class to which he belongs, or the alteration of his consciousness by the state, insofar as the latter is able to accomplish this. A standing army, with its traditions and its firm barracks discipline, is a powerful tool for altering human consciousness. However, this alteration requires a lot of time and is possible only on a limited scale. Modern warfare, which requires millions of men for mobilization and for reinforcing the armed front, cannot rely solely on the consciousness artificially created in the barracks, and only if the purposes of a war are clearly understood and close to broad segments of the public can we count on the armed forces fighting for long periods of time with a great deal of enthusiasm and pertinacity. If this is not the case, we would observe phenomena similar to those which took place in the Austrian infantry [in the First World War]: as soon as combat operations wiped off the barracks greasepaint, as soon as the cadres fell, as soon as the units were diluted with new men and as soon as the armed nation began to appear on the front, the combat-readiness of the Austrian infantry dropped quickly and abruptly and its members began surrendering en masse.[59]

By Svechin's criteria, the Red Army had not met the preconditions for its members to fight "with a great deal of enthusiasm and pertinacity," in June 1941. The barracks greasepaint had been wiped off at Khalkin-Gol, in Finland, and in Poland. The cadres, in the persons of experienced junior commanders and officers, had been falling since mid-1937 in the tens of thousands to purge and war. Units were diluted with new men on a regular basis. Firm barracks discipline came about too late. The term of service had only been raised from two to three years in 1939 and, under the circumstances, was still too short a time to alter the consciousness, even temporarily, of many soldiers, given the disaffection many felt.

The unexpectedness of the war was a problem for a great many soldiers and civilians. Antifascist propaganda in the Soviet media abruptly ceased in August 1939, after years of vilifying Germany. The sudden onslaught by Germany in June 1941 caught millions of average citizens and soldiers psychologically unprepared.[60] Initially, the purposes of the war were not, in Svechin's terms, "clearly understood nor close to broad segments of the population." The state launched a sudden and massive propaganda effort to reorient public attitudes.

The rapid expansion of the Red Army made it, for all intents and purposes, unmanageable. The lack of capable cadres of officers and noncommissioned officers resulted in generally poor training, not only of the enlisted men but also of the new junior leadership. Commanders' pervasive lack of talent and knowledge rendered the massive size of the armed forces largely ineffective and limited the usefulness of what first-class equipment it possessed.

On the eve of the war, the Red Army still had not decided how to fight at division level and higher, which further hindered the work of the platoon commanders. The army did not fight any of its three tests before Barbarossa using the guidelines of the 1936 Field Regulations (PU-36), which had been in effect for three years. The RKKA used three completely different techniques in the successful battle against the Japanese at Khalkhin-Gol, the invasion of Poland, and the war in Finland. At the regimental level, examples of the opening battles of the war with Germany show both a reversion to the typical nineteenth-century tactic of frontal assault and an inability by Red Army officers to adapt their thinking under pressure to follow new ideas that would have exploited the potential of their new technology. This reversion was due in part to a lack of guidance from the highest levels of the army. Stalin cannot be blamed for this. Neither he nor his cohort shaped the general atmosphere of politics and decision making such that no Soviet officer could make common-sense objections and advance ideas contrary to prevailing opinion. After the *Ezhovshchina*, people expressed fears of voicing independent views, but years before the terror the army had contributed to its own close-mindedness and called on Marx to legitimize it.

The doctrinal debates in the early thirties pitted Svechin and Verkhovskii, representatives of the old guard, who believed in the potential for continued wars of attrition and limited gain, against Tukhachevskii, representative of the new guard, who thought in terms of mass mechanized armies fighting wars of destruction and clear-cut victory. Rather than keep the debate on solely military grounds, Tukhachevskii attacked with citations from Lenin, Stalin, and Voroshilov. According to Jacob Kipp, Tukhachevskii "sought to stigmatize [Svechin and] those favoring a strategy of 'attrition' as class enemies, bourgeois theorists and idealists. In seeking to establish his own credibility by invoking ideological purity and party loyalty, Tukhachevskii contributed to the end of professional debate within the Red Army."[61] By the end of 1931, Svechin's ideas had been discredited politically, and the army turned its back on measures he endorsed that possibly would have mitigated the disaster of 1941. The army itself created an atmosphere that inhibited free exchange of ideas and controversy.

In this stultified atmosphere, between 24 and 31 December 1940, twenty-eight top leaders of the RKKA's ground and air forces conferred on how best to defend the USSR from German attack. The main argument concerned the style of defense to adopt, active or static. Those in favor of the static defense pointed out the success of the Finns just a year earlier. Those in favor of active defense—mobile armor oriented—had no concrete examples to cite. No one grasped with certainty what lessons could be drawn from the German victory over France. Although the conferees did not reach a decision, the army sent a confusing message, for it seemed to prepare for both defensive styles by constructing more fortified regions and organizing more mechanized corps.[62] In May 1941, the General Staff produced a plan for the defense of the USSR against both Nazi and Japanese aggression. Rather than devising strategy, it concentrated on delineating areas for military districts to defend and allocated forces to them.[63]

Battalion-level tactics promulgated in MTPP-33 were sound and applicable to the situation in 1941, yet it seems that commanders ignored them in the panic that gripped the army as it sought to plug gaps in the line to stem the German advance. A crisis of confidence brought on the reversion to typical Russian massed infantry attacks in disregard of established techniques. Inadequately trained officers at the company and battalion levels did not trust their men or themselves with the more decentralized formations and tactics of MTPP-33; instead, they opted for unit attacks that they could control more directly—that is, they had all the men line up and rush the objective. Regimental commanders seem also to have lacked confidence in their subordinate officers, and they initiated regimental attacks in which the regiments were massed to create centralized control under the regimental commander, rather than maneuvering battalions under their battalion commanders toward a regimental objective.

The ruinous effects of such lack of confidence, talent, and knowledge minimizes the importance of the defense industry's role in equipping the RKKA before the war. Having more and better equipment would not have made a substantial difference in the initial campaigns of the war, but knowing how to effectively employ existing weapons, old or new, would have. The Red Army overcame prewar problems in the defense industry, Stalin's interference, military-industrial conflicts, the general problems of the economy, and even the late start on increasing the rate of production in 1942. Even though the RKKA had more first-rate equipment in 1942 than in 1941, the Wehrmacht succeeded in pushing the Red Army back to Stalingrad without the advantage of surprise. It was not until 1944, when the Red Army became more adept in the use of its armor and aircraft, that it used these weapons to real effect, although the generals still relied more heavily on mass rather than maneuver.

CONCLUSION

The problem with the Red Army in June 1941 was a human problem. It was not a problem of enemy superiority, technology, or interference from a tyrannical supreme leader. The armed forces had outrun the capacity of a still predominantly peasant society to provide (on a mostly volunteer basis) cadres capable of leading and managing a modern mass army. Soviet society was no different from tsarist society in that the majority of its members showed aversion to military service in any capacity. What was different was that the Soviet regime, contrary to its intentions, had created a reservoir of ill will among potential conscripts through its social and economic policies of collectivization and dekulakization and had disrupted normal patterns of social development through rapid industrialization and urbanization. These policies hindered the assimilation of such state-promoted values as patriotism, obedience, and self-discipline, all necessary to a stable military.

According to Hans Speier, "A modern mass army is rendered helpless if the many specialized functions that it is supposed to perform are not properly coordinated."[64] This observation provides a framework for understanding why the RKKA failed in 1941. The men responsible could not get maps to commanders or fuel to tanks. Officers could not coordinate between arms. Rifle and tank unit commanders could not call on artillery or the air force for support. Before the war, the high command could not recruit, train, and retain a sufficiently large, dedicated, and educated corps of officers to master the many specialized functions of a modern mass army.

In some ways, the regime failed the army. It imposed requirements on it that detracted from the army's military endeavors. The regime failed to adequately fund the military for two decades yet expected maximum results. It politicized and purged the armed forces. In other ways, the army high command failed the soldiers. It did not train officers and men as well as it could have. It lost sight of the individual and his needs, forgetting that the foundation of military success is the motivated and trained soldier. Instead, the leadership thought in terms of mass and material and did not do a particularly good job in organizing them. The result was that the people of the USSR suffered more than they would have if the regime and military had done things differently.

It is doubtful that these problems could have been avoided entirely. The army mirrored the mainstream of Soviet society and indeed was a product of it. The army's failure was indicative of the overall failure of the Soviet regime to exercise caution, restraint, moderation, and pragmatism in the social, political, and economic spheres. The development of the Red Army serves as an example of the subordination of the reality of human limitation to the arbitrarily imposed political and ideological imperatives that pervaded all aspects of Stalinist society. The army consistently failed to properly estimate the human element, that is, the intelligence, education, motivation, moral character, dedication, and loyalty of both officers and enlisted men. It did little or nothing to improve these necessary qualities.

What choice did the army have but to accept the dictates of the government and party? It could, however, determine how fully it embraced those dictates. The high command and the soldiery, not being monolithic in outlook, showed considerable variability in their reactions to state policies, sometimes exhibiting alienation and resistance and at other times embracing them wholeheartedly, heedless of their consequences. At all times the military acknowledged its subordination to civilian authority, yet it sought to influence policy-making to satisfy its own interests and was often successful; thus, by selfish and short-sighted decision making, it in some ways promoted its own demise.

As of the end of March 1942, the old Red Army of the Revolution and Civil War ceased to exist. It did not die a sudden death but suffered a long, drawn-out ordeal in which the RKKA, like civilian society, dropped its revolutionary idealism and egalitarianism and instead adopted traditional authoritarian bureaucratic structures, behavior, and outlooks. By the end of the 1941–1942 winter offensive, most *krasnoarmeitsy* were dead, captured, too seriously wounded to return to duty, or swallowed up in a sea of newly conscripted servicemen (*voenno-sluzhashchii*) whose only experience of military life was the Second World War (which the army subsequently used to create an entirely new military tradition) and whose only purpose was to save the motherland. In many ways, the war created a second chance and a new beginning for the Soviet armed forces.

Introduction

1. See for example John Erickson, *The Soviet High Command: A Military-Political History* (New York: St. Martin's Press, 1962), and Seweryn Bialer, ed., *Stalin and His Generals* (New York: Pegasus, 1969).
2. Mark von Hagen, *Soldiers in the Proletarian Dictatorship: The Red Army and the Soviet Socialist State, 1917–1930* (Ithaca, N.Y.: Cornell University Press, 1990).

1. Organization and Training

1. Il'ia B. Berkhin, *Voennaia reforma v SSSR (1924–1925 gg)* (Moscow: Voenizdat, 1958), 78–87; Makhmut A. Gareev, *M. V. Frunze, Military Theorist* (McClean, Va.: Pergamon-Brassey's, 1988), 228–232. For a detailed treatment of the political infighting around the establishment of the mixed regular-territorial system, see Francesco Benvenuti, *The Bolsheviks and the Red Army, 1918–1922* (New York: Cambridge University Press, 1988), and Mark von Hagen, *Soldiers in the Proletarian Dictatorship: The Red Army and the Soviet Socialist State, 1917–1930* (Ithaca, N.Y.: Cornell University Press, 1990).
2. Although the regime decided in 1925 that the Red Army's regular forces would be established at 529,000 officers and men (down from its peak Civil War strength of five million) and its budget reduced to less than 2 percent of the national budget, the number of servicemen did not drop to that level until 1927. "K istorii territorial'no-militsionnogo stroitel'stva v Krasnoi Armii," *Voenno-istoricheskii zhurnal*, no. 11 (1960), 87–88; Nikolai Vishniakov and F. I. Arkhipov, *Ustroistvo vooruzhennykh sil SSSR* (Moscow: Voenizdat, 1926), 16–17; Gareev, *M. V. Frunze, Military Theorist*, 234–241; *15 let na strazhe Oktiabria* (Moscow: Gosvoenizdat, 1932), 56–58.
3. For a brief overview of the theories governing the organization and function of the army before the Frunze reforms, see William E. Odom, "Bolshevik Ideas on the Military's Role in Modernization," *Armed Forces and Society* 3, no. 1 (1976), 103–120.
4. N. F. Kuz'min, *Na strazhe mirnogo truda 1921–1940* (Moscow: Voenizdat, 1959), 13.
5. Robert W. Davies, *The Soviet Economy in Turmoil, 1929–1930* (Cambridge, Mass.: Harvard University Press, 1989), 443–451; Gareev, *M. V. Frunze, Military Theorist*, 248–250; Odom, "Bolshevik Ideas," 112.
6. *Harvard University Refugee Interview Project*, Soviet Interview Project Archives, 1980–1987, Record Series 24/2/50, University of Illinois Archives, no. 1, ML, A2/3, 6–7.

7. Vishniakov and Arkhipov, *Ustroistvo vooruzhennykh sil SSSR*, 85; Berkhin, *Voennaia reforma v SSSR*, 179.

8. *Harvard University Refugee Interview Project*, no. 1, ML, A2/3, 6–7.

9. Ibid., 6, 7; *Krasnaia zvezda*, 28 Aug., 1 Sept. 1935.

10. *Kievskii krasnoznamennyi* (Moscow: Voenizdat, 1974), 77, 91.

11. Boris I. Balinsky, *Memoir*, unpublished manuscript dated 1988, University of Illinois Archives (Record Series 15/35/57), 125; Nicholas DeWitt, *Education and Professional Employment in the USSR* (Washington, D.C.: National Science Foundation, 1961), 53; *Harvard University Refugee Interview Project*, no. 18, RF, A3, 8, 9.

12. In 1926, for example, peasants represented 82.5 percent of the draft cohort but 71.3 percent of the men actually conscripted. Workers comprised 12.1 percent of the available draft cohort but 18.1 percent of the conscripts. Men in the category "other" were the most overrepresented in the army. Comprising 10.6 percent of the conscripts, they were represented at nearly twice their number in society: 5.4 percent. In the twenties, the army debated the ratio of peasants to workers it could sustain in peace and war without disrupting the civilian economy. Many never ceased to wish for a predominantly worker army for ideological and practical reasons. Others, such as Aleksandr Svechin, saw the predominance of peasants as an advantage because this would enable the USSR to keep its skilled laborers at the workbench in time of war. See Alexandr A. Svechin, *Strategy*, ed. Kent D. Lee (Minneapolis, Minn.: East View Publications, 1992), 123, 124. Originally published as *Strategiia* (Moscow: Voennyi Vestnik, 1927).

13. Il'ia Berkhin, "O territorial'no-militsionnom stroitel'stve v Sovetskoi Armii," *Voenno-istoricheskii zhurnal*, no. 12 (1960), 16; *Krasnaia zvezda*, 15 July 1925.

14. Rossiiskii gosudarstvennyi voennyi arkhiv [formerly Tsentral'nyi gosudarstvennyi arkhiv Sovetskoi Armii, hereafter cited as RGVA] f. 9, op. 26, d. 490, ll. 29–30; f. 25893, op. 1, d. 292, ll. 68–69, 120–121.

15. Victor Kravchenko, *I Chose Freedom* (New York: Scribner's, 1946), 47.

16. RGVA f. 9, op. 26, d. 487, ll. 80–85; d. 490, l. 41; Semion Belitskii, *Besedy o voennom dele i Krasnoi Armii: sbornik dlia kruzhkov voennykh znanii na fabrikakh, zavodakh, pri klubakh i shkolakh* (Moscow: Voennyi Vestnik, 1926), 185–186; *Krasnoarmeets*, 20 Oct. 1927.

17. *Krasnoarmeets*, 10 Jan. 1930; B. Tal', *Istoriia Krasnoi armii* (Moscow: Gosizdat, 1929), 191; *Krasnaia zvezda*, 15 Dec. 1929; RGVA, f. 25893, op. 1, d. 292, ll. 12–14.

18. *Krasnaia zvezda*, 14 Nov., 14 Dec. 1929.

19. K. Voroshilov, L. Mekhlis, S. Budenny, G. Stern, *The Red Army Today: Speeches Delivered at the Eighteenth Congress of the C.P.S.U. (B), March 21, 1939* (Moscow: Foreign Language Publishing House, 1939), 15.

20. *British Foreign Office Russia: Correspondence 1781–1945, British Foreign Office File 371 (1906–1948)*, 1939, vol. 23688, 297; hereafter cited as *B.F.O. 371*.

21. *Krasnaia zvezda*, 11 Aug. 1936, 1 Sept. 1937, 1 Sept 1938; *B.F.O. 371*, 1936, vol. 20348.

22. *Krasnaia zvezda*, 9, 10, 28 May 1936; 28 April, 11 Sept. 1937; *Krasnoznamennyi Severo-kavkazskii* (Rostov: Rostovskoe knizhnoe izdat, 1971), 132; Philip Longworth, *The Cossacks* (New York: Holt, Rinehart and Winston, 1969), 327–328; N. I. Savinkin, *KPSS o Vooruzhennykh Silakh Sovetskogo Soiuza: Dokumenty 1917–1981* (Moscow: Voenizdat, 1981), 286.

23. RGVA f. 25880, op. 4, d. 4, l. 448.

24. *Krasnaia zvezda*, 10 Aug., 20 Sept. 1936, 14 July 1937.

25. Pitirim I. Shuktomov, *Druzhba skreplennaia v boiakh* (Moscow: Dosaaf, 1972), 35–44; John L. Scherer, *USSR Facts and Figures Annual*, vol. 1 (Academic International Press, 1977), 94; Peter A. Zaionchkovskii, *Samoderzhavie i russkaia armiia na rubezhe XIX–XX stoletii 1881–1903* (Moscow: Mysl', 1973), 119.

26. Tal', *Istoriia Krasnoi Armii*, 192–193; Belitskii, *Besedy o voennom dele i Krasnoi Armii*, 32–55.

27. V. S. Orlovskii, *Stavropol'skaia imeni Blinova* (Stravropol': Stavropol'skoe knizhnoe izdat, 1971), 128–130.

28. RGVA f. 25893, op. 1, d. 292, l. 88.

29. *Records of the Smolensk Oblast of the All-Union Communist Party of the Soviet Union, 1917–1941*, WKP 225, 34; hereafter cited as *Smolensk Archive*.

30. *Smolensk Archives*, WKP 225, 34; *Krasnaia zvezda*, 21 June 1933. The responsibility for preconscription training was consolidated in the thirties when the Society for Defense, Aviation and Chemistry (Osoaviakhim) took over most of the work with support from local military units. Even so, problems persisted. For more on Osoaviakhim, see Gal'ianov and Gorshenin, *Voennaia rabota komsomola* (Moscow: Molodaia gvardiia, 1931), 30; William E. Odom, *The Soviet Volunteers: Modernization and Bureaucracy in a Public Mass Organization* (Princeton: Princeton University Press, 1973), 144, 145.

31. Roberta T. Manning, *Government in the Soviet Countryside during the Stalinist Thirties: The Case of Belyi Raion in 1937*, The Carl Beck Papers in Russian and East European Studies, no. 301 (Pittsburgh: University of Pittsburgh, 1984), 29.

32. Arnol'd B. Kadishev, *Chto dolzhen znat' molodoi krasnoarmeets*, 13th ed. (Moscow/Leningrad: Gosizdat, 1930), 106–110.

33. Belitskii, *Besedy o voennom dele i Krasnoi Armii*, 53–55; I. Karpov, *XXI godovshchina Raboche-Krest'ianskoi Krasnoi Armii i Voenno-Morskogo Flota* (Leningrad: 1939), 60–64; N. Fedoseev, *Prava i Obiazannosti Krasnoarmeitsa. Kratkii spravochnik* (Moscow/Leningrad: Gosizdat, 1928), 65–72; Semen M. Budennyi, *Boets-grazhdanin* (Moscow: Partizdat, 1937), 16–17.

34. Vishniakov and Arkhipov, *Ustroistvo vooruzhennykh sil SSSR*, 15–30; Kadishev, *Chto dolzhen znat' molodoi krasnoarmeets*, 38–46.

35. *Dlia distsipliny net melochei* (Moscow: Gosizdat, 1927), 1–3, 9–11.

36. Kadishev, *Chto dolzhen znat' molodoi krasnoarmeets*, 48–56, 161–162.

37. Belitskii, *Besedy o voennom dele i Krasnoi Armii*, 188, 189; *Krasnoarmeets*, 20 March 1928.

38. A. Edel'shtein, *Alkogolizmu v Krasnoi armii net mesta* (Moscow, 1928), 1–12.

39. Leon Trotsky, *Military Writings* (New York: Merit Publishers, 1969), 69.

40. *Krasnaia zvezda*, 12 May, 2 June 1935.

41. *Krasnaia zvezda*, 10 May 1937, 18 April, 17 May 1938.

42. M. Vasilenko, *Boevaia slushba krasnoarmeitsa*, 7th ed. (Moscow: OGIZ, 1937), 22–23, 42–65, 79–81, 88–91, 103–107, 113–117.

43. *Krasnaia zvezda*, 8 May 1933.

44. *Metodika Takticheskoi Podgotovki Pekhoty-33 chast' I* and *Metodika Takticheskoi Podgotovki Pekhoty-33 chast' II* (Moscow: Voenizdat, 1933).

45. Ironically, three years later the army made a special effort to conscript new men

and mobilize *vnevoiskovniki* and reservists having specialized skills such as those of the men demobilized in 1930. *Smolensk Archive,* WKP 225, 30, 31; Vladimir F. Klochkov, *Krasnaia Armiia—shkola kommunisticheskogo vospitaniia sovetskikh voinov, 1918–1941* (Moscow: Nauka, 1984), 117.

46. Aleksei A. Epishev, *Partiia i armiia* (Moscow: Politizdat, 1977), 147.

47. Petro Grigorenko, *Memoirs* (New York: Norton, 1982), 59; Vladimir Unishevsky, *Red Pilot: Memoirs of a Soviet Airman* (London: Hurst and Blackett, 1939), 84.

48. *Istoriia Ural'skogo voennogo okruga* (Moscow: Voenizdat, 1970), 129; Epishev, *Partiia i armiia,* 147; *Krasnoznamennyi Severo-Kavkazskii,* 127.

49. *Krasnaia zvezda,* 3 June 1937.

50. James S. Corum, *The Roots of Blitzkrieg* (Lawrence: University Press of Kansas, 1992), 203–205; Victor Vogel, *Soldiers of the Old Army* (College Station: Texas A&M University Press, 1990), 98–104.

51. Lieutenant-General Sir Giffard Martel, *The Russian Outlook* (London: Michael Joseph Ltd., 1947), 20.

52. *Krasnaia zvezda,* 26 Oct. 1936.

53. *Krasnaia zvezda,* 9 May 1937, 22 Sept. 1938, 16 Nov. 1938, 7 March 1941.

54. *Krasnaia zvezda,* 1 June 1936, 8 Jan., 11 Jan., 9 May 1937, 27 Nov. 1938.

55. *Krasnaia zvezda,* 1 June 1936, 3 Feb. 1938, 18 Jan. 1939.

56. B. Baratov, *Die Rote Armee und das Territorialsystem* (Pokrovsk: Nemgosizdat, 1928), 30–32. [Translated from the Russian *Krasnaia armiia i territorial'nia sistema.*]

57. Berkhin, "O territorial'no-militsionnom stroitel'stve," 13; V. N. Koniukhovskii, *Territorial'naia sistema voennogo stroitel'stva* (Moscow: Voenizdat, 1961), 42; Kadishev, *Chto dolzhen znat' molodoi krasnoarmeets,* 283; *Krasnaia zvezda,* 12 July 1932.

58. Orlovskii, *Stavropol'skaia imeni Blinova,* 128–129; Ivan Shevchenko, *Deviataia Plastunskaia* (Moscow: Voenizdat, 1970), 99.

59. *Istoriia Ural'skogo voennogo okruga,* 119; *Sovetskaia Voennaia Entsiklopediia,* vol. 8 (Moscow: Voenizdat, 1980), 28–29; Aleksandr M. Vasilevskii, *Delo vsem zhizni* (Moscow: Politizdat, 1975), 59.

60. Berkhin, *Voennaia reforma v SSSR (1924–1925 gg),* 126, 129–132; *15 let na strazhe Oktiabria* (Moscow: Gosvoenizdat, 1932), 58–61.

61. Koniukhovskii, *Territorial'naia sistema voennogo stroitel'stva,* 41.

62. V. F. Loboda, *Komandnye kadry i zakonodatel'stvo o kadrakh razvitii vooruzhennykh sil SSSR* (Moscow: Voenizdat, 1960), 56.

63. Kuz'min, *Na strazhe mirnogo truda 1921–1940,* 31; "K istorii territorial'no-militsionnogo stroitel'stva v Krasnoi Armii," *Voenno-istoricheskii zhurnal,* no. 11 (1960), 93; Koniukhovskii, *Territorial'naia sistema voennogo stroitel'stva,* 71; *KPSS i stroitel'stvo Vooruzhennykh Sil SSSR* (Moscow: Voenizdat, 1959), 337.

64. Berkhin, "O territorial'no-militsionnom stroitel'stve v Sovetskoi Armii," 16.

65. *Krasnaia zvezda,* 17 July 1925.

66. T. H. Rigby, *Communist Party Membership in the USSR 1917–1967* (Princeton: Princeton University Press, 1968), 241; RGVA f. 1293, op. 5782, d. 6, l. 1.

67. *Smolensk Archives,* WKP 186, 49.

68. Iosif I. Geller, *Pod krasnoi zvezdoi: Krasnaia Armiia na fronte kollektivizatsii* (Samara: Gosizdat, 1931), 69; *Vsearmeiskie sovershchaniia politrabotnikov 1918–1940* (Moscow: Nauka, 1984), 176–177.

69. *Krasnaia zvezda*, 17 Feb. 1933.

70. *Krasnaia zvezda*, 5 March 1933.

71. *Kievskii krasnoznamennyi* (Moscow: Voenizdat, 1974), 91; *Sovetskie Vooruzhennye Sily* (Moscow: Voenizdat, 1978), 194.

72. *Sovetskie Vooruzhennye Sily*, 197; *KPSS i stroitel'stvo Vooruzhennykh Sil SSSR*, 337.

73. *Sovetskie Vooruzhennye Sily*, 236; L. M. Sandalov, "Stoiali Nasmert': Podgotovka voisk 4-i armii k otrazheniiu fashistskoi agressii," *Voenno-istoricheskii zhurnal*, no. 11 (1988), 6; Matei V. Zakharov, *General'nyi shtab v predvoennyi gody* (Moscow: Voenizdat, 1989), 177–180; *Odesskii krasnoznamennyi* (Kishinev: Kartia Moldoveniaskii, 1975), 39; *Ordena Lenina Moskovskii voennyi okrug*, 3d ed. (Moscow: Moskovskii rabochii, 1985), 168.

74. RGVA f. 25880, op. 4, d. 5, ll. 220, 221, 329, 596, 598.

75. Ibid., 555–562; Ignatii S. Prochko, *Artilleriia v boiakh za Rodinu* (Moscow: Voenizdat, 1957), 131; *50 let Vooruzhennykh sil SSSR* (Moscow: Voenizdat, 1968), 236; L. M. Sandalov, "Stoiali Nasmert'" 6; Nikolai D. Iakovlev, *Ob artillerii i nemnogo o sebe* (Moscow: Voenizdat, 1981), 50–52.

76. For a discussion of the debate over armor, see John Erickson, *The Soviet High Command: A Military-Political History* (New York: St. Martin's Press, 1962); Amnon Sella, "Red Army Doctrine and Training on the Eve of the Second World War," *Soviet Studies* 27, no. 2 (1975), 245–265; and Zakharov, *General'nyi shtab v predvoennyi gody*, 177–180.

77. Zakharov, *General'nyi shtab v predvoennyi gody*, 186–188; Sandalov, "Stoiali Nasmert'," 6.

78. O. A. Losik, *Stroitel'stvo i boevoe primenenie sovetskikh tankovykh voisk v gody Velikoi Otechestvennoi voiny* (Moscow: Voenizdat, 1979), 44–45; A. G. Khor'kov, "Tekhnicheskoe perevooruchenie Sovetski Armii, " *Voenno-istoricheskiizhurnal*, no. 6 (1987), 22; Pavel A. Rotmistrov, *Vremia i tanki* (Moscow: Voenizdat, 1959), 64, 84–88.

79. In 1940, 35 percent of conscripts had postsecondary, high school, or incomplete high school education. Another 55 percent had fourth- through sixth-grade education, and only 9 percent had fewer than four years of schooling. D. A. Voropaev and A. M. Iovlev, *Bor'ba KPSS za sozdanie voennykh kadrov, 1918–1941* (Moscow: Voenizdat, 1960), 161; Aleksandr N. Kolesnik, *Sovetskie voennye stroiteli* (Moscow: Voenizdat, 1988), 97; Konstantin P. Terekhin, Aleksandr S. Taralov, and Aleksandr T. Tomashevskii, *Voiny stal'nykh magistralei* (Moscow: Voenizdat, 1969), 70–73; E. P. Egorov, *Inzhenernye voiska Sovetskoi Armii 1918–1945* (Moscow: Voenizdat, 1985), 181.

80. *Narodnoe Khoziaistvo SSSR v 1959 godu* (Moscow: Gosizdat, 1960), 381.

81. RGVA f. 25880, op. 4, d. 5, ll. 555–562; Voroshilov et al., *The Red Army Today*, 60–63.

82. Svechin, *Strategy*, 204–205.

83. Robert Doughty, *The Seeds of Disaster: The Development of French Army Doctrine, 1919–1939* (Hamden, Conn.: Archon Books, 1985), 22, 24; Robert Doughty, "The French Armed Forces, 1918–1940," in Allan R. Millet and Williamson Murray, eds., *Military Effectiveness*, vol. 2 (Boston: Allen and Unwin, 1988), 43, 44, 64.

84. *Istoriia vtoroi mirovoi voiny 1939–1945*, vol. 3 (Moscow: Voenizdat, 1973), 441.

85. *Sbornik boevykh dokumentov Velikoi Otechestvennoi voiny* (Moscow: Voenizdat, 1958–1959).

86. Konstantin K. Rokossovskii, "Soldatskii Dolg," *Voenno-istoricheskii zhurnal*, no. 4 (1989), 52.

87. Vogel, *Soldiers of the Old Army*, 112–115.

2. Daily Life, Conditions of Service, and Discipline

1. *British Foreign Office Russia: Correspondence 1781– 1945, British Foreign Office File 371* (1906–1948), 1927, vol. 12585, 18–20; hereafter cited as *B.F.O. 371*; Stanislav G. Poplavskii, *Tovarishchi v bor'be* (Moscow: Voenizdat, 1974), 16.

2. *Krasnaia zvezda*, 6, 23 March 1932; Vladimir Unishevsky, *Red Pilot: Memoirs of a Soviet Airman* (London: Hurst and Blackett, 1939), 84–88.

3. *Krasnaia zvezda*, 6, 23 March, 10 July 1932, 27 March 1933; *Tyl Sovetskoi Armii* (Moscow: Voenizdat, 1968), 64.

4. *Krasnaia zvezda*, 1 Oct. 1925; 5 Oct. 1933.

5. N. Vishniakov and F. Arkhipov, *Ustroistvo vooruzhennykh sil SSSR* (Moscow: Voenizdat, 1926), 252–255.

6. *B.F.O. 371*, 1933, vol. 17256, 27.

7. Georgii Sofronov, *Nepodvlastnoe vremeni* (Moscow: Voenizdat, 1976), 335–336.

8. Georgii K. Zhukov, *Vospominaniia i Razmyshleniia* (Moscow: Novosti, 1969), 123.

9. Ibid., 128, 134.

10. Vsevolod V. Garshin, *From the Reminiscences of Private Ivanov and Other Stories*, trans. Peter Henry, Liv Tudge, Donald Rayfield, and Philip Taylor (London: Taylor Books, 1988), 163.

11. V. S. Orlovskii, *Stavropol'skaia imeni Blinova* (Stavropol': Stavropol'skoe knizhnoe izdat, 1971), 132–133.

12. Andre I. Eremenko, *Pomni Voinu* (Donetsk: Donbass, 1971), 98, 104.

13. Boris I. Balinsky, *Memoir* (Record Series 15/35/57, University of Illinois archives), 131.

14. Ivan Boldin, *Stranitsy zhizni* (Moscow: Voenizdat, 1961), 41.

15. John Scott, *Behind the Urals* (Bloomington: Indiana University Press, 1988), 55–56, 90, 104; Victor Kravchenko, *I Chose Freedom* (New York: Charles Scribner's Sons, 1946), 59–60, 79-80.

16. Teodor K. Gladkov and Luka E. Kizia, *Kovpak* (Moscow: Molodaia gvardiia, 1973), 50–53.

17. Scott, *Behind the Urals*, 38–42; Solomon Schwarz, *Labor in the Soviet Union* (New York: Praeger, 1951), 154; Leonard Hubbard, *Soviet Trade and Distribution* (London: MacMillan, 1938), 275; Kravchenko, *I Chose Freedom*, 178–179.

18. *Krasnaia zvezda*, 10 July, 15 July, 1 Aug. 1932.

19. *Krasnaia zvezda*, 6 March 1932; Scott, *Behind the Urals*, 42.

20. *Krasnaia zvezda*, 9 July 1934.

21. *Krasnaia zvezda*, 3 Dec. 1932; Schwarz, *Labor in the Soviet Union*, 142; Nikolai Iakovlev, *Ob artillerii i nemnogo o sebe* (Moscow: Voenizdat, 1981), 29.

22. *Krasnaia zvezda*, 22 June 1932.

23. *Krasnaia zvezda*, 3 Dec. 1932.

24. Ibid.

25. Rossiiskii gosudarstvennyi voennyi arkhiv (RGVA) f. 25893, op. 1, d. 292, l. 129.

26. RGVA f. 9, op. 26, d. 490, l. 2.

27. Schwarz, *Labor in the Soviet Union*, 143–144; Scott, *Behind the Urals*, 30–33, 37.

28. Semen M. Budennyi, *Boets-grazhdanin* (Moscow: Partizdat, 1937), 11; according to Alan Wildman, *The End of the Russian Imperial Army*, vol. 1 (Princeton: Princeton University Press, 1980), food in the old army was not really that bad, which lends credence to the idea that the Red Army was trying to make the old army look worse than it was so that the soldiers would feel better about serving in the Red Army despite its problems.

29. Elise K. Wirtschafter, "The Lower Ranks in the Peacetime Regimental Economy of the Russian Army 1796–1856," *Slavonic and East European Review* 64, no. 1 (January 1986), 40–65.

30. *Krasnaia zvezda*, 17 March 1933.

31. *Krasnaia zvezda*, 12 Nov. 1932.

32. *Krasnaia zvezda*, 17 Sept. 1932, 16 Jan., 2 April 1933.

33. *Krasnaia zvezda*, 9 Dec. 1932; Nikolai Voronov, *Na sluzhbe voennoi* (Moscow: Voenizdat, 1963), 71.

34. *Krasnaia zvezda*, 17 Dec. 1932, 26 March, 17 July, 23 July, 20 Aug. 1933.

35. *Krasnaia zvezda*, 9 Dec. 1932.

36. RGVA f. 25880, op. 4, d. 5, l. 182.

37. Vishniakov and Arkhipov, *Ustroistvo vooruzhennykh sil SSSR*, 242–245.

38. "Red Army—General Conditions, 1927," *U.S. MID Reports*, Reel 4, 76.

39. Vishniakov and Arkhipov, *Ustroistvo vooruzhennykh sil SSSR*, 366; *B.F.O. 371*, 1939, vol. 23688, 241–245.

40. *Harvard University Refugee Interview Project*, Soviet Interview Project Archives, 1980–1987, Record Series 24/2/50, University of Illinois Archives, no. 18, RF, A3, 43.

41. Arnol'd B. Kadishev, *Chto dolzhen znat' molodoi krasnoarmeets*, 13th ed., (Moscow/Leningrad: Gosizdat, 1930), 271–283; N. Fedoseev, *Prava i obiazannosti Krasnoarmeitsa* (Moscow: Gosizdat, 1928), 99.

42. *Krasnaia zvezda*, 20 Sept. 1929.

43. See Roberta T. Manning, *Government in the Soviet Countryside in the Stalinist Thirties: The Case of the Belyi Raion in 1937*, Carl Beck Papers in Russian and East European Studies, no. 301 (Pittsburgh, University of Pittsburgh, 1984) for the underdevelopment of rural administration in the thirties.

44. *Voennyi Vestnik*, 15 Feb. 1932.

45. *Krasnaia zvezda*, 12 July 1932.

46. *Krasnaia zvezda*, 21 Dec. 1932.

47. *Krasnaia zvezda*, 12 July 1933.

48. *Krasnaia zvezda*, 3 Oct. 1933.

49. Ibid.

50. *Krasnaia zvezda*, 15 May 1937.

51. RGVA f. 25990, op. 4, d. 4, ll. 439–444; 842.

52. Elise K. Wirtschafter, "Military Justice and Social Relations in the Preform Army," *Slavic Review* 44 (Spring 1985), 67–82.

53. Vishniakov and Arkhipov, *Ustroistvo vooruzhennykh sil SSSR*, 173.

54. Ibid., 174, 203.

55. Vladimir F. Klochkov, *Krasnaia Armiia—shkola kommunisticheskogo vospitaniia sovetskikh voinov, 1918–1941* (Moscow: Nauka, 1984), 204, 205.

56. RGVA f. 25893, op. 1, d. 292, ll. 108–110.

57. K. E. Voroshilov, *O molodezhi* (Leningrad: Molodaia gvardiia, 1937), 16–17.

58. K. E. Voroshilov and M. V. Frunze, *O molodezhi* (Moscow: Partizdat, 1936), 139; *Krasnaia zvezda*, 13 Feb. 1929.

59. *Krasnaia zvezda*, 15 July, 6 Oct. 1932.

60. RGVA f. 887, op. 1, d. 90, ll. 1–49; d. 96, ll. 1–69; d. 99, ll. 1–119.

61. Il'ia B. Berkhin, *Voennaia reforma v SSSR (1924–1925 gg)* (Moscow: Voenizdat, 1958), 248.

62. *Harvard University Refugee Interview Project*, no. 1, ML, A2/3, 30.

63. *Krasnaia zvezda*, 4, 5 Aug. 1932.

64. "Red Army Discipline and Morale, 1933–34," *U.S. MID Reports*, Reel 3, 325–329.

65. Nikolai A. Ivnitskii, *Klassovaia bor'ba v derevne i likvidatsiia kulachesta kak klassa (1929–1932 gg)* (Moscow: Nauka, 1972), 96–133, 271–279; Robert W. Davies, *The Socialist Offensive* (Cambridge, Mass.: Harvard University Press, 1980), 243–261.

66. *B.F.O. 371*, 1933, vol. 12756, 74; *Krasnaia zvezda*, 18 April 1929; "Insurrection in Siberia, November 15, 1930," *U.S. MID Reports*, Reel 10, 355–362.

67. "Political Unrest, September 22, 1936," *U.S. MID Reports*, Reel 10, 386–393.

68. Zhukov, *Vospominaniia i razmyshleniia*, 103.

69. Mikhail Soloviev, *My Nine Lives in the Red Army* (New York: David McKay, 1955), 39–48. For more on the Ukrainian famine, see Kravchenko, *I Chose Freedom*, 106–108, 111–129; *First Interim Report of Meetings and Hearings of and Before the Commission on the Ukraine Famine, held in 1986* (Washington, D.C.: U. S. Government Printing Office, 1987); Robert Conquest, *Harvest of Sorrow* (New York: Oxford University Press, 1986).

70. *Krasnaia zvezda*, 17 July 1925.

71. "Red Army Personnel—Relations with Civilians, May 31, 1927," *U.S. MID Reports,* Reel 3, 448; "Red Army Discipline and Morale, 1928–1929," Reel 3, 311–314; "Red Army Discipline and Morale, August 24, 1929," Reel 3, 450.

72. Vasilii Varenov, *Pomoshch' krasnoi armii v razvitii kolkhoznogo stroitel'stva (1929–1933 gg)* (Moscow: Nauka, 1978), 41.

73. Iosif I. Geller, *Pod krasnoi zvezdoi: Krasnaia Armiia na fronte kollektivizatsii* (Samara: Gosizdat, 1931), 72–77.

74. "Red Army Discipline and Morale, 1933–34," *U.S. MID Reports*, Reel 3, 326, 327; Kadishev, *Chto dolzhen znat' molodoi krasnoarmeets*, 258, 259.

75. Kadishev, *Chto dolzhen znat' molodoi krasnoarmeets*, 258–259; *Krasnaia zvezda*, 24 Nov. 1925.

76. Harold J. Berman and Miroslav Kerner, *Documents on Soviet Military Law and Administration* (Cambridge, Mass.: Harvard University Press, 1958), 85, 111, 112.

77. Ibid., 85, 111, 112.

78. Ibid., 85–94.

79. Kravchenko, *I Chose Freedom,* 134; Suvenirov, "Vsearmeiskaia Tragediia," *Voenno-istoricheskii zhurnal*, no. 3 (1989), 43.

80. Grigorenko, *Memoirs*, 75.

81. Scott, *Behind the Urals*, 195.

82. *Krasnaia zvezda*, 20, 29 March, 21 April, 24 June 1938.

83. *Krasnaia zvezda*, 5 Oct., 18 Dec. 1938.

84. *Krasnaia zvezda*, July–Dec. 1938.

85. Harold J. Berman and Miroslav Kerner, *Soviet Military Law and Administration* (Cambridge, Mass.: Harvard University Press, 1955), 72–87.

86. RGVA f. 25880, op. 4, d. 4, ll. 16–20, 196, 197, 268–270, 290; d. 5, ll. 301, 303–307, 316–324, 328, 545, 547, 595, 597.

87. *Distsiplinarnyi Ustav Krasnoi Armii* (Moscow: Voenizdat, 1941).

88. S. F. Petrov, *Doprizyvnaia Voennaia Podgotovka* (Moscow: Gosudarstvennoe uchebno-pedagogicheskoe izdatel'stvo Narkomprosa RSFSR, 1941), 45.

89. O. F. Suvenirov, "Prikaz Otmeniat' ne budem," *Voenno-istoricheskii zhurnal*, no. 4 (1989), 32–33.

90. "O rabote Politicheskogo Upravleniia Krasnoi Armii, Iz doklada Politicheskogo Upravleniia Krasnoi Armii Tsentralnomu Komitetu VKP(b) o rabote Politicheskogo Upravleniia Krasnoi Armii, 23 Maia 1940 g," *Isvestiia TsK KPSS*, no. 3 (1990), 200.

91. *Krasnaia zvezda*, 15 Oct. 1940.

92. RGVA f. 25880, op. 4, d. 5, l. 548; "O rabote Politicheskogo Upravleniia Krasnoi Armii," 200, 201.

93. *Krasnaia zvezda*, 27 June 1940.

94. "O rabote Politicheskogo Upravleniia Krasnoi Armii," 200.

95. Suvenirov, "Prikaz Otmeniat' ne budem," 32–34; *Krasnaia zvezda*, 27 June 1940.

96. *Krasnaia zvezda*, 27 June 1940.

97. Ibid.; according to Wildman (*End of the Russian Imperial Army*, 34), bread and water was the standard fare of the tsarist soldier while in the guardhouse—here we see another throwback to the old familiar ways.

98. Suvenirov, "Prikaz Otmeniat' ne budem," 34; "O rabote Politicheskogo Upravleniia Krasnoi Armii," 200–202. Disciplinary battalions were organized by military district headquarters.

99. *Krasnaia zvezda*, 22 Oct., 3 Nov. 1940.

100. A. T. Ukolov and V. I. Ivkin, "O Masshtabakh Repressii v Krasnoi Armii v predvoennye godu," *Voenno-istoricheskii zhurnal*, no. 1 (1993), 59.

3. PUR and the Army

1. P. Pavlovskii, *Kak Krasnaia armiia gotovit boitsa-grazhdanina* (Moscow/Leningrad: Gosizdat, 1929), 12.

2. V. Danilov, "Stroitel'stvo tsentral'nogo voennogo apparata v 1924–1928 gg," *Voenno-istoricheskii zhurnal*, no. 6 (1972), 83.

3. Nikolai P. Vishniakov and F. I. Arkhipov, *Ustroistvo vooruzhennykh sil SSSR* (Moscow: Voennyi Vestnik, 1926), 93–95.

4. I. Petukhov, *Partiinaia organizatsiia i partiinaia rabota v RKKA* (Moscow/Leningrad: Gosizdat, 1928), 75.

5. Iurii P. Petrov, *Stroitel'stvo politorganov partiinykh i komsomol'skikh organizatsii armii i flota (1918–1968)* (Moscow: Voenizdat, 1968), 244.

6. Zbigniew Brzezinski, *Political Controls in the Soviet Army* (New York: Research Program on the USSR, 1954), 31; A. S. Zheltova, *Imeni Lenina* (Moscow: Voenizdat, 1966), 75, 84.

7. Rossiiskii gosudarstvennyi voennyi arkhiv (RGVA) f. 54, op. 1, d. 1235, l. 17; f. 37837, op. 21, d. 23, l. 20.

8. "Political Training in the Red Army, 1931–32," *U.S. MID Reports*, Reel 4, 344.

9. Mikhail Soloviev, *My Nine Lives in the Red Army* (New York: David McKay, 1955), 95–97.

10. Ibid.

11. Vladimir Unishevsky, *Red Pilot: Memoirs of a Soviet Airman* (London: Hurst and Blackett, 1939), 98.

12. John Erickson, *The Soviet High Command: A Military-Political History* (New York: St. Martin's Press, 1962), 423.

13. RGVA f. 37837, op. 21, d. 23, l. 19; Petrov, *Stroitel'stvo politorganov partiinykh i komsomol'skikh organizatsii*, 233; Iu. I. Korablev and M. I. Loginov, eds., *KPSS i stroitel'stvo Vooruzhennykh Sil SSSR (1918–iiun 1941)* (Moscow: Voenizdat, 1959), 469.

14. T. H. Rigby, *Communist Party Membership in the USSR 1917–1967* (Princeton: Princeton University Press, 1968), 248; D. Milov, "Partiinaia organizatsiia RKKA pered XVI s"ezdom partii," *Voennyi Vestnik* 10, no. 17 (1930), 2.

15. "Partorganizatsiia i politprosvetrabota k XVI s"ezdu VKP(b): statisticheskii material," *Voennyi Vestnik* 10, no. 14 (1930), 80; *XV let Krasnoi Armii* (Arkhangel'sk: severnoe kraevoe gosizdat, 1933), 12. In 1928, military party membership comprised 41 percent workers, 32 percent peasants, and 25 percent others. In 1930, workers were even more overrepresented: over 58 percent of army party members were workers, only 29 percent were peasants, and 12 percent were others.

16. Arnol'd B. Kadishev, *Chto dolzhen znat' molodoi krasnoarmeets*, 13th ed., (Moscow/Leningrad: Gosizdat, 1930), 61–68; Littleton B. Atkinson, *Dual Command in the Red Army 1918-1942* (Maxwell Air Force Base, Ala.: Air University, 1950), 11.

17. Semion Belitskii, *Besedy o voennom dele i Krasnoi Armii: sbornik dlia kruzhkov voennykh znanii na fabrikakh, zavodakh, pri klubakh i shkolakh* (Moscow: Voennyi Vestnik, 1926), 68.

18. Boris I. Balinsky, *Memoir,* unpublished manuscript dated 1988, Record Series 15/35/54, University of Illinois Archives, 131.

19. *Harvard University Refugee Interview Project*, Soviet Interview Project Archives, 1980–1987, Record Series 24/2/50–51, University of Illinois Archives, no. 18 RF, A3, p. 15.

20. RGVA f. 9, op. 26, d. 490, l. 7; f. 25893, op. 1, d. 292, l. 164; *Harvard University Refugee Interview Project*, no.1, ML, A2/3, 30, 33.

21. RGVA f. 1293, op. 5782, d. 6, l. 14; *Harvard University Refugee Interview Project,* no. 1, ML, A2/3, 31.

22. RGVA f. 25893, op. 1, d. 292, ll. 153, 154; *Instruktsiia oblastnym, raionnym i rizovym komissiiam po chistke partii* (Moscow: Partizdat, 1934), 3–8. For an examination of the difference between party purges and repressive purges by terror, see J. Arch Getty, *The Origins of the Great Purge* (New York: Cambridge University Press, 1985), and J. Arch Getty and Roberta T. Manning, eds., *Stalinist Terror: New Perspectives* (New York: Cambridge University Press, 1993).

23. RGVA f. 887, op. 1, d. 86, ll. 6–7; f. 1293, op. 5782, d. 6, l. 25; *Krasnaia zvezda,* 6 Sept. 1929, 17 May 1934.

24. Victor Kravchenko, *I Chose Freedom* (New York: Scribner's, 1946), 134.

25. Ibid., 134; Roberta T. Manning, *Government in the Soviet Countryside in the Stalinist Thirties: The Case of the Belyi* Raion *in 1937,* The Carl Beck Papers in Russian and East European Studies, no. 301 (Pittsburgh: University of Pittsburgh, 1984), 16; Roberta T. Manning, "The Great Purges in a Rural District: Belyi *Raion* Revisited," *Russian History* 16, nos. 2–4 (1989), 411.

26. RGVA f. 887, op. 1, d. 86, ll. 6, 7, 9, 11–13.

27. *Krasnaia zvezda* 6 Sept. 1929, 17 Oct. 1933, 17 May 1934; Nikolai G. Liashchenko, *Gody v shineli* (Frunze: Kyrgyzstan, 1974), 144–145.

28. RGVA f. 1293, op. 5782, d. 6, ll. 49–50.

29. RGVA f. 887, op. 1, d. 86, ll. 6, 7, 9, 11–13, 24, 25; f. 25893, op. 1, d. 292, l. 104.

30. Records of the *Smolensk Oblast of the All–Union Communist Party of the Soviet Union, 1917–1941,* hereafter cited as *Smolensk Archive,* WKP 186, 151–156.

31. RGVA f. 887, op. 1, d. 86, ll. 6, 7.

32. "Chistka partii i zadachi partorganizatsii VVS," *Vestnik Vozdushnogo Flota,* no. 10 (1933), 9–11.

33. *Krasnaia zvezda,* 15 Nov. 1928.

34. *Krasnaia zvezda,* 2 June 1935.

35. *XX let raboche-krest'ianskoi krasnoi armii i voenno-morskogo flota* (Leningrad: Lenoblizdat, 1938), 95.

36. M. Lisenkov, "O likvidatsii negramotnosti v Krasnoi Armii (1918–1939)," *Voenno-istoricheskii zhurnal,* no. 7 (1977), 117.

37. Willis E. Brooks, "Reform in the Russian Army, 1856–1861," *Slavic Review* 43 (Summer 1984), 71; Forrestt A. Miller, *Dmitrii Miliutin and the Reform Era in Russia* (Nashville, Tenn.: Vanderbilt University Press, 1968), 89, 90.

38. Colin Stevenson, *Challenging Adult Illiteracy: Reading and Writing Disabilities in the British Army* (New York: Columbia University Press, 1985), 1–6.

39. *Pravda,* 5 March 1933.

40. RGVA f. 896, op. 2, d. 1, l. 48; f. 1293, op. 5782, d. 6, l. 1; B. Tal', *Istoriia Krasnoi armii* (Moscow: Gosizdat, 1929), 190; *Istoriia ordena Lenin Leningradskogo voennogo okruga* (Moscow: Voenizdat, 1974), 127.

41. Korablev and Loginov, eds., *KPSS i stroitel'stvo Sovetskikh Vooruzhennykh Sil SSSR,* 219; Vasilii Varenov, *Pomoshch' Krasnoi Armii v razvitii kolkhoznogo stroitel'stva (1929–1933 gg)* (Moscow: Nauka, 1978), 23; N. F. Kuz'min, *Na strazhe mirnogo truda 1921–1940, gg* (Moscow: Voenizdat, 1959), 29. PUR was also responsible for eradicating illiteracy in the territorial forces. In 1924, nearly one-fifth of all new recruits in the territorial units were illiterate; in some units, more than 50 percent. In the 21st Territorial Rifle Division, 67 percent of its candidates for district military schools were semiliterate in 1930. The army required candidates for regimental schools to have had at least three years of elementary education, but in order to procure the necessary number of junior commanders, this requirement had to be waived in many areas of the USSR.

42. *Krasnaia zvezda,* 23, 27 Aug. 1933, 17 Sept. 1935.

43. *Smolensk Archive:* WKP 40, 85–87; John Scott, *Behind the Urals* (Bloomington: Indiana University Press, 1988), 40.

44. F. Rodinova, *Krasnoarmeiskii antireligioznii uchebnik*, 2nd ed. (Moscow: Bezbozhnik, 1931), 230–233.

45. Ibid., 224–229.

46. Kapiton Paiusov, *Atiesticheskoe vospitanie sovetskikh voinov* (Moscow: Voenizdat, 1963), 6; Vladimir F. Klochkov, *Krasnaia Armiia—shkola kommunisticheskogo vospitaniia sovetskikh voinov, 1918–1941* (Moscow: Nauka, 1984), 65; for the civilian SVB movement, see Gladys Young, "Rural Religion and Soviet Power, 1921–1932" (Ph.D. diss., University of California at Berkeley, 1989), 37, 46–92.

47. *Krasnoarmeets*, 15 Oct. 1929, 15 Oct. 1930.

48. Nicholas S. Timasheff, *The Great Retreat* (New York: E. P. Dutton, 1946), 227. For more on Timasheff's view of antireligion in the USSR, see his *Religion in the Soviet Republic* (New York: 1942).

49. RGVA f. 9, op. 26, d. 487, ll. 69, 70; Varenov, *Pomoshch' Krasnoi Armii v razvitii kolkhoznogo*, 88–89.

50. Aleksandr P. Vrublevskii and Tat'iana S. Prot'ko, *Iz Istorii Repressii Protiv Belorusskogo Krest'ianstva 1929–1934 gg* (Minsk: Navuka i Tekhnika, 1992), 26; V. Varenov, "Uchastie Krasnoi Armii v sotsialisticheskom perestroistve derevni," *Voenno-istoricheskii zhurnal*, no. 10 (1972), 79–80; Iosif I. Geller, *Pod krasnoi zvezdoi: Krasnaia Armiia na fronte kollektivizatsii* (Samara: Gosizdat, 1931), 50–53; Ivan L. Zalesskii, *Kommunisticheskaia partiia—organizator pomoshchi Krasnoi Armii trudiashchemusia krest'ianstvu v sotsialisticheskom preobrazovanii sel'skogo khoziaistva v 1927–1932 godakh (Iz materialakh Krasnoznamennogo Severo-Kavkazskogo voennogo okruga)* (Rostov-on-Don: 1981), 18.

51. RGVA f. 9, op. 26, d. 490, l. 25; f. 1293, op. 5782, d. 6, l. 28; *Krasnaia zvezda*, 25 Oct. 1929.

52. *Krasnoarmeets*, 15 Sept. 1929.

53. RGVA f. 9. op. 26, d. 487, l. 50; Geller, *Pod krasnoi zvezdoi*, 40–53.

54. Varenov, *Pomoshch' Krasnoi armii v razvitii kolkhoznogo*, 32, 33, 50, 51.

55. RGVA f. 9, op. 26, d. 490, ll. 34, 41.

56. RGVA f. 9, op. 26, d. 487, ll. 85, 120; d. 490, ll. 41, 44, 52.

57. RGVA f. 9, op. 26, d. 487, l. 109.

58. RGVA f. 9, op. 26, d. 487, l. 26; d. 490, l. 44; f. 37837, op. 21, d. 23, l. 143.

59. Varenov, *Pomoshch' Krasnoi Armii v razvitii kolkhoznogo*, 139–145.

60. RGVA f. 9, op. 26, d. 490, ll. 21, 22, 30.

61. RGVA f. 9, op. 26, d. 487, ll. 51, 56–58; f. 9, op. 26, d. 490, ll. 27, 82, 113.

62. RGVA f. 9, op. 26, d. 487, ll. 26–29; f. 1293, op. 5782, d. 6, ll. 27; *Za liniiu partii protiv opportunisticheskikh shatanii: liniia partii v voprosakh kollektivizatsii v dokumentakh i materialakh* (Kharkov: Proletarii izdvo, 1930), 5–10; "Iz postanovleniia biuro sibkraikoma VKP (b) 'O proshenii fraktsii soiuza soiuzov o dopushchenii kulakov v kolkhozy,' 4 Oktiabr 1929 g," in A. A. Govorkova, *Kollektivizatsiia sel'skogo khoziastva zapadnoi sibiri 1927–1937 gg* (Tomsk: Zapadno-sibirskoe knizhnoe izdatel'stvo, 1972), 87–88.

63. RGVA f. 9, op. 26, d. 490, ll. 10, 22, 104–110, 121–128; d. 487, ll. 26, 29; f. 25893, op. 1, d. 292, l. 22.

64. RGVA f. 1293, op. 5782, d. 6, ll. 39–41.

65. RGVA f. 9, op. 26, d. 487, l. 57; d. 490, l. 24; f. 25893, op. 1, d. 292, l. 127; f. 1293, op. 5782, d. 6, l. 51; *Krasnaia zvezda*, 3, 5 Jan. 1930, 7 Feb. 1930.

66. RGVA f. 9, op. 26, d. 487, ll. 77, 78; d. 490, ll. 3, 9, 16, 113–115.

67. RGVA f. 9, op. 26, d. 490, l. 17; Oleg F. Suvenirov, "Narkomat oborony i NKVD v predvoennyi gody," *Voprosy istorii*, no. 6 (1991), 26.

68. RGVA f. 9, op. 26, d. 490, ll. 23–24; f. 887, op. 1, d. 86, l. 6; f. 25893, op. 1, d. 292, ll. 40, 47–49, 75.

69. RGVA f. 9, op. 26, d. 487, ll. 4–5.

70. RGVA f. 9, op. 26, d. 487, l. 30.

71. Geller, *Pod krasnoi zvezdoi*, 30–32; Varenov, *Pomoshch' Krasnoi Armii v razvitii kolkhoznogo stroitel'stva*, 159, 161.

72. RGVA f. 9, op. 26, d. 487, l. 31; f. 37837, op. 21, d. 23, l. 28; Danilov and Ivanitskii, *Dokumenty svidetl'stvuiut: Iz istorii derevni nakanune i v khode kollektivizatsii 1927–1932 gg*, 23, 32, 297.

73. RGVA f. 9, op. 26, d. 487, ll. 78, 87; Vrublevskii and Prot'ko, *Iz Istorii Repressii protiv Belorusskogo Krest'ianstva 1929-1934 gg*. 121–123.

74. Ibid., 127; Geller, *Pod krasnoi zvezdoi*, 30–32.

75. Pavlovskii, *Kak Krasnaia armiia gotovit boitsa-grazhdanina*, 24–25; "Letopis' stroitel'stva sovetskikh vooruzhennykh sil 1930 god (mai–iiun')," *Voenno-istoricheskii zhurnal*, no. 2 (1976), 118; Klochkov, *Krasnaia Armiia*, 116.

76. Dzyza, "Zadachi podgotovki 100,000 kolkhoznykh kadrov," *Voennyi Vestnik* 10, no. 15 (1930), 2–8.

77. Dzyza, "Krasnaia Armiia i zadachi kolkhoznogo stroitel'stva" *Voennyi Vestnik* 10, no. 4 (1930), 35; Moseichuk, "Komsomol i kolkhoznoe stroitel'stvo," *Voennyi Vestnik* 10, no. 1 (1930), 36, 37; Klochkov, *Krasnaia Armiia*, 116.

78. For a complete account of the 25,000er movement, see Lynne Viola, *The Best Sons of the Fatherland* (New York: Oxford University Press, 1987).

79. K. Voroshilov, L. Mekhlis, S. Budenny, G. Stern, *The Red Army Today: Speeches Delivered at the Eighteenth Congress of the CPSU (B), March 10–21, 1939* (Moscow: Foreign Language Publishing House, 1939), 47.

80. *Krasnyi Voin*, 28 Nov. 1934.

81. "O postanovke partiinoi propagandy v sviazi s vypuskom 'kratkogo kursa istorii VKP(b),'" *Voennaia mysl'* 2, no. 12 (1938), 3–18; *Istoriia Vsesoiuznoi Kommunisticheskoi partii (bol'shevikov)* (Moscow, 1938).

82. RGVA f. 1293, op. 5782, d. 6, l. 2; *Krasnaia zvezda*, 15 March, 18 March, 23 April 1937.

83. *Krasnaia zvezda*, 8 Jan, 6 June 1937.

84. *Krasnaia zvezda*, 5 March, 3 Oct., 15 Nov. 1937.

85. "O rabote Politicheskogo Upravleniia Krasnoi Armii," *Izvestiia Tsk KPSS*, no. 1 (1990),194; "Ob otbore 4,000 kommunistov na politrabotu v RKKA, 29 Avgust 1939 g," *Izvestiia TsK KPSS*, no. 1 (1990), 174, 175; "O voennyi perepodgotovke, pereattestovannii rabotnikov partiinykh kometetov i o poriadke ikh mobilizatsii v RKKA," *Izvestiia TsK KPSS*, no. 1 (1990), 175, 176.

86. Balinsky, *Memoir,* 35.

87. *Harvard University Refugee Interview Project*, no. 1, ML, A2/3, 31.

88. Ibid., 34.

89. *Harvard University Refugee Interview Project*, no. 18, RF, A3, 43.

90. Ibid., 9–10.

91. Ibid., 8, 28–30.

92. Danilov and Ivanitskii, *Dokumenty svidetl'stvuiut*, 458–464.

93. Mark von Hagen, *Soldiers in the Proletarian Dictatorship: The Red Army and the Soviet Socialist State, 1917–1930* (Ithaca, N.Y.: Cornell University Press, 1990), 271–343.

94. Allan K. Wildman, *The End of the Russian Imperial Army* (Princeton: Princeton University Press, 1980), 38, 39.

4. The Red Army Officer Corps

1. Rossiiskii gosudarstvennyi voennyi arkhiv (RGVA) f. 37837, op. 22, d. 41, l. 12; Petr A. Zaionchkovskii, *Samoderzhavie i russkaia armiia na rubezhe XIX–XX stoletii: 1881–1903* (Moscow: Mysl', 1973), 202–205; Norman Stone, *The Eastern Front 1941–1917* (New York: Scribner's, 1975), 21, 25; Allan K. Wildman, *The End of the Imperial Army: The Old Army and the Soldiers' Revolt (March–April 1917)* (Princeton: Princeton University Press, 1980), 19–24, 100–101; Peter Kenez, "A Profile of the Prerevolutionary Officer Corps," *California Slavic Studies*, no. 7 (1973), 121–158.

2. B. Tal', *Istoriia Krasnoi armii* (Moscow: Gosizdat, 1929), 189.

3. RGVA f. 37837, op. 21, d. 23, ll. 11, 29, 41; *Krasnaia zvezda*, 12 Nov. 1929.

4. The officer corps was, until the Second World War, identified by two terms, *komsostav* and *nachal'sostav*, both translated as "commanding personnel." The first term included officers in line units and, under certain circumstances, junior commanders in command positions. The second term included line officers, administrative officers, junior commanders, and PUR. The Red Army did not reintroduce the title officer (*ofitser*) until the Second World War.

5. See F. L. Carsten, *Revolution in Central Europe 1918-1919* (Berkeley: University of California Press, 1972) and *The Reichswehr in Politics* (London: Oxford, 1966), for the Weimar government's reliance on the old professional army instead of creating a new military force loyal to the ideals of the Republic.

6. Nikolai P. Vishniakov and F. I. Arkhipov, *Ustroistvo vooruzhennykh sil SSSR* (Moscow: Voenizdat, 1926), 126, 127.

7. Ibid., 126, 127; Viktor F. Loboda, *Komandnye kadry i zakonodatel'stvo o kadrakh razvitii vooruzhennykh sil SSSR* (Moscow: Voenizdat, 1960), 55.

8. *Kak Rabochemu i krest'ianinu postupit' v Voennuiu Shkolu* (Moscow: Voennyi Vestnik, 1927), 14.

9. D. A. Voropaev and A. M. Iovlev, *Bor'ba KPSS za sozdanie voennykh kadrov* (Moscow: Voenizdat, 1960), 130, 131.

10. Aleksei M. Iovlev, "Podgotovka komandnykh i politicheskikh kadrov Sovetskoi Armii v 1929–1933 godakh," *Voenno-istoricheskii zhurnal*, no. 5 (1960), 70; Mikhail Soloviev, *My Nine Lives in the Red Army* (New York: David McKay, 1955), 13–21; A. I. Radziev, *Akademiia imeni M. V. Frunze* (Moscow: Voenizdat, 1973), 87–88; A. Dragunskii, *Polevaia akademiia* (Moscow: Voenizdat, 1982), 3, 98–110.

11. Aleksei M. Iovlev, *Deiatel'nost KPSS po podogotovke voennykh kadrov* (Moscow: Voenizdat, 1976), 104.

12. Ivan A. Korotkov, *Istoriia sovetskoi voennoi mysli* (Moscow: Nauka, 1980), 47; Radziev, *Akademiia imeni M. V. Frunze*, 87, 113; Mikhail I. Kazakov, *Nad kartoi bylykh srazhenii* (Moscow: Voenizdat, 1971), 27–30.

13. In 1926, less than 7 percent of all officers had completed a secondary education. About 32 percent had between seven and ten years of schooling, and over 58 percent had only an elementary education. Three percent had had no formal education at all. Iovlev, "Podgotovka komandnykh i politicheskikh kadrov Sovetskoi Armii," 60, 70–71; "Social and Party Status of Red Army Personnel, July 20, 1927," *U.S. MID Reports*, Reel 3, 295; Konstantin A. Vorob'ev, *Vooruzhennye sily razvitogo sotsialisticheskogo obshchestva* (Moscow: Voenizdat, 1980), 172.

14. At the start of 1928, 90 percent of unit commanders in the Red Army and Fleet had had some form of military education. As of spring 1934, just over 81 percent of company grade officers had been commissioned through military schools, as had nearly 43 percent of senior officers. Iovlev, *Deiatel'nost KPSS po podogotovke voennykh kadrov*, 98; Loboda, *Komandnye kadry i zakonodatel'stvo o kadrakh razvitii vooruzhennykh sil SSSR*, 53; *Krasnaia zvezda*, 4 Feb. 1934; *Pravda*, 31 Jan. 1935.

15. *Krasnaia zvezda*, 23 Oct. 1929, 18 Aug. 1932; Iovlev, *Deiatel'nost KPSS po podogotovke voennykh kadrov*, 122.

16. Andrei S. Bubnov, *O Krasnoi Armii* (Moscow: Voenizdat, 1958), 130–33, 144.

17. "Social and Party Status of Red Army Personnel," 295.

18. RGVA f. 4, op. 1, d. 1120, ll. 4, 10, 13–15; Kliment E. Voroshilov, *O molodezhi* (Moscow: Molodaia gvardiia, 1937), 19, 53, 141; Mikhail M. Lisenkov, *Kul'turnaia revoliutsiia v SSSR i Armiia* (Moscow: Voenizdat, 1977), 109; *50 let Vooruzhennykh sil SSSR* (Moscow: Voenizdat, 1968), 213; A. Iovlev, "Podgotovka komandnykh i politicheskikh kadrov Sovetskoi Armii," 66; *Krasnaia zvezda*, 17 Feb. 1933 and 4 Feb. 1934; *Pravda*, 31 Jan. 1935.

19. *XV let Krasnoi Armii* (Arkhangel'sk: Severnoe kraevoe gosizdat, 1933), 11.

20. For representative works, see Littleton B. Atkinson, *Dual Command in the Red Army 1918–1942* (Maxwell Air Force Base, Ala.: Air University, 1950); Zbigniew Brzezinski, *Political Controls in the Soviet Army* (New York: Research Program on the USSR, 1954); Erich Wollenberg, *The Red Army* (London: Secker and Warburg, 1959); Mikhail Soloviev, *My Nine Lives in the Red Army* (New York: David McKay, 1955); Vladimir Unishevsky, *Red Pilot* (London: Hurst and Blackett, 1939).

21. RGVA f. 37837, op. 21, d. 23, l. 17; *Krasnaia zvezda*, 1 April 1930; Voropaev and Iovlev, *Bor'ba KPSS za sozdanie voennykh kadrov*, 90-91; Iu. Petrov, *Partiinoe stroitel'stvo v Sovetskoi Armii i Flote, 1918–1961* (Moscow: Voenizdat, 1964), 191–195.

22. Steven J. Main, "The Red Army and the Soviet Military and Political Leadership in the Late 1920s: The Case of the 'Inner-Army Opposition' of 1928," *Europe-Asia Studies* 47, no. 2 (1995), 337, 340–343.

23. Timothy Colton, *Commissars, Commanders and Civilian Authority* (Princeton: Princeton University Press, 1979), 59; Petro Grigorenko, *Memoirs* (New York: Norton, 1982), 59, 60.

24. *Harvard University Refugee Interview Project*, Soviet Interview Project Archives, 1980–1987, Record Series 24/2/50-51, University of Illinois Archives, no. 1, ML, A2/3, 30, 33.

25. Iovlev, *Deiatel'nost KPSS po podgotovke voennykh kadrov*, 97; Iovlev, "Podgotovka komandnykh i politicheskikh kadrov Sovetskoi Armii," 66, 67.

26. *Harvard University Refugee Interview Project*, no. 18, RF, A3, 14–15.

27. RGVA f. 896, op. 3, d. 10, ll. 1–7.

28. Vladmir Unishevsky, *Red Pilot: Memoirs of a Soviet Airman* (London: Hurst and Blackett, 1939), 26–42.

29. RGVA f. 9, op. 26, d. 487, l. 112.

30. Moshe Lewin, *Russian Peasants and Soviet Power: A Study of Collectivization* (New York: Norton, 1975), 397, 398.

31. Iu. I. Korablev, *KPSS i stroitel'stvo Vooruzhennykh Sil SSSR* (Moscow: Voenizdat, 1959), 276; Voroshilov, *O molodezhi*, 53, 54.

32. *Krasnaia zvezda*, 24 April 1929.

33. RGVA f. 4, op. 1, d. 1134, ll. 2, 3; f. 37837, op. 21, d. 23, ll. 49, 177, 194, 200, 201, 211, 281–287; Korotkov, *Istoriia sovetskoi voennoi mysli*, 44, 45.

34. RGVA f. 37837, op. 21, d. 23, ll. 49, 177, 194, 200, 201, 211.

35. RGVA f. 9, op. 26, d. 487, ll. 63–65, 107.

36. Ibid., l. 64.

37. Iovlev, "Podgotovka komandnykh i politicheskikh kadrov," 65, 74.

38. Ibid., 63.

39. Boris Tel'pukhovskii, *KPSS vo glave stroitel'stva Vooruzhennykh Sil SSSR* (Moscow: Politizdat, 1983), 115; Gal'ianov and Gorshenin, *Voennaia rabota Komsomola* (Moscow: Molodaia gvardiia, 1931), 37–41; Voropaev and Iovlev, *Bor'ba KPSS za sozdanie voennykh kadrov*, 132; *Sovetskie Vooruzhennye Sily* (Moscow: Voenizdat, 1978), 209, 210.

40. Records of the Smolensk Oblast of the All-Union Communist Party of the Soviet Union, 1917–1941, hereafter cited as *Smolensk Archive*, WKP 225, 67–68; WKP 229, 76–77.

41. Iovlev, "Podgotovka komandnykh i politicheskikh kadrov Sovetskoi Armii," 65.

42. RGVA f. 37837, op. 21, d. 23, l. 18.

43. *Krasnaia zvezda*, 21 Feb. 1932; 1, 8, 11, 14, 15 March 1932; 20 Aug. 1932.

44. *Krasnaia zvezda*, 14 July 1935, 9.

45. RGVA f. 37837, op. 21, d. 23, ll. 211, 275; *Krasnaia zvezda*, 28, 30 May, 3 June 1932; 18 May, 5 Oct. 1933; 3 June 1934, 26 May 1935.

46. "Red Army Discipline and Morale, November 1, 1927," *U.S. MID Reports*, Reel 3, 898.

47. Ibid., 899.

48. Unishevsky, *Red Pilot*, 85, 86.

49. *Krasnaia zvezda*, 1 Sept.–30 Dec. 1929.

50. RGVA f. 25893, op. 1, d. 292, ll. 108–110; f. 9, op. 26, d. 487, ll. 38–40, 44, 45, 49, 71-74, 93, 94, 103, 128, 138, 142, 156, 162; d. 490, ll. 91–101; f. 896, op. 3, d. 10, ll. 1–74; f. 887, op. 1, d. 90, ll. 29, 30; d. 96, l. 23, 32, 60, 61; d. 99, ll. 76, 78, 89, 118.

51. Moshe Lewin, *The Making of the Soviet System: Essays in the Social History of Interwar Russia* (New York: Pantheon, 1985), 216.

52. Ibid., 225.

53. RGVA f. 25893, op. 1, d. 292, l. 104; f. 25880, op. 4, d. 4, ll. 265, 344–348, d. 5, ll. 269, 595, 622; f. 887, op. 1, d. 99, l. 76; Unishevsky, *Red Pilot*, 26–42; *Krasnaia zvezda*, 16 Sept. 1925.

54. "Education and Training of Officers, December 21, 1934," *U.S. MID Reports*, Reel 5, 176.

55. Il'ia Berkhin, *Voennaia reforma v SSSR (1924–1925 gg)* (Moscow: Voenizdat, 1958), 181, 262.

56. The British Army was, however, short nearly 1,000 officers in 1937. J. M. Brereton, *The British Soldier: A Social History from 1661 to the Present Day* (London: Bath Press, 1986), 156; *League of Nations Armaments Yearbook 1929–30* (Geneva, 1930), 113, 433, 464; *League of Nations Armaments Yearbook 1936*, 334; S. J. Lewis, *Forgotten Legions: German Army Infantry Policy 1918–1941* (New York: Praeger, 1985), 36.

57. Dmitrii Fedotoff White, *The Growth of the Red Army* (Princeton: Princeton University Press, 1944), 304.

58. N. Kuibyshev, "Problema kadrov i sverkhsrochnik," *Voennyi vestnik* 10, no. 17 (1930), 4–7.

59. Zaionchkovskii, *Samoderzhavie i russkaia armiia*, 120, 121.

60. Karl Aru, *S rodnoi artilleriei* (Tallin: Eestu raamat, 1977), 93.

61. Oleg F. Suvenirov, "Vsearmeiskaia Tragediia," *Voenno-istoricheskii zhurnal*, no. 3 (1989), 39.

62. RGVA f. 37837, op. 21, d. 23, l. 64; "O Nakoplenii Nachal'stvuiushchego sostava i popolnenii im Raboche'—Krest'ianskaia Krasnoi Armii: Iz spravki-doklada nachal'nika Upravleniia po nachal'stvuiushchemu sostavu RKKA Narkomata Oborony SSSR E. A. Shchadenko, 20 Marta 1940 g," *Izvestiia TsK KPSS*, no. 1 (1990), 178.

63. Voropaev and Iovlev, *Bor'ba KPSS za sozdanie voennykh kadrov*, 129, 157.

64. "Iz doklada nachalnika general'nogo shtaba krasnoi armii Narodnomu Komissaru Oborony SSSR, 20 Iiunia 1940 g," *Rodina*, nos. 6–7 (1991), 28.

65. *Izvestiia*, 10 Dec. 1926.

66. Ibid.

67. RGVA f. 4, op. 1, d. 1134, ll. 2, 3, 6, 7; f. 54, op. 1, d. 1235, ll. 5–7, 11, 13, 16.

68. RGVA f. 37837, op. 21, d. 23, ll. 281–287.

69. William C. Fuller, *Civil-Military Conflict in Imperial Russia 1881–1914* (Princeton: Princeton University Press, 1985), 13, 14; Kenez, "A Profile of the Prerevolutionary Officer Corps," 129, 130.

70. Abram Bergson, *The Structure of Soviet Wages* (Cambridge, Mass.: Harvard University Press, 1944), 167; E. H. Carr, *Foundations of a Planned Economy 1926–1929*, vol. 1 (New York: Macmillan, 1969), 129.

71. John Scott, *Behind the Urals* (Bloomington: Indiana University Press, 1988), 148; Donald Filtzer, *Soviet Workers and Stalinist Industrialization* (London: Pluto Press, 1986), 212–222; Solomon Schwarz, *Labor in the Soviet Union* (New York: Praeger, 1951), 152.

72. *Harvard University Refugee Interview Project*, no. 1, ML, A2/3, 10; "Pay in the Red Army, January 24, 1934," *U.S. MID Reports*, Reel 3, 552–553; Filtzer, *Soviet Workers and Stalinist Industrialization*, 212–222.

73. RGVA f. 37837, op. 21, d. 23, l. 16.

74. Fuller, *Civil-Military Conflict in Imperial Russia 1881–1914*, 13, 14.

75. *Krasnoznamennyi Dal'nevostochnyi: Istoriia Krasnoznamennogo Dal'nevostochnogo voennogo okruga*, 3d ed. (Moscow: Voenizdat, 1975), 106.

76. *Krasnaia zvezda*, 5 Aug. 1932.

77. RGVA f. 9, op. 26, d. 487, l. 60; *Krasnaia zvezda*, 24 July 1933.

78. *Krasnaia zvezda*, 16 April 1932, 27 April 1933.

79. RGVA f. 9, op. 26, d. 487, l. 60; f. 37837, op. 21, d. 23, l. 16; *Harvard University Refugee Interview Project*, no. 1, ML, A2/3, 28.

80. Sergei M. Shtemenko, *General'nyi shtab v gody voiny*, vol. 1 (Moscow: Voenizdat, 1981), 46.

81. Ibid., 50–52.

82. Robert Doughty, "The French Armed Forces, 1918–1940," in *Military Effectiveness*, Allan R. Millett and Williamson Murray, eds. (Boston: Allen and Unwin, 1988), 44; Donald C. Watt, *Too Serious a Business: European Armed Forces and the Approach to the Second World War* (New York: Norton, 1975), 36, 37.

83. Brian Bond and Williamson Murray, "The British Armed Forces 1918–1939," in *Military Effectiveness*, Allan R. Millett and Williamson Murray, eds., 104.

84. Siegfried Knappe and Ted Brusaw, *Soldat: Reflections of a German Soldier, 1936–1949* (New York: Orion, 1992), 117.

85. Nicholas Timasheff, *The Great Retreat* (New York: E. P. Dutton, 1946), 362–367; Iovlev, *Deiatel'nost' KPSS po podgotovke voennykh kadrov*, 130.

86. *Krasnaia zvezda*, 26 Sept. 1935.

87. *Krasnaia zvezda*, 22 Sept. 1935.

88. *Izvestiia*, 10 Dec. 1926.

89. *Pravda*, 12 Oct. 1935.

5. The Purge and Further Expansion

1. A. T. Ukolov and V. I. Ivkin, "O masshtabakh repressii v Krasnoi Armii v predvoennye gody," *Voenno-istoricheskii zhurnal*, no. 1 (1993), 57, 58.

2. "O rabote Politicheskogo Upravleniia Krasnoi Armii," *Izvestiia TsK KPSS*, no. 3 (1990), 193.

3. Not all of the men in confinement were political prisoners. Several thousand were in the Gulag serving sentences of more than three years for criminal acts. Ukolov and Ivkin, "O masshtabakh repressii," 58, 59.

4. F. B. Komal, "Voennye Kadry Nakanune Voiny," *Voenno-istoricheskii zhurnal*, no. 2 (1990), 21; "O Nakoplenii Nachal'stvuiushchego sostava i popolnenii im Raboche-Krest'ianskoi Krasnoi Armii: Iz spravki–doklada nachal'nika Upravleniia po nachal'stvuiushchemu sostavu RKKA Narkomata Oborony SSSR E. A. Shchadenko, 20 Marta 1940 g," *Izvestiia TsK KPSS*, no. 1 (1990), 178–180.

5. "Ob otbore 4,000 kommunistov na politrabotu v RKKA, 29 Avgusta 1939 g," *Izvestiia TsK KPSS*, no. 1 (1990), 174–175; Iurii P. Petrov, *Stroitel'stvo politorganov partiinykh i komsomol'skikh organizatsii armii i flota (1918–1968)* (Moscow: Voenizdat, 1968), 249-250; Iurii Korablev and Mikhail Loginov, eds., *KPSS i stroitel'stvo Vooruzhennykh Sil SSSR (1918–iiun 1941)* (Moscow: Voenizdat, 1959), 469.

6. In 1962, John Erickson estimated that 25 to 30 percent of the officers had been purged, and in 1968, Robert Conquest estimated 50 percent. Both estimates are in sharp contrast to the actual figures; in the worst year, 1937, less than 8 percent of the Red Army's leadership was purged. Erickson and Conquest estimated the officer corps at 80,000 and 70,000, respectively, so while Erickson's estimates of between 20,000 and 30,000 men repressed is very near the mark, his estimate of the impact is far off, as is Conquest's estimate of 35,000 arrested officers out of a corps of 70,000,

and his minimum figure of 20,000 arrested PUR men— 300 percent higher than actual counts. In addition, both consider the majority of *Ezhovshchina* victims to have been arrested, not expelled and discharged, and did not realize how quickly and in what large numbers men were rehabilitated.

7. Oleg F. Suvenirov, "Narkomat oborony i NKVD v predvoennye godi," *Voprosy istorii*, no. 6 (1991), 27.

8. Ibid., 29; Erickson, *The Soviet High Command* (New York: St. Martin's Press, 1962), 449, 451, 452.

9. For biographies of eighty-four of the RKKA's top leaders killed in the *Ezhovshchina*, see Borys Levytsky, *The Stalinist Terror in the Thirties: Documentation from the Soviet Press* (Stanford, Calif.: Hoover Institution Press, 1974), 45–196.

10. *Krasnaia zvezda*, 26 Jan.–1 Feb. 1937, 11, 12, 14 June 1937.

11. *Krasnaia zvezda,* 16 June 1937.

12. Rossiiskii gosudarstvenno voennyi arkhiv (RGVA) f. 37837, op. 22, d. 41, l. 61.

13. Oleg F. Suvenirov, "Vsearmiia Tragediia," *Voenno-istoricheskii zhurnal*, no. 3 (1989), 43-44; "O rabote Politicheskogo Upravleniia Krasnoi Armii," 200.

14. "O rabote Politicheskogo Upravleniia Krasnoi Armii," 195.

15. Lev Mekhlis, *Rech' na XVIII s"ezde VKP(b), 14 Marta 1939 g* (Moscow: Gosvoenizdat, 1939), 14. It was natural that *kritika* and *samokritika* sessions were an integral part of the terror, because when these sessions were first introduced in fall 1928, *politruki* were instructed to use them to root out Trotskyites and other right deviationists, which they did. See Korablev and Loginov, eds., *KPSS i stroitel'stvo Vooruzhennykh Sil SSSR*, 284–290.

16. Ibid., 14.

17. Roberta T. Manning, "The Great Purges in a Rural District: Belyi *Raion* Revisited," *Russian History* 16, nos. 2–4 (1989), 410, 411.

18. "*Materialy k Protokolu zasedaniia Voennogo Soveta Kievskogo Voennogo Okruga No. 2 ot 26 Marta 1938 g,*" published in Suvenirov, "Vsearmeiskaia Tragediia," 47, 48.

19. I. T. Starinov, "Homecoming," in Seweryn Bialer, ed., *Stalin and His Generals* (New York: Pegasus, 1969), 78.

20. A. T. Stuchenko, "In the Frunze Military Academy," in Bialer, ed., *Stalin and His Generals*, 81.

21. "O rabote Politicheskogo Upravleniia Krasnoi Armii, 23 Maia 1940 g," 193.

22. Stepan A. Kalinin, *Razmyshliaia o minuvshem* (Moscow: Voenizdat, 1963), 120–122; Petro G. Grigorenko, *Memoirs* (New York: Norton, 1982), 70–85.

23. Aleksandr V. Gorbatov, *Years of My Life* (New York: Norton, 1965), 103, 108–151.

24. Starinov, "Homecoming," 75.

25. Oleg F. Suvenirov, "Esli b ne ta vakkhanaliia," *Voenno-istoricheskii zhurnal*, no. 2 (1989), 57, 58; K. Voroshilov, L. Mekhlis, S. Budenny, G. Stern, *The Red Army Today, Speeches Delivered at the Eighteenth Congress of the CPSU (B), March 10–21, 1939* (Moscow: Foreign Language Publishing House, 1939), 46; T. H. Rigby, *Communist Party Membership in the USSR 1917–1967* (Princeton: Princeton University Press, 1967), 217–219, 249 .

26. RGVA f. 37837, op. 22, d. 41, ll. 73–76, f. 896, op. 3, d. 10, ll. 9–15; Harold J.

Berman and Miroslav Kerner, *Soviet Military Law and Administration* (Cambridge, Mass.: Harvard University Press, 1955), 124–126; Oleg Suvenirov, "Narkomat oborony i NKVD v predvoennye gody," 29–34.

27. RGVA f. 37837, op. 21, d. 23, ll. 44, 45.

28. RGVA f. 896, op. 3, d. 10, ll. 16–53, 54–68, 72–28.

29. RGVA f. 37837, op. 22, d. 41, l. 10.

30. Komal, "Voennye Kadry Nakanune Voiny," 24.

31. RGVA f. 37837, op. 22, d. 41, ll. 6, 7, 11, 34, 35, 38, 89, 101–103, 104; op. 18, d. 777, ll. 1–49.

32. Kalinin, *Razmyshliaia o minuvshem*, 120–122.

33. RGVA f. 37837, op. 22, d. 41, ll. 31, 61, 63, 67, 68, 70, 100.

34. Ibid., l. 7.

35. Ibid., ll. 1–3, 61. What is most interesting about Savitskii's case is that Rozovskii himself had him discharged for his Trotskyite past in 1938 and less than a year later was petitioning for his reinstatement.

36. K. Voroshilov et al., *The Red Army Today*, 45.

37. *Krasnaia zvezda*, 29 Aug. 1937.

38. Timothy Colton, *Commissars, Commanders and Civilian Authority* (Princeton: Princeton University Press, 1979), 58–60.

39. *Krasnaia zvezda*, 14 May 1938.

40. *Sovetskie Vooruzhennye Sily* (Moscow: Voenizdat, 1978), 220.

41. *B. F. O. 371: Russia Correspondence 1939*, vol. 23688, 209–210.

42. Komal "Voennye Kadry Nakanune Voiny," 24.

43. Voroshilov et al., *The Red Army Today*, 47.

44. *Krasnaia zvezda*, 15 Jan., 14 Feb. 1939.

45. Mark von Hagen, "Soviet Soldiers and Officers on the Eve of the German Invasion: Towards a Description of Social Psychology and Political Attitudes," *Soviet Union/Union Sovetique* 18 nos. 1–3 (1991), 90–94.

46. *Krasnaia zvezda*, 16 Jan. 1936.

47. "O Nakoplenii Nachal'stvuiushchego sostava i popolnenii im Raboche-Krest'ianskoi Krasnoi Armii," 178.

48. N. M. Iakupov, "Stalin i Krasnaia Armiia (Arkhivnye nakhodki)," *Istoriia SSSR*, no. 5 (1991), 171, 172.

49. Dmitrii Volkogonov, *Triumf i tragediia: Politicheskii portret I. V. Stalin*, vol. 2, part I (Moscow: Novosti, 1989), 52, 55.

50. *50 let vooruzhennykh sil SSSR* (Moscow: Voenizdat, 1968), 235–236; Albert Z. Conner and Robert G. Poirer, *The Red Army Order of Battle in the Great Patriotic War* (Novato, Calif.: Presidio Press, 1985), 261–400; "O rabote za 1939 god: Iz otcheta nachal'nika Upravleniia po nachal'stvuiushchemu sostava RKKA Narkomata Oborony SSSR, E. A. Shchadenko, 5 May 1940," *Izvestiia TsK KPSS*, no. 1 (1990), 186.

51. Bialer, ed., *Stalin and His Generals*, 63.

52. Between 1939 and mid-1940, officers in new assignments as a percentage of all officers rose to 68.8 percent. The assignment or reassignment of officers involved 246,626 men, of whom 86,511 were given their first assignments, 111,939 were promoted to new assignments, and 48,186 were laterally transferred to similar assignments in different units. "O rabote za 1939 god," 186.

53. *Krasnaia zvezda*, 15 Jan., 2, 14, 17, 26, 28 Feb., 20 April 1937; Matvei V. Za-kharov, *General'nyi shtab v predvoennye gody* (Moscow: Voenizdat, 1989), 100, 101; Pavel P. Ganichev, *Voinskie zvaniia* (Moscow: Dosaaf, 1989), 45–62.

54. Grigorenko, *Memoirs*, 45–57, 67.

55. Evdokim E. Mal'tsev, *Akademiia imeni V. I. Lenina* (Moscow: Voenizdat, 1980), 75; "Ob otbore 4,000 kommunistov na politrabotu v RKKA, 29 Avgusta 1939 g." 174–175; Valentin O. Osipov, *Politruk Vasilii Klochkov* (Moscow: Voenizdat, 1984), 67–75, 97.

56. Iurii P. Petrov, *Stroitel'stvo politorganov partiinykh i komsomol'skikh organizat-sii armii i flota (1918–1968)* (Moscow: Voenizdat, 1968), 249-250; Korablev and Logi-nov, eds., *KPSS i stroitel'stvo Vooruzhennykh Sil SSSR*, 469.

57. Wilhelm Deist, *The Wehrmacht and German Rearmament* (Toronto: University of Toronto Press, 1981), 38.

58. Matthew Cooper, *The German Army 1933–1945: Its Political and Military Fail-ure* (New York: Stein and Day, 1978), 159.

59. Siegfried Knappe and Ted Brusaw, *Soldat: Reflections of a German Soldier, 1936–1949* (New York: Orion, 1992), 100, 104–106.

60. S. J. Lewis, *Forgotten Legions: German Army Infantry Policy 1918–1941* (New York: Praeger, 1985), 36.

61. Deist, *The Wehrmacht and German Rearmament*, 40.

62. Cooper, *The German Army 1933–1945*, 160.

63. *Krasnaia zvezda*, 6 Aug. 1937, 27 May 1938.

64. *Krasnaia zvezda*, 30 Dec. 1937, 15 Feb. 1938.

65. *Istoriia Ural'skogo voennogo okruga* (Moscow: Voenizdat, 1970), 137; *Krasnoz-nammenyi Ural'skii* (Moscow: Voenizdat, 1983), 92.

66. Shelby C. Davis, *The French War Machine* (London: Allen and Unwin, 1937), 76.

67. J. M. Brereton, *The British Soldier: A Social History from 1661 to the Present Day* (London: Bath Press, 1986), 142, 143.

68. Cooper, *The German Army 1933–1945*, 160–161; Gordon Craig, *The Politics of the Prussian Army 1640–1945* (Oxford: Clarendon Press, 1955), 482–484.

69. The British experienced some problems with this procurement system, in that too many unqualified men and ne'er-do-wells entered the OCTUs. In 1942, a three-day screening process was added, with psychological and intelligence tests followed by a six-week preparation course for those who passed screening; then they went on to OCTU. By the end of 1945, the British had commissioned 200,000 officers this way. Brereton, *The British Soldier*, 167.

70. Russell F. Weigley, *History of the United States Army* (New York: Macmillan, 1967), 428; James C. Shelburne and Kenneth J. Groves, *Education in the Armed Forces* (New York: Center for Applied Research in Education, 1965), 58, 59.

71. *Krasnaia zvezda*, 30 July 1938.

72. *Krasnaia zvezda*, 11 Oct. 1938.

73. *Krasnaia zvezda*, 30 Jan. 1938.

74. *Krasnaia zvezda*, 27 Aug. 1938.

75. *Krasnaia zvezda*, 22 May 1938.

76. *Krasnaia zvezda*, 27 Oct. 1939.

77. A. Cheremnykh, "Razvite Voenno-uchebnykh zavedenii v predvoennyi period (1937–1941 gg)," *Voenno-istoricheskii zhurnal*, no. 8 (1982), 75.

78. "O Nakoplenii Nachal'stvuiushchego sostava i popolnenii im Raboche-Krest'ian-skoi Krasnoi Armii," 180; *Istoriia ordena Lenina Leningradskogo voennogo okruga* (Moscow: Voenizdat, 1974), 147.

79. *Krasnaia zvezda*, 27 Oct., 12 Nov. 1939.

80. "O Nakoplenii Nachal'stvuiushchego sostava i popolnenii im Raboche-Krest'ian-skoi Krasnoi Armii," 179; Dmitrii Fedotoff White, *The Growth of the Red Army* (Princeton: Princeton University Press, 1944), 372.

81. Nikolai Ia. Golovanov, *Zhitomirskoe Krasnoznamennoe imeni Leninskogo komsomola* (Moscow: Voenizdat, 1977), 42–46, 48.

82. Ibid., 50, 51.

83. Suvenirov, "Vsearmeiskaia Tragediia," 45.

84. Nikolai D. Iakovlev, *Ob artillerii i nemnogo o sebe* (Moscow: Voenizdat, 1981), 6–38; Ivan M. Chistiakov, *Sluzhim Otchizne* (Moscow: Voenizdat, 1975), 23–41; Stanislav G. Poplavskii, *Tovarishchi v bor'be*, 2d ed. (Moscow: Voenizdat, 1974), 16–28; Konstantin P. Kazakov, *Artilleriiskii grom* (Moscow: Molodaia gvardiia, 1978), 17–42, 50–73; Grigorii D. Plaskov, *Pod grokhot kanonady* (Moscow: Voenizdat, 1969), 93–125; P. G. Kuznetsov, *General Cherniakhovskii* (Moscow: Voenizdat, 1969), 48, 49.

85. Vasilii S. Golubovich, *Marshal Malinovskii* (Kiev: Politizdat Ukraine, 1988), 3–23; R. M. Portugalskii, *Marshal I. S. Konev* (Moscow: Voenizdat, 1985), 3–59; V. E. Bystrov, ed., *Sovetskie polkovodtsy i voenachal'niki* (Moscow: Molodaia gvardiia, 1988), 242–255, 306–314.

86. RGVA f. 25880, op. 4, d. 5, ll. 382–386; Zakharov, *General'nyi shtab v predvoennyi gody*, 257.

87. Sergei I. Vasil'ev and Aleksei P. Dikan', *Gvardeitsy piatnadtsatoi* (Moscow: Voenizdat, 1960), 9–24.

88. K. E. Voroshilov, *Rech' na XVIII s"ezde VKP (b)* (Moscow: Gospolitizdat, 1939), 24.

89. "O rabote Politicheskogo Upravleniia Krasnoi Armii, 200.

90. For example, 9,100 officers went to recruiting and conscription duties, 6,000 were reassigned to PUR, and 1,420 were transferred to the NKVD. "O Nakoplenii Nachal'stvuiushchego sostava i popolnenii im Raboche-Krest'ianskoi Krasnoi Armii," 178, 180, 182.

6. The Last Eighteen Months

1. N. A. Mal'tsev, "Kadrovaia ili militsionnaia?" *Voenno-istoricheskii zhurnal*, no. 11 (1989), 38.

2. Rossiiskii gosudarstvenno voennyi arkhiv (RGVA) f. 25880, op. 4, d. 5, l. 3. Throughout the thirties, the French and British also overestimated the strength of the German armed forces to about twice their actual size. See Donald C. Watt, *Too Serious a Business: European Armed Forces and the Approach of the Second World War* (New York: Norton, 1975), 93, 94, 102.

3. Stepan A. Kalinin, *Razmyshliaia o minuvshem* (Moscow: Voenizdat, 1963), 123, 124.

4. Leon Trotsky, *Military Writings* (New York: Merit Publishers, 1969), 106–108.

5. William C. Fuller, *Civil-Military Conflict in Imperial Russia, 1881–1914* (Princeton: Princeton University Press, 1985), 48–52.

6. L. G. Ivashov, "V poslednie predvoennye," *Voenno-istoricheskii zhurnal*, no. 11 (1989), 12.

7. David Holloway, "Military Technology," in Ronald Amann, Julian Cooper, and R. W. Davies, eds., *The Technological Level of Soviet Industry* (New Haven: Yale University Press, 1977), 418; O. A. Losik, *Stroitel'stvo i boevoe primenenie sovetskikh tankovykh voisk v gody Velikoi Otechestvennoi voiny* (Moscow: Voenizdat; 1979), 24.

8. Robert A. Kilmarx, *A History of Soviet Airpower* (New York: Praeger, 1962), 128, 158–160; A. S. Iakovlev, *50 let sovetskogo samoleto stroeniia* (Moscow: Nauka, 1968), 28, 29.

9. A. S. Iakovlev, *Tsel' Zhizni: Zapiski aviakonstruktora* (Moscow: Politizdat, 1968), 166–168; A. G. Khor'kov, "Tekhnicheskoe perevooruzhenie Sovetskoi Armii nakanune Velikoi Otechestvennoi voiny," *Voenno-istoricheskii zhurnal*, no. 6 (1987), 15–21.

10. Ivan Petrov, "Ia vipolnial zadanie Stalina," *Rodina*, no. 5 (1992), 32; Leonid V. Belovinskii, *C russkim voinom cherez veka* (Moscow: Prosveshchenie, 1992), 106–108.

11. G. F. Krivosheev, *Grif Sekretnosti Sniat: Poteri Vooruzhennykh Sil SSSR v voinakh, voevykh deistviiakh i voennykh konfliktakh* (Moscow: Voenizdat, 1993), 70–76.

12. Vladimir Katuntsev, "Intsident: podopleka Khasanskikh sobytii," *Rodina*, nos. 6–7 (1991), 16–18; *Krasnoznamennyi Dal'nevostochnyi voennyi okrug*, 3d ed. (Moscow: Voenizdat, 1985), 118–126.

13. Krivosheev, *Grif Sekretnosti Sniat*, 76–85. These losses (23,926 men out of a total of 69,101 involved) represent 34 percent casualties. A unit that suffers such losses is not normally considered combat worthy, until replacements are secured.

14. Petro Grigorenko, *Memoirs* (New York: Norton, 1982), 108, 109; Marshal G. K. Zhukov, *Vospominaniia i razmyshleniia*, vol. 1, 11th ed. (Moscow: Novosti, 1992), 249–287. In this revised edition, parts omitted by the original censor are restored. In the chapter on Khalkin-Gol, the restored parts show that Zhukov blamed Mongolian units assigned to his army group for some of his problems.

15. Grigorenko, *Memoirs*, 110.

16. Krivosheev, *Grif Sekretnosti Sniat*, 85–92, 125. These losses seem very light. A total of 466,526 personnel participated in the campaign, suffering 3,522 casualties, which represents less than 1 percent of the forces involved. One must keep in mind, however, that the fighting only lasted some two weeks against a Polish army fighting on two fronts that had committed most of its forces against the Germans.

17. For a general overview of the war from the Soviet perspective, see *Istoriia ordena Lenina Leningradskogo voennogo okruga*, 3d ed. (Moscow: Voenizdat, 1988), and Seweryn Bialer, ed., *Stalin and His Generals* (New York: Pegasus, 1969). See also Carl Van Dyke, *The Soviet-Finnish War of 1939–1940: Anatomy of a Preventive War* (Ph.D. diss., Emmanuel College, 1994).

18. The figure for wounded includes nearly 18,000 frostbite casualties. The total number of men the Red Army committed to this short war was 848,570, and with total casualties of 391,783 (not including desertions) the losses equal 46 percent of the force. Not all units suffered equally, of course. The Thirteenth Army suffered 61.2 percent casualties, while the Eighth Army incurred 29.2 percent, the Fourteenth

Army 25 percent, and the Ninth between 20 percent and 30 percent. It is also interesting to note that the losses among officers between 30 November 1939 and 13
March 1940 are just slightly higher than those of the *Ezhovshchina*. Krivosheev, *Grif
Sekretnosti Sniat*, 93–126; P. A. Artekar', "Opravdanny li zhertvy?" *Voenno-istoricheskii zhurnal*, no. 3 (1992), 43–45.

19. M. I. Semiriaga, "Neznamenitaia voina," *Ogonek*, no. 22 (May 1989), 28–30.

20. Il'ia Belikov, *Imeni Dzerzhinskogo* (Moscow: Voenizdat, 1976), 73; *Odesskii
krasnoznamennyi*, 49; Evdokim E. Mal'tsev, *V gody ispytanii* (Moscow: Voenizdat,
1979), 43; Lauri Paanan and Eloise Engle, *The Winter War: The Russo-Finnish Conflict, 1939–1940* (New York: Scribner's, 1973), 160, 161.

21. "O Nakoplenii Nachal'stvuiushchego sostava im Raboche-Krest'ianskoi Krasnoi
Armii: Iz spravki-doklada Upravleniia po nachal'stvuiushchemu sostavu RKKA Narkomata Oborony SSSR E. A. Shchadenko, 20 Marta 1940 g," *Izvestiia TsK KPSS*, no. 1
(1990), 181; Evdokim E. Mal'tsev, *Akademiia imeni V. I. Lenina* (Moscow: Voenizdat,
1980), 86.

22. Sergei I. Vasil'ev and Aleksei P. Dikan', *Gvardeitsy piatnadtsatoi* (Moscow: Voenizdat, 1960), 9–24.

23. "Akt o Prieme Narkomata Oborony Soiuza SSR tov. Timoshenko S. K. ot tov.
Voroshilov K. E.," *Izvestiia TsK KPSS*, no. 1 (1990), 193–205.

24. RGVA f. 25880, op. 4, d. 4, ll. 754–759; John Erickson, *The Road to Stalingrad: Stalin's War with Germany* (London: Weidenfeld and Nicolson, 1975), 24. In
1932, some members of France's Chamber of Deputies wanted to save money by
canceling reserve training for one year. Colonel Fabray, chairman of the army commission to the Chamber of Deputies, "argued that sending men into battle without
sufficient training would be a 'crime against the nation' and would be the same as
sending them to the 'butcher.'" Robert A. Doughty, *The Seeds of Disaster: The Development of French Army Doctrine, 1919–1939* (Hamden, Conn.: Archon Books,
1985), 28.

25. *Krasnaia zvezda*, 8, 10 Oct. 1940.

26. Mark von Hagen casts serious doubt on the ability of the Red Army to reform
itself. The high command was able to discern only the symptoms of the problems
plaguing the army but failed to discover the real problems of the political, economic, and social system upon which the Red Army rested. Mark von Hagen, "Soviet Soldiers and Officers on the Eve of the German Invasion: Towards a
Description of Social Psychology and Political Attitudes," *Soviet Union/Union Sovetique* 18, nos. 1–3 (1991), 85, 86.

27. Williamson Murray, "The German Response to Victory in Poland: A Case Study
in Professionalism," *Armed Forces and Society* 7, no. 2 (1981), 285–298.

28. *Pravda*, 25 Aug. 1940.

29. L. M. Sandalov, "Stoiali Nasmert': Podgotovka voisk 4-i Armii k otrazheniiu
fashistskoi agressii," *Voenno-istoricheskii zhurnal*, no. 11 (1988), 3–4.

30. RGVA f. 25580, op. 4, d. 4, ll. 263, 850–852; d. 5, l. 6.

31. *Sovetskie Vooruzhennye Sily* (Moscow: Voenizdat, 1978), 505; "O rabote za
1939 god.: Iz otcheta nachal'nika Upravleniia po nachal'stvuiushchemu sostavu RKKA
Narkomata Oborony SSSR E. A. Shchadenko, 5 Maia 1940 g," *Izvestiia TsK KPSS*,
no. 1 (1990), 187.

32. B. P. Krikunov, "'Prostaia arifmetika' V. V. Shlykova," *Voenno-istoricheskii zhurnal*, no. 4 (1989), 41–43.

33. RGVA f. 25880, op. 4, d. 4, ll. 62, 226–62.

34. Ibid., l. 263; d. 5, l. 509.

35. RGVA f. 25880, op. 4, d. 5, l. 6

36. RGVA f. 25880, op. 4, d. 4, ll. 730, 731.

37. *Kievskii krasnoznamennyi: Istoriia krasnoznamennogo kievskogo voennogo okruga 1919–1972* (Moscow: Voenizdat, 1974), 138; Geoffrey Roberts, *The Unholy Alliance: Stalin's Pact with Hitler* (London: I. B. Taurus, 1989), 188–191.

38. This call-up has never been reported in the secondary literature and the records in the RGVA only allude to it, but there is no *opis'* or *delo* that deals with it as a single event, so the scope of it is still unknown.

39. RGVA f. 25880, op. 4, d. 4, ll. 48, 49.

40. Ibid., ll. 143–145, 188, 189, 671, 842.

41. Ibid., ll. 306, 385, 386.

42. Ibid., l. 667.

43. Aleksandr A. Svechin, *Strategy*, Kent D. Lee, ed. (Minneapolis, Minn.: East View Publications, 1992), 204. Originally published as *Strategiia* (Moscow: Voennyi Vestnik, 1927).

44. RGVA f. 25880, op. 4, d. 4, ll. 266, 339.

45. Ibid., l. 707.

46. Ibid., d. 5, ll. 145, 146, 182, 183, 220, 345.

47. Ibid., ll. 260, 344.

48. Ibid., l. 184.

49. Ibid., ll. 220, 221.

50. Ibid., ll. 555–562.

51. Ibid., ll. 329, 596, 598.

52. Ibid., ll. 324, 325, 605–607.

53. Ibid., ll. 219, 563, 564.

54. Ibid., l. 608.

55. RGVA f. 25880, op. 4, d. 4. ll. 16, 17, 391.

56. Ibid., ll. 143, 144.

57. Ibid., ll. 331, 707.

58. Ibid., d. 5, ll. 316, 320.

59. Ibid., l. 303.

60. Ibid., ll. 301, 328.

61. Ibid., ll. 304–307.

62. Ibid., ll. 321–324, 545, 547.

63. Ibid., ll. 545, 597.

64. Ibid., l. 595.

65. RGVA f. 25880, op. 4, d. 4, ll. 268–270.

66. Ibid., ll. 16–20, 196, 197.

67. Ibid., ll. 270, 595.

68. Ibid., l. 314.

69. Ibid., ll. 70, 71, 723.

70. Ibid., ll. 70, 71.

71. Ibid., ll.70, 71, 74.
72. Ibid., ll. 749–753.
73. RGVA f. 25880, op. 4, d. 5, ll. 449–451, 626.
74. Svechin, *Strategy*, 180, 181.

7. The Predictable Disaster

1. G. F. Krivosheev, *Grif Sekretnosti Sniat: Poteri Vooruzhennykh Sil SSSR v voinakh, voevykh deistviiakh i voennykh konfliktakh* (Moscow: Voenizdat, 1993), 143; *Small Unit Actions During the German Campaign in Russia*, Department of the Army Pamphlet no. 20-269 (Washington, D.C.: Department of the Army), 88.

2. Iu. I. Korablev and M. I. Loginov, eds., *KPSS i stroitel'stvo Vooruzhennykh Sil SSSR (1918–iiun 1941)* (Moscow: Voenizdat, 1959), 430. For a summary of these arguments in English, see Vladimir Petrov, *"22 June 1941": Soviet Historians and the German Invasion* (Columbia: University of South Carolina Press, 1968).

3. Robert Doughty, "The French Armed Forces, 1918–1940," in Allan R. Millet and Williamson Murray, eds., *Military Effectiveness*, vol. 2 (Boston: Allen and Unwin, 1988), 53.

4. Nikita S. Khrushchev, *The 'Secret' Speech* (Nottingham: Spokesman Books, 1976), 49; Lisann Maury, "Stalin the Appeaser," *Survey*, no. 76 (summer 1970), 56; Gustav Hilger, *The Incompatible Allies* (New York: Macmillan, 1953), 32, 33, 307.

5. John Erickson, "The Soviet Response to Surprise Attack: Three Directives, 22 June 1941," *Soviet Studies* 23, no. 4 (1972), 519–530.

6. Between 14 and 19 June, the NKO ordered military district commanders to reorganize their districts as fronts and on 19 June to camouflage airfields and troop concentrations. A. G. Khor'kov, *Nachal'nyi period Velikoi Otechestvennoi voiny* (Moscow: Voroshilov Academy of the General Staff, 1984), 11.

7. Hermann Plocher, *The German Air Force versus Russia, 1941*, USAF Historical Studies, no. 153, Harry R. Fletcher, ed., USAF Historical Division, Aerospace Studies Institute, Air University (New York: Arno Press, 1965), 41.

8. Seweryn Bialer, ed., *Stalin and His Generals* (New York: Pegasus, 1969), 183, 184; *Current Digest of the Soviet Press* 40, no. 33 (1988), 17, 18.

9. *Istoriia Velikoi Otechestvennoi Voiny Sovetskogo Soiuza, 1941–1945* (Moscow: Voenizdat, 1960), 475.

10. B. L. Vannikov, "In the People's Commissariat of Armaments," in Bialer, ed., *Stalin and His Generals*, 156.

11. V. S. Emelianov, "Trials of an Industrial Manager," in Bialer, ed., *Stalin and His Generals*, 104–114; B. L. Vannikov, "Obornnaia Promyshlennost' SSSR nakanune voiny (iz zapisok Narkoma)," *Voprosy istorii*, no. 10 (1968), 122.

12. Ivan Petrov, "Ia vypolnial zadanie Stalina," *Rodina*, no. 5 (1992), 32–35.

13. Jerry Hough, "The Historical Legacy in Soviet Weapons Development," in Jiri Valenta and William Potter, eds., *Soviet Decisionmaking for National Security* (London: Allen and Unwin, 1984), 88–89.

14. Ibid., 98–100.

15. Mark Harrison, *Soviet Planning in Peace and War 1938–1945* (Cambridge, Mass.: Harvard University Press, 1985), 7–11; Matvei Zakharov, *General'nyi shtab v predvoennyi gody* (Moscow: Voenizdat, 1989), 201.

16. Eugene Zaleskii, *Stalinist Planning for Economic Growth 1933–1952* (Chapel Hill: University of North Carolina Press, 1980), 164, 167.

17. Barbara Katz, "Purges and Production: Soviet Economic Growth, 1928–1940," *Journal of Economic History* 35, no. 3 (1975), 566–573; Mark Harrison, *Soviet Planning in Peace and War 1938–1945* (New York: Cambridge University Press, 1984), 10; Donald Filtzer, *Soviet Workers and Stalinist Industrialization* (London: Pluto Press, 1986), 127, 128.

18. Hough, "The Historical Legacy in Soviet Weapons Development," 88–90, 100–110.

19. The Red Army suffered an acute munitions shortage in the summer of 1941, not only because of transport problems due to the war but also because the military did not turn in its request for munitions production until the spring of 1941—months behind schedule. "Zapiska G. I. Kulika I. V. Stalinu, 19 iiunia 1941 g," *Izvestiia TsK KPSS*, no. 5 (1990), 203–206.

20. Vannikov, "Obornnaia Promyshlennost' SSSR nakanune voiny (iz zapisok Narkoma)," 122–124; "In the People's Commissariat of Armaments," in Bialer, ed., *Stalin and His Generals*, 153–156.

21. Donald C. Watt, *Too Serious a Business: European Armed Forces and the Approach to the Second World War* (New York: Norton, 1992), 74, 75, 92, 93.

22. S. Skryabin and N. Medvedev, "O tyle frontov v nachale Velikoi Otechestvennoi Voiny," *Voenno-istoricheskii zhurnal*, no. 4 (April 1984), 32–38; Alexandr Nekrich, "22 June 1941," in Petrov, "*22 June 1941*": *Soviet Historians and the German Invasion*, 130, 131.

23. Georgii K. Zhukov, *Vospominaniia i razmyshleniia* (Moscow: Novosti, 1969), 215.

24. Skryabin and Medvedev, "O tyle frontov v nachale Velikoi Otechestvennoi Voiny," 33.

25. Ibid., 32, 35.

26. A. S. Klemin, "Voennye Soobshchennia v godu Velikoi Otechestvennoi Voiny," *Voenno-istoricheskii zhurnal*, no. 3 (1985), 67, 73.

27. I. Volkotrubenko, "O planovom snabzheni Voisk vooruzheniem i boepripasami," *Voenno-istoricheskii zhurnal*, no. 12 (1983), 59, 60.

28. Doughty, "The French Armed Forces, 1918–1940," 45.

29. B. H. Liddell-Hart, *Europe in Arms* (London: Faber and Faber Ltd., 1937), 29.

30. "Combat Efficiency Estimate, 16 June 1941," *U.S. Military Intelligence Reports 1919–1941*, Reel V, 0770.

31. Zhukov, *Vospominaniia i razmyshleniia*, 214, 215.

32. "Pis'mo leitenanta A. N. Kozlova I. V. Stalinu, 30 iiulia 1941 g," *Izvestiia TsK KPSS*, no. 8 (1990), 222.

33. John A. English, *A Perspective on Infantry* (New York: Praeger, 1981), 110, 111; Aleksandr Dongarov, "Mezhdu Reinom i Volgoi," *Rodina*, no. 5 (1991), 43.

34. *Istoriia vtoroi mirovoi voiny 1939–1945* (Moscow: Voenizdat, 1974), vol. 3, 421, and vol. 4, 18; Zakharov, *General'nyi shtab v predvoennye gody*, 259, 260; A. G. Khor'kov, *Nachal'nyi period Velikoi Otechestvennoi voiny* (Moscow: Voroshilov Academy of the General Staff, 1984), 11, 13.

35. F. M. von Senger und Etterlin, *German Tanks of World War II* (New York: Galahad Books, 1969), 34–58; *Istoriia vtoroi mirovoi voiny 1939–1945*, vol. 3, 420; Douglas Orgill, *T-34 Russian Armor* (New York: Ballantine Books, 1971), 29.

36. In their invasion of the west, the Germans faced equal numbers of Allied troops armed with more artillery and tanks, especially heavy tanks. Here, as early in the Russian campaign, the credit for victory goes to superior tactics and training. James S. Corum, *The Roots of Blitzkrieg* (Lawrence: University Press of Kansas, 1992), 203.

37. Hermann Plocher, *The German Air Force versus Russia, 1941*, 39; Richard Muller, *The German Air War in Russia* (Baltimore, Md.: The Nautical and Aviation Publishing Company of America, 1992), 44, 45.

38. Doughty, "The French Armed Forces, 1918–1940," 51.

39. Omer Bartov, *The Eastern Front, 1941–1945, German Troops and the Barbarisation of Warfare* (London: Macmillan, 1985), 11.

40. *Small Unit Actions During the German Campaign in Russia*, 1, 2.

41. "Iz pis'ma riadogo 233-go pekhotnogo polka 102-i pokhotnoi divizii germanskoi armii K. Franka iz gospitalia sem'e 10 iiulia 1941 g," *Rodina*, nos. 6–7 (1991), 28.

42. Bartov, *The Eastern Front, 1941–1945*, 27–31; Wilhelm Prüller, *Diary of a German Soldier* (New York: Coward-McCann, 1963), 115, 116.

43. James Lucas, *War on the Eastern Front, 1941–1945: The German Soldier in Russia* (New York: Stein and Day, 1979), 129–131.

44. "Doklad komandovaniia Zapadnogo fronta I. V. Stalinu o prichinakh porazheniia 22–i armii, 3 Sentiabra 1941," *Istoricheskii Arkhiv*, no. 1 (1993), 58, 59.

45. "Opyt pervogo mesiatsa voiny s Germaniei: Doklad komandovaniia Iuzhnogo fronta, 21 iiulia 1941 g," *Izvestiia TsK KPSS*, no. 8 (1990), 213, 214; "Pis'mo leitenanta A. N. Kozlova I. V. Stalinu, 30 iiulia 1941 g," 222; Lucas, *War on the Eastern Front*, 193.

46. V. P. Krikunov, "Kuda delis' tanki?" *Voenno-istoricheskii zhurnal*, no. 11 (1988), 33.

47. Ibid.

48. Ibid., 33–35.

49. Ibid., 35–37.

50. Ibid., 37–39.

51. Ibid.

52. Ibid.

53. Ibid., 39.

54. Ibid; M. I. Kormilitsin, "Armii nuzhno goriuchee," *Voprosy istorii*, no. 12 (1969), 17–125.

55. Leon Trotsky, *Military Writings* (New York: Pathfinder, 1971), 107.

56. Moshe Lewin, *The Gorbachev Phenomenon: A Historical Interpretation* (Berkeley: University of California Press, 1988), 22.

57. Moshe Lewin, *The Making of the Soviet System: Essays in the Social History of Interwar Russia* (New York: Pantheon, 1985), 241–243.

58. William Moskoff, *The Bread of Affliction: The Food Supply in the USSR During World War II* (New York: Cambridge University Press, 1990), 6–10.

59. Aleksandr A. Svechin, *Strategy*, ed. and trans. Kent D. Lee (Minneapolis, Minn.: East View Publications, 1992), 177. Originally published as *Strategiia* (Moscow: Voennyi Vestnik, 1927).

60. Von Hagen discusses the effect of the Nazi-Soviet Nonaggression Pact in the years 1939–1941 in "Soviet Soldiers and Officers on the Eve of the German Invasion: Towards a Description of Social Psychology and Political Attitudes," *Soviet Union/Union Sovetique* 18, nos. 1–3 (1991), 98, 99.

61. Jacob Kipp, "Preface" to Svechin, *Strategy*, 50.

62. Zakharov, *General'nyi shtab v predvoennye gody*, 175, 176, 192–211.

63. Khor'kov, *Nachal'nyi period Velikoi Otechestvennoi voiny*, 11–14.

64. Hans Speier, *Social Order and the Risks of War* (Cambridge, Mass.: MIT Press, 1952), 257.

Select Bibliography

Archival Sources

British Foreign Office File 371 (1906–1948); *British Foreign Office Russia: Correspondence 1781–1945*
Record Group no. 165, Military Intelligence files: Russia; see the guide, *U.S. Military Intelligence Reports 1919–1941: Russia Military Intelligence Division War Department General Staff Military Attache Reports: Soviet Union*, National Archives and Record Service, Washington, D.C.
Rossiiskii gosudarstvennyi voennyi arkhiv (RGVA)
fond 4 Upravlenie delami pri narodnom kommissare oborony SSSR
    opis' 1, delo 1120
    opis' 1, delo 1134
fond 9 Politicheskoe upravlenie RKKA
    opis' 26, delo 487
    opis' 26, delo 490
fond 54 Glavnoe upravlenie RKKA
    opis' 1, delo 1235
fond 887 Upravlenie XVIII Strelkovo Korpusa
    opis' 1, delo 86
    opis' 1, delo 90
    opis' 1, delo 96
    opis' 1, delo 99
fond 896 Upravlenie XIV Strelkovo Korpusa
    opis' 2, delo 1
    opis' 3, delo 10
fond 1293 Upravlenie XXI Permskoi Strelkovoi Divizii
    opis' 5782, delo 6
fond 25880 Kievskii Osobyi voennyi okrug
    opis' 4, delo 4
    opis' 4, delo 5
fond 25893 Sibirskii voennyi okrug
    opis' 1, delo 292
fond 37837 Upravlenie po nachal'stvuiushchemu sostavu RKKA
    opis' 18, delo 777
    opis' 19, delo 37
    opis' 21, delo 23
    opis' 22, delo 41
    opis' 22, delo 99

Smolensk Archive: The Records of the Western Regional Committee of the Communist Party of the Soviet Union; see the guide, *Records of the Smolensk Oblast of the All-Union Communist Party of the Soviet Union, 1917–1941.* Washington, D.C.: The National Archives and Records Service, 1980.

Files WKP 40, WKP 129, WKP 186, WKP 225, and WKP 229

University of Illinois Archives; *Harvard University Refugee Interview Project: Soviet Interview Project Archives*, 1980–1987. Record Series 24/2/50-51.

Books and Articles

Alferov, S. "Strategicheskoe razvertyvanie sovetskikh voisk na zapadnom TVD v 1941 godu." *Voenno-istoricheskii zhurnal*, no. 6 (1980), 26–33.

Anfilov, Viktor A. *Nachalo Velikoi Otechestvennoi voiny (22 Iiunia—serednia iiulia 1941 goda).* Moscow: Voenizdat, 1962.

Artekar', P. A. "Opravdanny li zhertvy?" *Voenno-istoricheskii zhurnal*, no. 3 (1992), 43–45.

Aru, Karl. *S rodnoi artillerii.* Tallin: Eestu raamat, 1977.

Atkinson, Littleton B. *Dual Command in the Red Army 1918–1942.* Maxwell Air Force Base, Ala.: Air University Documentary Research Study, 1950.

Babakov, A. "Sovetskie Voennye Okruga." *Voenno-istoricheskii zhurnal*, no. 9 (1982), 62–67.

Bagramian, Ivan Kh. *Moi vospominaniia.* Erevan: Aiastan, 1980.

Baratov, B. *Die Rote Armee und das Territorialsystem.* Pokrovsk: Nemgosizdat, 1928.

Batekhin, L. "Meropriiatiia Kommunisticheskoi Partii po Razvitiiu Voenno-vozdushnykh Sil V Predvoennye Gody." *Voenno-istoricheskii zhurnal*, no. 8 (1983), 69–73.

Belikov, Il'ia. *Imeni Dzerzhinskogo.* Moscow: Voenizdat, 1976.

Belitskii, Semion M., et al. *Besedy o voennom dele i Krasnoi Armii: sbornik dlia kruzhkov voennykh znanii na fabrikakh, zavodakh . . .* Moscow: Voennyi Vestnik, 1926.

Beloborodov, Afanasii P. *Vsegda v boiu.* Moscow: Voenizdat, 1978.

Belovinskii, Leonid V. *S russkim voinom cherez veka.* Moscow: Prosveshchenie, 1992.

Benvenuti, Francesco. *The Bolsheviks and the Red Army, 1918–1922.* New York: Cambridge University Press, 1988.

Berkhin, Il'ia. "O territorial'no-militsionnom stroitelstve v Sovetskoi Armii." *Voenno-istoricheskii zhurnal*, no. 12 (1960), 3–20.

———. *Voennaia reforma v SSSR (1924–1925 gg).* Moscow: Voenizdat, 1958.

Berman, Harold J. and Kerner, Miroslav. *Documents on Soviet Military Law and Administration.* Cambridge, Mass.: Harvard University Press, 1955.

———. *Soviet Military Law and Administration.* Cambridge, Mass.: Harvard University Press, 1955.

Bialer, Seweryn, ed. *Stalin and His Generals.* New York: Pegasus, 1969.

Boldin, Ivan V. *Stranitsy zhizni.* Moscow: Voenizdat, 1961.

Bond, Brian. *British Military Policy Between the Two World Wars.* Oxford: Clarendon Press, 1980.

Brereton, J. M. *The British Soldier: A Social History from 1661 to the Present Day.* London: Bath Press, 1986.

Brzezinski, Zbigniew K., ed. *Political Controls in the Soviet Army.* New York: Research Program on the USSR, 1954.

Bubnov, Andre S. *O Krasnoi Armii.* Moscow: Voenizdat, 1958.

Budennyi, Semen M. *Boets-grazhdanin.* Moscow: Partizdat, 1937.

Bushnell, John. "Peasants in Uniform: The Tsarist Army as a Peasant Society." *Journal of Social History* 13 (1980), 565–574.

————."The Tsarist Officer Corps, 1881–1914: Customs, Duties, Inefficiency." *American Historical Review* 86, no. 4 (1981), 753–780.

Bystrov, V. E., ed. *Sovetskie polkovodtsy i voenachal'niki.* Moscow: Molodaiagvardiia, 1988.

Cheremnykh, A. "Razvite Voenno-uchebnykh zavedenii v predvoennyi period (1937–1941 gg)." *Voenno-istoricheskii zhurnal,* no. 8 (1982), 75–80.

Chistiakov, Ivan M. *Sluzhim Otchizne.* Moscow: Voenizdat, 1975.

"Chistka partii i zadachi partorganizatsii VVS." *Vestnik Vozdushnogo Flota,* no. 10 (1933), 9–11.

Clark, Alan. *Barbarossa: The Russian-German Conflict, 1941–45.* New York: William Morrow, 1965.

Colton, Timothy. *Commissars, Commanders and Civilian Authority.* Princeton: Princeton University Press, 1979.

Conner, Albert Z., and Poirer, Robert G. *The Red Army Order of Battle in the Great Patriotic War.* Novato, Calif.: Presidio Press, 1985.

Conquest, Robert. *The Great Terror.* New York: Macmillan, 1968.

Cooper, Matthew. *The German Army 1933–1945: Its Political and Military Failure.* New York: Stein and Day, 1978.

Corum, James S. *The Roots of Blitzkrieg: Hans von Seeckt and German Military Reform.* Lawrence: University Press of Kansas, 1992.

Craig, Gordon. *The Politics of the Prussian Army 1640–1945.* Oxford: Clarendon Press, 1955.

Danilov, V. "Stroitel'stvo tsentral'nogo voennogo apparata v 1924–1928 gg." *Voenno-istoricheskii zhurnal,* no. 6 (1972), 80–86.

Danilov, V. P., and Ivanitskii, N. A. *Dokumenty svidetel'stvuiut: Iz istorii derevni nakanune i v khode kollektivizatsii 1927–1932 gg.* Moscow: Politizdat, 1989.

Davies, Robert W. *The Socialist Offensive.: The Collectivization of Soviet Agriculture 1929–1930.* Cambridge, Mass.: Harvard University Press, 1980.

————. *The Soviet Economy in Turmoil, 1929–1930.* Cambridge, Mass.: Harvard University Press, 1989.

Davis, Shelby C. *The French War Machine.* London: Allen and Unwin, 1937.

Deist, Wilhelm. *The Wehrmacht and German Rearmament.* Toronto: University of Toronto Press, 1981.

Demin, Nikita S. *Voina i liudi.* Moscow: Voenizdat, 1972.

Desiat let Krasnoi Armii 1918–1928. Moscow: Voenizdat, 1928.

DeWitt, Nicholas. *Education and Professional Employment in the USSR.* Washington, D.C.: National Science Foundation, 1961.

Distsiplinarnyi Ustav Krasnoi Armii. Moscow: Voenizdat, 1941.

Dlia distsipliny net melochei. Moscow: Gosizdat, 1927.

Dongarov, Aleksandr. "Mezhdu Reinom i Volgoi." *Rodina,* no. 5 (1991), 39–43.

Doughty, Robert A. *The Seeds of Disaster: The Development of French Army Doctrine, 1919–1939.* Hamden, Conn.: Archon Books, 1985.

Dragunskii, A. *Polevaia academiia.* Moscow: Voenizdat, 1982.

XX let raboche-krest'ianskoi krasnoi armii i voennomorskogo flota. Leningrad: Lenoblizdat, 1938.

Dzyza. "Krasnaia Armiia i zadachi kolkhoznogo stroitel'stva." *Voennyi Vestnik* 10, no. 4 (1930), 35.

———. "Zadachi podgotovki 100,000 kolkhoznykh kadrov." *Voennyi Vestnik* 10, no. 15 (1930), 2–8.

Edel'shtein, A. O. *Alkogolizmu v krasnoi armii net mesta.* Moscow, 1928.

Efimov, N. *Prokhozhdenie sluzhby v RKKA.* Moscow/Leningrad: Gosizdat, 1927.

Egorov, E. P. *Inzhenernye voiska Sovetskoi Armii 1918–1945.* Moscow: Voenizdat, 1985.

English, John A. *A Perspective on Infantry.* New York: Praeger, 1981.

Epishev, Aleksai A. *Partiia i armiia.* Moscow: Politizdat, 1977.

Epishev, Aleksai A., ed. *Partiino-politicheskaia rabota v vooruzhennykh silakh SSSR, 1918–1973 gg. Istoricheskii ocherk.* Moscow: Voenizdat, 1974.

"Epoka v avtobiografiiakh." *Voenno-istoricheskii zhurnal,* no. 1 (1989), 74–77.

Eremenko, Andre I. *Pomni Voinu.* Donetsk: Donbass, 1971.

Erickson, John. *The Road to Stalingrad: Stalin's War with Germany.* London: Weidenfeld and Nicolson, 1975.

———. *The Soviet High Command: A Military-Political History.* New York: St. Martin's Press, 1962.

———. "The Soviet Response to Surprise Attack: Three Directives, 22 June 1941." *Soviet Studies* 23, no. 4 (1972), 519–530.

Fainsod, Merle. *Smolensk Under Soviet Rule.* Cambridge, Mass.: Harvard University Press, 1958.

Fedorenko, L. *Osnovy territorial'nogo stroitel'stva krasnoi konnitsy.* Leningrad: Voennaia tipografiia, 1926.

Fedoseev, N. *Prava i Obiazannosti Krasnoarmeitsa. Kratkii spravochnik.* Moscow/Leningrad: Gosizdat, 1928.

Fedotoff-White, Dmitrii. *The Growth of the Red Army.* Princeton: Princeton University Press, 1944.

Fitzpatrick, Sheila M. *Education and Social Mobility in the Soviet Union 1921–1934.* New York: Cambridge University Press, 1979.

Frunze, Mikhail V. *Izbrannye proizvedeniia.* Moscow: Voenizdat, 1965.

Fuller, William C. *Civil-Military Conflict in Imperial Russia 1881–1914.* Princeton: Princeton University Press, 1985.

Gaglov, Ivan I. *General Antonov.* Moscow: Voenizdat, 1978.

Gal'ianov and Gorshenin. *Voennaia rabota komsomola.* Moscow: Molodaia gvardiia, 1931.

Ganichev, Pavel P. *Voinskie zvaniia.* Moscow: Dosaaf, 1989.

Gareev, Makhmut A. *M. V. Frunze, Military Theorist.* McClean, Va.: Pergamon-Brassey's International Defense Publishers, 1988.

Geller, Iosif Isakovich. *Pod krasnoi zvezdoi: krasnaia armiia na fronte kollektivizatsii.* Samara: Gosizdat, 1931.

Getty, J. Arch. *The Origins of the Great Purge.* New York: Oxford University Press, 1985.

Getty, J. Arch, and Manning, Roberta T., eds. *Stalinist Terror: New Perspectives.* New York: Cambridge University Press, 1993.

Golovanov, Nikolai Ia. *Zhitomirskoe Krasnoznamennoe imeni Leninskogo komsomola.* Moscow: Voenizdat, 1977.

Golubovich, Vasilii S. *Marshal Malinovskii.* Kiev: Politizdat Ukraine, 1988.

Gorbatov, Aleksandr V. *Years of My Life.* New York: Norton, 1965.

Govorkova, A. A., ed. *Kollektivizatsiia sel'skogo khoziastva zapadnoi sibiri 1927–1937 gg.* Tomsk: Zapadno-sibirskoe knozhnoe izdatel'stvo, 1972.

Grigorenko, Petro G. *Memoirs.* New York: Norton, 1982.

Hardesty, Von. *Red Phoenix: The Rise of Soviet Air Power, 1941–1945.* Washington, D.C.: Smithsonian Institution Press, 1982.

Harrison, Mark. *Soviet Planning in Peace and War 1938–1945.* New York: Cambridge University Press, 1984.

Hilger, Gustav. *The Incompatible Allies.* New York: Macmillan, 1953.

Huntington, Samuel P. *The Soldier and the State.* Cambridge, Mass.: Harvard University Press, 1957.

Iakovlev, A. S. *50 let sovetskogo samoleto stroeniia.* Moscow: Nauka, 1968.

———. *Tsel' Zhizni: Zapiski aviakonstruktora.* Moscow: Politizdat, 1968.

Iakovlev, Nikolai D. *Ob artillerii i nemnogo o sebe.* Moscow: Voenizdat, 1981.

Iakubovskii, Ivan I. *Zemlia v ogne.* Moscow: Voenizdat, 1975.

Iakupov, N. M. "Stalin i Krasnaia Armiia (Arkhivnye nakhodki)." *Istoriia SSSR,* no. 5 (1991), 171–172.

Ianguzov, Z. Sh. *Komissary "Nashenskogo kraia."* Blagoveshchensk: Khabarovskoe, 1975.

Instruktsiia oblastnym, raionnym i rizovym komissiiam po chistke partii. Moscow: Partizdat, 1934.

Inzhenernye voiska v boiakh za Sovetskuiu Rodinu. Moscow: Voenizdat, 1970.

Iovlev, Aleksei M. "Deiatel'nost' Kommunisticheskoi partii po ukrepleniiu politiko-moral'nogo sostoianiia Krasnoi Armii (1928–1932 gg)." *Voenno-istoricheskii zhurnal,* no. 6 (1973), 73–79.

———. *Deiatel'nost' KPSS po podgotovke voennykh kadrov.* Moscow: Voenizdat, 1976.

———. "Podgotovka komandnykh i politicheskikh kadrov Sovetskoi Armii v 1929–1933 godakh." *Voenno-istoricheskii zhurnal,* no. 5 (1960), 63–75.

———. "Sovershenstvovanie voenno-uchebnykh zavedenii v 1921–1928 gg." *Voenno-istoricheskii zhurnal,* no. 2 (1976), 93–98.

———. "Tekhnicheskoe perevooruzhenie Krasnoi Armii v gody pervoi piatiletki." *Voenno-istoricheskii zhurnal,* no. 12 (1964), 3–13.

Iovlev, A., and Bokarev, V. "Stanovlenie i razvitie sistemy podgotovki Komandno-nachal'stvuiushchego sostava zapasa v mezhvoennyi period." *Voenno-istoricheskii zhurnal,* no. 8 (1983), 86–91.

Istoriia Krest'ianstva SSSR: Istoriia sovetskogo krest'ianstva. Moscow: Nauka, 1986.

Istoriia ordena Lenin Leningradskogo voennogo okruga. Moscow: Voenizdat, 1974.

Istoriia Ural'skogo voennogo okruga. Moscow: Voenizdat, 1970.

Istoriia Velikoi Otechestvennoi Voiny Sovetskogo Soiuza 1941–1945. Moscow: Voenizdat, 1960.

Istoriia vtoroi mirovoi voiny 1939–1945. Moscow: Voenizdat, 1973.

Ivashov, L. G. "V poslednie predvoennye." *Voenno-istoricheskii zhurnal,* no. 11 (1989), 12–18.

Ivnitskii, Nikolai A. *Klassovaia bor'ba v derevne i likvidatsiia kulachestva kak klassa (1929–1932 gg).* Moscow: Nauka, 1972.

Janowitz, Morris. *The Professional Officer.* New York: Free Press, 1971.

Jones, Ellen. *Red Army and Society.* Boston: Allen and Unwin, 1985.

Kabanov, Pavel A. *Stal'nye Peregony.* Moscow: Voenizdat, 1973.

Kadishev, Arnol'd. *Chto dolzhen znat' molodoi krasnoarmeets* 13th ed. Moscow/Leningrad: Gosizdat, 1930.

Kak Rabochemu i Krest'ianinu postupit' v Voennuiu Shkolu. Moscow: Voennyi Vestnik, 1927.

Kalinin, Nikolai V. *Vek moi, zhizn' moia.* Iaroslavl'v: Verkhne-Volzsk, 1971.

Kalinin, Stepan A. *Razmyshliaia o minuvshem.* Moscow: Voenizdat, 1963.

Karpov, I. *XXI godovshchina Raboche-Krest'ianskoi Krasnoi Armii i Voenno-morskogo Flota.* Leningrad: N.p., 1939.

Katuntsev, Vladimir. "Intsident: podopleka Khasanskikh sobytii." *Rodina,* nos. 6–7 (1991), 12–20.

Kazakov, Konstantin P. *Artilleriiskii grom.* Moscow: Molodaia gvardiia, 1978.

Kazakov, Mikhail I. *Nad kartoi bylykh srazheni.* Moscow: Voenizdat, 1971.

Khetagurov, Grigorii I. *Ispolnenie dolga.* Moscow: Voenizdat, 1977.

Khlepnikov, Nikolai M. *Pod grokhot soten batarei.* Moscow: Voenizdat, 1979.

Khor'kov, A. G. *Nachal'nyi period Velikoi Otechestvennoi voiny.* Moscow: Voroshilov Academy of the General Staff, 1984.

———. "Tekhnicheskoe perevooruchenie Sovetskii Armii nakanune Velikoi Otechestvennoi voiny." *Voenno-istoricheskii zhurnal,* no. 6 (1987), 15–24.

Khrushchev, Nikita S. *Khrushchev Remembers.* Trans. by Strobe Talbot. New York: Little, Brown, 1970.

———. *The 'Secret' Speech.* Nottingham: Spokesman, 1976.

Kievskii krasnoznamennyi: Istoriia krasnoznamennogo kievskogo voennogo okruga 1919–1972. Moscow: Voenizdat, 1974.

Kilmarx, Robert A. *A History of Soviet Airpower.* New York: Praeger, 1962.

"K istorii territorial'no-militsionnogo stroitel'stva v Krasnoi Armii." *Voenno-istoricheskii zhurnal,* no. 11 (1960), 87–97.

Klemin, A. S. "Voennye Soobshchennia v godu Velikoi Otechestvennoi Voiny." *Voenno-istoricheskii zhurnal,* no. 3 (1985), 66–74.

Klochkov, Vladimir F. *Krasnaia Armiia—shkola kommunisticheskogo vospitaniia sovetskikh voinov, 1918–1941.* Moscow: Nauka, 1984.

Kolesnik, Aleksandr N. *Sovetskie voennye stroiteli.* Moscow: Voenizdat, 1988.

Kolkowicz, Raymond. *The Soviet Military and the Communist Party.* Princeton: Princeton University Press, 1967.

Kolodny, Lev. "Sholokhov on Outrages during the Period of Collectivization." *Moscow News,* no. 28 (19–26 July 1987).

Komal, F. B. "Voennye Kadry Nakanune Voiny." *Voenno-istoricheskii zhurnal*, no. 2 (1990), 21.

Koniukhovskii, V. N. *Territorial'naia sistema voennogo stroitel'stva*. Moscow: Voenizdat, 1961.

Korablev, Iurii, and Loginov, Mikhail I., eds. *KPSS i stroitel'stvo Vooruzhennykh Sil SSSR (1918–iiun 1941)*. Moscow: Voenizdat, 1959.

Kormilitsin, M. I. "Armii nuzhno goriuchee." *Voprosy istorii*, no. 12 (1969), 117–35.

Korobchenko, A. "Voprosy Komsomol'skoi raboty." *Voennyi Vestnik* 10, no. 22 (1930), 39–40.

Korotkov, Ivan A. *Istoriia sovetskoi voennoi mysli*. Moscow: Nauka, 1980.

Kotikov, G. "Terstroitel'stvo v sviazi s kollektivizatsiei sel'skogo khoziaistva." *Voennyi Vestnik* 10, no. 2 (1930), 33–36.

Kozlov, V. A. *Dozornye Zapadnykh Rubazhei*. Kiev: Politizdat Ukraine, 1972.

Krasnoznamennyi Belorusskii voennyi okrug. Minsk: Belarus, 1973.

Krasnoznamennyi Dal'nevostochnyi voennyi okrug, 3d ed. Moscow: Voenizdat, 1985.

Krasnoznamennyi Severo-Kavkazskii. Rostov: Rostovskoe knizhnoeizdat, 1971.

Krasnoznamennyi Ural'skii. Moscow: Voenizdat, 1983.

Kravchenko, Victor. *I Chose Freedom*. New York: Scribner's, 1946.

Krikunov, V. P. "Kuda delis tanki?" *Voenno-istoricheskii zhurnal*, no. 11 (1988), 29–39.

———. "'Prostaia arifmetika' V. V. Shlykova." *Voenno-istoricheskii zhurnal*, no. 4 (1989), 41–44.

Krivosheev, G. F. *Grif Sekretnosti Sniat: Poteri Vooruzhennykh Sil SSSR v voinakh, voevykh deistviiakh i voennykh konfliktakh*. Moscow: Voenizdat, 1993.

Kuibyshev, N. "Problema kadrov i sverkhsrochnik." *Voennyi Vestnik* 10, no. 17 (1930), 4–7.

Kulish, V. M. *Korni pobedy i podazheniia*. Moscow: 1988.

Kuz'min, N. F. *Na strazhe mirnogo truda 1921–1940 gg*. Moscow: Voenizdat, 1959.

Kuznetsov, P. *General Cherniakhovskii*. Moscow: Voenizdat, 1969.

League of Nations Armaments Yearbook 1929–30. Geneva, 1930.

League of Nations Armaments Yearbook 1936. Geneva, 1937.

"Letopis' stroitel'stva sovetskikh vooruzhennykh sil 1930 god (mai-iiun')." *Voenno-istoricheskii zhurnal*, no. 2 (1976), 118.

Levytsky, Borys. *The Stalinist Terror in the Thirties: Documentation from the Soviet Press*. Stanford, Calif.: Hoover Institution Press, 1974.

Lewin, Moshe. *The Gorbachev Phenomenon: An Historical Interpretation*. Berkeley: University of California Press, 1988.

———. *The Making of the Soviet System: Essays in the Social History of Interwar Russia*. New York: Pantheon, 1985.

———. *Russian Peasants and Soviet Power: A Study in Collectivization*. New York: Norton, 1975.

———. "Russia/USSR in Historical Motion: An Essay in Interpretation." *Russian Review* 50, no. 3 (1991), 249–266.

Lewis, S. J. *Forgotten Legions: German Army Infantry Policy 1918–1941*. New York: Praeger, 1985.

Liashchenko, Nikolai G. *Gody v shineli*. Frunze: Kyrgyzstan, 1974.

Liddell-Hart, Basil H. *Europe in Arm*. London: Faber and Faber, 1937.

———. *The Red Army*. New York: Harcourt Brace, 1956.

———. *The German Generals Talk*. New York: Quill, 1979.

Lisenkov, M. "O likvidatsii negramotnosti v Krasnoi Armii (1928–1939)." *Voenno-istoricheskii zhurnal*, no. 7 (1977), 117.

Lobanov, M. M. *My-voennye Inzhenery*. Moscow: Voenizdat, 1977.

Loboda, Viktor Fedorovich. *Komandnye kadry i zakonodatel'stvo o kadrakh v razvitii vooruzhennykh sil SSSR*. Moscow: Voenizdat, 1960.

Losik, O. A. *Stroitel'stvo i boevoe primenenie sovetskikh tankovykh voisk v gody Velikoi Otechestvennoi voiny*. Moscow: Voenizdat, 1979.

Lucas, James. *War on the Eastern Front, 1941–1945: The German Soldier in Russia*. New York: Stein and Day, 1979.

Main, Steven J. "The Red Army and the Soviet Military and Political Leadership in the Late 1920s: The Case of the 'Inner-Army Opposition' of 1928." *Europe-Asia Studies* 47, no. 2 (1995), 337–355.

Mal'tsev, Evdokim E. *Akademiia imeni V. I. Lenina*. Moscow: Voenizdat, 1980.

———. *V gody ispytanii*. Moscow: Voenizdat, 1979.

Mal'tsev, N. A. "Kadrovaia ili militsionnaia? (O printsipakh komplektovaniia sovetskikh vooruzhennykh sil)." *Voenno-istoricheskii zhurnal*, no. 11 (1989), 30–40.

Manning, Roberta T. "Government in the Soviet Countryside in the Stalinist Thirties: The Case of Belyi *Raion* in 1937." *Carl Beck Papers in Russian and East European Studies*, no. 301. Pittsburgh: University of Pittsburgh, 1984.

———. "The Great Purges in a Rural District: Belyi *Raion* Revisited." *Russian History* 16, nos. 2–4 (1989), 409–433.

Martel, Lieutenant-General Sir Giffard. *The Russian Outlook*. London: Michael Joseph, 1947.

Maury, Lisann. "Stalin the Appeaser." *Survey*, no. 76 (Summer 1970), 56.

Mekhlis, Lev. *Rech' na XVIII s"ezde VKP(b), 14 Marta 1939 g*. Moscow: Gosvoenizdat, 1939.

Meretskov, Kirill A. *Na sluzhbe narodu*. Moscow, Voenizdat, 1968.

Metodika takticheskoi podgotovki pekhoty-33. Leningrad: Gosizdat, 1933.

Millett, Allan R., and Murray, Williamson, eds. *Military Effectiveness*. Boston: Allen and Unwin, 1988.

Milov, D. "Partiinaia organizatsiia RKKA pered XVI c"ezdom partii." *Voennyi Vestnik* 10, no. 17 (1930).

Minkevich, V. *Moskovskaia Proletarskaia*. Moscow: Moskovskii rabochii, 1978.

Moseichuk, "Komsomol i kolkhoznoe stroitel'stvo." *Voennyi Vestnik* 10, no. 1 (1930), 3.

Moskoff, William. *The Bread of Affliction: The Food Supply in the USSR During World War II*. New York: Cambridge University Press, 1990.

Moskovskii, V. *Voenno-vozdushnye sily SSSR (1918–1948 gg)*. Moscow: Voenizdat, 1948.

Muller, Richard. *The German Air War in Russia*. Baltimore, Md.: Nautical and Aviation Publishing Company of America, 1992.

Murray, Williamson. "The German Response to Victory in Poland: A Case Study in Professionalism." *Armed Forces and Society* 7, no. 2 (1981), 285–298.

Narodnoe Khoziaistvo SSSR v 1959 godu. Moscow: Gosizdat, 1960.

Nove, Alec. *An Economic History of the USSR, 1917–1991.* 3d ed. New York: Penguin, 1992.

Odesskii krasnoznamennyi. Kishinev: Kartia Moldoveniaske, 1975.

Odom, William E. "Bolshevik Ideas on the Military's Role in Modernization." *Armed Forces and Society* 3, no. 1 (1976), 103–120.

————. *The Soviet Volunteers: Modernization and Bureaucracy in a Public Mass Organization.* Princeton: Princeton University Press, 1973.

"O postanovke partiinoi propagandy v sviazi s vypuskom 'Kratkogo kursa istorii VKP(b).'" *Voennaia mysl'* 2, no. 12 (1938), 3–18.

Ordena Lenina Moskovskii voennyi okrug, 3d ed. Moscow: Moskovskii rabochii, 1985.

Orlovskii, V. S. *Stavropol'skaia imeni Blinova.* Stavropol: Stavropol'skoe: knizhnoe izdatel'stvo, 1971.

Osipov, Valentin O. *Politruk Vasilii Klochkov.* Moscow: Politizdat, 1984.

Paananen, Lauri, and Engle, Eloise. *The Winter War: The Russo-Finnish Conflict, 1939–1940.* New York: Scribner's, 1973.

Paiusov, Kapiton A. *Ateisticheskoe vospitanie sovetskikh voinov.* Moscow: Voenizdat, 1963.

Panov, N. N., and Karev, F. A., eds. *Kollektivizatsiia sel'skogo khoziaistva v Srednem Povolzh'e (1927–1937gg).* Kuibyshev: Kuibyshevskoe knizhnoe izdatelstvo, 1970.

"Partorganizatsiia i politprosvetrabota k XVI s"ezdu VKP(b): statisticheskii material." *Voennyi Vestnik* 10, no. 14 (1930), 80.

Patolichev, Nikolai S. *Ispytanie na zrelost'.* Moscow: Politizdat, 1977.

Pavlovskii, P. *Kak Krasnaia armiia gotovit boitsa-grazhdanina.* Moscow/Leningrad: Gosizdat, 1929.

Peresypkin, Ivan. *Sviaz' serdets boevykh.* Donetsk: Donbass, 1974.

Petrov, Iurii P. *Partiinoe stroitel'stvo v Sovetskoi Armii i Flote, 1918–1961.* Moscow: Voenizdat, 1964.

————. *Stroitel'stvo politorganov partiinykh i komsomol'sikh organizatsii armii i flota (1918–1968).* Moscow: Voenizdat, 1968.

Petrov, Ivan. "Ia vipolnial zadanie Stalina." *Rodina,* no. 5 (1992), 32–35.

Petrov, S. F. *Doprizyvanaia Voenaia Podgotovka.* Moscow: Gosudarstvennoe uchebno-pedagogicheskoe izdatel'stvo Narkomprosa RSFSR, 1941.

Petrov, Vladimir. *"22 June 1941": Soviet Historians and the German Invasion.* Columbia: University of South Carolina Press, 1968.

Petukhov, I. *Partiinaia organizatsiia i partiinaia rabota v RKKA.* Moscow/Leningrad: Gosizdat, 1928.

50 (Piat'desiat) let Vooruzhennykh sil SSSR. Moscow: Voenizdat, 1968.

15 let na strazhe Oktiabr. Moscow: Gospolitizdat, 1932.

XV let Krasnoi Armii. Arkhangel'sk: Severnoe Kraevoe Gosizdat, 1933.

Plaskov, Grigorii D. *Pod grokhot kanonady.* Moscow: Voenizdat, 1969.

Plocher, Hermann. *The German Air Force Versus Russia, 1941.* USAF Historical Studies no. 153, Harry R. Fletcher, ed. USAF Historical Division, Aerospace Studies Institute, Air University. New York: Arno Press, 1965.

Pogranichnye voiska SSSR 1929–1938: Sbornik dokumentov i materialov. Moscow: Nauka, 1972.

Poplavskii, Stanislav G. *Tovarishchi v bor'be,* 2d ed. Moscow: Voenizdat, 1974.

Portugalskii, R. M. *Marshal I. S. Konev.* Moscow: Voenizdat, 1985.

Prochko, Ignatii S. *Artilleriia v boiakyh za Rodinu.* Moscow: Voenizdat, 1957.

Radziev, A. I. *Akademiia imeni M. V. Frunze.* Moscow: Voenizdat, 1973.

Raftopullo, Anatolii A. *V atake "Tridtsat'chetverki."* Seratov: Privolzh, 1973.

Rapoport, Vitaly, and Alexeev, Yuri. *High Treason: Essays on the History of the Red Army, 1918–1938.* Durham, N.C.: Duke University Press, 1985.

Rigby, Thomas H. *Communist Party Membership in the USSR 1917–1967.* Princeton: Princeton University Press, 1968.

Roberts, Geoffrey. *The Unholy Alliance: Stalin's Pact with Hitler.* London: I. B. Taurus, 1989.

Rodinova, F. *Krasnoarmeiskii antireligioznyi uchebnik,* 2d ed. Moscow: Bezbozhnik, 1931.

Rokossovskii, Konstantin K. "Soldatskii Dolg." *Voenno-istoricheskii zhurnal,* no. 4 (1989), 52–55.

Rumiantsev, Nikolai M. *Geroi Khalkhin-Gola.* Moscow: Voenizdat, 1989.

Sandalov, L. M. "Stoiali Nasmert': Podgotovka voisk 4-i Armii k otrazheniiu fashistskoi agressii." *Voenno-istoricheskii zhurnal,* no. 11 (1988), 3–10.

Savinkin, N. I. *KPSS o Vooruzhennykh Silakh Sovetskogo Soiuza: Dokumenty 1917–1981.* Moscow: Voenizdat, 1981.

Scott, John. *Behind the Urals.* Bloomington: Indiana University Press, 1988.

Sella, Amnon. "Red Army Doctrine and Training on the Eve of the Second World War." *Soviet Studies* 27, no. 2 (1975), 245–265.

Semiriaga, M. I. "Neznamenitaia voina: razmyshleniia istorika o Sovetsko-Finliandskoi voine 1939–1940 godov." *Ogonek,* no. 22 (May 1989), 28–30.

Shevchenko, Ivan N. *Deviataia plastunskaia.* Moscow: Voenizdat, 1970.

Shkol'nikov, Semen S. *V ob'ektive-voina.* Moscow: Voenizdat, 1979.

Shtemenko, Sergei M. *General'nyi shtab v gody voiny,* vol. 1. Moscow: Voenizdat, 1981.

Shutov, Stepan F. *Krasnye streli.* Moscow: Voenizdat, 1963.

Skryabin, S., and Medvedev, N. "O tyle frontov v nachale Velikoi Otechestvennoi Voiny." *Voenno-istoricheskii zhurnal,* no. 4 (1984), 32–38.

Sofronov, Georgii P. *Nepodvlastnoe vremeni.* Moscow: Voenizdat, 1976.

Soloviev, Mikhail. *My Nine Lives in the Red Army.* New York: David McKay, 1955.

Sovetskie Polkovodtsy i voenachal'niki. Moscow: Molodaia gvardiia, 1988.

Sovetskie Vooruzhennye Sily: Istoriia stroitel'stva. Moscow: Voenizdat, 1978.

Speier, Hans. *Social Order and the Risks of War.* Cambridge, Mass.: MIT Press, 1952.

Stevenson, Colin. *Challenging Adult Illiteracy: Reading and Writing Disabilities in the British Army.* New York: Columbia University Press, 1985.

Suvenirov, Oleg F. "Esli b ne ta vakkhanaliia." *Voenno-istoricheskii zhurnal,* no. 2 (1989), 51–59.

———. "Narkomat Oborony i NKVD v predvoennye godi." *Voprosy istorii,* no. 6 (1991), 26–35.

———. "Prikaz Otmeniat' ne budem." *Voenno-istoricheskii zhurnal,* no. 4 (1989), 32–39.

———. "Vsearmeiskaia Tragediia." *Voenno-istoricheskii zhurnal,* no. 3 (1989), 39–47.

Svechin, Aleksandr A. *Strategy.* Ed. and trans. Kent D. Lee. Minneapolis, Minn.: East View Publications, 1992. (Originally published as *Strategiia.* Moscow: Voennyi Vestnik, 1927).

Tal', B. *Istoriia Krasnoi armii*. Moscow: Gosizdat, 1929.

Taschenbuch Russisches Heer: Bestimmt für den Gebrauch der Truppe im Felde. Oberkommando des Heeres, January 1941.

Tel'pukhovskii, Boris S. *KPSS vo glave stroitel'stva Vooruzhennykh Sil SSSR Oktiebr' 1917–1982g*. Moscow: Politizdat, 1983.

Terekhin, Konstantin P., et al. *Voiny stal'nykh magistralei*. Moscow: Voenizdat, 1969.

Thompson, Terry L., and Sheldon, Richard, eds. *Soviet Society and Culture*. Boulder, Colo.: Westview Press, 1988.

Timasheff, Nicholas S. *The Great Retreat: The Growth and Decline of Communism in Russia*. New York: Dutton, 1946.

Trotsky, Leon. *Military Writings*. New York: Merit Publishers, 1969.

Tyl Sovetskoi Armii. Moscow: Voenizdat, 1968.

Ukolov, A. T., and Ivkin, V. I. "O masshtabakh repressii v Krasnoi Armii v predvoennye gody." *Voenno-istoricheskii zhurnal*, no. 1 (1993), 56–59.

Unishevsky, Vladimir. *Red Pilot: Memoirs of a Soviet Airman*. London: Hurst and Blackett, 1939.

U.S. Army. *German Campaign in Russia: Planning and Operations (1940–1942)*. Department of the Army Pamphlet no. 20-261a. Washington, D.C.: Department of the Army, 1955.

———. *Russian Combat Methods in World War II*. Department of the Army Pamphlet no. 20-230. Washington, D.C.: Department of the Army, 1950.

———. *Small Unit Actions During the German Campaign in Russia*. Department of the Army Pamphlet no. 20-269. Washington, D.C.: Department of the Army, 1953.

Valenta, Jiri, and Potter, William. *Soviet Decisionmaking for National Security*. London: Allen and Unwin, 1984.

Van Dyke, Carl. *The Soviet-Finnish War of 1939–1940: Anatomy of a Preventive War*. Ph.D. dissertation, Emmanuel College, 1994.

Vannikov, B. L. "Obornnaia Promyshlennost' SSSR nakanune voiny (iz zapisok Narkoma)." *Voprosy istorii*, no. 10 (1968), 116–123, and no. 1 (1969), 122–135.

Varenov, Vasilii I. *Pomoshch' Krasnoi Armii v razvitii kolkhoznogo stroitel'stva (1929–1933 gg)*. Moscow: Nauka, 1978.

———. "Uchastie Krasnoi Armii v sotsialisticheskam pereustroistve derevni." *Voenno-istoricheskii zhurnal*, no. 10 (1972), 79–83.

Vashchenko, N. F., and Runov, V. A. "Voennaia Reforma V SSSR." *Voenno-istoricheskii zhurnal*, no. 12 (1989), 33–40.

Vasilenko, M. *Boevaia sluzhba krasnoarmeitsa*, 7th ed. Moscow: OGIZ, 1937.

Vasilevskii, Aleksandr M. *Delo vsei zhizni*. Moscow: Politizdat, 1975.

Vasil'ev, Sergei I., and Dikan', Aleksei P. *Gvardeitsy piatnadtsatoi*. Moscow: Voenizdat, 1960.

Vishniakov, Nikolai P., and Arkhipov, F. I. *Ustroistvo vooruzhennykh sil SSSR*. Moscow: Voenizdat, 1926.

Volkogonov, Dmitrii. *Triumf i tragediia: Politicheskii portret I. V. Stalin*. Moscow: Novosti, 1989.

Volkotrubenko, I. "O Planovom snabzheni voisk vooruzheniem i boepripasami." *Voenno-istoricheskii zhurnal*, no. 12 (1983), 59–61.

von Hagen, Mark. *Soldiers in the Proletarian Dictatorship: The Red Army and the Soviet Socialist State, 1917–1930.* Ithaca, N.Y.: Cornell University Press, 1990.

———. "Soviet Soldiers and Officers on the Eve of the German Invasion: Towards a Description of Social Psychology and Political Attitudes." *Soviet Union/Union Sovetique* 18, nos. 1–3 (1991), 79–101.

Vorob'ev, Konstantin A. *Vooruzhennye sily razvitogo sotsialisticheskogo obshchestva.* Moscow: Voenizdat, 1980.

Voronov, Nikolai N. *Na sluzhbe voennoi.* Moscow: Voenizdat, 1963.

Voropaev, D. A., and Iovlev, A. M. *Bor'ba KPSS za sozdanie voennykh kadrov, 1918–1941.* Moscow: Voenizdat, 1960.

Voroshilov, Kliment E. *O molodezhi.* Moscow: Molodaia gvardiia, 1937.

———. *Stat'i i rechi.* Moscow: Partizdat, 1936.

Voroshilov, Kliment E., Mekhlis, L., Budenny, S., and Stern, G. *The Red Army Today: Speeches Delivered at the Eighteenth Congress of the CPSU (B), March 10–21, 1939.* Moscow: Foreign Language Publishing House, 1939.

Voroshilov, Kliment E., and Frunze, Mikhail V. *O molodezhi.* Moscow: Partizdat, 1936.

Vrublevskii, Aleksandr P., and Prot'ko, Tat'iana S. *Iz Istorii Repressii protiv Belorusskogo Krest'ianstva 1929–1934 gg.* Minsk: Navuka i Tekhnika, 1992.

Vsearmeiskie soveshchaniia politrabotnikov, 1918–1940. Moscow: Nauka, 1984.

Watt, Donald C. *Too Serious a Business: European Armed Forces and the Approach of the Second World War.* New York: Norton, 1992.

Weigley, Russell F. *History of the United States Army.* New York: Macmillan, 1967.

Wildman, Allan. *The End of the Russian Imperial Army: The Old Army and the Soldiers' Revolt (March–April 1917).* Princeton: Princeton University Press, 1980.

Wollenberg, Erich. *The Red Army.* London: Secker and Warburg, 1959.

Za liniiu partii protiv opportunisticheskikh shatanii: liniia partii v voprosakh kollektivizatsii v dokumentakh i materialakh. Khark'ov: Proletarii izdvo, 1930.

Zakharov, Matvei V. *General'nyi shtab v predvoennyi gody.* Moscow: Voenizdat, 1989.

Zalesskii, Ivan L. *Kommunisticheskaia partiia—organizator pomoshchi Krasnoi Armii trudiashchemusia krest'ianstvu v sotsialisticheskom preobrazovanii sel'skogo khoziaistva v 1927-1932 godakh (Iz materialakh Krasnoznamennogo Severo-Kavkazskogo voennogo okruga).* Rostov-on-Don: n.p., 1981.

Zheltova, A. S. *Imeni Lenina.* Moscow: Voenizdat, 1966.

Zhukov, Georgii K. *Vospominaniia i razmyshleniia.* Moscow: Novosti, 1969.

———. *Vospminaniia i razmyshleniia: dopolnennoe po rukopisi avtora,* 11th ed. Moscow: Novosti, 1992.

Unpublished Memoirs

Balinsky, Boris I. *Memoir.* Record Series 15/35/57, University of Illinois Archives, 1988.

Published Documents

"Akt o Prieme Narkomata Oborony Soiuza SSR tov. Timoshenko S. K. ot tov. Voroshilov K. E." *Izvestiia TsK KPSS,* no. 1 (1990), 193–205.

"Doklad komandovaniia Zapadnogo fronta I. V. Stalinu o prichinakh porazheniia 22-i armii, 3 Sentiabra 1941." *Istoricheskii Arkhiv,* no. 1 (1993), 57–60.

"Iz doklada nachal'nika general'nogo shtaba krashoi armii Navodnomo Komissaru Oborony SSSR, 20 iiunia 1940 g." *Rodina,* nos. 6–7 (1991), 28.

"Iz pis'ma riadogo 233-go pekhotnogo polka 102-i pokhotnoi divizii germanskoi armii K. Franka iz gospitalia sem'e 10 iiula 1941g." *Rodina,* no. 6–7 (1991), 28.

"O nakoplenii nachal'stvuiushchego sostava i popolnenii im Raboche-Krest'ianskoi Krasnoi Armii: Iz spravki-doklada nachal'nika Upravleniia po nachal'stvuiushchemu sostavu RKKA Narkomata Oboronu SSSR E. A. Shchadenko, 20 Marta 1940 g." *Izvestiia TsK KPSS,* no. 1 (1990), 177–185.

"O rabote Politicheskogo Upravleniia Krasnoi Armii. Iz doklada Politicheskogo Up-ravleniia Krasnoi Armii Tsentral'nomu Komitetu VKP(b) o rabote Politicheskogo Upravleniia Krasnoi Armii, 23 Maia 1940 g." *Izvestiia TsK KPSS,* no. 3 (1990), 192–201.

"O rabote za 1939 god.: Iz otcheta nachal'nika Upravleniia po nachal'stvuiushchemu sostavu RKKA Narkomata Oborony SSSR E. A. Shchadenko, 5 Maia 1940 g." *Izvestiia TsK KPSS,* no. 1 (1990), 86–192.

"O voenni perepodgotovke, pereattestovannii rabotnikov partiinykh kometetov i o poriadke ikh mobilizatsii v RKKA." *Izvestiia TsK KPSS,* no. 1 (1990), 175–176.

"O vydvizhenii nachal'stvuiushchego sostava RKKA, 25 Marta 1940 g." *Izvestiia TsK KPSS,* no. 1 (1990), 178–179.

"Ob otbore 4000 kommunistov na politrabotu v RKKA, 29 Avgust 1939 g." *Izvestiia TsK KPSS,* no. 1 (1990), 174–175.

"Organizuetsia narodnoe opolchenie: Telegramma iz Kieva, 5 iiulia 1941 g." *Izvestiia TsK KPSS,* no. 7 (1990), 198.

"Opyt pervogo mesiatsa voiny s Germaniei: Doklad komandovaniia Iuzhnogo fronta, 21 iiulia 1941 g." *Izvestiia TsK KPSS,* no. 8 (1990), 213–214.

"Pis'mo leitenanta A. N. Kozlova I. V. Stalinu, 30 iiulia 1941 g." *Izvestiia TsK KPSS,* no. 8 (1990), 222.

"Rukopis' Stat'i M. N. Tukhachevskogo 'Voennye plany Gitlera' s pravkoi I. V. Stalina, 29 Marta 1935 g." *Izvestiia TsK KPSS,* no. 1 (1990), 161–170.

"Zapiska G. I. Kulika I. V. Stalinu, 19 iiunia 1941 g. *"Izvestiia TsK KPSS,* no. 5 (1990), 203–206.

Russian Newspapers

Izvestiia (Moscow, 1926–1941)

Krasnaia zvezda (Moscow, 1925–1940)

Krasnoe znamia (Tomsk)

Krasnyi Voin (1934)

Krasnoarmeets i Krasnoflotets (Moscow, 1928–1933)

Pravda (Moscow, 1925–1940)

Voennyi Vestnik (1930–1938)

Military Units

Index